Cambridge University Press

Cambridge English Language Assessment
Part of the University of Cambridge

Cambridge Official Preparation Material

Kid's Box

Updated Second Edition

CB126712

Teacher's Book 5

American English

Lucy Frino and Melanie Williams
with Caroline Nixon & Michael Tomlinson

Cambridge University Press
www.cambridge.org/elt

Cambridge Assessment English
www.cambridgeenglish.org

Information on this title: www.cambridge.org/9781316627044

First published 2009
Second edition 2015
Updated second edition 2017

Printed in Great Britain by CPI Group (UK) Ltd, Croydon CR0 4YY

A catalog record for this publication is available from the British Library

ISBN 978-1-316-62704-4 Teacher's Book 5
ISBN 978-1-316-62755-6 Student's Book 5
ISBN 978-1-316-62721-1 Workbook with Online Resources 5
ISBN 978-1-316-62727-3 Class Audio CDs 5 (3 CDs)
ISBN 978-1-316-62738-9 Teacher's Resource Book with Online Audio 5
ISBN 978-1-316-62791-4 Interactive DVD with Teacher's Booklet 5 (PAL/NTSC)
ISBN 978-1-316-62712-9 Presentation Plus 5
ISBN 978-1-316-63019-8 Posters 5

Additional resources for this publication at www.cambridge.org/elt/kidsboxamericanenglish

Contents

Language summary

	Key vocabulary	Key grammar and functions	Phonics	Review
Welcome to our ezine page 4	**School subjects:** *art, computer studies, English, French, geography, German, history, math, P.E., science, Spanish* **School:** *competition, dictionary, exam, language, lesson, prize, study, subject, timetable*	*Like/love* + *-ing* / nouns, *'d like* + infinitive **Simple present questions and short answers:** *Do you live close to your school? Yes, I do. / No, I don't. Is it on Thursday? Yes, it is. / No, it isn't.*	**Consonant sounds:** "j" (jump, orange) and "ch" (cheese, lunch)	simple past, simple present, school and school subjects, sports, activities, adjectives, superlative adjectives, *study, learn about, too* + adjective, *cool*, telling the time, *at, before, on, in, joke, neck, bone, museum*
1 Time for TV page 10	**Time:** *after, a quarter after, half, o'clock* **TV shows:** *cartoon, comedy, documentary, music video, news, quiz show, sports, weather* **TV:** *action movie, channel, episode, series, turn on* **Adjectives:** *amazing, bad, boring, exciting, funny, good, interesting*	**The time:** *What time is it? It's a quarter after one.* **Simple present for routines:** *I always ride my bike to school.*	Vowel sound: *"yoo"* (*usually, music*)	TV shows, *Should, Let's, golf*, days of the week, school subjects, sports, adjectives, telling the time
History Cartoons page 16				
2 People at work page 18	**Jobs:** *actor, artist, cook, dancer, dentist, doctor, farmer, firefighter, manager, mechanic, nurse, pilot, reporter, secretary, soccer player, sports commentator, swimmer, teacher, writer*	**Plans, intentions, and predictions:** *going to*	Short vowel sound: "er" (*manager, actor, treasure*)	jobs, actions, verbs for daily routines, sports, mixed tenses, questions, telling the time, adverbs, *a.m., p.m., going to*, comparatives
Science Teeth page 24		**Review** 1 and 2 page 26		
3 City life page 28	**City life:** *airport, bridge, castle, fire station, gym, hotel, museum, playground, police station, post office, prison, restaurant, road, stadium, street, taxi/cab, theater, zoo* **Directions:** *across, corner, down, past, left, right, straight ahead*	**Directions:** *Go down / across (Green Street), Take the first/second/third street on the left/right, Go straight ahead, Turn left onto (Blue Street), Turn right at the corner, Stop before you get to the (river), Walk past the (playground), What's at the end of (the street)?, be lost* **Prepositions:** *across from, behind, between, next to*	Consonant sounds: "s" (*socks*) and "sh" (*gosh, machine*)	cities, telling the time, simple past, imperatives, *map*, prepositions, superlatives, jobs, definitions with *who/that/where*, family, colors, *I can see …*
Geography Cities page 34				
4 Disaster! page 36	**Disasters:** *earthquake, hurricane, iceberg, lightning, storm, tsunami, volcano* **Verbs:** *break (leg), catch fire, cut, destroy, drop, erupt, fall down, hit, hurt, lose* **Months**	**Past progressive and simple past:** *I was having a picnic when it started to rain. What were you doing when the teacher saw you?*	Stressed syllables	the weather, adjectives, spelling for *-ing* endings, telling the time, *helicopter*, weather, daily activities, past narrative tenses, holiday activities, present progressive, simple past, past progressive
Geography The earth's surface page 42		**Review** 3 and 4 page 44		

Introduction

Kid's Box American English introduces students to the pleasures of learning English and enables them to consistently improve throughout the seven books in the series. All seven levels develop students' abilities in the four skills – listening, speaking, reading, and writing – as well as challenging them cognitively and helping them to feel a real sense of achievement in learning. As experienced teachers ourselves, we are aware of the demands and difficulties involved in managing a diverse and mixed-ability classroom. Teaching younger learners can be at once the most rewarding and the most soul-destroying of pursuits! Sometimes we can have very bad days, but it's the good days that give us an exhilarating sense of achievement, a sense of being part of a child's future development.

Plutarch reminds us that **"The mind is not a vessel to be filled, but a fire to be ignited,"** and this concept of learning underpins *Kid's Box American English*. Students learn when they are interested and involved: when they want to find something out, when they are playing a game, when they are listening to a story, when they are doing craft activities. Learning is an active process in every way, and *Kid's Box American English* makes sure that students are physically and mentally active and that they are encouraged to make sense of the language themselves. **"The art of teaching is the art of assisting discovery,"** Mark Van Doren.

The language syllabus of *Kid's Box American English* has been carefully selected and graded to suit the age and level of the students. Language is introduced in context and in manageable chunks, giving students plenty of opportunities to practice and become familiar with the meanings and the sounds. Language is recycled throughout the units, and students can practice the language in different contexts. They can also personalize it. Recycling is particularly important for young learners, who tend to forget quickly and who do not have the study skills of older learners. For this reason, there is constant review and recycling throughout the units and course.

The units in Level 5 are based around the new characters - Maria, Dan, and Alex. Characters give students a way of contextualizing the language and help them to make it meaningful and purposeful. The characters develop throughout the books so as to sustain the students' interest and motivation.

Cambridge English: Young Learners

In *Kid's Box American English* we have followed the syllabus for the *Cambridge English: Young Learners* tests so that each cycle of two levels corresponds to one of the tests. Therefore the material covered in the first cycle coincides with that which is required for Starters, cycle 2 with Movers, and cycle 3 with Flyers. *Kid's Box American English* covers all the relevant language structures, presents and practices the vocabulary, and includes examples of the task types from the tests. Where certain topics include a vocabulary list which is too comprehensive to include all of the lexical items in the Student's Book, additional activities have been offered in the Teacher's Resource Book.

Each *Cambridge English: Young Learners* test consists of three papers: Listening, Reading and Writing, and Speaking. These tests are child-friendly and motivating, and have been specially written for primary learners. They are taken by students all over the world, have international recognition, and are backed by the reputation and research of Cambridge English Language Assessment. They provide a gentle introduction to public exams, and research shows that children find the tests highly motivating. The tests can act as a stepping stone to other Cambridge English exams, as the highest level, *Cambridge English: Flyers*, is roughly equivalent in language level to *Cambridge English: Key for Schools*. The *Cambridge English: Young Learners* tests are an incentive; however, they should at no stage be seen as obligatory. For further information on the component papers for each test, visit: www.cambridgeenglish.org/exams

Common European Framework of Reference for Languages – Learning, Teaching, Assessment

Kid's Box American English has been written taking into account the proposals included in the Common European Framework of Reference (CEFR). The CEFR has been designed for language teachers and material developers to be able to define different levels of competence and performance. These objectives coincide with those of *Cambridge English: Young Learner English* tests.

Flyers	(at around Level A2 of the CEFR)
Movers	(at Level A1)
Starters	(below Level A1)

The framework places emphasis on values, such as student autonomy, proposing a task-based methodology with functional evaluation criteria. Although large parts of the CEFR are more relevant to older learners and have not been designed specifically for the elementary classroom, it includes two particularly useful parts, the Common Reference Levels and the English Language Portfolio.

The Common Reference Levels offer a description of what a language learner "can do" at different stages of the learning process. These levels can be consulted separately, but they have been mirrored here in the self-evaluation sections.

The Language Portfolio is designed as a compendium of skills acquired and work done that incorporates the "can do" checklists for self-assessment. This is important for student motivation and can also be shown to parents to inform them of the syllabus and objectives set for their children.

Course components

Levels 1 through 6 of *Kid's Box American English* include a Student's Book, Workbook, Class Audio CDs, Teacher's Book, Teacher's Resource Book, Presentation Plus, Online Resources, Interactive DVD, Tests, and Posters. There are also Flashcards for Levels 1 through 4. The new Starter Level offers a Class Book with CD-ROM, Class Audio CDs, Flashcards, Teacher's Book, Teacher's Resource Book, Presentation Plus, Interactive DVD, and Posters.

Student's Book

This 88-page full-color book consists of nine units. Each unit is six pages in length, with each page providing sufficient material for one lesson. After each unit there is a Content and Language Integrated Learning (CLIL) spread to learn about other subjects through English. The Review sections cover language from the two previous units. There is a phonics section within every unit. There are four Values pages at the end of the book to develop students' social awareness. Lessons include a variety of interesting and motivating activities, such as pairwork, role plays, craft activities, guessing games, songs, and chants. The series' strong cast of characters appears throughout the book. The adventures of Diggory Bones and his daughter, Emily, are played out in a picture story at the end of each unit.

Workbook

This 104-page book is designed to give students further practice with the new language and to help them consolidate their understanding. The students will have fun doing the activities, and you will find that they stimulate their creativity, too. The Workbook materials are designed to be integrated into the lessons, and there is guidance in the Teacher's Book as to how this works. This edition also features a full-page *Cambridge English: Young Learners* test practice activity for each unit.

Class Audio CDs

The Class Audio CDs contain all of the listening material for the Student's Book and Workbook, including all of the songs and stories. The songs are available in both sung and karaoke versions.

Teacher's Resource Book with Online Audio

The Teacher's Resource Book contains a wealth of photocopiable activities to help with mixed-ability classes. There are two Reinforcement and two Extension worksheets for every unit, as well as Song and Topic worksheets for further exploitation. The Teacher's Resource Book also includes extra *Cambridge English: Young Learners*–type tests with listening content online. The book also features word cards to reinforce target vocabulary.

Language Portfolio

In accordance with CEFR guidelines, there is a Language Portfolio of individual competencies to lead the student to self-evaluation and to record the learning experience of each student throughout the elementary school years. This is included in the Workbook.

Interactive DVD

As you navigate your way through our interactive DVD, you will find animated versions of the stories in the library, the songs with animation and video in the music room, video documentaries in the hall, interactive games in the computer room, and a quiz in the classroom.

Teacher's Book

This 208-page interleaved Student's and Teacher's Book provides teaching notes for each lesson, that include recording scripts for all listening activities, answer keys for all activities, an overview of the syllabus for each level, extra activities, photocopiable pages, extra project ideas, and evaluation activities.

Teaching notes

The teaching notes provide step-by-step guidelines for each page. Lesson objectives are clearly described, and the materials needed for each lesson are specified. Each lesson starts with a *Warmer* and finishes with an *Ending the lesson* activity. Activities from the Workbook are integrated with the Student's Book activities to provide a balanced range of appropriate activities. There are two *Extra activities* provided for each lesson for times when you need even more material. These Extra activities only appear in the Teacher's Book, and there are suggestions in the teaching notes as to when each activity should be used in the lesson. They are not designed only for the end of the lesson.

F towards: these activities introduce children to the Flyers test tasks to gain confidence in aspects of the task types.

F these activities are closer in format and content to the Flyers test tasks.

Evaluation activities

There are four evaluation pages for this level, one page to be used after each Review section. The format and design of the evaluation pages is similar to the tasks in the YLE tests. This is to help students become used to this type of evaluation and to be able to measure their own progress. At the end of this Introduction, there is a section on the specific Evaluation pages included in this book.

Photocopiable pages

There is a photocopiable page for each unit in the back of the Teacher's Book. These pages provide you with a range of manual activities to use with your students: for example, there are word cards, a survey, and a fill-in-the-blank activity. There are full instructions in the teaching notes on how to prepare the materials and when and how to use them in class.

Presentation Plus

Presentation Plus includes interactive whiteboard tools, a fully interactive Student's Book and Workbook, digital versions of the Teacher's Book and Teacher's Resource Book, a multimedia library including video from the DVD, Class Audio, and access to online teacher training support. This pack enables you to plan and deliver your lessons "paper-free" from a tablet or a computer.

Online Resources

The online platform includes games and extra grammar, vocabulary, and writing activities for every single unit, providing plenty of extra practice. All the students' online work can be tracked and reviewed by the teacher.

Tests

The Level 5 and 6 Tests and Audio allow you to regularly assess your students in different ways. You can choose the unit tests, review tests, and end-of-level tests, as customizable Microsoft Word documents. If you are preparing students for the *Cambridge English: Young Learners* tests, you can additionally select the *Cambridge English: Young Learners*–style unit tests, review tests, and end-of-level tests, as Adobe PDFs. cambridge.org/kidsbox/tests

Posters

These colorful and appealing posters aid review by giving students the chance to practice unit language in a different and fun context. They can be added to the classroom wall as you progress through the course to aid review. This pack includes eight posters with clear teaching notes available online.

What does *Kid's Box American English* offer?

"To awaken interest and kindle enthusiasm is the sure way to teach easily and successfully," Tyron Edwards.

Once students are interested, and ready and eager to learn, then the job of teaching them becomes so much easier. The materials in *Kid's Box American English* have been designed to do just that. Here's how and why it works:

- **Humour through the characters and the stories**

  "The important thing is not so much that every child should be taught, as that every child should be given the wish to learn," John Lubbock.

  For younger students, motivation is vital if the language acquisition process is to be successful. We have tried to include an element of humour in the presentations and, more particularly, in the story that rounds off each of the units. This story is designed to review what students have been studying and galvanize them to study more because they want to follow the adventures of the characters.

- **Creativity and learning through action and activity**
  "I hear and I forget. I see and I remember. I do and I understand," Chinese proverb.

  Young learners need a lot of meaningful, contextualized practice if they are to become successful language learners. In *Kid's Box American English* there is plenty of "hands-on" practice. Drawing, "make and do," songs, games, and chants are all activity types that form an integral part of the learning process. These enable students to be creative, and they help to anchor knowledge more effectively. It's only through repeated practice that skills, awareness, and understanding can be developed.
- **Connecting to the world outside the classroom**
  "A child educated only at school is an uneducated child," George Santayana.

  The CLIL sections bring the outside world into the classroom so that students learn about the world around them as they learn English. This helps them understand that English is more than a classroom subject and lets them realize ways in which English can be used as a tool for knowledge.

  "I like a teacher who gives you something to take home to think about besides homework," Lily Tomlin (Edith Ann).
- **Discovery and the development of learner autonomy**
  "The object of teaching a child is to enable him to get along without his teacher," Elbert Hubbard.
  For students to be able to learn effectively and to continue to learn, they need to be encouraged and enabled to find things out for themselves. *Kid's Box American English* includes self-correction and other activities to develop learner autonomy. Communicative activities, such as pairwork, group work, and role playing, give students the opportunity to work independently of the teacher. In these types of activities, the teacher's role is as a guide and facilitator. In this instance, we should stand back a little from the activity and monitor and assist when necessary.
- **Promoting tolerance and respect**
  "The highest result of education is tolerance," Helen Keller.
  The material and activities in the book help students to appreciate cultural diversity, respect differences, and develop human values. Respect for and protection of the natural environment goes hand in hand with the respecting of other human beings. This theme runs throughout the whole of *Kid's Box American English* and in particular in the Values sections of the Student's Book and the Workbook.

Learning styles / Multiple intelligences

"If a child can't learn the way we teach, maybe we should teach the way they learn," Ignacio Estrada.
We now understand that people learn in different ways. We don't talk about "intelligence" anymore, we talk about "intelligences." The activities in *Kid's Box American English* are designed to stimulate these different intelligences. This means there will always be something to appeal to every learner.

- **Linguistic intelligence:** sensitivity to the written and spoken word and the ability to learn languages.

  This is a core element of any language course, and in *Kid's Box American English* it is exploited in combination with the other intelligences.
- **Interpersonal intelligence:** effective communication with others.

  Communication activities have been incorporated from the Starter Level onwards. It is a vital aspect of language learning and is essential in making younger learners aware that language is a tool for communication and not just another school subject. Communication activities help interpersonal skills, encouraging children to work together and develop important communication strategies.
- **Intrapersonal intelligence:** expression of inner thoughts and feelings.

  Throughout the course there are various reflective activities, for example the "Do you remember?" and "Can do" sections help students become more aware of themselves.
- **Musical intelligence:** appreciation of rhythm and music.

  This intelligence runs almost parallel to linguistic intelligence, as Howard Gardner points out. Each unit of *Kid's Box American English* includes a song as well as occasional raps, rhymes, and chants.
- **Bodily-kinesthetic intelligence:** coordination and connection with the whole body.

  This is extremely important for the developing minds and bodies of younger learners, as there is a significant relation between mental and physical activity. In *Kid's Box American English* there are plenty of action songs and rhymes, which can help develop bodily-kinesthetic intelligence at the same time as offering a change of rhythm and activity to the ever-restless young learner.
- **Logical-mathematical intelligence:** problem solving and logical thought.

  There is a range of activity types for this intelligence in *Kid's Box American English*. These activities help develop logical reasoning, problem solving, and the detection of patterns. We feel they are vital and extremely motivating.
- **Visual-spatial intelligence:** expression and understanding through the visual world.

  This intelligence is one of the key ways that children learn. In *Kid's Box American English* there is a range of ways in which students' visual-spatial intelligence is supported and developed, such as the full-color illustrations in the Student's Books, the coloring activities, and the content from the Interactive DVD.

Tips for teachers

Preparation

- In order to guarantee a positive learning experience, students need to be properly prepared before doing any task. Ensure they have the language they need to carry out an activity and that they know exactly how to do it.
- Before starting an activity, demonstrate it. For pairwork activities, choose an individual student to help you. Do the first question of the pairwork task with the student for the class to get an idea. You can follow this up with an open-pair demonstration, choosing two students from the class to do another question and answer for the whole class.
- When you divide the class into pairs or groups, point to each student in turn and say, for example, *A–B, A–B, A–B* and so on, so they are in no doubt what their role is. You can follow this up with *As, raise your hands. Bs, raise your hands* as a further check. Try to give simple, clear instructions in English. Say, for example, *As ask the question, and Bs answer the*

question: A–B, A–B, A–B. Then Bs ask the question, and As answer the question: B–A, B–A, B–A.
- Always bring a few extra copies of the photocopiable worksheets to avoid tears if any students do it wrong and want to start again.

Classroom dynamics

"A good teacher, like a good entertainer, first must hold his audience's attention, then he can teach his lesson," John Henrik Clarke.

- Try to move around the classroom while explaining or doing the activities. Circulating among the students enables you more effectively to supervise and monitor those who may need more attention at times.
- In the same way that it is a good idea for teachers to move around, it is also advisable to move the students themselves around occasionally. By periodically changing seating arrangements, you can help group dynamics and break up potentially disruptive students. For example, weaker students could be put next to stronger ones, and more hard-working students next to disruptive ones. Students might benefit from working with learners they may not usually associate with.
- When forming pairs or groups, we suggest that, whenever possible, students just move their chairs. For group work, they can bring chairs around one or two tables, allowing them an easy environment for discussion and written work. For pairwork, they can position their two chairs to face each other. This allows a more realistic eye-to-eye communication situation. This change of seating prepares them for the oral work they are about to begin.

Noise

- While speaking activities which involve movement around the classroom can make the class more lively and dynamic, they will also generate a lot of excitement. When students are excited, they can become noisy and may even use their first language to talk about or discuss some aspect of the activity. Although it can be difficult to get used to it at first, noise in the classroom is tolerable if it is related directly to the activity and is an expression of interest or enthusiasm for the task at hand. You should ensure, however, that only English is used for the completion of tasks and for correction at the end of the activity.

Teaching and learning

"Mistakes are the portals of discovery," James Joyce.

- Making mistakes is a vital part of the learning process, so when students are asked to invent their own sentences, stories, chants, etc, we should not expect these to be perfect. Sometimes accuracy should be forfeited for the sake of creativity, enthusiastic participation and learning.
- Activities that students traditionally find engaging include: moving about, singing, playing games, doing puzzles and coloring in. Wherever possible, use these as effective teaching tools. In this way, young learners can use language to practice English, and work very hard, without being conscious of it. By setting them in meaningful contexts, the diverse disciplines of language learning, such as grammar, reading, pronunciation and communication can be taught with a dynamic and child-friendly approach.
- The Extra activities for each lesson can be used when you feel that students need more practice with some of the language, or when you think you will finish the lesson material before the end of the lesson.
- Try to avoid the immediate repetition of an activity simply because it has worked well in class and your students have enjoyed it. If you do this, the novelty will quickly wear off and students will become bored. Save it for a later occasion, and they will come back to it with fresh enthusiasm.
- When students are doing listening activities, it is usual for them to listen to the material twice. After the first listening, it is a good idea for students to check their answers with each other. This makes them feel more confident if they have the same answers, and is less intimidating if they don't. This approach also gives them a purpose for listening the second time: to confirm or to check again. When checking answers with the whole class, try to include as many students as you can and encourage them to say longer phrases rather than single words.
- Students are sometimes shy about speaking aloud. They say the answer quietly to the teacher, and then the teacher repeats it for the class. This is effective – but it does not help the students develop their speaking or listening skills. Whenever possible, you should encourage students to speak loudly and clearly and, if the rest of the class didn't hear what the student said, you should ask the student to repeat, rather than repeat it yourself.

"A teacher is a person who never says anything once," Howard Nemerov.

- Recycling is an important part of the learning process. Don't expect students to remember everything from a previous lesson in the next one. They will only absorb what attracts or interests them, and what they are ready to learn. *Kid's Box American English* builds in regular recycling and, as the students get older, they will come to realize that they can investigate something further by themselves if it really interests them.
- Be flexible within teaching. It is important to take time to listen to students and to connect with them. You should try to familiarize yourself with their likes and dislikes and identify both their learning and their emotional needs. If you can do this, then you will be better able to support them in their learning.

Assessment and evaluation

- With students of this age, it is best to use continuous assessment. This means we monitor their progress in the classroom and use this information to help us with our teaching. For example, we may find that we need to review language previously taught, or that we can add more challenging activities because students are ready for these.
- Children do not develop at the same rate, and they do not learn in the same way. So we need to assess each student as an individual and not compare them with the other students in the class. We should look for progress and development in every student. With young children, we should assess and monitor their social and emotional development, as well as their learning of English. This means we should praise effort, and encourage them to share and to work in pairs and groups, as well as giving them feedback on their English.

Discipline

"No life ever grows great until it is focused, dedicated, disciplined," Harry Emerson Fosdick.

- One of the most challenging aspects of teaching young learners is holding their interest in the classroom. Students have limitless energy, combined with an extremely limited attention span.

We have to juggle these factors to try to avoid boredom, restlessness, and demotivation, all of which lead to problems with discipline. By channelling students' innate energy to the good, we can often avoid unruliness and indiscipline. A lot of discipline problems arise when students are underchallenged and bored, or when activities are too repetitive. *Kid's Box American English* has been written by experienced teachers who at all times have borne in mind the needs and requirements of students and have included a variety of activities for them to enjoy.

- It is important that you establish a context of discipline in your class. Make sure students know what is acceptable and what is not and make sure you treat all students in the same way. Students are very aware when we are not "fair." Clear and fair discipline parameters create a "safe" classroom environment in which students can work confidently and freely. This makes for an ordered, busy classroom, rather than an anarchic one.

Songs, rhymes, and chants

- For the activities based around songs, rhymes, and chants, it is not always necessary for students to understand every word outside the key words being practiced. In these activities, we are more interested in students understanding the gist, and we are using the rhyme as a means with which to practice language, rhythm, and pronunciation. The visuals that accompany the rhymes, songs, and chants, and the actions included in some, should provide students with sufficient information to be able to understand the overall concept. It is important then, at this stage, not to spend precious class time on lengthy and complicated explanations of specific words.
- Get students to stand up when performing the songs, rhymes, or chants. It can make a tremendous difference to their performance and enjoyment.
- Songs, rhymes and chants can be presented in different ways to make them more interesting and challenging. These techniques are especially useful if you want to go back to previously-used material for review or further exploitation and want to avoid your students' reaction of "We've already done this!"
  - Whisper the rhyme or phrase while snapping your fingers. Repeat the rhyme, getting gradually louder each time and then reverse the process.
  - Say a rhyme or chant while clapping hands and tapping your foot in time to the rhythm.
  - Divide the class into groups and ask them to repeat the rhyme or chant in rounds. To do this, the first group starts to say the rhyme and then, at a suitable point, usually one or two lines into it, the second group starts to say the rhyme from the beginning.
  - With your class audio or video recorder, record the class performing. Be sure to give them a round of applause and encourage the class to do the same. Let your students listen to themselves. If they feel that they could improve on a second attempt, record them again.
- It can be extremely motivating for children to watch their own performances on video, but if you video or photograph your students, make sure you get written permission from parents or guardians first.

Competition

- An element of competition can make many students try harder. However, although a competition can be a good incentive for an otherwise unenthusiastic student, it can sometimes be demotivating for a less able but ordinarily hard-working one. Before playing a competitive game, it may be useful to explain to students that this is only a means of learning. Although they may not win the game, all students are "winners" if they know more English at the end than they knew at the beginning. Help students understand that when they play a game they can practice and learn more English, so they each win a prize and that prize is knowledge. Nonetheless, it is always a good idea to balance competitive games with cooperative ones and to include other activities so that you can reward and praise individuals according to their own needs and performance.

Display

- Students find it extremely motivating to have their work displayed and will generally work hard to produce work to the best of their ability if they know it is going to be seen by others. So try to arrange to display students' work around the classroom or school whenever possible. Don't forget to include work by all the students (not in every display, but over a period of time) and to change the displays regularly.

Craft activities: Storage of material

- It is useful to keep supplies for craft activities, for example scissors, glue, yarn, and crayons, in a large box in the classroom. Then when it is time for craft activities, you can put the box on a table, and students can come and collect what they need.
- Make sure students always clear up at the end of craft activities; that they put materials back in the box and that they throw their trash away. You will need to supply each student with an envelope for photocopiable activities, such as game cards. At the end of the activity, students write their name on their envelope and put their cards inside. With younger students, it is best if you keep the envelopes until the next time you want to use the cards.

Evaluation pages

The evaluation pages in *Kid's Box American English 5* are designed to be used after each Review section: Evaluation 1 after Review Units 1–2, Evaluation 2 after Review Units 3–4, Evaluation 3 after Review Units 5–6 and Evaluation 4 after Review Units 7–8. You will notice that the evaluation pages use similar task-types to those in the Cambridge English: Young Learners (YLE) Flyers Test. Over the four evaluation pages, students will be evaluated on their Reading, Writing, Listening, and Speaking. Tell the students that you are going to give them an evaluation activity, but make sure they don't become too nervous about it. Hand out a copy to each student and make sure they have the necessary materials (crayons, pencils, etc.). You should allow about ten minutes for each evaluation. Give the instructions in English. Monitor students as they do the activity and give encouragement. At the end of the activity, collect their work. Give each student feedback about their work, but always focus on what they can do and what they have done, rather than on what they can't do. For students of this age, feedback should be positive and encouraging whenever possible, and no individual student's performance should be compared with the performance of another student. The audio track can be found on the *Kid's Box American English* website.

A final word

We've had a lot of fun writing this course and sincerely hope that you and your students have as much fun using it.

Caroline Nixon and Michael Tomlinson, Murcia 2017

Evaluation 1 (page T114)

F towards

Instructions

Tell students to take out a pencil and their crayons and put them on their desks. Hand out Evaluation 1. Say *Read the instructions.* Give them time to read. Say *Are you ready? Remember you are going to hear the CD twice. The first one is an example.* Play the CD twice through without a pause. At the end, tell students to write their names. Collect the papers from students.

Feedback: There are five stars at the bottom of the page. Color one for each correct answer. Draw a smiley face in the circle to the right. Congratulate students when you hand back their work. Don't grade the evaluation and don't rank students in order.

CD 3, 39

NARRATOR: Look at the picture. Listen and look. There is one example.
MAN: Hello, Jenny. Would you like to color this picture?
JENNY: Yes, please. They're making a TV program!
MAN: Yes. What would you like to color first?
JENNY: Um, the man who's holding a paintbrush, I think.
MAN: The one who's talking to a reporter. Color his hat.
JENNY: OK. I'll color it black.
NARRATOR: Can you see the man's black hat? This is an example. Now you listen and color and write.

NARRATOR: 1
JENNY: What should I color now?
MAN: Let me think. Can you see the children over there?
JENNY: Yes, I can. They're watching the police dog.
MAN: Well, look at the girl who's taking a picture.
JENNY: Should I color her T-shirt yellow?
MAN: OK. I like that color.

NARRATOR: 2
MAN: Can you see the chairs? There are two on the stage, close to the big camera.
JENNY: Should I color one?
MAN: No. Write on the smaller one. Write the word "actor" on it.
JENNY: I'm writing that now.

NARRATOR: 3
MAN: Would you like to write something else?
JENNY: Yes, please. I like writing.
MAN: Can you see the poster on the wall?
JENNY: The one above the clock?
MAN: Yes. Write "Television" under the letters A B C.
JENNY: That's a good idea.

NARRATOR: 4
MAN: I think you should color something now.
JENNY: OK.
MAN: There are two people looking at a poster on the wall.
JENNY: Should I color the woman's hair?
MAN: Yes. What color, do you think?
JENNY: I think red.
MAN: Do that color then.

NARRATOR: 5
MAN: Last thing now. There are two men sitting next to the photographer.
JENNY: Yes. One of them's wearing glasses. Should I color his jacket?
MAN: Yes. Color it blue.
JENNY: OK. Is that all?
MAN: Yes. It looks good, doesn't it?

NARRATOR: That is the end of the evaluation.

Evaluation 2 (page T115)

Instructions

If you are working with one student at a time, show them Parts A and B, but then take back Part B and tell them this is your copy. Ask questions using the simple past to elicit the information the student has on their sheet. Then the student asks the questions to find out the information you have. Alternatively, students can do the activity in pairs.

Feedback: There are ten stars at the bottom of the page. Color each one according to how well the student completed the task: one star for each correct question and answer. Draw a smiley face in the circle to the right.

Evaluation 3 (page T116)

Instructions

Hand out Evaluation 3. Say *Read the instructions.* Give students time to read. Say *Are you ready? Remember you can use one, two, three, or four words for your answers. Use the example to help you.* Students work individually. Give them about seven minutes to complete the evaluation.

Collect the papers from students. Make sure they have written their names.

Feedback: There are seven stars at the bottom of the page. Color each one according to how well the student completed the task: one star for each correct answer. Draw a smiley face in the circle.

Key (possible answers): 1 cages, 2 the rabbits, 3 kitchen, 4 played with Jerry, 5 close the door, 6 carrots and cheese, 7 in his bowl

Evaluation 4 (page T117)

Instructions

Hand out Evaluation 4. Say *Read the instructions.* Give students time to read. Say *Are you ready? Remember to read the whole letter before you start and to write one word in each blank. Use the example to help you.* Students work individually. Give them about seven minutes to complete the evaluation.

Collect the papers from students. Make sure they have written their names.

Feedback: There are five stars at the bottom of the page. Color each one according to how well the student completed the task: one star for each correct answer. Draw a smiley face in the circle.

Key: 1 by, 2 best, 3 that, 4 won, 5 soon

Welcome to our ezine

Show what you know! What school words can you remember?

Listening **1** 02 CD1 Listen and check (✓) the school words you hear.

2 03 CD1 Listen again. Who said it?

1 Did you have a good vacation? (Dan.)
2 What's an ezine?
3 It's an internet magazine.
4 Can we write about sports and computers?
5 Let's write our first ezine on our school.
6 See you outside school at four o'clock.

3 Answer the questions.

1 What are the children's names?
2 Where are they?
3 Where's the poster?
4 What's an ezine?
5 What's the prize for?
6 What can they write about?

LOOK

Nice to meet you.

OBJECTIVES: By the end of the lesson, students will have reviewed introductions, suggestions, and how to exchange personal information.

• TARGET LANGUAGE

Key language: *Hello, Hi, Nice to meet you, Let's ... , Should we ... ? We can ... , Show what you know, ezine, internet magazine, competition, prize*

Additional language: character names, *See you! sneakers, wifi, do a search*

Review: simple past, simple present, *can* for ability and permission, school vocabulary

• MATERIALS REQUIRED

Extra activity 1: A sheet of paper for each student, colored pencils

Extra activity 2: A large sheet of paper for each group of four students

Optional: *Kid's Box AE Workbook 5 Language Portfolio,* pages 89 and 90

Warmer

- Greet the students and introduce yourself. Put students into pairs. They find out each other's names and then one piece of interesting information about each other, e.g., where their partner went on vacation. Go around the class, asking students to introduce their partner and tell the class the piece of information, e.g., *This is Charley. He has a baby brother.* Don't overcorrect.

SB4. SHOW WHAT YOU KNOW! *What school words can you remember?*

- Write *School* on the board and draw a circle around it. Say *Show what you know ... about school.* Brainstorm in two minutes all the school words the students remember onto a mind map on the board. Students copy it into their notebooks.

SB4. ACTIVITY 1. *Listen and check (✓) the school words you hear.*

- Tell students to open their Student's Books to page 4. Focus them on the pictures and introduce the characters (girl Maria, blond boy Dan, and Alex). Elicit where they are (a school) and its name (City School). Elicit/Pre-teach *ezine* (see tapescript below). Focus students on the activity instruction. They check the words they hear in their School mind maps.
- Play the CD. Students listen and check. They check in pairs. Use the mind map on the board to check with the class.

CD 1, 02

DAN: Hi, Maria. Did you have a good vacation?

MARIA: Yeah. Nice, thanks, Dan. Do you know Alex? He lives close to me and he's new in school.

DAN: Hi, Alex. Nice to meet you.

ALEX: Hi, Dan.

ALEX: What's that on the board?

MARIA: It's a poster about a new school ezine.

DAN: What's an ezine?

MARIA: It's an internet magazine.

DAN: Oh!

DAN: Look. It's a competition for the best ezine in the school.

MARIA: Oh, that's interesting. And there's a prize! Should we try and write one?

ALEX: Good idea, but what should we write about?

ALL: Hmm.

ALEX: Oh! Can we write about sports and computers?

DAN: We can write about anything we like.

MARIA: Let's write our first ezine on our school, so Alex can learn about it.

DAN: OK.

ALEX: Great!

DAN: See you outside school at four o'clock.

ALEX AND MARIA: See you!

SB4. ACTIVITY 2. *Listen again. Who said it?*

- Focus students on Activity 2 and on the activity instructions. Write the characters' names (Dan, Maria, Alex) on the board.
- Play the CD. Students listen and write the name for each one. They check in pairs. Play the CD again. Check with the class.
- Focus students on the Look box. Elicit who said this to whom (Dan to Alex). Get the class to repeat after you. Provide a short dialogue for practice: A: *Hi. I'm* (name). B: *Hi. I'm* (name). *Nice to meet you.* Students practice with classmates.

Key: Dan: 2, 6; Maria: 3, 5; Alex: 4

CD 1, 03

SB4. ACTIVITY 3. *Answer the questions.*

- Ask *Do they want to enter the competition? What do they get for the best ezine?*
- Focus students on Activity 3. In pairs, students answer the questions orally. Elicit answers, reminding students to use full sentences. Students write the full answers in their notebooks.

Key: 1 Their names are Dan, Maria and Alex. 2 They are at school. 3 It's on the board / in the school corridor. 4 It's an internet magazine. 5 The prize is for the best ezine. 6 They can write about anything they like.

WB4. ACTIVITY 1. *Put the words in groups.*

- Pre-teach *sneakers* and *wifi.*

Key: Things we read: comic book, newspaper, magazine; Things we wear: coat, sweater, sneakers; Computer things: wifi, screen, Internet

WB4. ACTIVITY 2. *Match the sentences with Dan, Maria, and Alex.*

Key: 2 Alex, 3 Dan, 4 Alex, 5 Maria, 6 Dan

WB4. ACTIVITY 3. *Read and complete.*

- Make sure students understand *(do a) search on the Internet.*

Key: 2 store, 3 Internet, 4 sports, 5 pictures, 6 music, 7 videos, 8 ezine

WB4. ACTIVITY 4. *Correct the sentences.*

Key: 2 No, you can't. You can find it on the Internet. 3 No, it isn't. *Kid's Box* is a new ezine. 4 No, they aren't. They're named Maria, Dan, and Alex. 5 No, there isn't. There's a prize for the best ezine.

Extra activities: see page T98 (if time)

Language Portfolio

- Students complete pages 89 and 90 of *Kid's Box AE Workbook 5 Language Portfolio* (My languages and Language Portfolio language skills: My progress).

Ending the lesson

- Review with students what they learned in this lesson, e.g., *What did we do today? What new words did you learn?* Do this orally. Say *See you on* (day). Students reply with the same.

OBJECTIVES: By the end of the lesson, students will have reviewed daily routines, likes, and preferences.

• TARGET LANGUAGE

Key language: simple present for routines, *like/love …- ing, 'd like*, question words, short answers, *so, before*
Additional language: character names
Review: sports, activities, school, superlative adjectives

• MATERIALS REQUIRED

Extra activity 1: A sheet of paper for each student
Optional: *Kid's Box AE Workbook 5 Language Portfolio*, page 95

Warmer

- Write the names *Dan, Alex, Maria* on the board. Elicit, using mind maps, information that the students remember about these three characters from the previous lesson. Ask questions with *interested in*, e.g., *Who do you think is interested in sports/art/music/clothes?* Elicit what else they'd like to know about the characters (to predict the content of this lesson).

SB5. ACTIVITY 4. *Read and answer.*

- Tell students to open their Student's Books to page 5. Focus students on the pictures and check who is who. Ask a student to read the introduction aloud. Write these gist reading questions on the board: *1 Who wants to write about nature? 2 Who's 11? 3 Who likes singing and music?* Students read the texts quickly to find the answers. They check in pairs. Check with the class (1 Maria, 2 Alex, 3 Dan). Focus students on the eight questions on the page. They re-read the texts and then answer the questions orally in pairs. Check with the class.

Key: 1 An ezine. 2 Alex. 3 City School. 4 He always rides his bike. 5 Ten. 6 Music and clothes. 7 Drawing and taking photos. 8 Alex.

SB5. ACTIVITY 5. *Listen and say the name.*

- Focus students on the activity instruction and on the example. Play number 1 on the CD as a demonstration. Check understanding of this type of short answer. Play the rest of the CD. Pause to give students time to check for the answer and to whisper the answer to their partner. Play the CD again. Elicit responses from pairs of students.

Key: 2 Dan does. 3 Alex does. 4 Maria does. 5 Alex does. 6 Dan does. 7 Maria does. 8 Alex does.

CD 1, 04

1. Who lives close to the school?
2. Who lives outside the town?
3. Who has breakfast in school?
4. Who walks to school?
5. Who loves playing soccer and basketball?
6. Who likes singing?
7. Who wants to write about the natural world?
8. Who wants to write about computers?

SB5. ACTIVITY 6. *Ask and answer.*

- Focus students on the activity instruction and check understanding. Elicit questions for some or all of the prompts as necessary. Students write the questions in their notebooks. They then take turns to asking and answering in pairs. Check students remember to use the short answers *Yes, I do. / No, I don't.* in this activity. Monitor and help where necessary. Students need to make notes of their partner's responses.

SB5. *Now think of some more questions.*

- Students think of at least two more questions each to ask and answer in their pairs.

WB5. ACTIVITY 5. *Read and order the text.*

- When students have found the correct order, they write the correct version in their notebooks.

Key: 2, 4, 9, 12, 7, 5, 3, 1, 6, 10, 8, 11

WB5. ACTIVITY 6. *Read and complete the questions.*

- Remind students to look at the answers to the questions before they try to choose the question word.

Key: 2 How many, 3 What, 4 When, 5 Why, 6 Where

WB5. ACTIVITY 7. *Write the correct sentences.*

- Each sentence is made up of three parts as in the example.

Key: 2 Dan lives in the country. 3 Maria walks to school every day. 4 Alex's the oldest of the children. 5 Alex lives close to Maria. 6 Dan and Maria are both ten.

Extra activities: see page T98 (if time)

Language Portfolio

- Students complete page 95 of *Kid's Box AE Workbook 5 Language Portfolio* (Learning English: Outside the classroom).

Ending the lesson

- Say some true/false sentences about Alex, Maria, and Dan. If the sentence is true, students stand up (or sit down). If it's false, they don't move. Example sentences: *Maria lives in the country.* (false). *Alex sometimes goes to the school breakfast club* (true).

4 Read and answer.

Kid's Box is an exciting new ezine for young people. Let's meet the writers, Dan, Alex, and Maria. They all go to the same school. It's called "City School."

Alex

I'm eleven years old. I always ride my bike to school. I sometimes have breakfast with the school breakfast club before my classes. I love playing soccer and basketball. I'm also interested in computers. I'd like to write about sports and computers in the ezine.

Dan

I'm ten. I live in the country outside the town, so I catch a bus to school every morning. I like singing and music. I love playing the guitar and the piano. I'd like to write about music and clothes in the ezine.

Maria

I'm ten. I live close to the school, so I walk in every day. I have lunch in school with my friends. I love drawing and taking pictures, so I want to put my pictures in the ezine and write about the natural world.

1 What's *Kid's Box*?
2 Who's interested in computers?
3 Which school do they go to?
4 How does Alex go to school?
5 How old is Dan?
6 What would Dan like to write about?
7 What does Maria love doing?
8 Who's the oldest, Alex, Maria, or Dan?

5 Listen and say the name.

04 CD1

Who lives close to the school? — Maria does.

6 Ask and answer.

Do you live close to your school? — No, I don't.

~~live / close to school~~
lunch / home
play / musical instrument

like / sports
read / magazines
use / the Internet

Now think of some more questions.

Reading **7** Read and think. What's your favorite school subject? Why?

http://www.cambridge.org/elt/kidsbox/ezine

Kid's Box Ezine!

home | reports | games | world | email

Kid's Box reports – Our School

For our first ezine we went around our school to find out more about what we learn.
We all study these school subjects: math, English, science, music, P.E., art, and computer studies.

a

Older students have to study more school subjects and take important exams.

b We study a second language. We can choose French, German, or Spanish.

c

We use the dictionaries in the school library to help us understand new words.

d

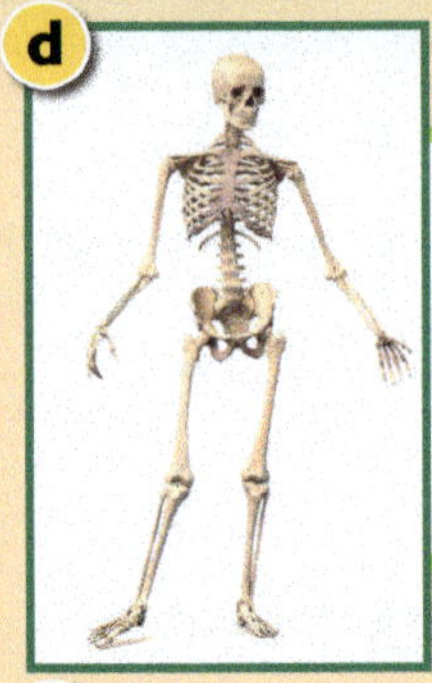

Science is an important subject, so we do it every day. This year we're learning about plants and the human body.

e In our geography classes we learn about different people and their countries.

f

The best subject is history. We love learning about the past!

We all agree that the best thing about school right now is the new ezine competition.
We all want to win that prize!

science | history | geography | language | school subjects | exam | dictionary

8 05 CD1 Listen. Repeat the word and say the letter. 1 History. History. That's "f."

9 Read again and say "same" or "different."

1 At City School they all study music.
2 Older students take important exams.
3 They can choose a second language.
4 There are dictionaries in the school library.
5 They study science every day.
6 They think history is better than geography.

OBJECTIVES: By the end of the lesson, students will have read about school subjects, chosen their favorites and given reasons for their choices.

● TARGET LANGUAGE

Key language: school subjects, numbers, adjectives, *second language, dictionary, exam*, simple present / simple past

Additional language: *We all agree that … , We all want … , the past*

Review: known school subjects

● MATERIALS REQUIRED

Extra activity 1: A large sheet of paper for each group of four students, colored markers

Extra activity 2: Dictionaries, paper

Optional: *Kid's Box AE Teacher's Resource Book 5* Welcome unit Reinforcement worksheets 1 and 2 (pages 9 and 10)

Warmer

- Write six known school subjects as anagrams on the board. Students work in pairs and race to unscramble them. Elicit the correct spellings. Elicit other subject names that students know in English.

SB6. ACTIVITY 7. *Read and think. What's your favorite school subject? Why?*

- Tell students to open their Student's Books to page 6. Focus them on Activity 7 and on the activity instructions. Make sure they notice the words at the bottom of the webpage. Ask a student to read them aloud. Elicit students' responses to the question and their reasons.
- Focus students on the heading, the photographs and on the accompanying texts. They read the texts silently. Check comprehension by asking, e.g., *Which are the subjects everyone has to study at City School? What are the students learning about in science this year?* After each question, ask the class *What about our school?* to get them to relate the information to their own school context. Check understanding of *second language*. Check students understand the relationship between the texts and the pictures.

SB6. ACTIVITY 8. *Listen. Repeat the word and say the letter.*

- Focus students on the Activity 8 instructions. Play the example to check students know what to do. Play the rest of the CD. Students repeat the word in chorus and then write the letter in their notebooks the first time they listen. Play the CD again. Students repeat the word and say the letter.

Key: 2 science. That's "d." 3 geography. That's "e." 4 Language. That's "b." 5 Exam. That's "a." 6 Dictionary. That's "c."

CD 1, 05

1 history, 2 science, 3 geography, 4 language, 5 exam, 6 dictionary

SB6. ACTIVITY 9. *Read again and say "same" or "different."*

- Focus students on Activity 9. Students take turns reading the statements around the class for the class to say *Same* or *Different* according to what happens in their school. Elicit more ideas for statements from students. They each write four more statements. Monitor and help where necessary. In pairs, students take turns reading a statement aloud and saying *Same* or *Different* with reference to their school. When students say *Different*, they say what happens in their school. If they go to different schools, they can compare their schools. Finish the activity in groups of four: pairs say one of their own statements to another pair.

WB6. ACTIVITY 8. *Choose words from the box to label the pictures.*

- Discuss what is in the picture clues with the class.

Note: There are two extra words in the box.

Key: 2 geography, 3 history, 4 exam, 5 language, 6 dictionary

WB6. ACTIVITY 9. *Follow the school words.*

- Go through the examples.
- Pre-teach *elbow* and check understanding of *knee*.

Key: math, English, computer studies, exam, dictionary, science, art, P.E., music, teacher, board, subject

WB6. ACTIVITY 10. *Now complete the chart with words from Activity 9.*

- Early finishers can add other words to the three categories.

Key: The body: back, beard, knee, ears, mustache, elbow; Food: beans, rice, potatoes, salad, soup, pasta; The natural world: ocean, cave, mountain, lake, river, field; Words that don't belong: dress, pants; Group: Clothes.

WB6. ACTIVITY 11. *Answer the questions.*

- Encourage students to answer in full sentences.

Key: Students' own answers

Extra activities: see page T98 (if time)

Optional activity

- Welcome unit Reinforcement worksheets 1 and 2 from *Teacher's Resource Book 5* (see pages 8, 9 and 10).

Ending the lesson

- Play a word association game. Say, e.g., *science*. Students call out words which they associate with it, e.g., *experiments, Tuesday, animals*. After about six words, call out a new subject word, e.g., *math*. Students can play this game in groups of six.

OBJECTIVES: By the end of the lesson, students will have had further practice with school subjects and sung a song.

• TARGET LANGUAGE

Key language: definitions, rhyming words, *computer studies, art*
Additional language: *field hockey, map*
Review: school subjects, simple present, *study, learn about, too* + adjective, *cool*

• MATERIALS REQUIRED

Extra activity 1 and 2: Paper
Optional: *Kid's Box AE Teacher's Resource Book 5* Welcome unit Song worksheet (page 13)

Warmer

- Call out school subjects one by one for students to spell aloud. Alternatively, they can write the words in their notebooks.

SB7. ACTIVITY 10. *Listen and say the subject.*

- Tell students to open their Student's Books to page 7. Focus on the activity instruction. Tell them they will hear clues. Play the CD twice, checking with the class after the second listening. Elicit what they heard, as well as the subject and what the clues were.

Key: 2 music, 3 math, 4 science, 5 history, 6 computer studies, 7 P.E., 8 language/French

CD 1, 06

1. A lot of people think the capital of Australia is Sydney, but it isn't. It's Canberra.
2. [Sound of recorders]
3. One nine is nine. Two nines are eighteen. Three nines are twenty-seven …
4. Plants have green leaves. They use their leaves to get food from the sun. Plants give us oxygen.
5. Magellan was the first man to sail around the world. He sailed around the world in 1642.
6. OK, Mary, now hold the mouse in your hand and click on the left button.
7. [Sound of bouncing balls and referee's whistle blowing]
8. Bonjour. Je m'appelle Peter. Bonjour. Je m'appelle Ann.

SB7. ACTIVITY 11. *Read and choose the right words.*

- In pairs, students read the sentences and choose the correct word. Pairs check with pairs. Check with the class.

Key: 1 history, 2 languages, 3 a dictionary, 4 science, 5 geography, 6 exams

SB7. ACTIVITY 12. *Listen and match. Check and sing.*

- Focus students on the song. They work in pairs to match the icons with the words. When everyone is ready, play the CD.
- Students listen again and check their work. Check with the class.
- Play the CD again. Students repeat line by line and then verse by verse. Students stand up. They sing the song right through, once with the first version on the CD and once with the karaoke version. Divide the class into two groups: one sings the verses, and the other the chorus. Swap and repeat.

Key: 2g, 3a, 4d, 5f, 6h, 7e, 8b

CD 1, 07

As in Student's Book

CD 1, 08

Now sing the song again. (Karaoke version)

SB7. ACTIVITY 13. *Read about the school words. What are they?* [F] toward

- Focus students on Activity 13 and on the instructions. Elicit the answers from the class.

Key: languages, science, geography, dictionary

SB7. ACTIVITY 14. *Write three more definitions. Ask and answer.* [F] toward

- Focus students on the Activity 14 instructions and check they know what to do. Brainstorm ideas to make definitions for other school subjects, e.g., music, computer studies, P.E. Students work individually and write at least three more definitions beginning with the phrases in bold in Activity 13. Monitor and help/advise.
- Make pairs or groups of four. Focus students on the dialogue prompts for this activity. Remind them to use *What is it?* and to respond with a *yes/no* question each time. Students take turns reading their definitions to the group. The other students take turns guessing.

WB7. ACTIVITY 12. *Read and complete the school schedule.*

- Remind students to read all the information through, before they try to complete the schedule.

Key:

	Monday	Tuesday	Wednesday	Thursday	Friday
9:00–10:00	science	computer studies	geography	math	science
10:00–11:00	math	science	P.E.	science	computer studies
11:00–12:00	computer studies	geography	music	English	English
lunch					
13:00–14:00	geography	art	art	art	history
14:00–15:00	history	P.E.	English	music	music
15:00–16:00	English	math	math	history	P.E.

WB7. ACTIVITY 13. *Now write about Jim's Monday schedule.*

- Students use sentences from Activity 12 as their models.

Key: Students' own answers

WB7. ACTIVITY 14. *Write about the schedule of your favorite school day.* [F] toward

- Early finishers can also say why this is their favorite day.

Key: Students' own answers

Extra activities: see page T98 (if time)

Optional activity

- Welcome unit Song worksheet from *Teacher's Resource Book 5* (see pages 8 and 13).

Ending the lesson

- Students sing the song from earlier in the lesson again.

10 Listen and say the subject.

06 CD1

1 A lot of people think the capital of Australia is Sydney, but it isn't. It's Canberra.

Geography.

11 Read and choose the right words.

1 We study the past in **science / geography / history.**
2 French, Spanish, and German are **languages / exams / math.**
3 When we don't understand a word, we can use **a book / a dictionary / art.**
4 We study plants and the human body in **math / P.E. / science.**
5 We learn about people and countries in **geography / computer studies / music.**
6 Teachers sometimes find out what we know by giving us **subjects / computers / exams.**

12 Listen and match. Check and sing.

07 CD1

a

b

Because school is cool, it's where we go
From Monday through Friday, I'm sure you know.
We study and we play, that's what we do.
We do it in the morning and the afternoon!

c

d

I really love (1)geography,
And I enjoy (2)history.
I like to study (3)science, too!
My favorite subject in the afternoon.

Before lunch we have (4)music,
And then (5)computer studies,
And on Wednesday we do (6)sports.
That's a class that is too short!

e

f

And I like to do (7)languages,
Spanish, French and Japanese.
A lot of words in the (8)dictionary,
For me to study and to read.

g

h
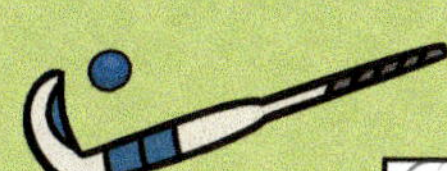

13 Read about the school words. What are they?

With this subject we can learn to talk to people from another country.

In this class we learn about plants and the human body.

When we study this, we learn about different countries and people.

We use this to learn new words.

14 Write three more definitions. Ask and answer.

With this subject we can learn about numbers and shapes. What is it?

Is it math?

Yes, it is.

15 Focus on phonics

Jill likes geography and German,
Her favorite subjects in school.
Charlie likes French, eating lunch,
And jumping in the pool!

Speaking 16 Play the game. Guess it in ten.

MY SCHOOL SCHEDULE

	Monday	Tuesday	Wednesday	Thursday	Friday
8:00–9:00	history	math	music	science	math
9:00–10:00	English	computer studies	geography	P.E.	
			recess		
11:00–12:00	art	science	science	French	English
12:00–13:00		music	computer studies	history	geography
			lunch		
14:00–15:00	French	P.E.	history	English	computer studies
15:00–16:00	geography		math	art	French

Is it on Thursday? Yes, it is.

Is it before lunch? No, it isn't.

Is it at three o'clock? Yes, it is.

Is it art? Yes, it is.

Joke Corner

Why doesn't the elephant like computer studies?

He's afraid of the mouse.

Writing 17 Write your school schedule.

OBJECTIVES: By the end of the lesson, students will have practiced identifying and differentiating between the phonemes /ʤ/ and /ʧ/. They will also have written their school schedule.

• TARGET LANGUAGE

Key language: *schedule/timetable*, *yes/no* questions and short answers, punctuation: *capital letter, period*

Review: school subjects, telling the time, *at, before, on, in, joke*

• MATERIALS REQUIRED

Extra activity 1: A large sheet of paper for each group of four students, glue

Extra activity 2: Paper for each student

Optional: *Kid's Box AE Workbook 5 Language Portfolio*, page 97

Warmer

- Write the words *kitchen, question* and *cheese* on the board. Ask students which sound all three words have in common. Say the words aloud. Students discuss in pairs. Elicit suggestions. Repeat the words, emphasising the /ʧ/ sounds. Underline them on the board (*kitchen, question, cheese*). Repeat with the words *Julia, giraffe, juice*. Elicit the sound /ʤ/. Tell students they will be practising recognising and telling the difference between these two sounds in today's lesson.

SB8. ACTIVITY **15.** *Focus on phonics*

- Tell students to open their Student's Books to page 8. Focus them on Activity 15. Elicit/Tell the class that this is the pronunciation activity. Play the CD. Students repeat after each line and then after the whole rhyme. Repeat once more. In pairs, students practice saying the rhyme together.

CD 1, 09

As in Student's Book

SB8. ACTIVITY **16.** *Play the game. Guess it in ten.*

- Focus students on Activity 16 and elicit that this is a guessing game. Demonstrate the game for students. Choose a subject on a day from the schedule without telling the class. Students take turns asking questions, as in the example, to guess the subject. They can have only ten questions. Check they remember to use *yes/no* questions. Students work in pairs. Student A chooses a subject and day and Student B has ten guesses. If Student B guesses correctly in less than ten, he/she gets a point. At the end of the game, the student with the most points is the winner.

SB8. ACTIVITY **17.** *Write your school schedule.*

- Focus students on Activity 17. Elicit some ideas for subjects. Make the schedule shape similar to their own, e.g., the number of lessons in a day, any half days they have. Students work individually and draw their own schedule on a sheet of paper.

SB8. JOKE CORNER.

- Focus students on the Joke Corner and review the meaning of *joke*. Play the CD as students read the joke in their books. Play the joke a second time and explain if necessary.

CD 1, 10

As in Student's Book

WB8. ACTIVITY **15.** *Write the words in the columns.*

- Tell students to open their Workbook to page 8. Check they know the meaning of all the words in the box. Read out the heading of each column. Make sure students know which sound goes in which column, using the example. Elicit the first word in the "j" column, if necessary. Students complete the activity in pencil. Tell them to say the words aloud to help.

WB8. ACTIVITY **16.** *Listen, check, and say.*

- Play the CD for students to listen and check. They compare answers in pairs. Check with the class. Play the CD again for students to listen and repeat.

Key: See audioscript below

CD 1, 11

"ch" sound: children, watch, French, question, picture

"j" sound: January, village, German, bridge, dangerous

WB8. ACTIVITY **17.** *Find 17 mistakes in the text.*

- Before students do the activity, focus them on the Write it right box and preteach *capital letter* and *period* using an example sentence with the class, e.g., *I don't have english on mondays*

Key: See Activity 18 key

WB8. ACTIVITY **18.** *Now write the text correctly.*

Key: On Mondays I have English, math and history in the morning. After lunch I only have two classes. They are science and art. Art is my favorite subject.

On Tuesdays I don't have English or math but I have P.E., which is great. After P.E. I have history and then in the afternoon I have geography and science. I love doing experiments in science.

WB8. ACTIVITY **19.** *Write about your dream school schedule.*

- Brainstorm ideas with students before they write. Students swap and check each other's drafts for mistakes before they write their final versions.

Key: Students' own answers

Extra activities: see page T98 (if time)

Language Portfolio

- Students complete page 97 of *Kid's Box AE Workbook 5 Language Portfolio* (About me).

Ending the lesson

- Do the phonics rhyme again with the class. Students stand up. Do it quickly and quietly and then quickly and loudly.

OBJECTIVES: By the end of the lesson, students will have read a story, reviewed language from the unit and completed a self-evaluation.

• TARGET LANGUAGE

Key language: language in the story, *Diggory Bones, dig, rocks, stones, archeology, archeologist, Sir Doug Bones, dinosaur, skeleton, ancient, the Rosetta Stone, program*

Additional language: *School of Archeology, classes, Egyptian hieroglyphics*

Review: *neck, bone, museum*, adjectives, language from the unit

• MATERIALS REQUIRED

Extra activity 2: The text from Workbook Activity 21 written on a large sheet of paper with blanks for certain words as below:

Egyptian hieroglyphics were one of the first kinds of [1]__________, but modern people couldn't [2]__________ them. Ancient people wrote important things on the [3]__________ Stone in three different [4]__________. In 1822, a very smart man named Jean-François Champollion used two of the [5]__________ to [6]__________ the third, the Egyptian hieroglyphics. The [7]__________ Stone helped us [8]__________ the [9]__________ better.

Optional: *Kid's Box AE Teacher's Resource Book 5* Welcome unit Extension worksheets 1 and 2 (pages 11 and 12) and/or Topic worksheet (page 14)

Warmer

- Review *history* and introduce the topic of *archeology*. Brainstorm (using a mind map) students' ideas about what people do / find out through archeology. Elicit/Provide *bones, dig, rocks, stones.*

SB9. STORY. *Diggory Bones.*

- Tell students to open their Student's Books to page 9. Elicit where the characters are (museum) and what is in the museum (dinosaur skeletons). Say *Look at the dinosaur bones. How many knees does this dinosaur have? Do you think this dinosaur has elbows?* (no) *Look at the dinosaur in the poster. Does it have elbows?* (Yes, it does.) Focus on the story in general, using this to introduce the context (*archeology, archeologist*). Set the questions: *What's the story called? What's the old man's name? What's the young man's name? What's the girl's name? Are they related?* Play the CD. Students listen and read to find the answers. They check in pairs. Check with the class (Diggory Bones. Sir Doug Bones. Diggory (Bones). Emily (Bones), Yes – Doug is Diggory's father and Emily's grandfather).
- Play the CD again. Students listen and read. Stop after each frame for students to repeat. At the end, check general comprehension by asking, e.g., *What's the name of the dinosaur? Is it small? What's Sir Doug Bones doing? What does Diggory Bones do? What is he teaching at the moment? Who's on the phone? What happened? What's The Baloney Stone?* Provide information in L1 for students about The Rosetta Stone. Elicit from students in L1 examples of ancient languages, what they know about dinosaurs and about archeology finds around the world.

CD 1, 12

As in Student's Book

WB9. ACTIVITY 20. *Read and answer.*

- Remind students to re-read the story as they answer the questions. It's not a test of memory.

Key: 2 It's almost 30 meters long. 3 They're learning about The Rosetta Stone. 4 It helped us understand ancient languages. 5 It was in his classroom. 6 She's Diggory's daughter.

WB9. ACTIVITY 21. *Read the text. Then look at the code and write the secret message.*

- Check understanding of *hieroglyphics* before/when students read the text.

Key: Very old languages are a kind of code. Use this code to write messages.

WB9. DO YOU REMEMBER?

- Students try to do the activity first without looking back through the unit. Once they have tried to complete all the sentences, they can look back through the unit to find the answers.

Key: 2 dictionary, 3 geography, 4 science, 5 Students' own answers, 6 period

WB9. CAN DO

- Focus students on the *Can do* section of the page. Ask a student to read the first sentence. Elicit what this means with examples and elicit/remind them of the activities they did in this unit when they talked about school subjects. Review what the three faces mean (not very well / OK / very well). Remind students they circle the one they think is true for them. Repeat for the second sentence, eliciting/reminding them of the activities when they asked their friends about school schedules. Students circle the appropriate face. Repeat for the third sentence, eliciting what *capital letters* and *periods* are and when students use them.
- Say *Now show and tell your friends.* Students work in groups of three and take turns showing their work for / talking about each one.

Extra activities: see page T98 (if time)

Optional activity

- Welcome unit Extension worksheets 1 and 2 and/or Topic worksheet from *Teacher's Resource Book 5* (see pages 8, 11, 12 and 14).

Ending the lesson

- Ask students which rhyme/song they'd like to do again from the unit. Do it together to end the lesson.

DIGGORY BONES

12 CD1

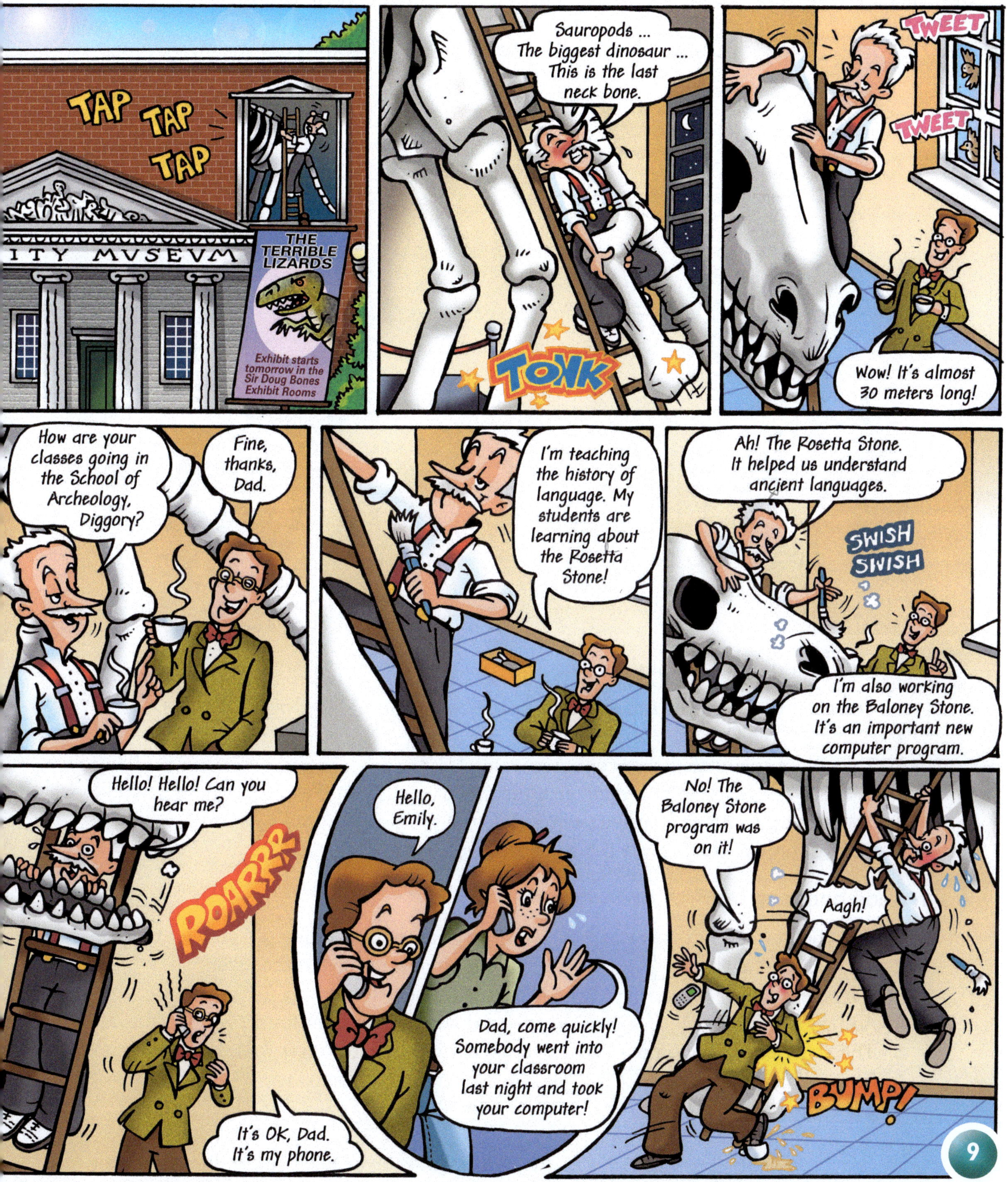

1 Time for TV

Show what you know! What TV words can you remember?

Listening **1** 13 CD1 Listen and check (✓) the TV words you hear.

2 14 CD1 Listen again. Say "yes" or "no."

1. The children are in the supermarket at the beginning of the story. (No.)
2. *Fun time* is on TV at ten after four.
3. They want to watch a show about animals.
4. The kids arrive home at a quarter after five.
5. The kids go to Alex's house to watch TV.
6. Mr. Nelson wants to watch the same show as them.

3 Read and match.

1. The children are in the library
2. They leave the library
3. *Fun time* is on TV1
4. *Animals* is on TV2
5. The children arrive home
6. The golf finishes

a. at ten after four.
b. at twenty-five after seven.
c. at ten to four.
d. at twenty after four.
e. at a quarter after four.
f. at five to four.

LOOK

It's **a quarter to** four. It's **a quarter after** four.

OBJECTIVES: By the end of the lesson, students will be able to tell the time and will have reviewed TV shows they know.

• TARGET LANGUAGE

Key language: time: *o'clock*, *after* (e.g., *ten*, *a quarter*), half past, *to* (e.g., *a quarter*, *twenty*)

Additional language: *just in time*

Review: character names, TV shows, suggestions: *Should/ Let's*; *golf*

• MATERIALS REQUIRED

Extra activity 1: Two sheets of colored paper or thin cardboard (white and blue) for each pair

Optional: *Kid's Box AE Teacher's Resource Book 5* Unit 1 Reinforcement worksheet 1 (page 16)

Warmer

- Greet the students. Say you have forgotten your watch and ask them to tell you what the time is. Write the time (if it isn't exactly *o'clock*) on the board, e.g., *2:05*. Elicit/Tell students how to say this in English, e.g., *Five after two*. Ask them what time the lesson finishes and do the same with this.

Presentation

- Tell students what time you had breakfast today, e.g., *7:45 a.m.* Draw the time on a clock and teach *A quarter to eight*. Do the same for when you, e.g., arrived at school: *8:15 a.m.*, and teach *A quarter after eight*. Use a circle on the board (to represent a clock) to show *after* and *to*. Use different colors. Draw clocks with different times on the board to practice how to tell the time, e.g., *12:00*, *1:25*, *4:50*, *3:15*, *9:45*, *5:30*. Use the colors on the circle on the board to remind students of *after* and *to*. Elicit/Teach *a.m.* and *p.m.* Tell students to open their Student's Books to page 10 and focus them on the Look box.

SB10. SHOW WHAT YOU KNOW! *What TV words can you remember?*

- Write *TV* on the board and draw a circle around it. Say *Show what you know … about TV.* Brainstorm all the different things students can say about TV in two minutes and create a mind map on the board. Supply words in English where necessary. Students copy the mind map into their notebooks.

SB10. ACTIVITY 1. *Listen and check (✓) the TV words you hear.*

- Focus students on the Activity 1 pictures. Elicit the names of the characters and what they're looking at in picture 1 (a TV magazine). Focus students on the activity instruction and check understanding. Remind them they do the same as for the "Show what you know" in the previous unit (check off the words they hear in the TV mind maps in their notebooks).
- Play the CD. Students listen and check. They check in pairs. Use the mind map on the board to check with the class.

CD 1, 13

NARRATOR: It's ten to four. Dan, Maria and Alex are in the library.

ALEX: Look at this, Dan. *Fun time* is on TV1 at ten after four. Should we watch it?

DAN: Wait a minute. *Animals* is on TV2 at twenty after four.

MARIA: Let's watch that because we all like it.

DAN: Yeah, that's a good idea, but what time is it now?

MARIA: It's five to four. If we want to watch it, we have to leave now.

ALEX: Come on, then. Let's go!

DAN: Phew. Just in time. It's a quarter after four.

MARIA: Hi, Dad. Can we put TV2 on, please? We want to watch *Animals*.

MR. NELSON: Oh, I'm sorry, Maria. Not today. Golf's on TV3 and you know I love golf.

ALEX: What time does it finish, Mr. Nelson?

MR. NELSON: Oh, don't worry. It finishes at twenty-five after seven!

THREE CHILDREN: Oh.

MARIA: Well, boys, I think we can watch TV another day.

ALEX: You're right. Let's go and write something about TV for our ezine.

DAN: Yeah. We can't watch TV, but we can write about it.

MR. NELSON: Shhhh!

THREE CHILDREN: Ooh!

SB10. ACTIVITY 2. *Listen again. Say "yes" or "no."*

- Focus students on Activity 2. Play the CD. Students listen and whisper the answers. Play the CD again. Pause after each one to elicit the response. For "no" answers, elicit the corrections. Elicit what the time is in each of the four pictures and who the man in pictures 3 and 4 is.

Key: 2 Yes, 3 Yes, 4 No (a quarter after four), 5 No (Maria's house), 6 No (He wants to watch golf.)

CD 1, 14

SB10. ACTIVITY 3. *Read and match.*

- Focus students on Activity 3. In pairs, they try to match the actions with the times. They draw the different times in their notebooks. Play the CD again for students to check. Check with the class.

Key: 1c, 2f, 3a, 4d, 5e, 6b

WB10. ACTIVITY 1. *Match the clocks with the pictures.*

Key: 2e, 3b, 4d, 5c, 6a

WB10. ACTIVITY 2. *Write the times.*

Key: 2 half past five/five thirty, 3 twenty-five after three, 4 five to eight, 5 a quarter to nine, 6 ten after seven

WB10. ACTIVITY 3. *Read and draw the times on the clocks.*

- Students read each sentence and draw the appropriate time on the same number clock.

Extra activities: see page T99 (if time)

Optional activity

- Unit 1 Reinforcement worksheet 1 from *Teacher's Resource Book 5* (see pages 15 and 16).

Ending the lesson

- Choose about eight TV words. Write them in scrambled form on the board for students to reorder.

OBJECTIVES: By the end of the lesson, students will have had more practice telling the time and talked about school routines.

• TARGET LANGUAGE

Key language: time, *What time is it?*, simple present for routines (affirmative), simple past (questions and affirmative)
Review: days of the week, school subjects

• MATERIALS REQUIRED

Photocopiable 1 (see page T90), one copy for each student
Extra activity: Strips of paper
Optional: *Kid's Box AE Teacher's Resource Book 5* Unit 1 Extension worksheet 1 (page 18)

Warmer

- Draw eight clocks on the board and draw a different time on each. Number the clocks. Students draw a 2 x 2 grid in their notebooks. They choose four of the clocks and write the corresponding number in each grid square, e.g., 4. Call out the times at random, keeping a note of which ones you have said. Students cross out a square if they have chosen the time you say. The first student(s) to cross out all four shout(s) *Bingo!* Elicit the times to check.

SB11. ACTIVITY **4.** *Read and label the clock.*

- Tell students to open their Student's Books to page 11. Focus them on the clock and the times. They label the clock using the times in the box. Students check in pairs. Check with the class.

Key: (clockwise from top) five after, ten after, twenty-five to, a quarter to

SB11. ACTIVITY **5.** *Do the actions. Tell the time.*

- Focus students on the Activity 5 instructions. Demonstrate the activity, holding your arms to show a time. Repeat, with students asking you the question as in the example. Practice with the class. Students secretly write six times in their notebooks before they do the activity in pairs. They take turns asking and demonstrating the time.

SB11. ACTIVITY **6.** *Look at the clocks. Ask and answer.*

- Make new pairs. Focus students on the Activity 6 instructions and speech bubbles, and check understanding. They take turns saying one of the three times. Their partner says *a*, *b*, or *c*. Monitor students to check they are telling the time correctly.

SB11. ACTIVITY **7.** *Listen and say the letter.*

- Focus students on the Activity 7 instruction and check understanding. They listen to the CD and look at the clocks in Activity 6. Remind students to whisper the letter to their friend (or write it) the first time they listen. Play the CD. Students listen and whisper/write. Play the CD again to check answers.

Key: 2c, 3b, 4b

CD 1, 15

1.
INTERVIEWER: Where do you have lunch?
BOY: I have it in school.
INTERVIEWER: What time do you have it?
BOY: I have lunch at a quarter to one every day.

2.
INTERVIEWER: What time do you get up during the week?
BOY: On school days, I have to get up early. I get up at twenty after seven.
INTERVIEWER: Ooh, that's earlier than me!

3.
INTERVIEWER: Do you walk home from school?
BOY: No, I catch the bus.
INTERVIEWER: Do you have to wait for it?
BOY: Sometimes, but the bus usually comes at twenty-five after four.

4.
INTERVIEWER: Do you study geography in school?
BOY: Yes, it's my favorite subject.
INTERVIEWER: When do you have it?
BOY: At ten to ten on Tuesdays and Fridays.

SB11. ACTIVITY **8.** *Play the game. Ask and answer.*

- Focus students on the Activity 8 instructions and on the prompts. Give students five minutes to write a sequence of times during the day when they do different things. Demonstrate the game first with the class. Make pairs. Students take turns playing the game using the prompts. Monitor and help. Check some questions and answers using open pairs.

Photocopiable 1 (see pages T88 and T90)

WB11. ACTIVITY **4.** *Match the clocks with the sentences for Dan's day yesterday. Put the sentences in order.*

Key: b6, c2, d7, e8, f1, g4, h3
Order: 2c, 3h, 4g, 5a, 6b, 7d, 8e

WB11. ACTIVITY **5.** *Find the past of these verbs and write them.*

Key: came, had, caught, woke up, got up, ate, drank, put, took

WB11. ACTIVITY **6.** *Answer the questions about yesterday.*

Key: Students' own answers

WB11. ACTIVITY **7.** *Now choose your favorite day of last week and write about what you did.*

Key: Students' own answers

Extra activity: see page T99 (if time)

Optional activity

- Unit 1 Extension worksheet 1 from *Teacher's Resource Book 5* (see pages 15 and 18).

Ending the lesson

- Play another game of Clock bingo to end the lesson.

4 Read and label the clock.

ten after	five after	twenty-five to	a quarter to

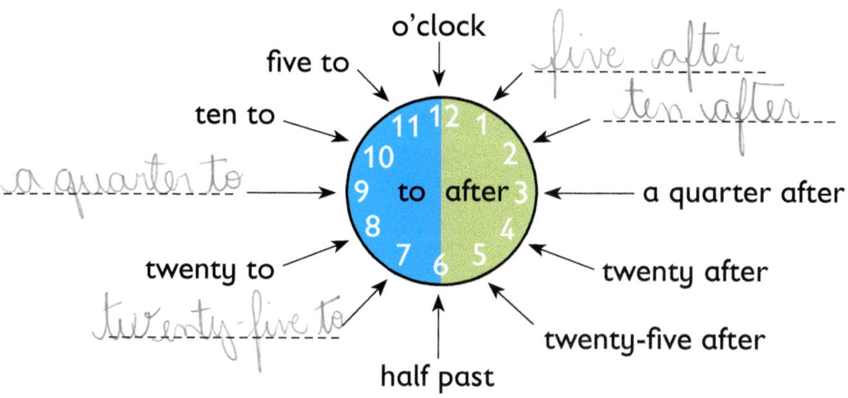

5 Do the actions. Tell the time.

What time is it?

It's nine o'clock.

6 Look at the clocks. Ask and answer.

What time is it?

It's a quarter after one.

1 – b

1

3 twenty-five after four

2

twenty after seven

4

ten to ten

7 Listen and say the letter.

15 CD1

1 … I have lunch at a quarter to one every day.

a

8 Play the game. Ask and answer.

I get up at this time on Mondays. What time is it?

A quarter to eight.

No.

I start my classes at this time. What time is it?

Nine o'clock.

Yes.

*Photocopiable – page T90

Reading 9 Read and think. What's your favorite TV show? Why?

http://www.cambridge.org/elt/kidsbox/ezine

Kid's Box Ezine!

home | reports | games | world | email

Most children love watching TV. So today's ezine is about TV. There are a lot of channels on TV and many different kinds of shows.

Kid's Box reports TV

a

Cartoons are moving pictures. Children love them. They can be short shows or complete movies. They're usually funny.

b

We watch the weather to find out if it is sunny, rainy, windy, or cloudy. What's the weather like today?

c

A documentary is a show that tells us about our world. It can be about animals, history, or geography.

d

A comedy is a funny show that makes us laugh. What's your favorite comedy?

e

The news is about all the things that happen in the world. It is on TV every day. What time is the news on in your country?

f

A quiz is a kind of competition. One person asks others a lot of different questions. The winner is the person with the most points.

g

The most popular sports shows in our country are baseball, basketball, and tennis. What are they in your country?

h

We watch a series in parts. These parts are called "episodes." You can sometimes watch an episode every day.

cartoon | weather | documentary | news | comedy | series | sports | quiz

10 CD1 16 Listen. Repeat the word and say the letter. 1 Quiz. — Quiz. That's "f."

11 Read again and answer.

1 Which show is in episodes?
2 Which show is funny?
3 Which show is a kind of competition?
4 Which show can be short or a complete movie?
5 Which show can tell us things about animals?
6 Which show can tell us to take an umbrella with us?

OBJECTIVES: By the end of the lesson, students will have read and talked about TV shows.

• TARGET LANGUAGE

Key language: TV shows: *cartoon, weather, documentary, comedy, news, quiz, sports, series, TV channel, episode*
Additional language: *webpage*
Review: sports, adjectives

• MATERIALS REQUIRED

Extra activity 2: Digital or video camera, props for making short excerpts of TV shows, paper
Optional: *Kid's Box AE Teacher's Resource Book 5* Unit 1 Reinforcement worksheet 2 and Extension worksheet 2 (pages 17 and 19)

Warmer

- Elicit types of TV show in English or L1. Write them on the board. Make sure you include the show types featured on Student's Book page 12.

SB12. ACTIVITY **9.** *Read and think. What's your favorite TV show? Why?*

- Tell students to open their Student's Books to page 12. Focus them on Activity 9 and on the activity instructions. Ask a student to read them aloud. Check understanding.
- Focus students on the text and elicit that it's a webpage. They read the text silently and think about their answers to the question in the instructions. Discuss their ideas as a class, reminding them to say why, as well as choosing a show. Check comprehension of vocabulary by referring students back to the texts and encouraging them to work out the meanings for themselves, e.g., *episode*. Discuss students' answers to the questions in the text. Check general comprehension by asking, e.g., *What does the weather tell us? Which series do you like?* Check students realize that *news* is singular.

SB12. ACTIVITY **10.** *Listen. Repeat the word and say the letter.*

- Focus students on the Activity 10 instructions. Play the example to check students know what to do. Play the rest of the CD. Students repeat the word in chorus and then write the letter in their notebooks the first time they listen. Play the CD again. Students repeat the word and say the letter.

Key: 2 Weather. That's "b." 3 Documentary. That's "c." 4 News. That's "e." 5 Comedy. That's "d." 6 Series. That's "h." 7 Sports. That's "g." 8 Cartoon. That's "a."

CD 1, 16

1 quiz, 2 weather, 3 documentary, 4 news, 5 comedy, 6 series, 7 sports, 8 cartoon

SB12. ACTIVITY **11.** *Read again and answer.*

- Focus students on Activity 11. They work in pairs and take turns reading out a question and saying the answer. They don't have to ask the questions in order. Check with the class, eliciting examples where possible. Students write the answers as full sentences in their notebooks.

Key: 1 series, 2 comedy/cartoon, 3 quiz, 4 cartoon, 5 documentary, 6 weather

WB12. ACTIVITY **8.** *Choose words from the box to label the pictures.*

Note: There are two extra words in the box.

Key: 2 documentary, 3 comedy, 4 news, 5 sports, 6 series

WB12. ACTIVITY **9.** *Write the shows.*

Key: 2 comedy, 3 weather, 4 news, 5 documentary, 6 series

WB12. ACTIVITY **10.** *Read and answer the questions.*

Key: 2 Channel 1 and Channel 3. 3 The weather. 4 *Count to ten* and *Answer first*. 5 (1) Animals of Africa, (2) Explorers, (3) Our body. 6 1.15.

WB12. ACTIVITY **11.** *Write a TV page with your favorite shows and times.*

Key: Students' own answers

Extra activities: see page T99 (if time)

Optional activity

- Unit 1 Reinforcement worksheet 2 and Extension worksheet 2 from *Teacher's Resource Book 5* (see pages 15, 17 and 19).

Ending the lesson

- Play a mime game to end the lesson. Mime something related to one of the show types. Students try to guess. Students then take turns doing similar mimes (using their own ideas) for the rest of the class to guess.

OBJECTIVES: By the end of the lesson, students will have had further practice reading and talking about TV shows and sung a song.

• TARGET LANGUAGE

Key language: TV shows, *music videos, action movies*, comparative and superlative adjectives: *interesting, exciting, boring, good, bad, funny, amazing*; simple past, *turn on, wait*
Additional language: *not my thing, the rest, until, the swings*
Review: time, comparatives, superlatives

• MATERIALS REQUIRED

Extra activity 1: A copy of the TV page from a newspaper/ TV guide for each group of four. Ten questions about the shows, e.g., *What's on at 8:30 on Channel 5? What's the name of the news show? What time's the movie on?* One set of questions for each group of four, paper
Optional: *Kid's Box AE Teacher's Resource Book 5* Unit 1 Song worksheet (page 20)

Warmer

- Name TV shows students know for them to guess the genre. Introduce *music videos* and write it on the board.

SB13. ACTIVITY 12. *Listen and say the show.*

- Tell students to open their Student's Books to page 13. Focus them on the text and pictures, and on the activity instruction. Play the CD. Students point to / say the show quietly to their friend. Play the CD again. Check with the class.

Key: 2 quiz show, 3 documentary, 4 cartoon, 5 weather, 6 music videos, 7 comedy show, 8 news

CD 1, 17

1. **COMMENTATOR:** Goal!
   CROWD: Yeah!
2. **QUIZMASTER:** Question one. What's the capital of Venezuela?
   BOY: Caracas.
   QUIZMASTER: Yes. Two points.
3. This is a forest. There are a lot of birds hiding in its trees. Let's go and find them.
4. Meow! Meeeooow!
5. **WEATHER PRESENTER:** Good morning. It was sunny yesterday, but today it's raining.
6. School is cool, it's where we go, From Monday to Friday, I'm sure you know. We study and we play, that's what we do. We do it in the morning and the afternoon!
7. **COMEDIAN 1:** Why didn't the skeleton go to the park?
   COMEDIAN 2: It had no body to go with!
8. **NEWS READER:** The Education Minister is visiting a new library in Springfield today. The library has one million books.

SB13. ACTIVITY 13. *Choose words to talk about the different shows.*

- Focus students on the word box and dialogue prompts. Pre-teach *amazing*. Elicit some comments about the shows, using the prompts. Make sure they use comparatives and superlatives correctly. If necessary, write the adjective forms on the board. Make groups of four. Students take turns making comments about the shows.
- Each student then writes six sentences about the shows in their notebooks, using the comparative or superlative.

SB13. ACTIVITY 14. *Listen and complete. Check and sing.*

- Focus students on the song and on the Activity 14 instructions.
- When everyone is ready, play the CD. Students listen and draw the clock hands. Check with the class. Play the CD again. Check understanding of the song, e.g., how many shows the person watches and the meaning of *not my thing*. Students repeat it line by line and then verse by verse. Students stand up. They sing the song right through. Divide the class into two groups: one sings the first verse, the other the second. Swap and repeat.

Key: ten after three, five to two, seven o'clock, half past three, a quarter after four, ten after seven

CD 1, 18

As in Student's Book and key

CD 1, 19

Now sing the song again. (Karaoke version)

SB13. ACTIVITY 15. *Read and complete.* F toward

- Focus students on Activity 15. Set the question: *What's the name of the show Tim and Jen wanted to watch?* (Friendly). Students quickly read to find the answer. They check in pairs. Students read the text in more detail to fill the blanks using the words in the box. They check in pairs. Ask why Tim and Jen didn't see the show.

Key: 2 past, 3 waited, 4 arrived, 5 turned on, 6 news

WB13. ACTIVITY 12. *Read and complete the chart.*

Key:

Name	Sophia	Emma	Frank	Harry
Kind of show	Cartoon	Quiz	Sports	Documentary
Show name	Quacky Duck	Who wants to be a billionaire?	Sunday sports	World around us
Show time	4:20	3:50	4:45	4:10

WB13. ACTIVITY 13. *Now answer the questions.*

Key: 2 *Who wants to be a billionaire?* 3 3:50, 4 Emma's, 5 Harry, 6 4:20

WB13. ACTIVITY 14. *Answer the questions.* F toward

Key: Students' own answers

WB13. ACTIVITY 15. *How many words can you find in "documentaries"?*

Key: Students' own answers

Extra activities: see page T99 (if time)

Optional activity

- Unit 1 Song worksheet from *Teacher's Resource Book 5* (see pages 15 and 20).

Ending the lesson

- Students sing the song from earlier in the lesson again.

12 Listen and say the show. (17 CD1)

1 Goal! Sports.

a cartoon (4)
b weather (5)
c sports (1)
d documentary (3)
e news (8)
f music videos (6)
g comedy show (7)
h quiz show (2)

13 Choose words to talk about the different shows.

interesting exciting boring good bad funny amazing

I think quiz shows are more interesting than the weather.

I think music videos are the best.

14 Listen and complete. Check and sing. (18 CD1)

I don't like TV, I don't like it much,
But there are some shows that
I sometimes watch.
On channel one at ten after three,
There's a really good documentary
About animals and where they live,
What they do and what they eat,
And on channel four at five to two,
They put on a great cartoon.
At one o'clock and then at seven o'clock,
They show the news and then the weather.
They're not my thing, they're not for me,
But I like the sports at half past three.
But what I like, what I love the best,
Are the action movies, more than the rest.
They're on at a quarter after four,
And at ten after seven, but I want more.

15 Read and complete.

news turned on waited
~~four~~ arrived past

Tim and Jen went to the park last Saturday. They ran on the grass, played with a ball, and went on the swings. At ten to (1) four they sat down because they were tired. They saw a newspaper on the bench. They opened it at the TV page and looked to see what was on the different channels. Tim wanted to go home and watch *Friendly* at half (2) past four. They went to the bus stop and (3) waited. The bus didn't come until a quarter after four. They (4) arrived home at twenty-five to five, ran into the living room, and (5) turned on the TV. The show wasn't *Friendly*, it was the (6) news. They looked at the newspaper again. It was an old one! They showed *Friendly* on Friday, not on Saturday.

16 Focus on phonics

The students usually use computers
At the university on Tuesdays.
But today they're at the museum,
Playing beautiful music!

Speaking 17 Ask your friend.

Questionnaire

1	How often do you watch TV?	Three times a week.
2	What's your favorite show?	
3	What kind of show is it?	
4	What day's it on?	
5	What time's it on?	
6	Why do you like it?	

Writing 18 Write about your friend.

Peter watches TV three times a week. His favorite show is ...

Joke Corner

What's the worst time to play soccer?

When it's five to one.

OBJECTIVES: By the end of the lesson, students will have practiced the phoneme /juː/ and completed a writing activity.

• TARGET LANGUAGE

Key language: the phoneme /juː/, simple present, *review*
Review: TV shows

• MATERIALS REQUIRED

Extra activity 1: Large sheet of paper for each group of four, colored markers

Optional: *Kid's Box AE Teacher's Resource Book 5* Unit 1 Topic worksheet (page 21)

Warmer

- Write the words *you*, *computer*, and *usually* on the board. Ask students which sound all three words have in common. Say the words aloud. Students discuss in pairs. Elicit suggestions. Repeat the words emphasising the /juː/ sounds. Elicit the sound. Underline the sound on the board (*you, computer, usually*). Tell students they will be practising recognising this sound and looking at different spellings for the sound in today's lesson.

SB14. ACTIVITY 16. *Focus on phonics*

- Tell students to open their Student's Books to page 14. Focus them on Activity 16. Play the CD. Students repeat after each line and then after the whole rhyme. Repeat once more, making sure students say the /juː/ sound correctly. In pairs, students practice the rhyme.

CD 1, 20

As in Student's Book

SB14. ACTIVITY 17. *Ask your friend.* F toward

- Focus students on the first question and example answer in the questionnaire. Prompt different students to ask this first question around the class and for different students to answer (open pairs). Students read the other questions aloud. Check for correct pronunciation and intonation of the questions. Students work in pairs. They write their partner's answers on the lines.

SB14. ACTIVITY 18. *Write about your friend.*

- Focus students on Activity 18. Ask one student *What did you find out?* Elicit one or two sentences about their friend, prompting use of the third person. Repeat for one or two other students, to check understanding of the activity. Students work individually and write about their partner in their notebooks.

SB14. JOKE CORNER

- Focus students on the Joke Corner and review the meaning of *joke*. Play the CD as students read the joke in their books. Play the joke a second time and explain if necessary.

CD 1, 21

As in Student's Book

WB14. ACTIVITY 16. *Complete the sentences.*

Key: 2 usually, 3 documentary, 4 computer, 5 university, 6 amazing

WB14. ACTIVITY 17. *Listen, check, and say.*

- Play the CD for students to listen and check. They compare answers in pairs. Check with the class. Play the CD again for students to listen and repeat.

Key: See audioscript below

CD 1, 22

1. After you see a movie, you can write a review about it.
2. I usually wake up at 8.30 in the morning.
3. Let's watch the documentary about monkeys on TV tonight.
4. On Tuesday afternoon the students have computer studies.
5. My sister is going to university next year.
6. Look at Daisy's beautiful new jacket!

WB14. ACTIVITY 18. *Read the text and answer the questions.*

- Before students do the activity, focus them on the Write it right box and discuss the questions. Pre-teach/Show examples of reviews.

Key: 2 It's about a police officer and his adventures. 3 Ben Jones is in it. 4 It's on Channel 4. 5 It's on at half past five on Saturday afternoons. 6 Because it's really fast and exciting, and it's funny too.

WB14. ACTIVITY 19. *Use the questions and answers to write a review of a TV show or movie.*

Key: Students' own answers

Extra activities: see page T99 (if time)

Optional activity

- Unit 1 Topic worksheet from *Teacher's Resource Book 5* (see pages 15 and 21).

Ending the lesson

- Do the rhyme again from the beginning of the lesson.

OBJECTIVES: By the end of the lesson, students will have read a story, reviewed language from the unit, and completed a self-evaluation.

• TARGET LANGUAGE

Key language: language in the story, *TV screen, cameraman, thief, password, treasure, reporter,* simple past

Additional language: *I have no time to lose, of course*

Review: language from the unit

• MATERIALS REQUIRED

Extra activity 2: Paper

Optional: *Kid's Box AE Teacher's Resource Book 5* Unit 1 Topic worksheet (page 21)

Warmer

- Review the story with students. Write words randomly across the board, e.g., *archeology, Diggory, Emily, bones, Rosetta Stone.* Elicit what they can remember about the story without looking in their books.

SB15. STORY. *Diggory Bones.*

- Tell students to open their Student's Books to page 15. Focus them on the story. Preteach *thief* and *TV screen* and set the questions: *Why is the Baloney Stone important? What happens to the TV screen? Who is on the TV?* Play the CD with books closed. Students listen to find the answers. They check in pairs with books open. Check with the class. (It's the most important computer program of old languages in the world. / You can find the world's most beautiful treasures with it. It goes black when the news is on. Brutus Grabbe.) Play the CD again. Students listen and read. Stop after each frame for students to repeat. At the end, check comprehension by asking, e.g., *What time is the news on? How is Brutus Grabbe on the TV? What does Diggory want and what does Brutus want?* Check that students understand why Brutus wants Diggory's password.

CD 1, 23

As in Student's Book

WB15. ACTIVITY 20. *Read and answer.*

Key: 2 It's on Diggory's computer. / Brutus Grabbe has it. 3 At half past nine. 4 The news. 5 Brutus Grabbe. 6 The professor's secret password.

WB15. ACTIVITY 21. *Read the story so far and then write it in the past.*

Key: The reporter and the cameraman arrived. The reporter asked Diggory some questions. Diggory said that he didn't want the thief to use the Baloney Stone to find treasure. At half past nine Diggory asked Emily to turn on the TV because he wanted to watch the news. Brutus Grabbe came onto the TV screen and laughed. He was the TV cameraman from the college! He wanted Diggory's secret password for the computer program.

WB15. DO YOU REMEMBER?

- Students try to do the activity first without looking back through the unit. Once they have tried to complete all the sentences, they can look back through the unit to find the answers.

Key: 2 twenty-five after eight, 3 documentary, 4 comedies, cartoons, 5 Students' own answers, 6 end

WB15. CAN DO

- Focus students on the *Can do* section of the page. Ask a student to read the first sentence. Elicit what this means with examples and elicit/remind them of the activities they did in this unit when they told the time. Review what the three faces mean (not very well / OK / very well). Remind students they circle the one they think is true for them. Repeat for the second sentence, eliciting/reminding them of the activities when they talked about different kinds of TV shows. Students circle the appropriate face. Repeat for the third sentence, eliciting what they wrote about for their reviews.
- Say *Now show and tell your friends.* Students work in groups of three and take turns showing their work for / talking about each one.

Extra activities: see page T99/T100 (if time)

Optional activity

- Unit 1 Topic worksheet from *Teacher's Resource Book 5* (see pages 15 and 21)

Ending the lesson

- Ask students which rhyme/song they'd like to do again from the unit. Do it together to end the lesson.

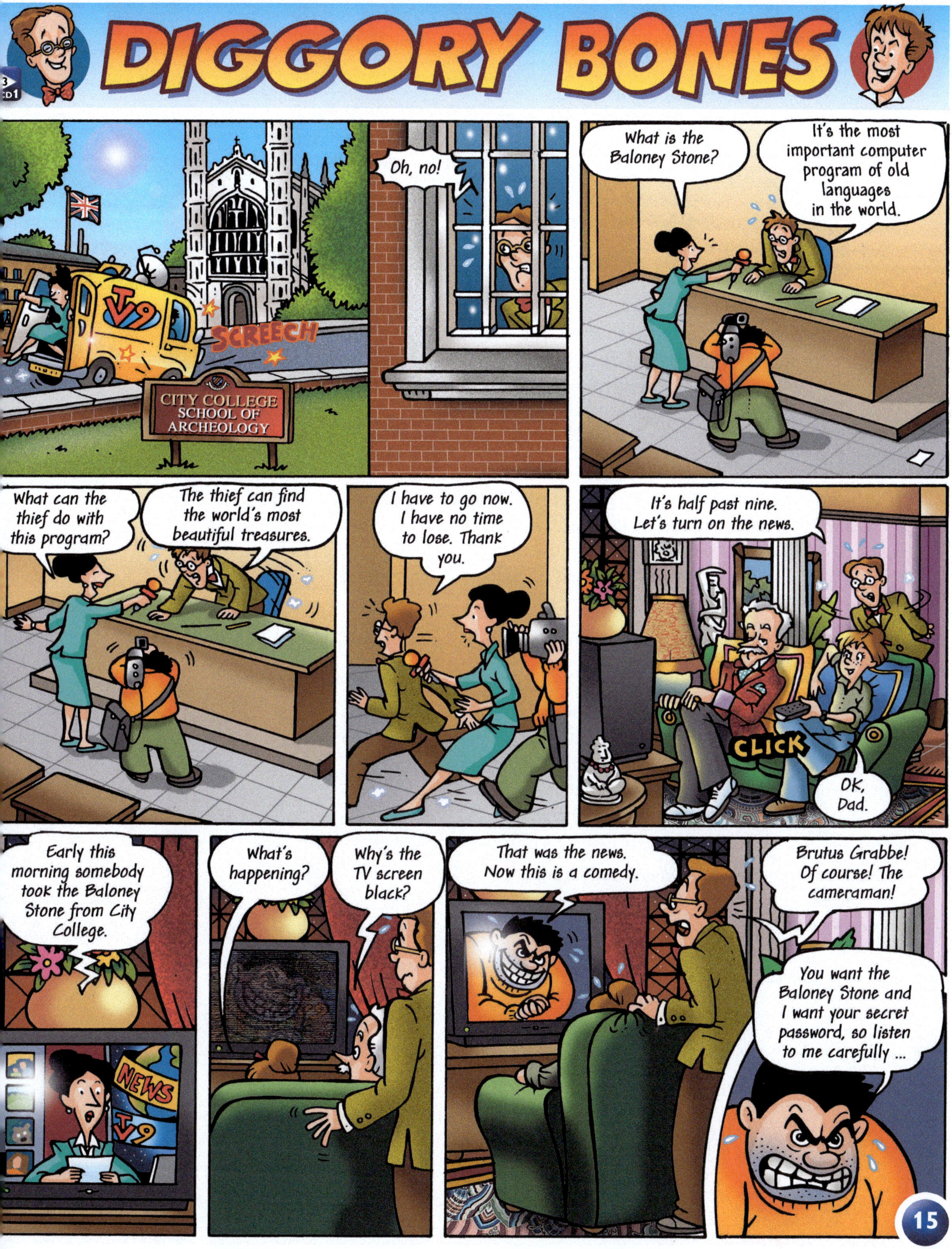
DIGGORY BONES
SCREECH
CITY COLLEGE
SCHOOL OF
ARCHEOLOGY
Oh, no!
What is the Baloney Stone?
It's the most important computer program of old languages in the world.
What can the thief do with this program?
The thief can find the world's most beautiful treasures.
I have to go now. I have no time to lose. Thank you.
It's half past nine. Let's turn on the news.
CLICK
OK, Dad.
Early this morning somebody took the Baloney Stone from City College.
NEWS
What's happening?
Why's the TV screen black?
That was the news. Now this is a comedy.
Brutus Grabbe! Of course! The cameraman!
You want the Baloney Stone and I want your secret password, so listen to me carefully ...

History | Cartoons

FACT: ***The Simpsons*** **started in 1987. It's the longest-running cartoon series.**

1 Ask and answer.

Do you watch cartoons? Who's your favorite cartoon character?

2 Look and say.

Do you know the names of these cartoons? Which characters are in them?

a

b

c

3 Read and answer.

Movies and cartoons are made of a lot of different images. In movies the different images are called frames, and in cartoons they are called cels. In a movie there are usually 24 frames per second, and in a cartoon there are 12 cels per second. Our eyes do not see the space between each frame or cel.

1 How many frames do you need for 15 seconds of movie?

2 How many cels do you need for one minute of animation?

There are lots of different ways to make cartoons. The first cartoons were made using hand-drawn pictures. Today, some cartoons are drawn using cel animation. For these, artists have to draw pictures on clear plastic. This means that to change the cels they only have to redraw the parts of the picture that move.

Other cartoons, such as *Wallace and Gromit*, use models. Artists move the models and take a photograph. They have to take a lot of photographs!

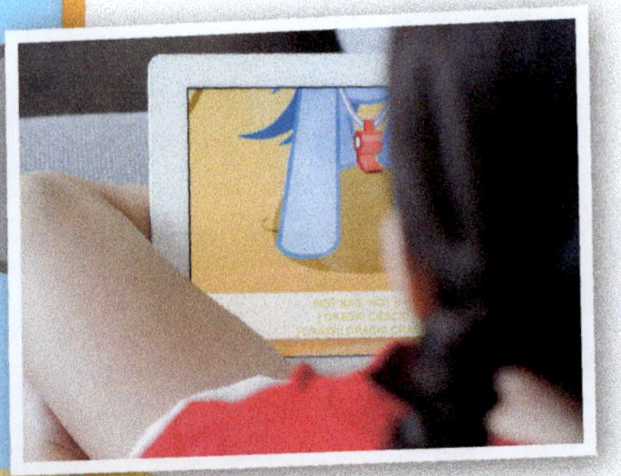

3 Which method of making a cartoon do you think would take the longest? Why?

These days, most cartoons are made using special techniques with a lot of help from computers. Now, anyone can make a cartoon using cartoon-making websites. You could make a cartoon, too.

4 Can you think of an idea for a cartoon?

OBJECTIVES: By the end of the lesson, students will have read about cartoons and animation and suggested ideas for a cartoon.

• TARGET LANGUAGE

Key language: *longest running, animation, image, frames, cels, hand-drawn, per (second), clear plastic, method, special techniques, are made, were made, artist,* simple past

Additional language: *The Simpsons, Wallace and Gromit*

Review: simple present

• MATERIALS REQUIRED

A DVD of a short cartoon and/or pictures/drawings of cartoon characters

Extra activity 1: Paper for display

Extra activity 2: Large sheets of paper, paper

Optional: *Kid's Box AE Interactive DVD 5: The school hall* "Making a cartoon" episode

Warmer

- Show a short cartoon on DVD and/or display pictures of cartoon characters in the classroom. Elicit what these are called. Tell students that today's topic is cartoons and how they are made.

SB16. FACT

- Tell students to open their Student's Books to page 16. Focus them on the top of the page and say *Did you know …?* Ask a student to read the fact to the class. Elicit if any of them know the series *The Simpsons* and some of the character names if they do. Elicit who they can see in the picture. Check understanding of *longest running* and elicit how many years it is from then until now.

SB16. ACTIVITY 1. *Ask and answer.*

- Focus students on the questions in Activity 1. If necessary, they write the questions in their notebooks. Students move around the room, asking their friends the two questions. They don't need to write the answers. Students go back to their places. Discuss with the class what they found out and make a tally of favorite cartoon characters on the board.

SB16. ACTIVITY 2. *Look and say.*

- Focus students on the pictures for Activity 2 and on the questions. Discuss as a class. Elicit the names of the characters on the rest of the page and on page 17 (Mickey Mouse, Bugs Bunny, Wallace and Gromit, Felix the cat, Shrek).

Key: a Pikachu and Ash Ketchum; b Tom and Jerry; c *Despicable me* (Gru and Agnes)

SB16. ACTIVITY 3. *Read and answer.*

- Preteach key vocabulary for the reading: *cel, frame, per (second), hand-drawn, animation.*
- Ask a student to read out questions 1 and 2. Check understanding. Students read the first paragraph silently and quickly to find the answers. They check in pairs. Check with the class. Help students with pronunciation of the large numbers. Students take turns reading the first paragraph aloud around the class. Repeat for question 3 and the corresponding paragraph. Read the final paragraph around the class before reading question 4. Students discuss their ideas in pairs or groups of three and then share them with the class. Discuss their general responses and reactions to the text in English and L1.

Key: 1: 360, 2: 720, 3 and 4: Students' own answers

WB16. ACTIVITY 1. *Answer the questions.*

Key: Students' own answers

WB16. ACTIVITY 2. *Answer "yes" or "no."*

Note: Students will not be able to do this activity until they have listened to the interview on Track 24 of the CD, *Students Book* (page 17), Activity 4.

Key: 2 yes, 3 no, 4 no, 5 yes, 6 yes

WB16. ACTIVITY 3. *Plan a report about the history of animation.*

- Before students do the activity, focus them on the plan for the report and on the sections for planning (introduction/middle/end).

Key: Students' own answers

WB16. ACTIVITY 4. *Now write your report.*

Key: Students' own answers

Extra activities: see page T100 (if time)

Optional activity

- The "Making a cartoon" episode from *Kid's Box AE Interactive DVD 5* (*The school hall* section). See pages 8–11 of the Teacher's Booklet for the Interactive DVD.

Ending the lesson

- Review with students what they have done and what they learned about in today's lesson.

OBJECTIVES: By the end of the lesson, students will have listened to more information about cartoons and cartoon characters and completed a project.

• TARGET LANGUAGE

Key language: *animated, timeline, flipbook, less (drawing), sound, 3D,* simple past, pronunciation of years, e.g., *1910, 1990s*
Additional language: cartoon characters
Review: cartoons

• MATERIALS REQUIRED

For each student, heavy paper or cardboard, pencils, scissors, crayons or markers, a stapler or big clip; a ready-made flipbook
Extra activity 1: A large sheet of paper for each student

Warmer

- Provide definitions of key words from the previous lesson. Students give you the words, e.g., *the name of an image in a movie, when a cartoon's drawn with a pencil, it's ... .*

SB17. ACTIVITY 4. *Listen and choose the answer.*

- Tell students to open their Student's Books to page 17. They read through the sentences. Play the CD. Students listen and choose the answer. They check in pairs. Play the CD again. Check with the class. Check understanding of key vocabulary and also of how to pronounce the years.

Key: 1a, 2b, 3b, 4b, 5a, 6c

CD 1, 24

PRESENTER: Hello and welcome to today's show about the history of cartoons. Here to tell us all about this interesting subject is Peter Jones.
PETER: Hello. Thanks for having me.
PRESENTER: Who was the first popular cartoon character?
PETER: Well, the first cartoon character that people liked in different countries was *Felix the Cat.*
PRESENTER: *Felix the Cat?*
PETER: That's right. *Felix the Cat* started in the 1920s and was very popular. The only problem was that Felix didn't speak.
PRESENTER: Do you mean that there wasn't any sound?
PETER: Yes.
PRESENTER: So what was the first cartoon with sound?
PETER: Ooh, that was a cartoon in 1928 called *Steamboat Willie*, and it was by Walt Disney.
PRESENTER: Walt Disney? Really? And who was in it?
PETER: The star of the cartoon was Mickey Mouse. Over the next ten years, Walt Disney also made cartoons with Pluto the dog and Donald Duck.
PRESENTER: There are a lot of animal cartoon characters, aren't there?
PETER: Uh, yes. Yes, there are. Anyway, in 1932, they made the first cartoons in color.
PRESENTER: 1932! Wow! Are cartoons today very different from the first ones?
PETER: Well, yes, they are. But the biggest change was in the 1990s, when people started to use computers to help them make cartoons. The first 3D computer movie was *Toy Story*, and that came out in 1995.
PRESENTER: That's right. And then, in 2001, *Shrek* won a prize for the best animated movie, didn't it?
PETER: Yes, it did and that really was a great movie! Now there are a lot of fantastic new animated movies every year. It's an exciting time for cartoons!
PRESENTER: Well, Peter, thank you very much for being here today.

SB17. ACTIVITY 5. *Listen again and put the information on the timeline.*

- Check students understand *timeline* by drawing one on the board to show *last year, this year, next year.* Give students thinking and reading time before they listen. Play the CD again (without stopping). Students try to mark the information on the timeline. They check in pairs. Draw the timeline on the board and elicit the information. Play the CD again for a final check.

Key: 1928: sound, 1932: color, 1990s: computers, 1995: *Toy Story*, 2001: *Shrek*

CD 1, 25

SB17. PROJECT. *Make a flipbook cartoon.*

- Show students a flipbook you have made. Read the project information through with the class, showing the materials they need. Check understanding of the procedure. Hand out the materials. Students work individually to make their flipbooks.
- Students show each other their flipbooks.

WB17. ACTIVITY 5. FLYERS Listening, Part 5. *Listen and color and write. There is one example.* (F)

CD 1, 26

Example: Hello, Michael. Would you like to color this picture? / Yes, please. It's a picture of a school cafeteria, isn't it? / That's right. What do you want to color first? / Umm ... Should I color the man who's standing behind the food? / OK. Color his hair black. / Alright.

Can you see the man's black hair? This is an example. Now you listen and color and write.

1. Now what should I color? / Well, can you see the three children standing over there, close to the food? / Yes, I can. They're all waiting. / Yes. Look at the boy who's got some food on his plate. He's wearing a jacket. / Oh, yes. I can see him well. Should I color his jacket green? / Good idea. Green's a nice color.
2. Can you see the man standing under the clock? / Which one? The one with a spoon? / No, the man who's carrying a bowl. Can you color the bowl red, please? / OK. Now he has a red bowl.
3. What should I do now? / Do you like writing? / Yes, I love writing. I'm better at that than drawing. / Good. Then can you write the word "FIRE" next to the word "EXIT" above the door? / Yes, I can do that. That's easy.
4. I'd like you to write something else now. Let's see. Find the book on the table. / Which one? The smaller one or the bigger one? / The bigger one, next to the boy's glass. Write the word "MATH" on it, please. / OK. I think he loves that subject.
5. Can you see the woman behind the food? / The one with the long hair? / Yes. That's right. She's holding a bottle. Would you like to color it? / Yes. Can I color it blue? / Of course. Now your picture looks really good. Good job!

Extra activities: see page T100 (if time)

Ending the lesson

- Ask students what activities they liked best.

4 Listen and choose the answer.

1 The first important cartoon character was
a) Felix the Cat. b) Shrek. c) Mickey Mouse.

2 A lot of cartoon characters are
a) teachers. b) animals. c) flowers.

3 Walt Disney made the first cartoon in color in
a) 1910. b) 1932. c) 1956.

4 In the 1990s cartoonists started to use
a) color. b) computers. c) sound.

5 *Shrek* won a prize for the best
a) animated movie. b) character. c) music.

6 There are a lot of fantastic new animated movies every
a) week. b) month. c) year.

5 Listen again and put the information on the timeline.

computers sound color ~~Felix the Cat~~ *Shrek* *Toy Story*

- 1920s Felix the Cat
- 1928 sound
- 1932 color
- 1990s computers
- 1995 Toy Story
- 2001 Shrek

Project Make a flipbook cartoon.

HW

You need:

- 2 sheets of heavy paper or thin cardboard
- A pencil and scissors
- Crayons or markers
- A big stapler or a big clip

How to make the flipbook:

1 Cut each sheet of thin card into six squares.

2 Number the cards from 1 to 12 and draw the same bounce line on all 12 cards. Then draw a ball on the bounce line to the left of the first card. Draw the same ball on each card just to the right of the one before.

3 Put the cards in order. Staple one side.

4 Now flip through your cartoon book.

2 People at work

Show what you know! What jobs can you remember?

Listening 1 27 CD1 Listen and check (✓) the jobs you hear.

2 28 CD1 Listen again. Complete the sentences.

1 They're looking at an exhibit on ________ .
2 Dan thinks he's going to be a ________ .
3 Maria thinks she's going to be a ________ .
4 Maria hopes the ________ isn't going to burn down.
5 Alex's going to be a ________ .
6 They're going to write about famous people's ________ .

3 Read and order the words.

1 write about / What / for our ezine? / are / we / going to
2 going to / a nurse / be / when I'm older. / I'm
3 a doctor. / going to / Alex / be / isn't
4 The school / isn't / burn down. / going to
5 win / prize! / We're / that / going to
6 do / you / What / tomorrow? / are / going to

LOOK

I'm **going to be** a dentist.
Alex **isn't going to be** a nurse.
What **are we going to write** about?

OBJECTIVES: By the end of the lesson, students will have talked about people's jobs and be able to talk about plans and intentions using *going to*.

• TARGET LANGUAGE

Key language: plans and intentions: *going to* (affirmative, negative, interrogative), *I think I'm going to …* , jobs: *nurse, firefighter, teacher, dentist; burn down, exhibit*
Review: jobs

• MATERIALS REQUIRED

Extra activities 1 and 2: Paper
Optional: *Kid's Box AE Teacher's Resource Book 5* Unit 2 Reinforcement worksheet 1 (page 23)

Warmer

- Mime a known job for students to guess. Invite one or two students to mime jobs for the class. The class can guess using only *yes/no* questions. Elicit the word *Jobs* and write it on the board.

SB18. SHOW WHAT YOU KNOW! *What jobs can you remember?*

- Draw a circle around the word *Jobs* on the board and elicit the ones from the warmer to start the mind map. Say *Show what you know … about jobs.* Brainstorm jobs in two minutes and create a mind map on the board. Supply words in English where necessary. Students copy it into their notebooks.

SB18. ACTIVITY 1. *Listen and check (✓) the jobs you hear.*

- Tell students to open their Student's Books to page 18. Focus students on the Activity 1 pictures. Elicit the names of the characters and where they are. Preteach/Check *exhibit.* Focus students on the activity instruction and check understanding. Remind them they check off the words they hear in the Job mind maps in their notebooks.
- Play the CD. Students listen and check. They check in pairs. Use the mind map on the board to check with the class.

CD 1, 27

DAN: What are we going to write about for our ezine this week?

MARIA: I don't know. Do you have any ideas, Alex?

ALEX: Uh, no, but let's take a look at the exhibit on jobs and think about it.

DAN: Look at this nurse! That's an interesting job. I think I'm going to be a nurse when I'm older.

MARIA: Hmm. A nurse is OK, but I think I'm going to be a dentist. What are you going to do, Alex?

ALEX: I'm not sure, but I'm going to have an exciting job.

TEACHER: Everybody has to leave the school building now, please. Walk quickly, but don't run.

MARIA: Oh, no! I hope the school isn't going to burn down.

TEACHER: It's OK, everybody. It's only a fire drill.

ALEX: That's a really exciting job. I'm going to be a firefighter.

MARIA: Well, now we know what we're going to write about in this week's ezine! Jobs.

DAN: Let's write about famous people's jobs.

MARIA AND ALEX: Yeah!

DAN: Yee ha! We're going to win that prize!

SB18. ACTIVITY 2. *Listen again. Complete the sentences.*

- Focus students on the Activity 2 instructions. Give them reading and discussion/prediction time. Play the CD. Students complete the sentences. Play the CD again and check with the class.
- Write up on the board two or three example sentences from the audioscript which include *going to.* Focus students on the concept, form, and use of *going to* in the sentences. Elicit if the people are talking about now or the future. Check understanding, e.g., *Is Dan a nurse now? Does he want to be a nurse in the future?* Elicit students' plans for jobs / the future, e.g., *I think I'm going to be (a doctor).* Focus on the Look box. Practice using open pairs, e.g., ask a student *What job are you going to do when you're older?* The student answers using *going to.* Ask a third student to report on what the student said. The third student asks a different student in the class. Pretend sometimes that you misheard to elicit the negative, e.g., Teacher: *Is Tom going to be a teacher?* Student: *No, he isn't going to be a teacher. He's going to be a pilot.*

Key: 1 jobs, 2 nurse, 3 dentist, 4 school, 5 firefighter, 6 jobs

CD 1, 28

SB18. ACTIVITY 3. *Read and order the words.*

- Students work in pairs to reorder the sentences. They write the correct sequence in their notebooks. Check with the class.

Key: 1 What are we going to write about for our ezine? 2 I'm going to be a nurse when I'm older. 3 Alex isn't going to be a doctor. 4 The school isn't going to burn down. 5 We're going to win that prize! 6 What are you going to do tomorrow?

WB18. ACTIVITY 1. *Write the words in the sentences.*

Key: 2 be, 3 read, 4 listen, 5 wear, 6 play

WB18. ACTIVITY 2. *Match the questions with the answers.*

Key: 2f, 3c, 4a, 5b, 6d, 7h, 8g

WB18. ACTIVITY 3. *Look at this code. Write the secret message.*

Key: Are you going to come to my party?

WB18. ACTIVITY 4. *Now write another message for your friend in your notebook.*

Key: Students' own answers

Extra activities: see page T100 (if time)

Optional activity

- Unit 2 Reinforcement worksheet 1 from *Kid's Box AE Teacher's Resource Book 5* (see pages 22 and 23).

Ending the lesson

- Write a message on the board in the code from Workbook Activity 3, e.g., *Goodbye. See you tomorrow.*

OBJECTIVES: By the end of the lesson, students will have had more practice using *going to* for plans and intentions and have sung a song.

• TARGET LANGUAGE

Key language: plans, intentions, and present evidence: *going to*, rhyming words, question words: *where, who, when, what time?*, telling the time, *brush (her) teeth, show, good rules, diary*

Additional language: *sold out, pajamas*

Review: actions, verbs for daily routines, sports

• MATERIALS REQUIRED

Extra activity 1: Paper for display, colored markers

Optional: *Kid's Box AE Teacher's Resource Book 5* Unit 2 Song worksheet (page 27)

Warmer

- Play a Bingo game to revise the time. Draw eight clocks on the board showing different times. Write numbers *1–8* under them. Students draw a 2 x 2 grid in their notebooks and write one number in each square (to represent a clock). Call out the times at random. If students have written the corresponding number, they cross out the square. The first student to cross out all four squares shouts *Bingo!* Check by eliciting the times.

SB19. ACTIVITY **4.** *Listen and order. Check and sing.*

- Tell students to open their Student's Books to page 19. Focus them on the first part of the activity instructions (*Listen and order*). Give them time to read the song and make predictions about the order. Play the CD. Students listen and order. They check in pairs. Play the CD again. Stop after each one to check and for students to repeat. Play the CD again, with students joining in. Students repeat the song as a class and then in seven groups, each group singing one section.

Key: a4, b6, c7, d3, e5, f2

CD 1, 29

He's going to do the job,
He's going to work all day.
He's going to do his best,
Then sleep and play. Sleep and play. (x3)
She's going to show the kids,
She's going to teach good rules.
She's going to help them all,
And work in schools. Work in schools. (x3)
They're going to do the job,
They're going to work all day.
They're going to do their best,
Then sleep and play.
They're going to do the job,
Then work all day,
Then sleep and play. (Repeat)

CD 1, 30

Now sing the song again. (Karaoke version)

SB19. ACTIVITY **5.** *Look and say. What are they going to do?*

- Focus students on the Activity 5 instructions. Elicit what they can see in, e.g., the first frame (a girl in the bathroom) and ask *What's she going to do?* Students respond, e.g., *She's going to brush her teeth.* Point out the girl's pajamas. Write the word on the board and get students to read it aloud. Ask them to raise their hand if they wear pajamas. Students do the activity in pairs, taking turns asking and answering questions about the pictures. Check with the whole class.

Key (possible answers): a She's going to brush her teeth. b They're going to go roller-skating. c They're going to buy a computer. d He's going to play soccer. e They're going to have lunch. f He's going to go to bed/sleep.

SB19. ACTIVITY **6.** *Correct the sentences.*

- Focus students on the Activity 6 example. Check they realize the sentences are about the pictures in Activity 5. In pairs, students take turns reading out a sentence and correcting it. Check with the class. Students write the corrected sentences in their notebooks.

Key: 2 No, they aren't going to go to a music festival. They're going to go roller-skating. 3 No, they aren't going to turn on a computer. They're going to buy a computer. 4 No, she isn't going to wash her face. She's going to brush her teeth. 5 No, they aren't going to watch TV. They're going to have lunch. 6 No, he isn't going to wake up. He's going to go to bed/sleep.

SB19. ACTIVITY **7.** *Ask your friend.* F toward

- Focus students on the questions and on the question words. Make new pairs. Students take turns asking all their questions to their partner. They note the answers. Monitor and check.

SB19. *Now think of some more questions.*

- Each student writes four more questions in their notebook, each using one of the question words. They ask and answer in pairs.

WB19. ACTIVITY **5.** *Look at the pictures and answer the questions.*

Key: 2 She's going to brush her teeth. 3 He's going to watch TV. 4 They're going to catch a bus. 5 He's going to do his homework. 6 She's going to go to sleep.

WB19. ACTIVITY **6.** *Make negative sentences.*

Key: 2 She isn't going to go skiing. 3 They aren't going to play tennis. 4 She isn't going to have a cookie. 5 They aren't going to see the movie. 6 They aren't going to drive the car.

WB19. ACTIVITY **7.** *Look at Sam's calendar for the weekend. Ask and answer the questions.*

Key: 2 a) What's Sam going to do on Friday afternoon? b) He's going to play soccer. 3 a) What time is Sam going to visit his grandma? b) He's going to visit her at 10:45 / quarter to eleven. 4 a) What's Sam going to buy on Saturday afternoon? b) He's going to buy some pajamas. 5 a) Where's Sam going to walk on Sunday morning? b) He's going to walk in the hills. 6 a) What's Sam going to do on Sunday afternoon? b) He's going to go to the movie theater.

Extra activities: see page T100 (if time)

Optional activity

- Unit 2 Song worksheet from *Kid's Box AE Teacher's Resource Book 5* (see pages 22 and 27).

Ending the lesson

- Sing the song again with the class.

4 Listen and order. Check and sing.

29 CD1

a She's going to help them all,
And work in schools … 4

b They're going to do their best,
Then sleep and play. 6

c They're going to do the job,
Then work all day,
Then sleep and play … 7

d She's going to show the kids,
She's going to teach good rules. 3

e They're going to do the job,
They're going to work all day. 5

f He's going to do his best,
Then sleep and play … 2

g He's going to do the job,
He's going to work all day. 1

5 Look and say. What are they going to do?

a) She's going to brush her teeth. b) They're going to go roller-skating. c) They're going to buy a computer.

a

b

c

d

e

f

d) He's going to play soccer. e) They're going to have lunch. He's going to go to bed / sleep.

6 Correct the sentences.

No, she isn't going to wash her face.
She's going to brush her teeth.

Key

a) She's going to wash her face.
b) They're going to go to a music festival.
c) They're going to turn on a computer.
d) He's going to play tennis.
e) They're going to watch TV.
f) He's going to wake up.

7 Ask your friend.

1. Where are you going to go after school?
2. Who are you going to see this evening?
3. When are you going to do your homework?
4. What time are you going to go to bed tonight?

Now think of some more questions.

Reading 8 Read and think. What's the most exciting job? Why?

http://www.cambridge.org/elt/kidsbox/ezine

Kid's Box Ezine!

home | reports | games | world | email

★ In today's ezine we're going to look at some interesting people and their jobs.

Kid's Box reports Jobs

a

John Travolta is a famous actor. His movies include *Grease* and *Hairspray*. He is also a pilot. This is his hobby. He has five planes, and he can fly all of them.

b

People remember George Orwell because he was an important writer. Two of his most famous novels are *Animal Farm* and *1984*. He was also a reporter, and wrote for different newspapers.

c

When Mia Hamm was young, she was a soccer player. She scored more than 100 goals for the U.S.A. and won the Women's World Cup. In 1999, she started the Mia Hamm Foundation. It helps girls start playing soccer.

d

Jamie Oliver is a famous cook who also works on TV. In his show *Jamie's School Dinners*, he made children's school meals healthier.

e

Formula 1 is a car racing competition. It's a team sport. One of the most important people on the team is the mechanic. Steve Matchett was a Formula 1 mechanic. He had to repair cars during the race. Now Steve works as a sports commentator on TV.

f

Mrs. Barbara Blackburn was a secretary. She was one of the best in the world. She had a special typewriter, and she could type faster than any other typist. She could type 150 words in a minute. Amazing!

secretary | soccer player | actor | reporter | cook | writer | mechanic | pilot

9 (31 CD1) Listen. Repeat the word and say the name of the person.

1 Cook.

Cook. That's Jamie Oliver.

10 Read again and answer.

1 What did the soccer player win?
2 What did the cook do in *Jamie's School Dinners*?
3 Why is the secretary famous?
4 What did Steve Matchett repair?
5 Who is a pilot and an actor?
6 What different jobs did George Orwell have?
7 How many of these people are on TV?

OBJECTIVES: By the end of the lesson, students will have had more practice talking about people and the jobs they do.

• TARGET LANGUAGE

Key language: jobs: *teacher, driver, dancer, skater, writer, singer, painter, photographer, farmer, tennis player, runner, swimmer, actor, pilot, reporter, soccer player, cook, mechanic, secretary, typist, scientist, manager, designer; novel,* pronunciation: *photograph/photographer*

Additional language: *school meals, repair, typewriter, Amazing!, design, manage*

Review: mixed tenses, questions

• MATERIALS REQUIRED

Extra activity 1: If possible, write one of the shorter texts or part of one of the longer texts from Student's Book Activity 8 on a hidden part of the board before the lesson.

Optional: *Kid's Box AE Teacher's Resource Book 5* Unit 2 Reinforcement worksheet 2 (page 24)

Warmer

- Give students one minute to write a list of as many jobs as they can. Students stop writing. They make groups of four and write a "master" list of all the jobs they have. Elicit the jobs from the class onto a mind map on the board. The group with the most jobs is the winner.

SB20. ACTIVITY 8. *Read and think. What's the most exciting job? Why?*

- Tell students to open their Student's Books to page 20. Focus them on Activity 8 and on the activity instructions. Ask a student to read them aloud. Check understanding.
- Focus students on the text and elicit that it's a webpage for the *Kid's Box* ezine. Make sure they notice the jobs at the bottom of the webpage. They read the texts silently and think about their answers to the question. Elicit the people's different jobs from students and discuss their ideas as a class, reminding them to say why the job they chose is the most exciting. Check comprehension of vocabulary by referring students back to the texts. Focus on each text one at a time, giving students reading time and then checking general comprehension by discussing the person and the job(s) they do.
- Students compare their lists from the warmer with the jobs mentioned in Activity 8.

SB20. ACTIVITY 9. *Listen. Repeat the word and say the name of the person.*

- Focus students on the Activity 9 instructions and the example. Elicit the names of the six people, helping students with pronunciation. Play the CD. Pause after each one for students to find the name in the text. They point to the name the first time. Play the CD again and elicit choral responses.

Key: 2 Actor. That's John Travolta. 3 Soccer player. That's Mia Hamm. 4 Reporter. That's George Orwell. 5 Secretary. That's Barbara Blackburn. 6 Pilot. That's John Travolta. 7 Mechanic. That's Steve Matchett. 8 Writer. That's George Orwell.

CD 1, 31

1 cook, 2 actor, 3 soccer player, 4 reporter, 5 secretary, 6 pilot, 7 mechanic, 8 writer

SB20. ACTIVITY 10. *Read again and answer.*

- Check understanding of the Activity 10 instruction. Students work in pairs. They take turns asking their partner questions. They don't have to ask them in order. Check using open pairs.

Key: 1 The Women's World Cup. 2 He made school meals healthier. 3 She could type faster than any other typist. 4 Formula 1 cars. 5 John Travolta. 6 Writer and reporter. 7 Two (Jamie Oliver and Steve Matchett).

WB20. ACTIVITY 8. *Choose words from the box to label the pictures.*

- Pre-teach *manager.*

Note: There are two extra words in the box.

Key: 2 soccer player, 3 manager, 4 actor, 5 reporter, 6 mechanic

WB20. ACTIVITY 9. *Complete the chart.*

- Make sure students notice changes in spelling, e.g., doubling of consonant.
- Pre-teach *designer, design,* and *manage.*

Key: driver, dance, skater, designer, singer, painter, photographer, manage, play tennis, run, swimmer

WB20. ACTIVITY 10. *Read and write the words in the puzzle.*

Key: 2 cook, 3 firefighter, 4 dentist, 5 nurse, 6 pilot, 7 mechanic, 8 artist, 9 actor; Mystery job: scientist

WB20. ACTIVITY 11. *Now write a definition for this job.*

Key: Students' own answers

Extra activities: see page T100 (if time)

Optional activity

- Unit 2 Reinforcement worksheet 2 from *Kid's Box AE Teacher's Resource Book 5* (see pages 22 and 24)

Ending the lesson

- Students look back through the lesson to see how many different jobs they can find that they talked about in the lesson.

OBJECTIVES: By the end of the lesson, students will have had further practice using *going to* to talk about people's jobs.

• TARGET LANGUAGE

Key language: plans, intentions, and predictions: *going to*, present continuous, simple present, jobs, *overalls*, *uniform*, *mask*, *bounce*, *repair*, *dirty*, *airport*, *machine*

Review: days of the week, *gloves*, *candy*, *a.m.*, *p.m.*

• MATERIALS REQUIRED

Optional: *Kid's Box AE Teacher's Resource Book 5* Unit 2 Extension worksheet 1 (page 25)

Warmer

- Review jobs by playing a spelling game, e.g. Teacher: *Give me an "s"* (s), *Give me a "k"* (k), *Give me an "a"* (a), *Give me a "t"* (t), *Give me an "e"* (e), *Give me an "r"* (r) *What does that spell?* (skater)

SB21. ACTIVITY 11. *Listen and match. Say the job.*

- Tell students to open their Student's Books to page 21. Focus them on the pictures and ask students what they can see and the job. Check understanding of the activity instructions. Play the CD. Students listen and whisper. Play the CD again. Elicit answers.

Key: 2 Dentist. That's f. 3 Cook. That's c. 4 Mechanic. That's b. 5 Actor. That's a. 6 Reporter. That's d.

CD 1, 32

1. **PILOT:** Good evening. This is Captain Bird speaking. Welcome aboard flight 241 from Dublin to London.
2. **DENTIST:** Hello, Bill. Please sit down. OK, open your mouth, please. That's good. Great. You brush your teeth very well. I can see you always brush your teeth three times a day after meals because they're nice and white. That's fine. No problems there.
3. **COOK:** Now, let me see. Three eggs, 500 grams of flour, half a liter of milk, 250 grams of sugar, and some chocolate. I'm going to mix it all together in a bowl and put it in a big cake pan. Then I'm going to cook it for half an hour. It's going to be a nice chocolate cake. Mmm!
4. **MECHANIC:** Good morning, Mr. Hamilton. This is Jack's Garage here. I looked at your car and I can see why it isn't working. I'm going to repair it now, so you can come and pick it up at half past ten.
5. **MOVIE DIRECTOR:** Action!
   ACTOR: I'm gonna look for a place to stay in this town. I'm tired, I'm hungry, and I'm thirsty. I have to find a hotel soon. Come on, GG.
   MOVIE DIRECTOR: Cut! Fantastic! Thank you, everybody. We're going to stop now.
6. **REPORTER:** That was a great game! I'm going to speak to the man of the game, John Brown. He put the ball through the basket 12 times. Here he comes and he's bouncing a ball.

SB21. ACTIVITY 12. *Listen again and choose the right words.*

- Focus students on the sentences. Give them reading time before they listen. Play the CD. Students listen and choose. They check in pairs. Play the CD again, pausing to check students' answers.

Key: 1 London, 2 well, 3 chocolate cake, 4 half past ten, 5 hungry, 6 basketball player

CD 1, 33

SB21. ACTIVITY 13. *Play the game. Guess it in ten.*

- Demonstrate the game. Think of a job, e.g., *reporter*. Students take turns asking *yes/no* questions. Remind them they can only have ten guesses. Help them focus their questions.
- Students play in pairs. Student A secretly writes a job and Student B asks questions. If B guesses in ten, he/she wins a point. Students take turns.

SB21. ACTIVITY 14. *Read and think. Ask and answer.*

- Focus students on the chart. Elicit that this is information about what these people like to do now. Students predict what the person is going to be. Students take turns talking about the different people, using the prompt. They make guesses about the possible jobs, using the information given. Discuss their predictions as a class.

Key: Student's own answers

SB21. ACTIVITY 15. *Think about somebody you know who has an interesting job. Answer the questions.*

- Focus students on the instructions and elicit ideas. Students write the answers in their notebooks. Supply the job in English.

Key: Student's own answers

SB21. *Now ask your friend the questions.*

- In pairs, students take turns finding out about the interesting job their partner wrote about. Discuss as a class.

WB21. ACTIVITY 12. *These four children are going to have different jobs. Write the numbers.*

Key: a: 4, 6, 8; b: 3, 5, 10; c: 1, 2, 7; d: 9, 11, 12

WB21. ACTIVITY 13. *Slim Jim's a famous singer. Read and complete his calendar.*

- Ask *Where does a soccer player play soccer?* to elicit *a soccer stadium*. Ask students if they can name famous stadiums in their country or in the world. Ask *Can you go to a soccer stadium to see a music festival?*

Key:

	Monday	Tuesday	Wednesday	Thursday	Friday
am	Arrive London	Music store	Open school	TV interview	Fly to Spain
	lunch	lunch	lunch	lunch	lunch
pm	Hospital	Dinner with actors	Sing in soccer stadium	Movie theater	Meet manager

WB21. ACTIVITY 14. *Answer the questions.*

Key: Students' own answers

Extra activities: see page T100 (if time)

Optional activity

- Unit 2 Extension worksheet 1 from *Kid's Box AE Teacher's Resource Book 5* (see pages 22 and 25)

Ending the lesson

- Elicit which is the favorite job from today and why.

11 Listen and match. Say the job.

CD1 32

1 Good evening. This is Captain Bird speaking. Welcome aboard flight 241 from Dublin to London.

Pilot. That's "e."

a

b

c

d

e

f

12 Listen again and choose the right words.

CD1 33

1 The plane is flying to **New York / London / Paris**.
2 Bill brushes his teeth **well / badly / on Saturdays.**
3 The cook is making a **chocolate cake / carrot cake / cheesecake.**
4 Mr. Hamilton can get his car at **ten o'clock / half past nine / half past ten.**
5 The cowboy is **happy / hungry / cold.**
6 The reporter is going to interview a **soccer player / swimmer / basketball player.**

13 Play the game. Guess it in ten.

Do you work at the fire station?

No, I don't.

Do you wear a uniform?

Yes, I do.

14 Read and think. Ask and answer.

What's Teresa going to be when she grows up?

She's going to be a cook.

Teresa	loves making cakes and working in the kitchen.
Richard	loves studying science and the human body.
William	loves drawing and painting.
Helen	likes working with children. She loves reading them stories.
Robert	loves animals and going to the country. He's very strong.
Katy	loves playing with cars and building things.

15 Think about somebody you know who has an interesting job. Answer the questions.

1 Who does this job?
2 What's his/her job?
3 What does he/she do at work?
4 Why do you think it's interesting?

Now ask your friend the questions.

16 CD1 34 Focus on phonics

Manager, actor, swimmer, writer,
Older, taller, stronger, faster.

Farmer, teacher, doctor, dancer,
Treasure, picture, paper, answer!

Speaking 17 Ask and answer.

Writing 18 Write your plans for next week. Don't repeat any verbs!

On Monday after school I'm going to play
with my friends.
On Tuesday ...

CD1 35 Joke Corner

A man went to the doctor with bananas in his ears and a carrot in his nose. What did the doctor say?

He said, "You're sick because you aren't eating right."

OBJECTIVES: By the end of the lesson, students will have practiced words ending in /ər/ and completed a writing activity.

• TARGET LANGUAGE

Key language: The phoneme /ər/, *treasure, picture, answer, apostrophe*

Review: *going to*, jobs, comparatives

• MATERIALS REQUIRED

Photocopiable 2 (page T91), copied twice and cut up into cards

Optional: *Kid's Box AE Teacher's Resource Book 5* Unit 2 Extension worksheet 2 (page 26)

Warmer

- Write the words *teacher, doctor, picture,* and *faster* on the board. Ask students which sound all four words have in common. Say the words aloud. Students discuss in pairs. Elicit suggestions. Repeat the words emphasising the /ər/ sound at the end of each word. Elicit the sound. Underline the sound on the board (*teacher, doctor, picture, faster*). Tell students they will be practising recognising this sound and looking at different spellings for the sound in today's lesson.

SB22. ACTIVITY 16. *Focus on phonics*

- Tell students to open their Student's Books to page 22. Focus them on Activity 16. Play the CD. Students repeat after each line and then after the whole rhyme. Repeat once more. In pairs, students practice the rhyme.

CD 1, 34

As in Student's Book

Photocopiable 2 (see pages T88 and T91 and the notes for Activity 17 below)

SB22. ACTIVITY 17. *Ask and answer.*

- Copy Photocopiable 2 (see page T91) twice, onto thin cardboard. Cut out the cards for the number of students in your class before the lesson. For example, if you have a class of 26, you will only need to use 13 of the cards from Photocopiable 2 – two copies of each. Hand out one card to each student. On the board write in example speech bubbles, *What are you going to do on ... ?* and, *I'm going to ... .* Tell students they need to find the person who has the same plans as they have on their card. The class mingle and ask and answer questions to find out who their partner is. Monitor and make sure they are speaking English and not simply comparing cards. When students have found their partner, they check with you and then sit down.

SB22. ACTIVITY 18. *Write your plans for next week. Don't repeat any verbs!*

- Focus students on the activity instructions. Ask a student to read the first sentence. Check students know to write a sentence for each day of the week, using a different verb each time (some sentences should be real and some should be imagined). Elicit some examples to give students ideas.
- Students then work with their partner from Activity 17. Set a time limit for the class of approximately five minutes. The pairs take turns writing their plans for the following week on a shared piece of paper. Students can't repeat any of the verbs used. At the end of the set time, the pairs count how many sentences they have written. The pair with the most sentences reads them aloud to the class. The pairs that are listening say whether the sentences are grammatically correct or not and then vote on whether they think they are true. Pairs win a point for each correct guess. The pair with the most points at the end of the activity wins.

SB22. JOKE CORNER

- Focus students on the Joke Corner and review the meaning of *joke*. Play the CD as students read the joke in their books. Play the joke a second time and explain if necessary.

CD 1, 35

As in Student's Book

WB22. ACTIVITY 15. *Can you remember? Complete the sentences.*

Key: 2 stronger, 3 treasure, 4 picture, 5 doctor, 6 answer

WB22. ACTIVITY 16. *Listen, check, and say.*

- Play the CD for students to listen and check. They compare answers in pairs. Check with the class. Elicit the words in each sentence with the /ər/ sound. Play the CD again for students to listen and repeat.

Key: See audioscript below

CD 1, 36

1. The manager is older than the actor.
2. The swimmer is stronger than the writer.
3. The farmer found some treasure.
4. The teacher showed her students a picture.
5. The doctor is writing on some paper.
6. The dancer knows the answer.

WB22. ACTIVITY 17. *Find 13 mistakes in the text.*

- Before students do the activity, focus them on the Write it right box and check they understand how, where and why apostrophes are used in English.

Key: See Activity 18 key

WB22. ACTIVITY 18. *Now write the text correctly.*

Key: My dad's a cook in a restaurant. It's called Pete's Diner. The restaurant's big. It has more than 20 tables and five cooks. Dad likes his job, but he doesn't have many vacations. He isn't working today, but he's cooking dinner for me and my sister. He doesn't always cook at home because he's often tired when he finishes work. Mom's a great cook too, but she doesn't get any money for cooking. She's a history teacher.

WB22. ACTIVITY 19. *Write about a job someone in your family does.*

Key: Students' own answers

Extra activity: see page T101 (if time)

Optional activity

- Unit 2 Extension worksheet 2 from *Kid's Box AE Teacher's Resource Book 5* (see pages 22 and 26)

Ending the lesson

- Do the rhyme from the beginning of the lesson again.

OBJECTIVES: By the end of the lesson, students will have read a story, reviewed language from the unit and completed a self-evaluation.

• TARGET LANGUAGE

Key language: language in the story, *pirate, have/has to, secretary*

Review: character names, language from the unit

• MATERIALS REQUIRED

Extra activity 2: Paper for each student

Warmer

- Review the story so far with students. Write the character names on the board. Students suggest adjectives that apply to them. If the class doesn't agree with any adjective, the student has to give the reason why he/she chose it.

SB23. STORY. *Diggory Bones.*

- Tell students to open their Student's Books to page 23. Focus them on the story. Tell them to read quickly and find evidence of any of the adjectives suggested for the characters in the warmer. Set the questions: *What does Brutus Grabbe want to be? Where must Diggory go to meet Brutus? What is Diggory's mistake?* Play the CD with books closed. Students listen to find the answers. They check in pairs with books open. Check with the class. (Brutus wants to be very rich. To the Old City Library at 10:45. He goes to the wrong library.) Play the CD again. Students listen and read. Stop after each frame for students to repeat. At the end, check comprehension by asking, e.g., *Was Brutus a good student? What did he study? What does he love? What time's the meeting? Who has the letter? What does it say?*

CD 1, 37

As in Student's Book

WB23. ACTIVITY 20. *Read and answer.*

Key: 2 at the Old City Library, 3 because he only loves money, 4 at 10:45 (a quarter to eleven), 5 No, he isn't. 6 the secretary

WB23. ACTIVITY 21. *Read and order the text.*

Key: From left to right: 3, 5, 1, 6, 8, 7, 2, 4

WB23. DO YOU REMEMBER?

- Students try to do the activity first without looking back through the unit. Once they have tried to complete all the sentences, they can look back through the unit to find the answers.

Key: 2 repairs, 3 dentist, 4 going to, 5 Students' own answers, 6 letter

WB23. CAN DO

- Focus students on the *Can do* section of the page. Ask a student to read the first sentence. Elicit what this means with examples and elicit/remind them of the activities they did in this unit when they used *going to*. Review what the three faces mean (not very well / OK / very well). Remind students they circle the one they think is true for them. Repeat for the second sentence, eliciting/reminding them of the activities when they talked about people at work. Students circle the appropriate face. Repeat for the third sentence, eliciting examples of words with apostrophes.
- Say *Now show and tell your friends.* Students work in groups of three and take turns showing their work for / talking about each one.

Extra activities: see page T101 (if time)

Ending the lesson

- Ask students which rhyme/song they'd like to do again from the unit. Do it together to end the lesson.

DIGGORY BONES
Who's Brutus Grabbe?
He was a student of mine. He was very smart, but he was ... very bad.
I studied dinosaurs' teeth, but I'm not an archeologist and I'm not a dentist.
No, you're a pirate! You only love money.
Yes, and I'm going to be very rich.
If you want the Baloney Stone, meet me at the Old City Library at 10:45 tomorrow.
He's going to use my program.
Oh, no, he isn't! We're going to stop him.
DONG DONG
CITY LIBRARY
Come on, Dad! It's a quarter to 11. We have work to do !
I'm going to get you, Brutus Grabbe!
He isn't here.
Yoo-hoo! Doctor Bones! I have a letter for you.
SECRETARY
This is the wrong library, Doctor Bones. I said the Old City Library. You have to think a little more. Brutus Grabbe.
This is the wrong library, Doctor Bones. I said the Old City Library. You have to think a little more.
Brutus Grabbe

Science Teeth

FACT: **People cleaned their teeth with wood and animal hair before William Addis invented the first toothbrush in 1780.**

1 Read and match.

a 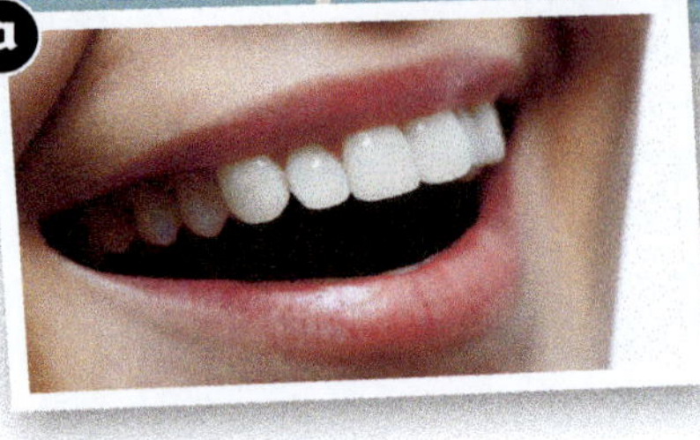

b 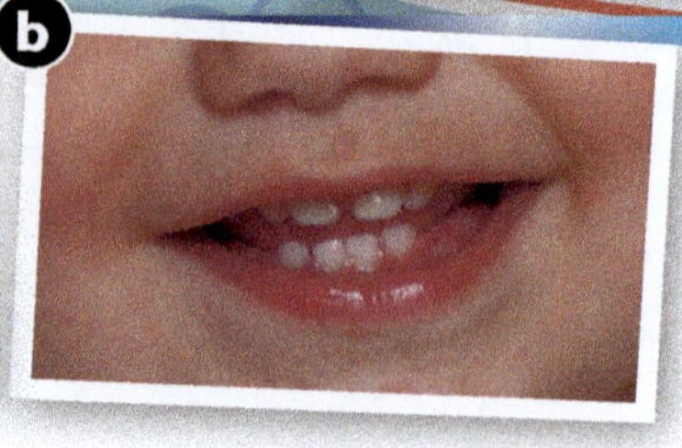

c 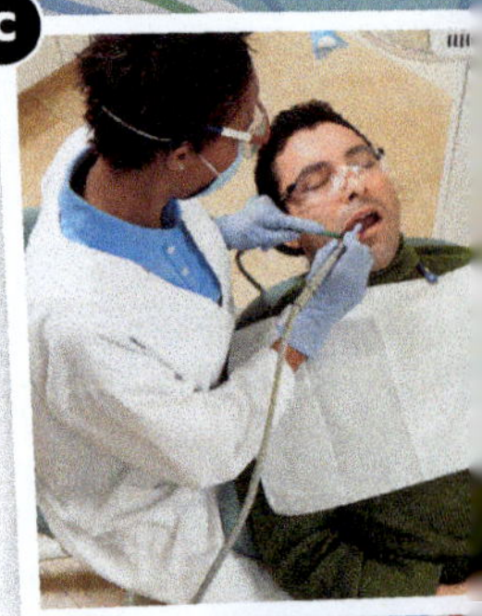

Our dentist

We start going to our dentist when we are very young because dentists help us take care of our teeth. Healthy teeth help us eat, speak clearly, and look good.

Our baby teeth

We get 20 baby teeth when we are between six months and three years old. Then we lose these teeth and get a permanent set of about 32 teeth.

Our permanent teeth

The first 28 permanent teeth appear when we are between six and 13. The final four molars, or wisdom teeth, usually come when we are between 16 and 21. Not everyone gets wisdom teeth. Do you know if your parents got theirs?

2 Read and label the diagram.

Our different teeth

We have four kinds of teeth, which do different things:

- We have eight **incisors** at the front of our mouths. They're the sharpest teeth because they cut our food.
- The four **canine** teeth are next to the incisors. They hold and tear food, so they have very long roots.
- Our eight **premolars** are behind our canine teeth. We use them to chew food, so premolars are flatter on the top.
- The **molars** are at the back of our mouths. Molars are much bigger than the premolars. Their job is to chew food into smaller pieces so it can be swallowed.

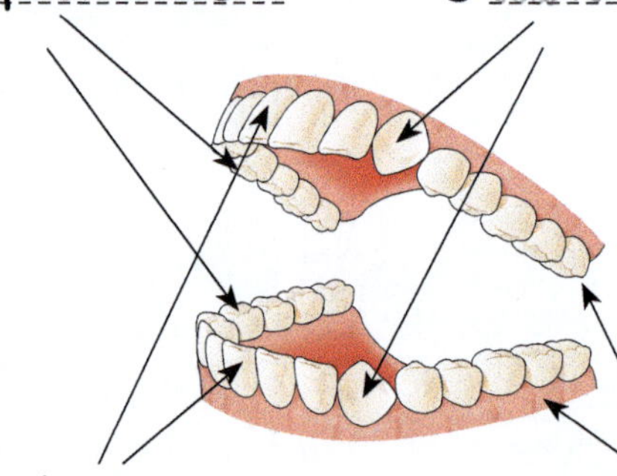

3 Match the sentences with the picture.

Tooth structure

A tooth has two parts: the crown and the root.

1 The **crown** is the part we can see when we smile or open our mouth.

2 We can't see the **root** because it is in the gums. It is about two-thirds of the tooth's total length.

3 The hard white part that covers the outside of the tooth is called the **enamel**.

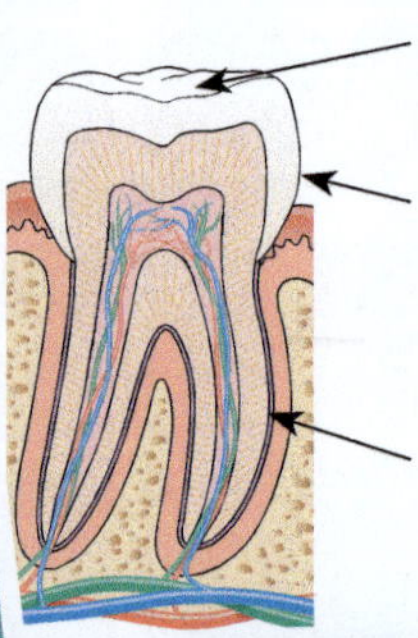

OBJECTIVES: By the end of the lesson, students will have read about teeth and their structure.

● TARGET LANGUAGE

Key language: *toothbrush, teeth, baby teeth, permanent, molars, wisdom teeth, appear, incisors, canines, premolars, chew, tear, flat(ter), swallow, crown, root, gum, enamel*
Review: *healthy, dentist,* numbers, adjectives

● MATERIALS REQUIRED

Extra activity 2: Reference books on animals, the Internet, large sheets of paper, colored markers

Warmer

- Ask students to count the number of teeth they have. They check with their partners to see if they have the same number. Tell them how many teeth you have. Ask *Do small babies have teeth?* (No, they don't.) Ask *How old are babies when their first teeth appear?* (About six months old.) Explain that *appear* means the same as *come*. Write it on the board and ask a student to spell it.

SB24. FACT

- Tell students to open their Student's Books to page 24. Focus them on the top of the page. Ask a student to read the fact to the class. Elicit their reactions. Elicit what students' own toothbrushes are made of.

SB24. ACTIVITY **1.** *Read and match.*

- Focus students on the Activity 1 instructions and on the pictures. If students try to guess before they read, don't tell them if they are right or wrong. Students read the text quickly (and silently) to match the pictures with the headings in the text. They check in pairs. Check with the class.

Key: a Our permanent teeth, b Our baby teeth, c Our dentist

SB24. ACTIVITY **2.** *Read and label the diagram.*

- Focus students on the Activity 2 instruction and on the diagram. They read the text to check which teeth are which and then label the diagram. They check in pairs. Check with the class and review what the functions of these different kinds of teeth are.
- Read the first two parts of the text through with the class, with students taking turns reading sections aloud. Discuss the information in each section with the class and check pronunciation of new words, e.g., *incisor*, and understanding of key vocabulary, e.g., *swallow.* Elicit what kinds of food the different types of teeth help us eat.

Key: 2 incisors, 3 canines, 4 molars

SB24. ACTIVITY **3.** *Match the sentences with the picture.*

- Check students understand what to do for Activity 3. They read the text and try to match the sentences with the picture, first on their own. Then they check with their partner. Draw the diagram on the board and check with the class. Check understanding and pronunciation of key words, e.g., *enamel, gums, crown, root.*

Key: 1 enamel, 2 crown, 3 root

WB24. ACTIVITY **1.** *Teeth quiz. Read and choose the right words.*

Key: 2b, 3c, 4a, 5c, 6c

WB24. ACTIVITY **2.** *Complete the teeth mind map.*

Note: Students will not be able to complete the activity until they have read both pages 24 and 25 of the Student's Book.

Key: (see below)

WB24. ACTIVITY **3.** *Answer the questions.*

Key: Students' own answers

WB24. ACTIVITY **4.** *Use the answers to write about your teeth.*

Key: Students' own answers

Extra activities: see page T101 (if time)

Ending the lesson

- Review with students what they have done and what they have learned about in today's lesson.

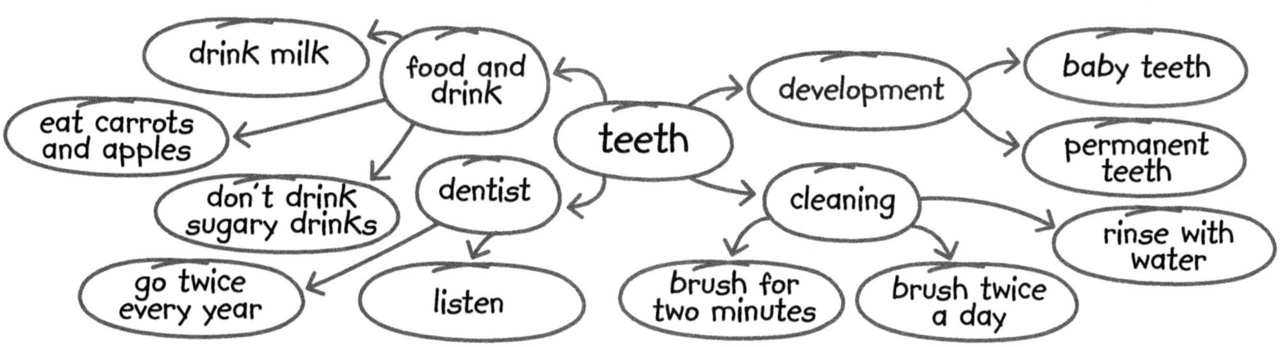

OBJECTIVES: By the end of the lesson, students will have learned more about teeth and oral hygiene and completed a project.

● TARGET LANGUAGE

Key language: *tooth care, sugary, healthy, between, diet, rinse, cavity (cavities), circular, fluoride, experiment, tongue, then, lastly, next, vinegar, hard-boiled eggs, minerals, acid, bubble, shell, appear*

Review: food

● MATERIALS REQUIRED

For each group of four: two hard-boiled eggs, two clear plastic cups. For the class: one tube of toothpaste with fluoride, two to four toothbrushes, two bottles of vinegar.
Extra activity 1: If possible, a watch with a timer or alarm
Optional: *Kid's Box AE Teacher's Resource Book 5* Unit 2 Topic worksheet (page 28)

Warmer

- With books closed, review some of the facts students learned about teeth in the previous lesson, e.g., *How many teeth do babies have? What about young children? What are their teeth called? How many teeth do adults have? What are the four different kinds of teeth called and what do they do?*

SB25. ACTIVITY **4.** *Read and complete.*

- Tell students to open their Student's Books to page 25. Focus them on Activity 4 and on the title (Tooth care). Elicit what students think this means. Ask a student to read the introduction aloud (*To have healthy teeth and gums, you must:*). Students work individually. They read the text and complete it with the words. They check in pairs. Check with the class by asking different students to read parts of the text aloud. Check understanding of each section by asking, e.g., *So what is it OK to eat? Give me an example of a sugary food. Is it good for our teeth?*

Key: 1 before; 2 shouldn't, between, hungry, brush, finish; 3 dentist, better, healthy

SB25. ACTIVITY **5.** *Read and order the text.*

- Focus students on the Activity 5 instruction and check understanding. Students work alone on this problem-solving activity. Remind them to use the sequencing words to help them. Don't hurry them, but give them plenty of time to think and re-read. They can ask you or their partner if there is anything they don't understand. Check the sequence with the class. Ask a student to read paragraph 1 aloud. Then elicit from students what they think paragraph 2 is and ask one to read it aloud. Ask the class if it sounds right and if they agree. Repeat for the other paragraphs. Finally, write the number sequence on the board to confirm the order. Check general comprehension and also the meaning of any key vocabulary. Draw students' attention to the sequencing words, e.g., *Then, Next, Lastly.*
- Show the students how long two minutes are by using the alarm on your watch or a clock.

Key: 8, 2, 9, 1, 6, 7, 4, 5, 3

SB25. PROJECT. *Do a dentist's experiment.*

- Show students the materials you have brought for the project (toothpaste, toothbrushes, cups, vinegar, eggs). Tell them they are going to be dentists today! Read the project information through with the class, showing the materials as they are mentioned. Elicit their predictions for the final question (Which egg do you think is going to start to bubble?). Check students understand what to do. Put students in groups of four and hand out the materials. Students do the experiment in their groups, following the instructions. Monitor and check/help where necessary. Elicit what actually happened and if they were correct about their predictions. Discuss why that egg bubbled first and how the result is connected with teeth, the dentist and fluoride.

WB25. ACTIVITY **5.** FLYERS **Reading and Writing, Part 6.** *Read the letter and write the missing words. Write one word on each line.* **F** toward

- Tell students to open their Workbooks to page 25. Read the activity instructions and make sure students realize they need to use just one word in each space. Students read and complete the text individually, then compare answers in pairs. Check with the class. Go through any new vocabulary.

Key: 1 than, 2 answer, 3 good/bad, 4 to, 5 some

Extra activities: see page T101 (if time)

Optional activity

- Unit 2 Topic worksheet from *Kid's Box AE Teacher's Resource Book 5* (see pages 22 and 28)

Ending the lesson

- Review with students what they talked and read about in today's lesson and which activities they liked best from this and the previous lesson.

4 Read and complete.

healthy between finish
~~after~~ shouldn't before hungry
brush dentist better

Tooth care

To have healthy teeth and gums, you must:

1 brush your teeth every day after________ meals and __________ bed.
2 eat a good diet. You __________ eat sugary foods __________ meals. If you are __________, eat an apple, a banana, or a carrot.
Don't drink lemonade. Drink milk! If you eat between meals, __________ your teeth when you __________.
3 visit the __________ twice a year. A dentist can clean your teeth __________ than you so that your mouth is __________.

5 Read and order the text.

How to brush your teeth

☐ To finish, rinse out your mouth with water.

☐ Always start and finish in the same place in your mouth. A good place to start is the outside of the back molars, which need the most time and brushing.

☐ All of that should take two minutes.

1 Brushing your teeth is very important. It cleans your teeth and gums, and helps against cavities.

6 Then repeat all of this on your bottom teeth.

☐ Lastly, don't forget the top of your mouth and your tongue.

☐ Next brush the inside of your teeth and gums using the same circular movement.

☐ When you finish the inside and outside of your top teeth, quickly brush along the chewing part of your teeth.

3 Gently brush the back molars and gums using a small circular movement. Then move slowly around your mouth brushing all your teeth.

Project Do a dentist's experiment.

You need:

- A toothbrush
- Toothpaste with fluoride
- 2 eggs
- A bottle of white vinegar
- 2 clear plastic cups

What to do:

1 Brush one of the eggs with fluoride toothpaste.
2 Put 10 cm of vinegar into both cups. Put the "fluoride" egg into one cup of vinegar and the other egg into the other cup of vinegar.

What happens:

Bubbles start to appear on one egg as the vinegar (an acid) attacks the minerals in the egg shell. Which egg do you think bubbles are going to appear on?

Review Units 1 and 2

1 Sarah is talking to her mother, Mrs. Smith. Read the conversation and choose the best answer. You do not need to use all the letters.

- **a** Can we go out to the park?
- **b** Yes, please. Can I phone Katy to see if she can come?
- **c** My favorite comedy's on at twenty-five after five.
- **d** I think it's about half past eleven.
- **e** All right, then. Can I call Peter?
- **f** Thanks, Mom. Can you hand me the phone?
- **g** Which ones should I wear? My sneakers?
- **h** Does Peter like history?

Example

Mrs. Smith: What time is it, Sarah?
Sarah: d

Questions

1 **Mrs. Smith:** What do you want to do?
Sarah: ....

2 **Mrs. Smith:** OK. Put your shoes on.
Sarah: ....

3 **Mrs. Smith:** Yes, the blue ones. Listen, do you want to go with a friend?
Sarah: ....

4 **Mrs. Smith:** I think Katy's studying for an exam this afternoon.
Sarah: ....

5 **Mrs. Smith:** OK. Call him and see if he wants to come, too.
Sarah: ....
Mrs. Smith: Here you are. Tell Peter to bring his bike!

2 Tell your friend the story. There is one example. (It's morning. The boy is going to scho

3 Now write the story.

OBJECTIVES: By the end of the lesson, students will have reviewed language from Units 1 and 2 and told and written a story.

• TARGET LANGUAGE

Key language: vocabulary and language from Units 1 and 2

Additional language: *platform*

• MATERIALS REQUIRED

Key vocabulary from Units 1 and 2, each word written on a small piece of paper, enough for each student in the class.

Warmer

- Make groups of six. Hand out a word from Unit 1 or 2 to each student. They keep their word secret. They take turns providing a definition of their word for the other students in their group to guess. If time, regroup students and repeat.

SB26. ACTIVITY **1.** *Sarah is talking to her mother, Mrs. Smith. Read the conversation and choose the best answer. You do not need to use all the letters.* F toward

- Tell students to open their Student's Books to page 26. Focus them on the Activity 1 instructions. Ask a student to read them aloud. Elicit what *best answer* means and check that students know what to do (complete the conversation). Students work individually to read the conversation and complete it. They check in pairs. Check with the class by asking pairs to read sections of the conversation aloud. Focus them on the key words which give them clues for the answers each time. Teach some techniques for this kind of activity, e.g., looking at the line that comes after the blank, looking at nouns, verbs, pronouns, etc. to check for coherence.

Key: 1a, 2g, 3b, 4e, 5f

SB26. ACTIVITY **2.** *Tell your friend the story.* F toward

- Focus students on Activity 2 and on the pictures. Give them time to look at the pictures and work out what is happening in the story. Elicit useful words for each picture as well as several sentences to describe what is happening in each picture. , e.g., *It's 8:30, and Peter is waiting on the platform for the train. He's going to be late, and he's not happy.* Encourage students to bring the story to life by giving the characters names, and to "fill in" the story between the pictures, e.g., *Peter runs out of the house. He is thinking about his homework.* Put students into pairs. They take turns telling the story (one picture each), saying at least two sentences for each picture and one sentence for in between the pictures. Remind them to use adjectives and adverbs to make the story more interesting. Go around the class, monitoring and listening in to the storytelling.

Key: Students' own answers

SB26. ACTIVITY **3.** *Now write the story.* F toward

- Focus students on the activity instruction. They write a draft of their story on paper or in their notebooks. Remind them to give the story a title, to give the people names, to write at least two sentences for each picture, to fill in between the pictures, and to use adjectives and adverbs to make it more interesting. Students write their first draft individually. They swap their work with a partner. They suggest corrections and improvements for each other's work. Students then write a final draft in their notebooks.

Note: In the real test, there are only three pictures.

WB26. ACTIVITY **1.** *Read the story. Choose words from the box to complete the sentences.* F toward

Note: There are five extra words in the box.

Key: 2 jobs, 3 firefighter, 4 painted, 5 going

WB26. ACTIVITY **2.** *Choose a title for this episode of* Friendly. F toward

Key: a) Modern art

WB26. ACTIVITY **3.** *Draw and color Sue's painting.*

WB26. ACTIVITY **4.** *Match the questions with the answers.*

Key: 3, 6, 4, 1, 2, 5

Extra activities: see page T101 (if time)

Ending the lesson

- Review *going to* by asking around the class what students are going to do that evening and on the weekend.

OBJECTIVES: By the end of the lesson, students will have reviewed language from Units 1 and 2 and played a board game.

• TARGET LANGUAGE

Key language: vocabulary and language from Units 1 and 2
Revision: language for playing games

• MATERIALS REQUIRED

Board game: Dice, colored counters
Optional: *Kid's Box AE Interactive DVD 5: The classroom* Quiz 1, *Kid's Box AE Teacher's Resource Book 5* Test Units Welcome–2 (pages 76–90), *Kid's Box AE Workbook 5 Language Portfolio* page 91

Warmer

- Revise telling the time with the class. Students make pairs. One sits with their back to the board, holding their notebook and a pencil. The other faces the board. Draw six numbered clocks on the board showing different times. Students whisper the number of each clock and then the time to their friend. The friend draws the time on the clock in their notebook. Students look and check. Pairs swap roles. Draw six more numbered clocks on the board showing different times.

SB27. ACTIVITY **4.** *Play the game.*

- Tell students to open their Student's Books to page 27. Elicit that this is a board game. Focus them on the instructions and check understanding. Students play in groups of three. One member of the group is the secretary and the other two are the players. The players take turns throwing the dice and moving around the board. When they land on a square, they say the time and what they're going to do at that time, as in the first example. The secretary makes a secret note of what is said. The next time it is their turn, they have to say the new time and then remember what they have planned to do the next day before adding the new activity, as in the second example. If they make a mistake or cannot remember the activity that goes with each time, they have to go back to the start. After the game, the players swap roles so that there is a new secretary.

WB27. ACTIVITY **5.** *Complete the sentences. Count and write the letters.*

Key: 2 history 7, 3 quarter 7, 4 art 3, 5 best 4, 6 geography 9, 7 quiz 4, 8 mechanic 8, 9 subject 7, 10 computer 8, 11 half 4, 12 math 4, 13 artist 6, 14 play 4

WB27. ACTIVITY **6.** *Now complete the crossword. Write the message.*

Key:

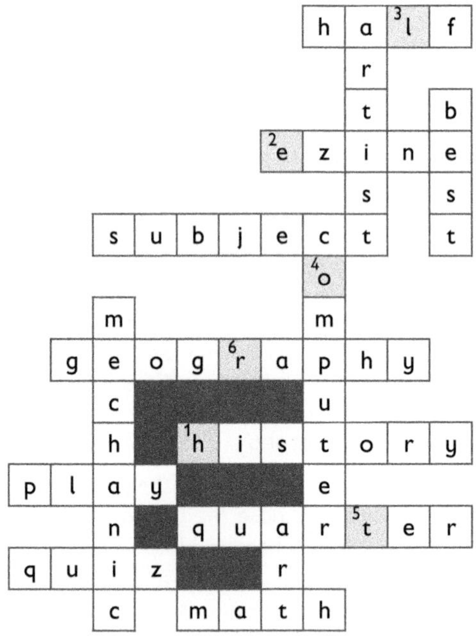

Message: hello there

WB27. ACTIVITY **7.** *Quiz time!*

Key: 1 They can study French, German, or Spanish, 2 science, 3 twelve, 4 a dentist, 5 writer and reporter, 6 four

WB27. ACTIVITY **8.** *Write questions for your quiz in your notebook.*

Key: Students' own answers

Extra activities: see page T101 (if time)

Optional evaluations

- Quiz 1 from *Kid's Box AE Interactive DVD 5* (*The classroom* section). This quiz can be done as a whole-class activity or as a team competition. See pages 36 and 37 of the Teacher's Booklet for the Interactive DVD.
- The test for Units Welcome–2 from *Kid's Box AE Teacher's Resource Book 5* (see pages 76–90) F toward

Language Portfolio

- Students complete page 91 of *Kid's Box AE Workbook 5 Language Portfolio* (I can ... Units 1 and 2).

Ending the lesson

- Students work in groups of three. They find the *Can do* Workbook sections for Units 1 and 2 (pages 15 and 23) and write the six statements on a large piece of paper. They discuss and give examples for each *Can do* statement, checking back in the Student's Book, the Workbook, or their notebooks if necessary. Elicit some examples from volunteer students in the class for each one.
- Ask students which lessons, topics and/or activities were their favorites.

4 Play the game.

What are you going to do tomorrow?

Instructions

- Go around the board. Say the time and what you are going to do at that time.
- Think of a different activity for each time.
- To keep playing you have to remember the activity that goes with each time. If you cannot remember, then go back to START and wait for another turn.

That's a quarter to seven. Tomorrow I'm going to wake up at a quarter to seven.

That's nine o'clock. Tomorrow I'm going to wake up at a quarter to seven and go to school at nine o'clock.

3 City life

Show what you know! What city words can you remember?

Listening **1** 02 CD2 Listen and check (✓) the city words you hear.

2 03 CD2 Listen again. Choose the right words.

1. They arrive at **ten after two** / **twenty to three**.
2. They want information for their **ezine** / **school homework**.
3. They decide to visit a **bridge** / **museum** first.
4. They start outside the **station** / **school**.
5. They're lost because of problems with the **map** / **bus**.
6. Tower Bridge is **behind** / **across** the street.

3 Read and complete the sentences.

1. We have to go along this road.
2. We don't go across the river. We turn left here.
3. Now we're at a corner.
4. I think we take the third street on the right, then walk past this park.
5. Let's go straight ahead.
6. It's just across the street.

LOOK

right left straight ahead
corner past across along

OBJECTIVES: By the end of the lesson, students will be able to understand and give simple directions and will have reviewed city vocabulary.

• TARGET LANGUAGE

Key language: directions: *right, left, straight ahead, (at/on the) corner, past, across, along; to get lost, turn, traffic lights*

Additional language: *just (across the street)*

Review: city and town vocabulary, telling the time, simple past, imperatives, *map*

• MATERIALS REQUIRED

Extra activity 1: Paper for making labels

Extra activity 2: Paper for each student

Warmer

- Provide a definition of city for students to guess the word, e.g., *I'm thinking of a place where people live. It's very busy. There are a lot of cars, stores, houses, and offices. There are parks, too.* Give clues until students guess. Provide a similar definition for *town*. Discuss briefly with students where they prefer to live (city or town) and why. Tell students the theme of Unit 3 is City life and write it in the center of the board.

SB28. SHOW WHAT YOU KNOW! *What city words can you remember?*

- Draw a circle around City life on the board and write one or two of the words you said in the warmer to start a mind map. Say *Show what you know … about city life.* Brainstorm with the class in two minutes the city words they can remember to add to the mind map on the board. Supply words in English where necessary. Students copy the mind map into their notebooks.

SB28. ACTIVITY 1. *Listen and check (✓) the city words you hear.*

- Tell students to open their Student's Books to page 28. Focus students on the Activity 1 pictures. Elicit the names of the characters and where they are. Focus students on the activity instruction and check understanding. Remind them to do the same as for the Show what you know in the previous units (check off the words they hear in the City life mind map in their notebooks).
- Play the CD. Students listen and check. They check in pairs. Use the mind map on the board to check with the class.

CD 2, 02

MR. GRAY: OK, kids. We're going to meet back here at half past five. Don't get lost!

DAN: No problem, Dad! It's ten after two now, so we have more than three hours.

MARIA: We want to get some interesting information for our ezine, so where should we go first?

ALEX: Tower Bridge is the most famous bridge in London. Let's go there.

MARIA: How do we get there?

ALEX: Let's look at the map … Now, we're outside the station. That's here.

DAN: We have to go straight along this road. We don't go across the river. We turn left here.

DAN: OK, now we're at a corner. Do we want to go left or right, Alex?

ALEX: Um, I don't know. I think we take the third street on the right, then walk past this park.

MARIA: Uh, boys … turn the map around! We're going in the wrong direction!

MARIA: Excuse me. Can you tell us how to get to Tower Bridge, please?

WOMAN: Look, dear. It's just across the street. It's behind you.

SB28. ACTIVITY 2. *Listen again. Choose the right words.*

- Focus students on the Activity 2 instructions and on the sentences. Give them reading and discussion/prediction time. Play the CD. Students choose the correct option. They check in pairs. Play the CD again and check answers with the class.

Key: 1 ten after two, 2 ezine, 3 bridge, 4 station, 5 map, 6 across

CD 2, 03

Presentation

- Draw a simple map on the board to pre-teach the directions *right, left, straight ahead, (on the) corner, past, across, along.* Focus students on the Look box to help check the concepts. Invite a student to the front. Give simple directions for the map on the board for the student to follow with a finger. Repeat.
- Play the CD from Activity 1 again. When students hear directions, they put their hands up. Stop the CD and elicit what was said. Get students to mime or point to the Look box to check understanding.

SB28. ACTIVITY 3. *Read and complete the sentences.*

- Focus students on Activity 3. They write the sentences in their notebooks. They check in pairs. Play the CD for a final check.

Key: 1 (straight) along, 2 left, 3 corner, 4 right, past, 5 straight ahead, 6 across

WB28. ACTIVITY 1. *Read and answer the questions.*

Key: 1 three, 2 twice, 3 thirteen

WB28. ACTIVITY 2. *Check (✓) or cross (✗) the sentences.*

Key: 1 ✗, 2 ✓, 3 ✗, 4 ✗

WB28. ACTIVITY 3. *Read and complete the sentences.*

Key: 2 right, 3 straight ahead, 4 on the corner, 5 left, 6 down

Extra activities: see page T101 (if time)

Ending the lesson

- Say the directions words again for students to mime with their hands.

OBJECTIVES: By the end of the lesson, students will have had further practice with using maps and understanding and giving simple directions.

• TARGET LANGUAGE

Key language: directions, imperatives, *You are here, across from, on the left/right, at the end of ..., bank, stadium, gym*
Review: city vocabulary, prepositions

• MATERIALS REQUIRED

Extra activity 1: The following directions written on a large sheet of paper. Don't write the answers (they are for you).

1 *Go straight ahead. Take the third street on the right. Walk past the shoe store and the candy store. Turn right. Go straight across Green Street. Go the the corner of Blue Street and the bank is on the left.* (Wrong: The bank is on the right. The bicycle store is on the left.)
2 *Walk up the High Street. Take the first street on the right and then take the first left. Take the second street on the left and the bus station is on the right.* (Wrong: The movie theater is on the right.)
3 *Go up the High Street. Walk across Blue Street and turn right at the book store. Cross Low Road. The supermarket is on the left.* (Wrong: The supermarket is on the right. The computer store is on the left.)

Optional: *Kid's Box AE Teacher's Resource Book 5* Unit 3 Reinforcement worksheets 1 and 2 (pages 30 and 31)

Warmer

- Draw a simple map on the board with features marked, e.g., station, library, museum. Ask students to come up one at a time and follow your directions. They also give directions, e.g., from the station to the museum.

SB29. ACTIVITY 4. *Look at the map. Read the directions and answer.*

- Tell students to open their Student's Books to page 29. Focus them on the map. Check understanding of vocabulary by asking, e.g., *Can you see the stadium? Can you see the gym?* Check they know where to start (red dot marked You are here). Students work individually and follow the directions to find the places on the map. They check in pairs, one reading the directions aloud, and the other following with their finger. Check with the class in the same way.

Key: 1 the stadium, 2 the candy store, 3 the school

SB29. ACTIVITY 5. Listen to the directions and answer.

- Focus students on the Activity 5 instruction. Remind them to start in the same place each time. Play the CD. They write the answer in their notebook each time. They check in pairs. Play the CD again. Check with the class.

Key: 2 the park, 3 the computer store, 4 the candy store, 5 the bus station

CD 2, 04

1. Go straight ahead. Take the second street on the left. What's at the end of the street?
2. Go up the High Street. Take the first street on the left and go across the river. What's on the right?
3. Go up the High Street. Take the second street on the right and go straight ahead. Cross Low Road. What's on the left?
4. Go straight ahead. Take the third street on the right. Walk past the shoe store and stop. What's on the right?
5. Go up the High Street. Take the first street on the right. Next, take the first street on the left and go across Green Street. Then take the first street on the right. What's on the left?

SB29. ACTIVITY 6. Play the game.

- Focus students on the Activity 6 instruction and on the example. Check they know what to do. Write useful words and phrases on the board, e.g., *on the left, on the right, at the end of ... , across from, next to, behind.* Students work individually for about five minutes, writing at least four sets of directions (plus the answers). Make pairs. Students take turns giving directions to each other and following them on the map. Make new pairs. Students repeat.

SB29. ACTIVITY 7. *Write the directions to (1) the bank and (2) the gym.*

- Students work individually to write the directions, but check with their partner if they get stuck. Check with the class.

Key (possible answers): (1) Go up High Street. Turn right on Blue Street. The bank is on the left corner, before you go across Low Road. (2) Go up High Street. Go across Red Street. The gym is on the left on the corner, opposite the movie theater.

WB29. ACTIVITY 4. *Follow the directions and write the message.*

Key: London is the biggest city in the U.K. There are a lot of interesting places to see and every year 29 million people visit it.

WB29. ACTIVITY 5. *Put these buildings on the map.*

Key: From left to right: castle, movie theater, library, school, fire station, stadium

WB29. ACTIVITY 6. *Find these buildings in Activity 5.*

Key: 1 the library, 2 the stadium

WB29. ACTIVITY 7. *Now write two sets of directions for a friend to follow.*

Key: Students' own answers

Extra activities: see page T101/T102 (if time)

Optional activity

- Unit 3 Reinforcement worksheets 1 and 2 from *Kid's Box AE Teacher's Resource Book 5* (see pages 29–31).

Ending the lesson

- Play a guessing game with some of the city vocabulary. Say, e.g., *I'm thinking of a place in the city. You can't shop there. You can read there, but you can't talk. Where is it?* (library). Repeat with *You go here to get money.* Students can take turns being the callers.

4 Look at the map. Read the directions and answer.

1 Go up High Street. Take the third street on the left and stop after the river. What's on the right? the stadium

2 Go up High Street and turn right onto Blue Street. Turn left onto Low Road, and then go across Green Street. What's on the corner, on the left, across from the movie theater? the candy store

3 Go up High Street, and take the second street on the left. Walk past the playground. What's next to it? the school

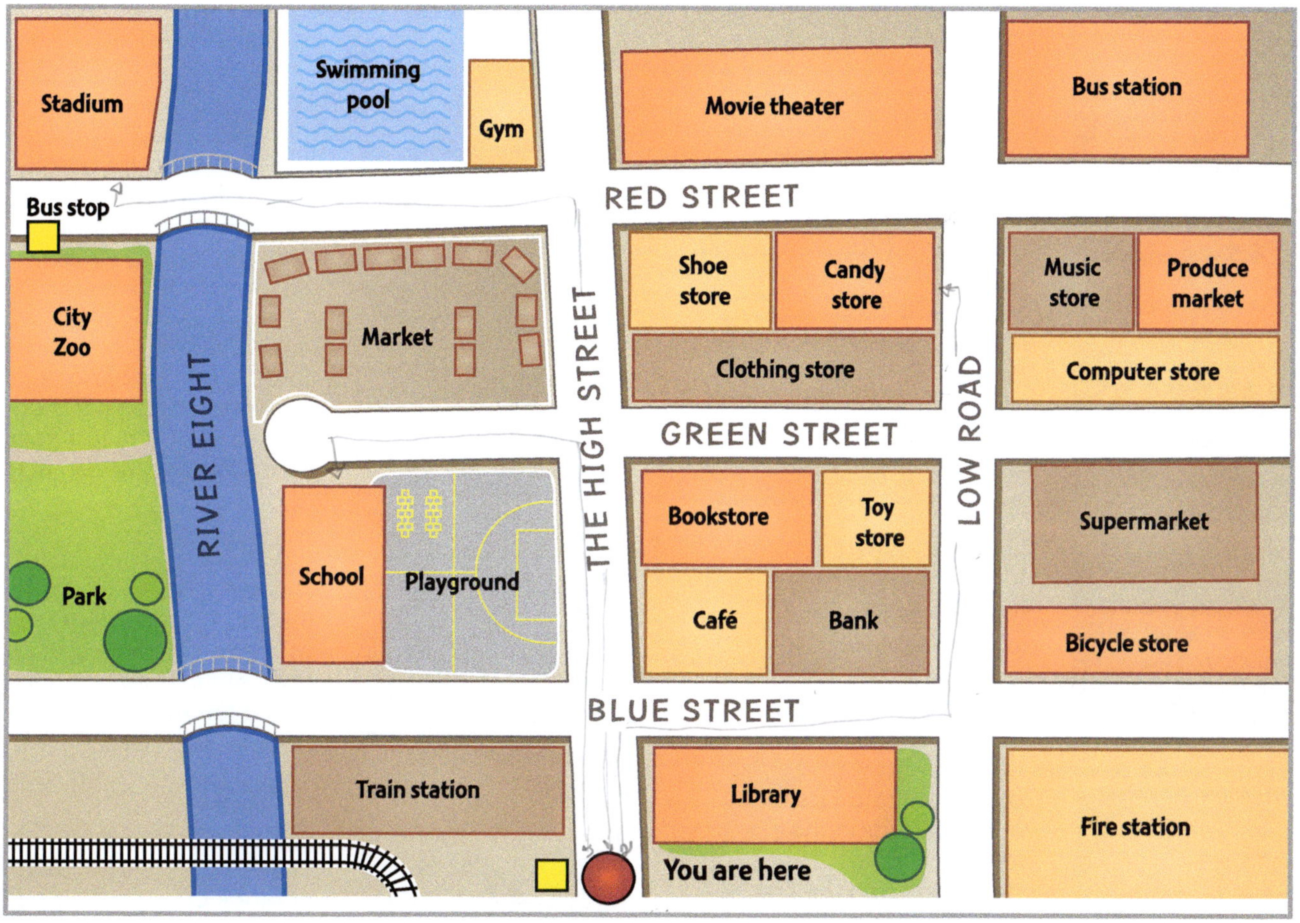

5 Listen to the directions and answer.

04 CD2

1 Go straight ahead. Take the second street on the left. What's at the end of the street?

The river.

6 Play the game.

Go up the High Street and take the third street on the right. Go across Low Road, and it's next to the music store.

Is it the produce market?

Yes, it is!

7 Write the directions to (1) the bank and (2) the computer store.

Possible answers:
1) Go up High Street. Turn right on Blue Street. The bank is on the left corner, before you across Low Road. 2) Go up High Street. Go across Red Street. The gym is on the left on the corner, opposite the movie theater.

Reading 8 Read and think. Is London an exciting city? Why?

http://www.cambridge.org/elt/kidsbox/ezine

Kid's Box Ezine!

home | reports | games | world | email

Kid's Box reports London

Yesterday we went to London and saw a lot of interesting places. Here are some of our pictures.

a

New Scotland Yard is one of the most famous police stations in the world. A king of Scotland lived in the first Scotland Yard.

b

This is the British Museum. There are six million objects here. One of them is the Rosetta Stone.

c

This is the new Globe Theater. The first Globe Theater was famous because William Shakespeare showed his plays there.

d

You can buy stamps for your postcards in the Trafalgar Square post office. They sold the first sticker stamps in this post office in 2001.

e

This is Brown's. It's a hotel and restaurant. It's the oldest hotel in London. Rudyard Kipling wrote *The Jungle Book* here.

f

London has six airports. This is Heathrow. It is the busiest airport in the world. 64 million people use this airport every year!

g

This castle is next to Tower Bridge. It's called the Tower of London. It looks beautiful now, but for many years it was a terrible prison. Many people died here.

h

This is a London taxi. It's called a black cab. Drivers of black cabs have to pass a test to show that they know all the streets in London.

taxi | hotel | police station | airport | restaurant | museum | castle | theater | post office

9 05 CD2 Listen. Repeat the word and say the name of the place.

1 Castle.

Castle. That's the Tower of London.

10 Read again and correct these sentences.

1. You can see the Rosetta Stone at the Natural History Museum.
2. William Shakespeare showed his movies here.
3. They sold the first postcards here.
4. Brown's is a store and hotel.
5. London has seven airports.
6. London buses are called black cabs.

OBJECTIVES: By the end of the lesson, students will have learned more vocabulary to talk about cities and read about London.

• TARGET LANGUAGE

Key language: *police station, theater, play (n.), stamps, post office, taxi, hotel, airport, restaurant, museum, castle, prison, black cab, is called*

Additional language: *the Globe Theater, William Shakespeare, Trafalgar Square, Brown's, Rudyard Kipling, The Jungle Book, New Scotland Yard, Tower Bridge, the Tower of London, Heathrow, the British Museum*

Review: city vocabulary, superlatives, telling the time

• MATERIALS REQUIRED

Photocopiable 3 (see page T92), one copy for each pair, cut into A and B

Extra activity: A large sheet of paper for each group of four, reference materials / the Internet to research London (past and present), colored markers

Optional: *Kid's Box AE Workbook 5 Language Portfolio*, page 98; *Kid's Box AE Teacher's Resource Book 5* Unit 3 Extension worksheet 1 (page 32)

Warmer

- Write London on the board. Give students two minutes in pairs to think/talk quietly about what they know about London. Then elicit/discuss what they know. Find out if anyone has visited London and, if they have, ask them where they went and what they saw.

SB30. ACTIVITY 8. *Read and think. Is London an exciting city? Why?*

- Tell students to open their Student's Books to page 30. Focus them on Activity 8 and on the activity instructions. Ask a student to read them aloud. Check understanding.
- Focus students on the text and elicit that it's a webpage for *Kid's Box* ezine. Make sure they notice the key words for places at the bottom of the webpage. They read the texts silently and think about their answers to the question. Elicit the places mentioned in the text and discuss their ideas as a class, reminding them to say why they think London is an exciting city. Check comprehension of vocabulary. Focus on each text one by one, giving students reading time, and then checking comprehension by discussing the information.

SB30. ACTIVITY 9. *Listen. Repeat the word and say the name of the place.*

- Focus students on the Activity 9 instructions and on the example. Elicit the names of the places mentioned in the text, e.g., *New Scotland Yard*, and what it is (a police station). Help students with pronunciation. Play the CD. Pause after each place for students to find the information. They point to the place the first time. Play the CD again. Elicit a choral response each time. Elicit what's in the British Museum (the Rosetta Stone).

Key: 2 Hotel. That's Brown's. 3 Police station. That's New Scotland Yard. 4 Airport. That's Heathrow. 5 Museum. That's the British Museum. 6 Theater. That's the Globe Theater. 7 Post office. That's Trafalgar Square post office. 8 Taxi. That's a black cab. 9 Restaurant. That's Brown's.

CD 2, 05

1 castle, 2 hotel, 3 police station, 4 airport, 5 museum, 6 theater, 7 post office, 8 taxi, 9 restaurant

SB30. ACTIVITY 10. *Read again and correct these sentences.*

- Focus students on the Activity 10 instruction. Students re-read the texts to find the correct information. They write the corrected sentences in their notebooks.

Key: 1 You can see the Rosetta Stone at the British Museum. 2 William Shakespeare showed his plays here. 3 They sold the first sticker stamps here. 4 Brown's is a hotel and restaurant. 5 London has six airports. 6 London taxis are called black cabs.

Photocopiable 3 (see pages T88 and T92)

WB30. ACTIVITY 8. *Choose words from the box to label the pictures.*

Note: There are two extra words in the box.

Key: 2 restaurant, 3 theater, 4 police station, 5 castle, 6 airport

WB30. ACTIVITY 9. *Unscramble and write the words.*

Key: 2 theater, 3 castle, 4 police station, 5 museum, 6 hotel

WB30. ACTIVITY 10. *Complete the chart. Look in the Student's Book to find the names of the places.*

Key: 10:30: Went for a boat trip on the River Thames. 12:45: Had a picnic lunch in Hyde Park. 2:30: Went to the new Globe Theater. 4:30: Went to look at the Tower of London. 5:30: Took a cab from Tower Bridge to the hotel. 5:50: Arrived at Brown's Hotel.

WB30. ACTIVITY 11. *Look at the letters on the clock and write the words.*

Key: 2 school, 3 stadium, 4 park, 5 shore, 6 road

Extra activity: see page T102 (if time)

Language Portfolio

- Students complete page 98 of *Kid's Box AE Workbook 5 Language Portfolio* (A city I know).

Optional activity

- Unit 3 Extension worksheet 1 from *Kid's Box AE Teacher's Resource Book 5* (see pages 29 and 32).

Ending the lesson

- Say the places from the reading again for students to provide the names, e.g., Teacher: Castle. Students: The Tower of London.

OBJECTIVES: By the end of the lesson, students will have had further practice giving directions and will have sung a song.

• TARGET LANGUAGE

Key language: city vocabulary, directions

Review: jobs, simple past, prepositions of place, giving definitions with *who, that, where*

• MATERIALS REQUIRED

Optional: *Kid's Box AE Teacher's Resource Book 5* Unit 3 Extension worksheet 2 and/or Song worksheet (pages 33 and 34)

Warmer

- Teach the simple chant below to revise city vocabulary.

  London, London, what a great city!
  There's a lot to see for you and me.
  Parks, castles, museums, theaters,
  There's a lot to see for you and me.

  Make small groups to suggest lines between each chorus by adding places, e.g., the Tower of London.

SB31. ACTIVITY **11.** *Listen and complete. Check and sing.*

- Tell students to open their Student's Books to page 31. Focus them on the Activity 11 song and on the words in the box. Give them a few minutes to read through the song and try to guess where the words go. Play the CD. They listen and check their work and complete the words in the song. They check in pairs. Check general comprehension of the song. Play the CD again. Stop for students to repeat, line by line, verse by verse. Play the CD again for students to join in with the song. Play the first version on the CD and then the karaoke version. Practice the song with students as a whole class, in large groups and in small groups (one group for each verse).

Key: theater, Bridge, castle, park, zoo, restaurant, street, taxi, station

CD 2, 06

As in Student's Book and key

CD 2, 07

Now sing the song again. (Karaoke version)

SB31. ACTIVITY **12.** Ask and answer.

- Focus students on the words in the box for Activity 12 and on the activity instruction. Give them thinking/checking time. Students work in pairs and take turns asking and answering, using the prompts as a model. Check with the class. Be ready to accept original answers.

Key (possible answers): A firefighter goes to a fire station. A manager goes to an office. An actor goes to a theater. A bus driver goes to a bus station. A doctor goes to a hospital. A teacher goes to a school. A pilot goes to an airport. A police officer goes to a police station.

SB31. ACTIVITY **13.** *Look at the map. Ask and answer.*

- Review prepositions *next to, between, behind, across from,* using classroom objects. Focus students on the Activity 13 map. Check they remember the names of all the places. Demonstrate the activity, using open pairs. Students continue, taking turns asking and answering in closed pairs. Monitor to check they are using the correct prepositions.

SB31. ACTIVITY **14.** *Think of a place you know. Give directions how to get there from your school. Can your friend guess?*

- Focus students on the Activity 14 instructions and check understanding. Read the sample text aloud around the class to make sure students know what to do. Brainstorm a few ideas of places with the class. Students work individually and write their directions. Go around the class, checking students have all thought of a place. Make suggestions if they haven't. In pairs, students take turns giving their directions and guessing the destination.

WB31. ACTIVITY **12.** *Write "who," "that" or "where."*

Key: 2 who, 3 that, 4 where, 5 who, 6 where, 7 where, 8 where, 9 who, 10 where

WB31. ACTIVITY **13.** *Now find the words from Activity 12.*

Key: 2 pilot, 3 ticket, 4 theater, 5 cook, 6 museum, 7 airport, 8 bank, 9 mechanic, 10 bridge

WB31. ACTIVITY **14.** *Write a definition of these words.*

Key (possible answers): 1 A place where you can catch a bus. 2 Someone who helps sick people in the hospital.

WB31. ACTIVITY **15.** *Put these places on your map.*

Key: Students' own answers

WB31. ACTIVITY **16.** *Now write directions from the castle to three places on the map.*

Key: Students' own answers

WB31. ACTIVITY **17.** *Ask your friend to follow your directions.*

Key: Students' own answers

Extra activities: see page T102 (if time)

Optional activities

- Unit 3 Extension worksheet 2 from *Kid's Box AE Teacher's Resource Book 5* (see pages 29 and 33).
- Unit 3 Song worksheet from *Kid's Box AE Teacher's Resource Book 5* (see pages 29 and 34).

Ending the lesson

- Sing the song from earlier in the lesson again with the class.

11 Listen and complete. Check and sing.

06 CD2

castle	zoo	restaurant	taxi
~~museum~~	station	theater	
Bridge	street	park	

Theater, movies,
Restaurant and hotel,
Museum, castle,
A story to tell.

I went to London,
To have a nice day.
To go to a museum and
The theater for a play.

I saw Tower Bridge
And the castle, too.
Walked in the park
And went to the zoo.

I went to a restaurant
On the corner of the street.
I sat outside and
I had something to eat.

I took a taxi
Because it was late.
My train was in the station.
It was half past eight.

12 Ask and answer.

To Dictation

cook	firefighter	manager
actor	bus driver	doctor
teacher	pilot	police officer

Who goes to work in a restaurant or hotel?

A cook.

13 Look at the map. Ask and answer.

Where's the theater?

It's between the gym and the library.

14 Think of a place you know. Give directions how to get there from your school. Can your friend guess?

Go out of the door, turn left, take the second street on your right, and walk past "Flower's Restaurant." What can you see?

Is it the stadium?

Yes, it is.

15 Focus on phonics

Sally: I need some socks, Scott.
Scott: But there aren't any stores at the bus station, Sally.
Sally: Look! What's that?
Scott: Gosh! It's a sock machine!

Speaking 16 Find ten differences.

In the first picture there's a green bus, but in the second picture there's a red bus.

Writing 17 Choose one of the pictures and write about it.

The first picture is of a town.
I can see ...

Joke Corner

What starts with "p," ends with "e," and has thousands of letters in it?

A post office.

OBJECTIVES: By the end of the lesson, students will have practiced the phonemes /s/ and /ʃ/ and completed a writing activity.

• TARGET LANGUAGE

Key language: the phonemes /s/ and /ʃ/, describing pictures, *there's a, in the background, in the foreground, on the left, on the right, at the top, at the bottom*

Review: the phoneme /ʧ/, family, city vocabulary, colors, *I can see …*

• MATERIALS REQUIRED

Extra activity 2: Card divided into 12 squares with the words from Workbook Activity 18 written (with underlining), one in each square (one photocopy for each pair of students)

Warmer

- Write the sentence *She sells sea shells on the sea shore* on the board. Check comprehension. Say the sentence for students to repeat. Get them to say it faster and faster. Elicit the two sounds practiced in the tongue twister (/s/ and /ʃ/). Tell students they will be practising recognising these sounds and looking at some different spellings in today's lesson. Elicit other words they can think of which have the same sound.

SB32. ACTIVITY 15. *Focus on phonics*

- Tell students to open their Student's Books to page 32. Focus them on Activity 15. Play the CD. Students repeat after each line and then after the whole rhyme. Repeat once more, making sure students say the /s/ and /ʃ/ sounds correctly. In pairs, students practice the rhyme.

CD 2, 08

As in Student's Book

SB32. ACTIVITY 16. *Find ten differences.* F toward

- Focus students on the pictures for Activity 16. Check they realize that there are differences between them. Students work in pairs, using the model. Write the following on the board:
  In the first picture there's / there are … , but in the second picture there's / there are …
- Students find the differences before they start the oral part of the activity. Check with the class.

Key: In the first picture there's a castle, but in the second picture there's a bridge.
In the first picture there's a woman and girl going into the post office, but in the second picture there's a woman and boy coming out of the post office.
In the first picture there's a police station next to the post office, but in the second picture there's a theater next to the post office.
In the first picture it's 3:15, but in the second picture it's 3:45.
In the first picture there's a man walking with a big dog, but in the second picture there's a man walking with a little dog.
In the first picture it's sunny, but in the second picture it's cloudy.
In the first picture there's a girl sitting on a bench, but in the second picture there's a girl running.
In the first picture there's a hungry boy, but in the second picture there's a thirsty boy.
In the first picture there's a café, but in the second picture there's a hotel.

SB32. ACTIVITY 17. *Choose one of the pictures and write about it.*

- Do the activity orally with the class first. Draw a picture frame on the board to check language: *in the background, in the foreground, on the left, on the right, at the top, at the bottom.* Students work individually to write their descriptions. They swap their first draft with a partner. They check each other's work. Students write their final draft in their notebooks.

SB32. JOKE CORNER

- Focus students on the Joke Corner. Play the CD as students read. Play the joke a second time and explain if necessary.

CD 2, 09

As in Student's Book

WB32. ACTIVITY 18. *Write the words in the columns.*

- Tell students to open their Workbook to page 32. Check they know the meaning of all the words in the box. Read out the heading of each column. Make sure students know which sound goes in which column, using the example. Remind students that they practiced the sound /ʧ/ (the third column) in the Welcome unit and tell them to focus on the sound of the words, not the spelling. Students complete the activity in pencil. Tell them to say the words aloud again to help.

WB32. ACTIVITY 19. *Listen, check, and say.*

- Play the CD for students to listen and check. They compare answers in pairs. Check with the class. Play the CD again for students to listen and repeat.

Key: See audioscript below

CD 2, 10

's' sound: *listen, stop, castle, place*
'sh' sound: *information, machine, shopping, directions*
'ch' sound: *children, watched, question, adventure*

WB32. ACTIVITY 20. *Find 14 spelling mistakes in the text.*

- Before students do the activity, focus them on the Write it right box and check they understand the spelling rules that are listed.

Key: See Activity 21 key

WB32. ACTIVITY 21. *Now write the text correctly.*

Key: In this picture we can see a lot of children playing. Three boys are sitting on the ground and playing with their toys. They have some toy trucks and a bus. They're close to two ladies who are sitting on chairs. These ladies are the boys' moms. Some older children are flying their kites. One boy's kite is in a tree. He's climbing up the tree, and he's trying to get it down.

WB32. ACTIVITY 22. *Describe your school playground.*

Key: Students' own answers

Extra activities: see page T102 (if time)

Ending the lesson

- Do the Phoneme rhyme from the beginning of the lesson again.

OBJECTIVES: By the end of the lesson, students will have read a story, reviewed language from the unit, and completed a self-evaluation.

• TARGET LANGUAGE

Key language: language in the story, *ancient world, cave, mountains (of secret treasure)*
Additional language: *Alexandria*
Review: language from the unit

• MATERIALS REQUIRED

Extra activity 2: Paper for making labels
Optional: *Kid's Box AE Interactive DVD 5: The school hall* "Visiting York" episode

Warmer

- Review the story so far. Pretend to misremember what has happened before, so students can correct you, e.g., *In the last episode, they went to meet Brutus at the British Museum* (No, they went to meet him at the library).

SB33. STORY. *Diggory Bones.*

- Tell students to open their Student's Books to page 33. Focus them on the story. Elicit who is going to be in this episode (Diggory, Emily, Sir Doug Bones, Brutus). Set the questions: *Which country are they going to? What's the name of the city? Why was the library famous? How are they going to get there?* Play the CD with books closed. Students listen to find the answers. They check in pairs with books open. Check with the class (Egypt. Alexandria. It was the most important library in the ancient world. By plane). Play the CD again. Students listen and read. Stop after each frame for students to repeat. At the end, check general comprehension by asking, e.g., *Where is the secret writing? How can The Baloney Stone help Brutus? What job is Brutus doing? How does Diggory change in the story?*

CD 2, 11

As in Student's Book

WB33. ACTIVITY 23. *Read and answer.*

Key: 2 He means Alexandria. 3 They are going to fly to Alexandria. 4 There is a cave. 5 There is secret writing. 6 Brutus Grabbe.

WB33. ACTIVITY 24. *Who said it? Read and match.*

Key: b3, c3, d4, e1, f2

WB33. DO YOU REMEMBER?

- Students try to do the activity first without looking back through the unit. Once they have tried to complete all the sentences, they can look back through the unit to find the answers.

Key: 2 hotel, 3 across, 4 left, 5 Students' own answers, 6 leaves

WB33. CAN DO

- Focus students on the *Can do* section of the page. Ask a student to read the first sentence. Elicit what this means, with examples, and elicit/remind them of the activities they did in this unit when they talked about places around town. Review what the three faces mean (not very well / OK / very well). Remind students they circle the one they think is true for them. Repeat for the second sentence, eliciting/reminding them of the activities in which they gave and understood directions. Students circle the appropriate face. Repeat for the third sentence, eliciting spelling rules for plural nouns.
- Say *Now show and tell your friends*. Students work in groups of three and take turns showing their work for / talking about each one.

Extra activities: see page T102 (if time)

Optional activity

- The "Visiting York" episode from *Kid's Box AE Interactive DVD 5 (The school hall* section). See pages 12–15 of the Teacher's Booklet for the Interactive DVD.

Ending the lesson

- Ask students which rhyme/song they'd like to do again from the unit. Do it together to end the lesson.

DIGGORY BONES

Geography Cities

FACT **Istanbul, in Turkey, is the only city that is on two continents. It's called the "bridge between Asia and Europe."**

1 Can you name these cities?

a 

b 

c 

d 

2 Read and answer "true" or "false."

1 During the Stone Age, cavemen started fishing.
2 Cities started growing where there were markets.
3 Cities stopped growing because of the Industrial Revolution.
4 Four thousand people lived in Mohenjo-Daro 40,000 years ago.
5 London is smaller than New York.
6 New York has more skyscrapers than Tokyo.

3 Read and order the events.

a) London was the biggest city in the world. ☐
b) People started building cities. ☐
c) New York was bigger than London. ☐
d) Cavemen started farming. 1
e) Tokyo is the biggest city in the world. ☐
f) Rome was the most important city in the world. ☐

Why did the first cities start?

During the Stone Age, cavemen started farming. As they got better at farming, they started growing more food than they could eat. They bought and sold the extra food in markets. Cities started growing around these markets.

Living in cities made people feel safe. People often lived close to castles and built walls around their houses. Two hundred years ago, cities started growing much faster. This was because of the Industrial Revolution. People went to work in the cities because there was more money.

Where were the first cities?

Mohenjo-Daro in the Indus Valley, in Pakistan, was one of the first cities. It was built more than 4,000 years ago. About 40,000 people lived there. If we look at a map of Mohenjo-Daro, we can see the streets were straight and that there were a lot of houses and big buildings.

About 2,000 years later, the biggest city in the world was Rome. It was the capital of the Roman Republic and Empire for a thousand years. About a million people lived there.

London was the first city to have more people than Rome. It was the biggest city in the world between 1831 and 1925. Then New York grew bigger. Now the biggest city in the world is Tokyo, but New York has more skyscrapers.

OBJECTIVES: By the end of the lesson, students will have read about the history of cities around the world.

• TARGET LANGUAGE

Key language: *continent, stone age, cavemen, start … - ing, Industrial Revolution, safe, Pakistan, was built, Rome, capital, republic, empire, New York, Tokyo, skyscraper*

Additional language: *Mohenjo-Daro, Indus Valley, Stratford-upon-Avon, Royal Shakespeare Theater*

Review: simple past, city vocabulary, comparatives, superlatives

• MATERIALS REQUIRED

Warmer: Prepare labels for about 12 cities in different parts of the world, e.g., New York, Alexandria, London, Tokyo, Rio de Janeiro, Istanbul, Sydney, Delhi, Cape Town, etc. (you need one label for every pair of students), a world map, sticky tack. Extra activity 2: Reference books / the Internet for students to find out about the Industrial Revolution, a large sheet of paper for each group of four students, colored markers

Warmer

- Hand out the city labels to pairs of students. Give them thinking time before you display the world map. Pairs come to the front one by one, say the name of their city, and then stick the label to the map. Elicit any other city names students know in countries other than their own and where they are on the map.

SB34. FACT

- Tell students to open their Student's Books to page 34. Focus them on the fact about Istanbul. Ask a student to read the fact to the class. Elicit where Istanbul is on the map in the classroom and show them how it straddles two continents. Ask if any students have been there.

SB34. ACTIVITY 1. *Can you name these cities?*

- Focus students on the Activity 1 pictures and instruction. Don't let them shout out their answers. Put students in groups of four to discuss their answers. Elicit the answers from the class and ask students to describe what they can see in the pictures.

Key: a Rome, b London, c Tokyo, d New York

SB34. ACTIVITY 2. *Read and answer "true" or "false."*

- Pre-teach the following vocabulary, using pictures where possible, before students read the text: *cavemen, stone age, Industrial Revolution, capital, skyscraper.* Set the following gist questions for the first reading: (first section) *Why did cities start growing faster 200 years ago?* (second section) *How old is Mohenjo-Daro? For how many years was London the biggest city in the world?* Students read the text silently and quickly to find the answers. They check in pairs. Check with the class (Because of the Industrial Revolution, more than 4,000 years old, 94). Elicit any other interesting information that students noticed.
- Focus students on the Activity 2 instruction and on the statements. Students re-read the text to find the answers. They check in pairs. Check with the class, eliciting corrections, and discuss the true statements. Check comprehension of other key vocabulary as you do this.

Key: 1 false (They started farming.), 2 true, 3 false (They started to grow faster.), 4 false (40,000 people / 4,000 years ago), 5 true, 6 true

SB34. ACTIVITY 3. *Read and order the events.*

- Focus students on Activity 3 and check understanding (chronological sequence). Remind students to read the sentences before looking back at the text to sequence them. Students work individually and then check in pairs. Check with the class, eliciting where in the text they found the information.

Key: a4, b2, c5, d1, e6, f3

WB34. ACTIVITY 1. *City quiz. Read and choose the right words.*

Key: 2c, 3a, 4c, 5b, 6a

WB34. ACTIVITY 2. *Read this report about Stratford-upon-Avon.*

WB34. ACTIVITY 3. *Complete the Stratford-upon-Avon mind map.*

Key: (see below)

WB34. ACTIVITY 4. *Now draw a mind map about your town or city.*

Key: Students' own answers

WB34. ACTIVITY 5. *Use the information from Activity 4 to write your report.*

Key: Students' own answers

Extra activities: see page T102 (if time)

Ending the lesson

- Review with students what they have done and what they have learned about in today's lesson.

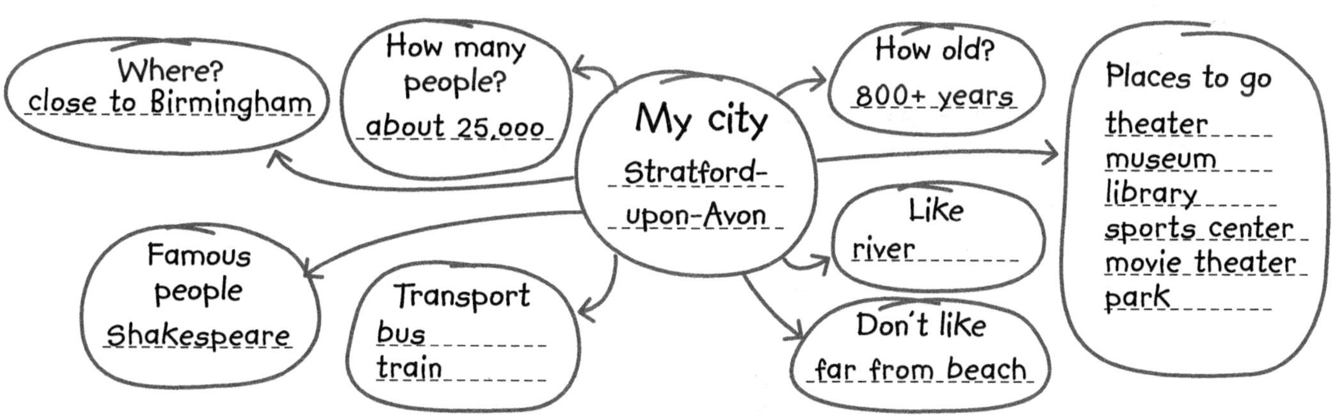

OBJECTIVES: By the end of the lesson, students will have learned more about cities and completed a project.

• TARGET LANGUAGE

Key language: comparatives, *want, need*
Review: city vocabulary, expressing opinions

• MATERIALS REQUIRED

Reference materials (leaflets and brochures) for a local city, paper for each group of four
Project: for each group of four: paper, a large piece of card, colored paper, colored markers, glue, scissors
Optional: *Kid's Box AE Teacher's Resource Book 5* Unit 3 Topic worksheet (page 35)

Warmer

- With Student's Books closed, review what students learned about the history of cities in the previous lesson. They don't need to recall exact dates and precise information. Prompt them if they need help, e.g., *Is Rome the biggest city in the world at the moment?* (No. It's Tokyo.)
- Elicit the name of a city close to where they live that you think they will know about.

SB35. ACTIVITY **4.** *In groups talk about a city you know.*

- Tell students to open their Student's Books to page 35. Focus them on the activity instruction and on part a). Make sure they notice that the mind map mostly has general categories (transportation) rather than specifics (e.g., trains). Make groups of four. Hand out leaflets and brochures about the local city you have chosen. Groups create a mind map on a piece of paper. Monitor as they work to provide support. Elicit ideas to create a shared mind map on the board.
- Focus students on part b). Ask one or two students to read the instructions aloud to check understanding. Give clear timings for each stage of the activity, e.g., five minutes for the lists, five minutes for the discussion, and suggestions for improvement. Elicit a few ideas of "good" and "bad" things before students start, but remind them that these words are subjective (one student might think something is "bad," and another might think it is "good"). Provide some prompts for discussion on the board:
  I think (…) are good because … / I don't agree. / I agree with you. / Good idea. / What about (…)? / We can make things better by … -ing
- Elicit ideas for improvements, group by group.

SB35. PROJECT. *Design a new city.*

- Focus students on the project and tell them they are going to be city planners and politicians. Read the questions on the left and have a general discussion of these points first. Check they understand the difference between want and need. Students work in their groups of four and write notes in answer to each question. Encourage them to be creative and imaginative.
- After sufficient planning and discussion time, focus on the instructions on the right. Check students understand what they have to do. Hand out the materials. Remind them to plan the city map carefully before they start drawing it on the card. Monitor and support where necessary.
- Groups take turns coming to the front and presenting their cities to the class. At the end, vote for the best new city.

WB35. ACTIVITY **6.** FLYERS **Listening, Part 2.** *Listen and write. There is one example.* F

Key: 1 Windsor, 2 Museum, 3 0207 541 4672, 4 Old, 5 half past three

CD 2, 12

Hello, George. Can I ask you some questions? / Yes, what about? / Well, you went to London last month, didn't you? Can you tell me about your vacation? / Yes, of course. / Well, first, how did you go there? / We went by train. It was cheap and quick. / Good. Let me write this down.

Can you see the answer? Now you listen and write.

What other questions do you have, Betty? / Well, I also want to know the name of the hotel. / The hotel? Sure, it's called The Windsor. / Can you spell that for me? / Um, yes. W-I-N-D-S-O-R. It is a nice hotel. / That's great. Why do you like it? / The rooms are very big and it's in a really good location. / Is it? Where? / Well, it's next to the British Museum. / I'd like to go there. Oh, one more thing. Do you know the phone number for the hotel? / Oh, yes. It's 0207 541 4672. / OK, thank you for that. Now I want to know where you visited. / Well, we went to a lot of places! / Really? Which did you like the best? / My favorite visit was when we went to the theater. / The theater? / Yes, it was called The Old Theater, and we saw a play called *The Mouse*. / Did you say "The Old Theater"? / That's right. / Was that in the evening? / No, we went to the play on Sunday afternoon. It started at half past three. / Hmm … I think that's a good idea. I want to go to that too. Thanks for all the information. / You're welcome, Betty! Bye! / Bye!

Extra activities: see page T102 (if time)

Optional activity

- Unit 3 Topic worksheet from *Kid's Box AE Teacher's Resource Book 5* (see pages 29 and 35).

Ending the lesson

- Review with students what they talked and read about in today's lesson and which activities they liked best from this and the previous lesson.

4 In groups talk about a city you know.

a) What can you find in your city? Make a mind map.

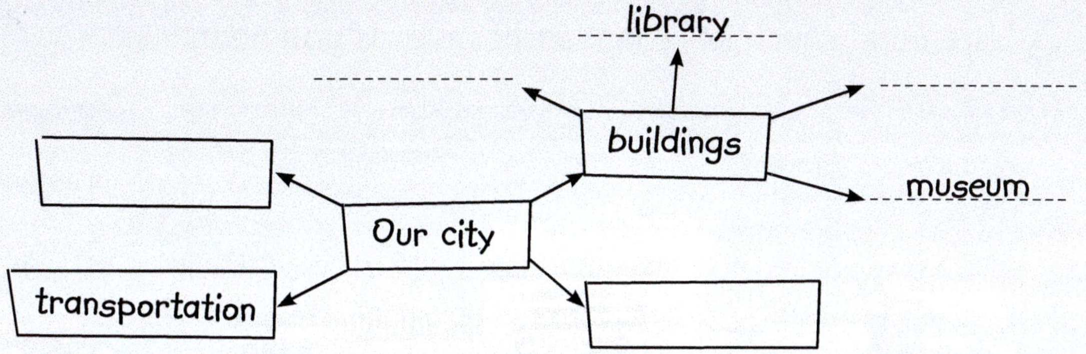

b) Make two columns in your notebook and write a list of the "good" things and the "bad" things about your city. Talk about why you think they are good or bad. How can you make the bad things better?

Our city	
Good	Bad
park	cars

Project

Design a new city.

Work in groups. Ask and answer.

- What do you want in your city?
- What do you need in your city?
- Where do you want to put parks, schools, houses, stores, markets?
- How can people go from their home to school, to stores, and to work?

How to make your city:

1. Make a map of your city on a big piece of cardboard.
2. Write the names of the places in your city on pieces of colored paper. Put them on your map to show where you want them.
3. Think of a name for your city and tell the other groups about it.

4 Disaster!

Show what you know! What weather words can you remember?

Listening **1** 13 CD2 Listen and check (✓) the weather words you hear.

2 14 CD2 Listen again. Who said it?

1 Now we have a great project for our ezine … disasters! Alex
2 We decided to sail to this small island for a picnic with my dad.
3 When we were sailing to the island, the sky went dark.
4 The radio was on, but we weren't listening to the weather. We were listening to music.
5 We were walking up the beach, looking for somewhere safe to stay, when lightning hit the boat.
6 It was really exciting when the helicopter came to get us.

LOOK

Were you **listening** to the weather on the radio?
We **weren't listening** to the radio.
We **were listening** to music.

3 Read and match.

1 They were sailing to the island
2 They were waiting on the island
3 The radio was on,
4 When the storm started,
5 They were walking away from the boat
6 They were getting warm

a they were waiting on the island.
b when the lightning hit it.
c when the sky went dark.
d when the reporter arrived.
e when the helicopter appeared.
f but they weren't listening to the weather.

OBJECTIVES: By the end of the lesson, students will be able to talk about the past, using the simple past and the past progressive.

• TARGET LANGUAGE

Key language: simple past and past progressive, *disaster, storm, island, beach, catch fire, lightning*

Review: the weather, adjectives, spelling for *-ing* endings, *helicopter*

• MATERIALS REQUIRED

Extra activity 1: The CD script from Student's Book Activity 1 written on a large sheet of paper

Optional: *Kid's Box AE Teacher's Resource Book 5* Unit 4 Reinforcement worksheet 1 (page 37)

Warmer

- Invent or tell students a short story of a disaster that happened to you which is weather-related, e.g., a flood in your house, your house was struck by lightning. At the end, say *It was a disaster / It was terrible*. Elicit if students have experienced any similar disasters. Tell students the theme of Unit 4 is *Disaster* and write it on the board. Draw a line from *Disaster* and write *Weather*. Tell students a lot of disasters are caused by the weather.

SB36. SHOW WHAT YOU KNOW! *What weather words can you remember?*

- Draw a circle around *Weather* on the board and write one or two of the words you mentioned in the warmer to start the mind map. Say *Show what you know … about weather words.* Brainstorm weather words and create a mind map on the board. Students copy the mind map into their notebooks.

SB36. ACTIVITY 1. *Listen and check (✓) the weather words you hear.*

- Tell students to open their Student's Books to page 36. Focus them on the Activity 1 pictures. Elicit the names of the characters and where they are.
- Play the CD. Students listen and check. They check in pairs. Use the mind map on the board to check with the class.

CD 2, 13

MARIA: That was amazing!
ALEX: It was really scary, too.
ALEX: Now we have a great project for our ezine … Disasters!
MARIA AND DAN: Yeah!
REPORTER: Well, hello, children. Are you getting warm?
MARIA, DAN, AND ALEX: Yes!
REPORTER: Can you tell me what happened?
MARIA: It was hot and sunny this morning, so we decided to sail to the small island for a picnic with my dad.
ALEX: When we were sailing to the island, the sky went dark.
REPORTER: Were you listening to the weather on the radio?
DAN: The radio was on, but we weren't listening to the weather. We were listening to music.
REPORTER: Why didn't you go back to the beach?
DAN: Because we were very close to the island. We decided to wait there for the weather to get better ... but it didn't. A storm started.
MARIA: We were walking up the beach, looking for somewhere safe to stay, when lightning hit the boat and it caught fire.
REPORTER: What a disaster!
MARIA: We couldn't leave the island, so Dad had to phone for help.
ALEX: At first the phone didn't work. But then he tried again and it was OK. Phew!
REPORTER: Were you afraid?
MARIA, DAN, AND ALEX: Yes!
DAN: But it was really exciting when the helicopter came to get us.
MARIA AND ALEX: Yeah, that was great!

SB36. ACTIVITY 2. *Listen again. Who said it?*

- Read the sentences through with the class. Play the CD. Students write the name in their notebooks. They check in pairs.

Key: 2 Maria, 3 Alex, 4 Dan, 5 Maria, 6 Dan

CD 2, 14

Presentation

- Write sentence 3 from Student's Book Activity 2 on the board. Underline the simple past in one color and the past progressive in another. Use a timeline to show that the past progressive happened over a period of time and was interrupted by the simple past action. Do the same using sentence 5. Elicit the names of the two tenses. Students copy the timeline into their notebooks.
- Play the CD from Activity 1 again. When students hear the past progressive, they raise their hands. Stop the CD and elicit what was said. At the end, elicit a story summary from students.
- Focus students on the Look box.

SB36. ACTIVITY 3. *Read and match.*

- Students do the activity in pairs. Check with the class.

Key: 1c, 2e, 3f, 4a, 5b, 6d

WB36. ACTIVITY 1. *Match the pictures with the text.*

Key: From left to right: 3, 6, 5, 1, 2, 4

WB36. ACTIVITY 2. *Write the verbs in the chart. Look at the spelling.*

Key:

taking	sailing	running
moving, living waking up, losing	enjoying, shouting cooking, carrying	cutting, stopping swimming, getting

WB36. ACTIVITY 3. *Read and choose the right words.*

Key: 2 climbing, 3 rang, 4 was, 5 when

Extra activities: see page T102 (if time)

Optional activity

- Unit 4 Reinforcement worksheet 1 from *Kid's Box AE Teacher's Resource Book 5* (see pages 36 and 37).

Ending the lesson

- Elicit from students what they remember about disaster stories from the warmer.

OBJECTIVES: By the end of the lesson, students will have had more practice using the simple past and past progressive to talk about interrupted past actions and will have sung a song.

• TARGET LANGUAGE

Key language: simple past and past progressive, *feel sick*
Review: weather vocabulary, telling the time, daily activities

• MATERIALS REQUIRED

Optional: *Kid's Box AE Teacher's Resource Book 5* Unit 4 Extension worksheet 1 and/or Unit 4 Song worksheet (pages 39 and 41)

Warmer

- Review the past progressive by asking different students, e.g., *What were you doing at eight o'clock yesterday evening?*

SB37. ACTIVITY 4. *Listen and complete. Check and sing.*

- Tell students to open their Student's Books to page 37. Remind them of the unit theme (disasters) and focus them on the questions. Ask different students to read them aloud. Check understanding of these questions. In pairs, students read the song with blanks and try to predict/guess what the missing words are, using the words in the box. They can compare ideas in pairs. Play the CD for students to check. Check with the class. Play the CD again for students to follow the complete text in their books. Play it a third time for students to repeat, line by line and then verse by verse. Students sing it as a class and then in three groups (one for each section). Play the first version on the CD and then the karaoke version. Groups swap roles and repeat.

Key: skating, playing, eating, swimming, sailing, climbing, sitting

CD 2, 15

As in Student's Book and key

CD 2, 16

Now sing the song again. (Karaoke version)

SB37. ACTIVITY 5. *What were you doing when these things happened? Write three sentences.*

- Focus students on the Activity 5 instructions. Elicit an example from students, using one of the pictures and one piece of text, e.g., *I was making sandwiches when I cut my hand.* Write it on the board with a timeline as in the previous lesson, using the same colors as previously for the two tenses. Ask students *What was happening over a longer time?* (making sandwiches). *What happened suddenly / interrupted it?* (cut my hand). Elicit another example if you think students need it. Students copy the example(s) into their notebooks under the timeline, using the appropriate colors. Check students understand the key vocabulary, e.g., the difference between *feel* and *fell*. Students work in pairs and orally make as many sentences as they can. Remind them to change the pronouns (*your* to *my*). Monitor and support where necessary. Elicit the sentences from the pairs to check.
- Students write at least three sentences in their notebooks. Encourage them to be creative with the matching.

SB37. ACTIVITY 6. *Play the game. Guess it in five.*

- Focus students on the Activity 6 instructions and on the example. Check understanding and demonstrate using open pairs. Make pairs. Students play the game, using the sentences they wrote for Activity 5.

WB37. ACTIVITY 4. *Write questions and answers about Paul's day.*

Key: 2 What was Paul doing at half past four? He was doing his homework. 3 What was Paul doing at a quarter after five? He was playing soccer. 4 What was Paul doing at half past six? He was taking a shower. 5 What was Paul doing at eight o'clock? He was eating dinner. 6 What was Paul doing at ten after ten? He was brushing his teeth.

WB37. ACTIVITY 5. *Read and complete the chart.*

Key:

Name	David	Betty	Katy	William
Clothes	red sweater, long scarf	short skirt, green shoes	jeans, T-shirt	gray pants, blue shirt
Where?	playground	playground	classroom	outside
What doing?	talking to friends	reading a book	jumping around	playing soccer

Who broke the chair? Katy.

Extra activities: see page T102/T103 (if time)

Optional activities

- Unit 4 Extension worksheet 1 from *Kid's Box AE Teacher's Resource Book 5* (see pages 36, 39, and 41).
- Unit 4 Song worksheet from *Kid's Box AE Teacher's Resource Book 5* (see pages 36 and 41).

Ending the lesson

- Students sing the song from the beginning of the lesson again in three groups.

4 Listen and complete. Check and sing.

swimming · skating · sitting · eating · ~~walking~~ · climbing · playing · sailing

What were you doing when the storm began?
When the lightning hit and the water ran.
Where were you when the rain came down?
On the mountain, at the beach, in the forest or the town.

I was walking up the mountain,
He was skating over the lake,
We were playing in the park,
She was eating a piece of cake.

They were swimming in the river,
He was sailing on the ocean,
She was climbing up a wall,
I was sitting under a tree.

5 What were you doing when these things happened? Write three sentences.

hurt your knee · teacher saw you · dropped your cell phone · cut your hand · lightning hit the tree · started to rain · shoe fell off · mother took a picture of you · started to feel sick · lost your watch

I was having a picnic lunch when it started to rain.

6 Play the game. Guess it in five.

What was I doing when it started to rain?

Were you having a picnic lunch?

Yes, I was.

Reading **7** Read and think. Which was the worst disaster? Why?

http://www.cambridge.org/elt/kidsbox/ezine

Kid's Box Ezine!

home | reports | games | world | email

Disasters sometimes happen, as we recently found out. We decided to find out about some famous disasters.

Kid's Box reports Disasters

a

This ship is called the Titanic. On April 14, 1912, it was traveling across the Atlantic Ocean when it hit an iceberg. They couldn't see the iceberg because of the fog.

b

The Hindenburg was one of the biggest airships ever built. On May 6, 1937, when it was arriving in the U.S.A., it caught fire. People think this happened because lightning hit it during a storm.

c

Hurricanes are very dangerous storms with strong winds. The worst Atlantic hurricane in history was the Great Hurricane in 1780, from October 10 through 16.

d

When a volcano erupts, it throws hot liquid rock and gases into the air through the hole at the top. When Krakatoa erupted on August 26, 1883, it made the loudest sound ever heard.

e

On November 1, 1755, an earthquake hit Lisbon, in Portugal. The ground moved for ten minutes. The earthquake destroyed most of the buildings in the city.

f

On December 28, 1908, a tsunami hit Messina, in Italy. The enormous wall of seawater was about ten meters high. How high do you think the seawater is in this picture?

tsunami | hurricane | volcano | earthquake | iceberg | storm

8 17 CD2 Listen and say "yes" or "no." Repeat or correct.

1 The tsunami was on December 28, 1908.

Yes. The tsunami was on December 28, 1908.

9 18 CD2 Listen and repeat the chant.

January, February, March,
April, May, June,
July, August, September,
October, November, December.

OBJECTIVES: By the end of the lesson, students will have read about disasters around the world and reviewed ordinals and months of the year.

• TARGET LANGUAGE

Key language: ordinals, months, superlatives, *iceberg, hurricane, volcano, erupt, liquid rock, gas, hole, enormous, earthquake, destroy, tsunami, in/on* (for dates)
Additional language: *Titanic, Hindenburg*
Review: weather, past narrative tenses

• MATERIALS REQUIRED

Optional: *Kid's Box AE Teacher's Resource Book 5* Unit 4 Reinforcement worksheet 2 and/or Extension worksheet 2 (pages 38 and 40)

Warmer

- Write *Disasters* on the board. Elicit recent disasters that have happened around the world, giving students clues if necessary. Write them on the board, introducing the new vocabulary, if appropriate, e.g., *hurricane, flood, tsunami.* Ask *What can you see at the top of a volcano?* to elicit *hole.* Write it on the board and ask a student to spell it. Explain that *enormous* is an adjective and that it has the same meaning as *huge.* Ask students to say words for things that are enormous. Elicit/Discuss what they know about the disasters.

SB38. ACTIVITY 7. *Read and think. Which was the worst disaster? Why?*

- Tell students to open their Student's Books to page 38. Focus them on Activity 7 and on the activity instructions. Ask a student to read them aloud. Check understanding.
- Focus students on the text and elicit that it's a webpage for *Kid's Box* ezine and that it's about disasters. Focus students on the key words at the bottom of the webpage and read them through with the class. Check they can say them correctly. Students read the texts silently and think about their answers to the question. Elicit each disaster one by one, when it happened and if students have heard about it before (perhaps they have seen a movie about it). Discuss their opinions as a class, reminding them to say why they think it is the worst disaster. Take a class vote for which is the worst disaster.
- Focus on each text one at a time, giving students reading time and then checking general comprehension by discussing the disaster in detail and their reactions to it.
- To check understanding of years, elicit the sequence of the disasters (which happened first / which most recently).
- Focus students on the first text (about the *Titanic*). Ask *Why couldn't they see the iceberg?* to elicit *Because of the fog.* To practice this structure, give prompts, e.g., *tennis/rain, swim in the ocean/enormous waves, wear our hats/the wind,* to elicit *We couldn't play tennis because of the rain,* etc.

SB38. ACTIVITY 8. *Listen and say "yes" or "no." Repeat or correct.*

- Focus students on the Activity 8 instruction. Play the CD. Pause after each statement to give students time to think. They whisper the answer to their partner the first time. Play the CD again. Elicit a choral response each time. Write up two examples to show/remind students when to use *in* with dates and when to use *on*, e.g., *on August 26, in February.*

Key: 2 Yes. The volcano Krakatoa erupted on August 26. 3 No. The Great Hurricane was in 1780. 4 Yes. The Hindenburg disaster was on May 6, 1937. 5 No. The Titanic hit an iceberg on April 14, 1912. 6 Yes. The Lisbon earthquake was on November 1.

CD 2, 17

1. The tsunami was on December 28, 1908.
2. The volcano Krakatoa erupted on August 26.
3. The Great Hurricane was in 1870.
4. The Hindenburg disaster was on the May 6, 1937.
5. The Titanic hit an iceberg on January 14, 1912.
6. The Lisbon earthquake was on November 1.

SB38. ACTIVITY 9. *Listen and repeat the chant.*

- Focus students on the Activity 9 chant. Play the CD. They listen the first time. Play it again for them to join in. Students repeat the chant as a class, and in groups. Make sure they pronounce the words correctly.

CD 2, 18

As in Student's Book

WB38. ACTIVITY 6. *Choose dates from the box to label the pictures.*

Key: 2 April 14, 1912, 3 May 6, 1937, 4 October 10, 1780, 5 August 26, 1883, 6 December 28, 1908

WB38. ACTIVITY 7. *Read and write the dates.*

Key: 2 the twenty-second, 3 the twenty-fifth, 4 the twenty-ninth, 5 the twenty-fourth, 6 the twenty-seventh

WB38. ACTIVITY 8. *Complete the sentences.*

Key: 2 March, 3 May, 4 July, 5 November, 6 December

WB38. ACTIVITY 9. *Unscramble and write the months. Put them in order.*

Key: 4 April, 6 June, 9 September, 10 October, 3 March, 12 December, 5 May, 7 July, 1 January, 11 November, 8 August, 2 February

Extra activities: see page T103 (if time)

Optional activities

- Unit 4 Reinforcement worksheet 2 from *Kid's Box AE Teacher's Resource Book 5* (see pages 36 and 38).
- Unit 4 Extension worksheet 2 from *Kid's Box AE Teacher's Resource Book 5* (see pages 36 and 40).

Ending the lesson

- Students repeat the Months chant from SB Activity 9.

OBJECTIVES: By the end of the lesson, students will have had more practice with months, ordinal numbers, and narrative past tenses.

• TARGET LANGUAGE

Key language: months

Review: weather, vacation / daily activities, present continuous, simple past, past progressive

• MATERIALS REQUIRED

Photocopiable 4 (see page T93), one copy cut in half for each pair

Extra activity: World map or globe

Warmer

- Invite 12 students to come to the front of the class. Whisper one different month to each one. They quickly form a line to show the sequence of the months. Each student then says their month and the class says if the order is correct. Repeat, but this time students must stand in alphabetical order.

SB39. ACTIVITY 10. *Listen and say the months.*

- Tell students to open their Student's Books to page 39. Focus them on the pictures for the 12 months. Ask a student to read the activity instruction aloud and check understanding. Play the CD. The first time, students point to the picture of the month / whisper it to their friend. Play the CD again. Elicit the month in chorus from students.
- Discuss with the class what the children are doing in the different pictures to check vocabulary. Ask students if this is what they do during the different months. Elicit some other ideas (prompt them to use simple present).

Key: 2 April, 3 March, 4 August, 5 May, 6 November, 7 February, 8 June, 9 December, 10 July, 11 January, 12 October

CD 2, 19

1. It's sunny and windy. There are a lot of red apples on the trees. They're falling and there are some on the ground.
2. It's sunny and windy. The children are flying their kites in a field. There are a lot of small, yellow flowers.
3. It's sunny and raining. There are a lot of big, yellow flowers in the field and there's a rainbow in the sky.
4. It's hot and sunny. The children are having a picnic next to the river and there are some apples on the blanket.
5. It's sunny, but there are some clouds and a rainbow in the sky. The children are in a field. They're reading comic books on a blanket.
6. It's gray and foggy. The children are playing in the yard. They're jumping in the leaves. There's a fire because their father's burning leaves. He's wearing an old brown hat.
7. It's gray and foggy. Outside we can see that there aren't any leaves on the trees in the yard. The children are reading comic books next to the fire in the living room.
8. It's sunny, but there are some clouds in the sky. Some boats are sailing on the lake.
9. The children are eating sandwiches next to the fire in the living room. Outside we can see it's foggy and snowing heavily.
10. It's sunny. The children are having a picnic at the beach. Some boats are sailing on the ocean.
11. The children are playing in the yard. There's a lot of snow and they're making a snowman. It has a carrot for a nose and an old brown hat on its head.
12. It's cloudy and windy. There are a lot of leaves on the trees in the yard. They're red, orange, and yellow. They're falling on the ground.

SB39. ACTIVITY 11. *Ask and answer.*

- Focus students on the Activity 11 instruction and on the example. They play the game in pairs, using the prompts as an example.

SB39. ACTIVITY 12. *Cross out the extra word.*

- Focus students on the Activity 12 instruction. Do the first one as an example with the class. Check they know what to do. Students work individually and cross out the incorrect word in each one. They check in pairs. Check with the class.

Key: 1 to, 2 many, 3 was, 4 do, 5 the, 6 the, 7 did, 8 very

SB39. ACTIVITY 13. *Read the notes and write about what happened.*

- Focus students on Activity 13 and read the introduction. Ask a student to read the prompts for the first line of the story aloud. Ask another to read the first line of text (at the bottom of the page) and check students understand that this is made from the line of prompts. Students work in pairs and orally complete the story first. Elicit the story from pairs around the class. Students then write the complete story in their notebooks. Monitor and help if necessary. Elicit from students if they think Friday 13 is a lucky or an unlucky day.

Key: She fell down and broke her leg. An ambulance came and took her to the hospital. When the nurses were carrying Jane into the hospital, they dropped her. Now Jane is in the hospital with a broken leg and a broken arm.

Photocopiable 4 (see pages T88 and T93)

WB39. ACTIVITY 10. *Answer the questions.*

Key: Students' own answers

WB39. ACTIVITY 11. *Match the words with the pictures.*

Key: 6, 1, 8, 3, 4, 2, 5, 7

WB39. ACTIVITY 12. *Now match the words and pictures with the definitions.*

Key: b3, c5, d8, e7, f6, g2, h4

WB39. ACTIVITY 13. *Keep a weather diary.*

Key: Students' own answers

Extra activity: see page T103 (if time)

Ending the lesson

- Elicit from students what their favorite month of the year is and why. Find out which month is the class's favorite.

10 Listen and say the months. (19 CD2)

1 It's sunny and windy. There are a lot of red apples on the trees …

September.

2. April 3. March 4. August 5. May 6. November 7. February 8. June 9. December 10. July 11. January 12. October

11 Ask and answer.

It's February. What can you see?

Some children are reading comic books. They're sitting in their living room next to the fire.

12 Cross out the extra word.

1 What were they to doing on Wednesday, November 13?
2 There was a many bad storm on May 31.
3 They couldn't see because of was the fog.
4 Why was do he running?
5 The lightning hit the my car on August 19.
6 My birthday was in the January.
7 The fire did started on June 29.
8 In Antarctica there's a very lot of ice.

13 Read the notes and write about what happened.

HW

Friday March 13 was a terrible day for Jane. What happened?

when / go / downstairs / put / foot / on / toy / car
fall / down / break / leg
ambulance / come / take / to / hospital
when / nurses / carry / Jane / into / hospital / drop / her
now / Jane / in / hospital / with / broken / leg / and / broken / arm

She fell down and broke her leg. An ambulance came and took her to the hospital. When the nurses were carrying Jane into the hospital, they dropped her. Now Jane is in the hospital with a broken leg and a broken arm.

When Jane was going downstairs, she put her foot on a toy car.

* Photocopiable – page T-93

14 20 CD2 Focus on phonics

There's a **bad storm** with **thun**der and **rain**,
An **aw**ful **earth**quake is **shak**ing a **train**.

A vol**ca**nic e**rup**tion **makes** a **ter**rible **sound**,
While a **dan**gerous **hur**ricane **blows** all a**round**!

Speaking 15 Complete the questions. Ask and answer.

What were you doing at …		Name ________	Name ________	Name ________
1	8:45 yesterday morning?			
2	4:15 ________ ?			
3	______ last Sunday morning?			
4	________			
5	________			

Writing 16 Write your diary for last week.

Monday
I was watching TV when John came over. It was a great surprise! We played on the computer, and he stayed for dinner.

21 CD2 Joke Corner

What place is in this joke?

The Red Sea.

OBJECTIVES: By the end of the lesson, students will have practiced weak forms (unstressed syllables) and strong forms (stressed syllables) and completed a writing activity.

• TARGET LANGUAGE

Key language: weak forms (unstressed syllables), strong forms (stressed syllables), disasters, weather, *eruption*, simple past, past progressive, *diary*

Review: telling the time

Warmer

- Elicit what one of the students wrote under the timeline for Student's Book page 37 Activity 5. Write it on the board. Say it naturally (with the appropriate unstressed and stressed syllables and words). Ask students what they notice about the way you say it. Repeat it several times. If they find the activity difficult, focus them on one part of the sentence, e.g., the auxiliary *was* (/wəz/) or *were* (/wər/), and ask them to notice how it sounds (weak/unstressed). Do the same for the strong/stressed words and syllables.

SB40. ACTIVITY 14. *Focus on phonics*

- Tell students to open their Student's Books to page 40. Focus them on Activity 14. Check comprehension of *blow* and *shake* and teach/review *eruption*. Play the CD. Students repeat after each line and then after the whole rhyme. Repeat once or twice more, making sure students say the weak/unstressed and strong/stressed parts of the sentences correctly. In pairs, students practice the rhyme.

CD 2, 20

As in Student's Book

SB40. ACTIVITY 15. *Complete the questions. Ask and answer.*

- Focus students on Activity 15 and on the chart. Say the prompt (*What were you doing at …*) and tell students they are going to ask their friends some questions for a class survey. They copy the chart into their notebooks and write in times and days in the left column. Demonstrate the activity with one or two students to check that they know what to do, that they use the unstressed form of *were* in the question and that they answer correctly using the past progressive. Students go around the class and ask the questions of three friends. They note their answers on the chart.

SB40. ACTIVITY 16. *Write your diary for last week.*

- Draw five large circles on the board. Write *Monday* in one, *Tuesday* in another, etc. Elicit from students by asking, e.g., *Paul, tell us about last Monday. What were you doing in the evening? Did anything happen?* Continue, eliciting ideas and experiences from other students in the class and noting ideas in the circles if appropriate. Focus students on the Activity 16 instruction and on the example. Check understanding of *diary*. In their notebooks, students write a few sentences for each school day of the previous week. Monitor and give suggestions/help where necessary.

SB40. JOKE CORNER

- Focus students on the Joke Corner and review the meaning of *joke*. Play the CD as students read the joke in their books. Play the joke a second time and explain if necessary.

CD 2, 21

As in Student's Book

WB40. ACTIVITY 14. *Write the words in the columns.*

- Tell students to open their Workbook to page 40. Check they know the meaning of all the words in the box. Copy the dots from the column headings on the board and make sure students realize that the large dots represent strong (stressed) syllables and the small dots weak (unstressed syllables). Elicit/Write some example words with the stress patterns below each set of dots on the board (e.g., *yes, father, yesterday, volcano*). Students complete the activity in pencil. Tell them to say the words aloud again to help.

WB40. ACTIVITY 15. *Listen, check, and say.*

- Play the CD for students to listen and check. They compare answers in pairs. Check with the class. Play the CD again for students to listen and repeat.

Key: See audioscript below

CD 2, 22

1. storm, stopped
2. story, wanted
3. terrible, dangerous
4. disaster, decided

WB40. ACTIVITY 16. *Find the 22 simple past and past progressive verbs and 4 sequencing words in this story.*

- Before students do the activity, focus them on the Write it right box and check they understand the three points discussed with reference to telling a story.

Key: Verbs: was, happened, were running, had, jumped, was, got, started, was, wasn't, was, was trying, jumped, were fighting, went, pushed, stopped, hit, called, pulled, said, laughed
Connecting and sequencing words: Then, After that, Next, Then

WB40. ACTIVITY 17. *Answer the questions.*

Key: 2 He was on a really high building. 3 The driver and Hard were fighting. 4 The driver of the motorcycle. 5 Hard told a joke and everybody laughed.

WB40. ACTIVITY 18. *Write about a scene from your favorite movie.*

Key: Students' own answers

Extra activities: see page T103 (if time)

Ending the lesson

- Do the rhyme from the beginning of the lesson again.

OBJECTIVES: By the end of the lesson, students will have read a story, reviewed language from the unit, and completed a self-evaluation.

• TARGET LANGUAGE

Key language: language in the story, *is called, too dangerous, New Year*

Additional language: *Canis Major, Sirius*

Review: language from the unit

• MATERIALS REQUIRED

Extra activity 2: Paper, sticky tack. One large piece of paper. Draw the largest circle you can on the paper. Draw a small circle in the center and write *Birthdays* inside it. Connect the inner to the outer circle with 12 lines (making 12 segments). Label each of these on the outer edge with the name of a month.

Warmer

- Review the story so far with students. Elicit which city they were in in the last episode (Alexandria) and which country that city is in (Egypt). Elicit who was there and what job Brutus was doing. Ask what students remember about the secret cave. Ask students if they think Brutus is going to find it in this episode.

SB41. STORY. *Diggory Bones.*

- Tell students to open their Student's Books to page 41. Focus them on the story. Tell them to read quickly and find out if they get to the secret cave (Yes, they do). Set the questions: *What's the date? What is special about the date? What disaster happened in Ancient Alexandria?* Play the CD with books closed. Students listen to find the answers. They check in pairs with books open. Check with the class (July 21, It's the beginning of the Ancient Egyptian year. A volcanic eruption, and a tsunami). Play the CD again. Students listen and read. Stop after each frame for students to repeat. At the end, check general comprehension by asking, e.g., *What is Sirius? What time of day is it? What's the weather like? Why was it hot in the cave, do you think? What happened at the end of the episode?*

CD 2, 23

As in Student's Book

WB41. ACTIVITY **19.** *Read and answer.*

Key: 2 It's called Sirius. 3 July 21, 4 when they were looking at the stars, 5 a volcanic eruption, 6 a tsunami

WB41. ACTIVITY **20.** *Complete the sentences from the story. Match them with the pictures.*

Key: 2 storm, 3 dangerous, 4 secret, 5 hot, 6 light
From left to right: 5, 2, 1, 3, 6, 4

WB41. DO YOU REMEMBER?

- Students try to do the activity first without looking back through the unit. Once they have tried to complete all the sentences, they can look back through the unit to find the answers.

Key: 2 lightning, 3, 4, and 5 Students' own answers, 6 then, after that

WB41. CAN DO

- Focus students on the *Can do* section of the page. Ask a student to read the first sentence. Elicit what this means with examples and elicit/remind them of the activities they did in this unit when they talked about the weather and disasters. Review what the three faces mean (not very well / OK / very well). Remind students they circle the one they think is true for them. Repeat for the second sentence, eliciting/reminding them of the activities when they talked about things that were happening in the past. Students circle the appropriate face. Repeat for the third sentence, eliciting parts of the stories they told.
- Say *Now show and tell your friends.* Students work in groups of three and take turns showing their work for / talking about each one.

Extra activities: see page T103 (if time)

Ending the lesson

- Ask students which rhyme/song they'd like to do again from the unit. Do it together to end the lesson.

DIGGORY BONES
Give me the Baloney Stone! You ... you ...
You can have the stone back when you help me get what I want.
That group of stars is called the "Canis Major," which means "the big dog."
And the brightest star on the dog's nose is called "Sirius."
What's the date today, Emily?
WHOOSH
July 21, why?
Today is the beginning of the Ancient Egyptian year.
There's the cave over there!
WHOOSH
Night's falling and a storm's coming. It's going to be very dark!
Is it too dangerous for you, Bones?
No ... I understand these places better than you, Brutus. I'm not afraid.
WHOOSH
In the Ancient Egyptian calendar, Sirius showed the opening of the New Year.
Today, it's going to show us the "opening" of the secret cave!
It's really hot down here.
PLOP
BUBBLE
When we were looking at the stars, I remembered the terrible disaster.
A volcanic eruption destroyed ancient Alexandria and then a tsunami covered the city with water.
PLOP
PLOP
BUBBLE
BOOM
Aagh! We're walking near a volcano!
CRACK
Run to the light, Emily!
CRACK
BOOOM
Aagh!

Geography The earth's surface

FACT: The word *volcano* comes from the Roman god of fire, Vulcan.

1 Read and answer.

1. What is the name for the outside of the earth?
2. What are plates?
3. What does the Richter scale measure?
4. Where are most tsunamis?

2 Read again and choose a title.

a) Plates and bowls

b) Natural disasters

c) Wave problems

3 Complete the sentences.

1. Two of the worst natural disasters are ...... and tsunamis.
2. The ...... of the earth is a solid rock layer called the crust.
3. The crust has different parts that are called ....
4. People use a seismometer to ...... how strong an earthquake is.
5. A ...... is a series of enormous waves.
6. About ...... out of every ten tsunamis happen in the Pacific Ocean.

A natural disaster is the name we give to something that happens because of natural forces and not because of the actions of people. Two of the worst natural disasters are earthquakes and tsunamis. They happen when land moves, and they're very frightening.

The outside of the earth is a solid rock layer called the crust. The crust has different parts that are called plates. The line where plates meet is called a plate boundary. Earthquakes and tsunamis often happen on or close to the plate boundaries.

Earthquakes

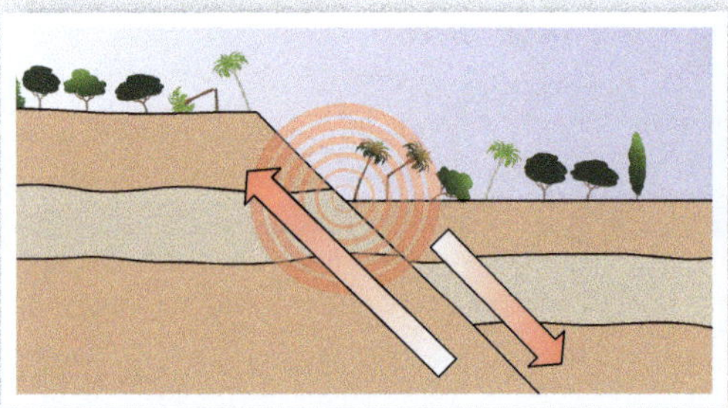

An earthquake is a sudden movement of the earth's surface. The plates under the earth are always moving slowly, but sometimes they stick and can't move until they move suddenly. This can cause an earthquake. People use a seismometer to measure how strong an earthquake is. A seismometer uses the Richter scale when it measures an earthquake. The Richter scale is numbered 0–10. Very bad earthquakes have a high number.

Tsunamis

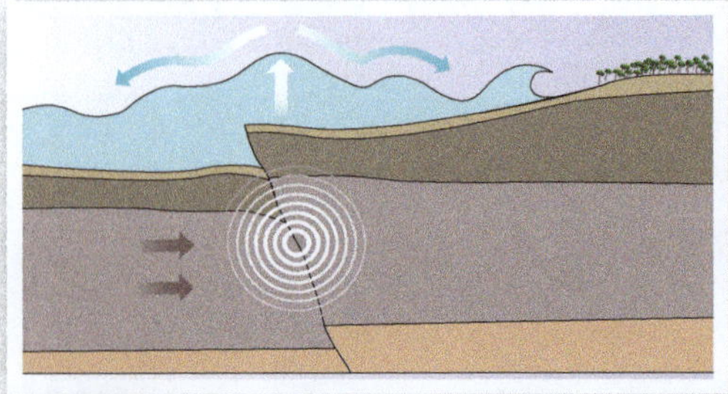

A tsunami is a series of enormous waves. Most tsunamis happen because of a big underwater earthquake. The earthquake must be over 6.75 on the Richter scale. About nine out of every ten tsunamis happen in the Pacific Ocean. Tsunamis are different from normal waves because they move a lot more quickly and the distance between one wave and the next is bigger.

OBJECTIVES: By the end of the lesson, students will have read about volcanoes, tsunamis, and earthquakes.

• TARGET LANGUAGE

Key language: *solid, layer, crust, plates, plate boundary, seismometer, frightening*

Additional language: *Richter Scale*

Review: disasters, *earth, measure, outside*

• MATERIALS REQUIRED

Map of the world and reference books

Optional: *Kid's Box AE Teacher's Resource Book 5* Unit 4 Topic worksheet (page 42), Extension worksheet 2 (page 40)

Warmer

- Write *volcanoes, tsunami, earthquakes* on the board. Ask students to discuss in pairs how they think these three types of disaster are connected. Elicit and discuss their ideas and prompt them to make connections.

SB42. FACT

- Tell students to open their Student's Books to page 42. Focus them on the top of the page. Ask a student to read the fact to the class. Elicit if they know any other words that come from the names of ancient gods or places. Ask students what this tells us about the Romans and their beliefs.

SB42. ACTIVITY **1.** *Read and answer.*

- Focus students on the Activity 1 instruction and on the pictures. Elicit what each picture is (volcano, earthquake, tsunami). Focus students on the four questions and ask volunteers to read them aloud. If students try to guess the answers before they read, don't tell them if they are right or wrong. Students read the text quickly (and silently) to see if they can find the answers. They check in pairs. Check with the class.
- Read the text through with the class, with students taking turns reading sections aloud. Discuss the information in each section with the class. Students don't need to understand all the words, but they do need to understand key vocabulary. Check understanding of *frightening*. Give them a synonym: *scary*. Ask them to tell you some things that they think are frightening. Write them on the board and ask students to spell them aloud. If appropriate, ask if anyone has personally experienced any of these phenomena.

Key: 1 The crust. 2 They are different parts of the crust. 3 How strong an earthquake is. 4 In the Pacific Ocean.

SB42. ACTIVITY **2.** *Read again and choose a title.*

- Focus students on the Activity 2 instruction and on the three titles. They re-read the text silently and then, in pairs, choose the best title. They find evidence in the text to support their choice. Discuss choices and reasons with the class.

Key: b) Natural disasters

SB42. ACTIVITY **3.** *Complete the sentences.*

- Focus students on Activity 3 and check they know what to do. They cover the text with a piece of paper and try to complete the sentences without re-reading the text. Then they look at the text and check in pairs. Check with the class.

Key: 1 earthquakes, 2 outside, 3 plates, 4 measure, 5 tsunami, 6 nine

WB42. ACTIVITY **1.** *Disasters quiz. Read and choose the right words.*

Key: 2a, 3c, 4b, 5c, 6b

WB42. ACTIVITY **2.** *Choose words from the box to complete the text.*

Note: There are four extra words in the box.

Key: 2 earthquake, 3 underwater, 4 Ocean, 5 hundred, 6 dangerous

WB42. ACTIVITY **3.** *Find out about a volcano, tsunami, or earthquake. Make notes about it.*

Key: Students' own answers

WB42. ACTIVITY **4.** *Now use the information to write your report.*

Key: Students' own answers

Extra activities: see page T103 (if time)

Optional activity

- Unit 4 Topic worksheet and Extension worksheet 2 from *Kid's Box AE Teacher's Resource Book 5* (see pages 36, 40, and 42).

Ending the lesson

- Review with students what they have done and what they have learned about in today's lesson.

OBJECTIVES: By the end of the lesson, students will have read about volcanoes and completed a project.

● TARGET LANGUAGE

Key language: *magma, liquid rock, lava, crater, vent, flour*
Review: disaster vocabulary, simple present, simple past, past progressive

● MATERIALS REQUIRED

Project: For each pair: one empty plastic water bottle, tape, thin cardboard, newspaper, flour, a bowl, paint, scissors

Warmer

- With books closed, review with students what they learned about in the previous lesson. Review some of the key words and concepts.

SB43. ACTIVITY 4. *Read and label the diagram.*

- Tell students to open their Student's Books to page 43. Focus them on Activity 4 and on the instruction. Elicit what the diagram is of (a volcano). Read the text through with the class. They don't label the diagram at this point. Students work in pairs and label the diagram in pencil. They check with another pair. Check with the class.

Key: 1 lava, 2 magma, 3 crater, 4 vent

SB43. ACTIVITY 5. *Listen. What is Mount Saint Helens?*

- Focus students on the Activity 5 instructions. If any students think they know, tell them not to say anything until after they have listened to the CD. Play the CD. Students listen for the answer. They check in pairs. Check with the class.

Key: A volcano in the USA.

CD 2, 24

NICK: Good morning, everyone. And good morning, Dr. Brosnan. Welcome to our series on world disasters.

DR. BROSNAN: Good morning, Nick.

NICK: Now, today's show is about volcanoes. Which volcano are you going to tell us about first?

DR. BROSNAN: Well, today I'm going to tell you about Mount Saint Helens here in the U.S.A.

NICK: Was that the worst volcano eruption ever?

DR. BROSNAN: No, it wasn't. The worst eruption was in Tambora in Indonesia in 1815. It was 100 times worse than the eruption at Mount Saint Helens.

NICK: So, why is Mount Saint Helens important?

DR. BROSNAN: Well, it wasn't the worst eruption in the world, but it was the worst eruption in the U.S.A.

NICK: When was it?

DR. BROSNAN: On May 18, 1980.

NICK: How did it start?

DR. BROSNAN: Well, scientists were watching the mountain because one side of it was growing by two meters a day. At half past eight in the morning, it erupted. There was no noise, so it was a big surprise for all the people there.

NICK: What happened?

DR. BROSNAN: The sky turned black and there was lightning. A big cloud of hot gas went 19 kilometers into the air.

NICK: Did you say 19 kilometers?

DR. BROSNAN: That's right, and in two days, the cloud of gas arrived in New York.

NICK: Was that the last time Mount Saint Helens erupted?

DR. BROSNAN: No, but 1980 was by far the worst eruption.

SB43. ACTIVITY 6. *Listen again and choose the answer.*

- Focus students on Activity 6 and on the questions. Give them reading and thinking time before they listen again. Some students may want to try to guess the answers. Play the CD. Students listen and choose the answers. They check in pairs. Play the CD again. Check with the class. Ask students which fact surprised them most about the volcano.

Key: 1 U.S.A, 2 the U.S.A, 3 May 18, 1980, 4 8:30, 5 19 km

CD 2, 25

SB43. PROJECT. *Make a volcano.*

- Tell students that they are going to make a volcano. Show and name the materials you have brought for the project (water bottle, tape, thin cardboard, newspaper, flour, bowl, paint). Read the project information through with the class before handing anything to the students, showing the materials as they are mentioned. Make sure they notice that they will not be able to complete the project in this lesson. Check students understand what to do. Put students in pairs and hand out the materials. Students work in their pairs, carefully following the instructions. Monitor and check/help where necessary. Show students where to put their volcano shapes (step 5) to dry. They need to be in a safe place for several hours. They will paint their volcanoes in the next lesson.

WB43. ACTIVITY 5. FLYERS Reading and Writing, Part 2 *Read the conversation and choose the best answer. Write a letter (A–E) for each answer. There is one example.*

(F) toward

- Tell students to open their Workbook to page 43. Direct them to the activity instructions and check understanding. Go through the example. Students work in pairs. They read the lines of dialog and write the letter of the correct response. Monitor students as they work. Check with the class. Ask students how they worked out the correct answer.

Key: 1B, 2E, 3A, 4C

Extra activities: see page T103 (if time)

Ending the lesson

- Review with students what they talked and read about in today's lesson and which activities they liked best from this and the previous lesson.

4 Read and label the diagram.

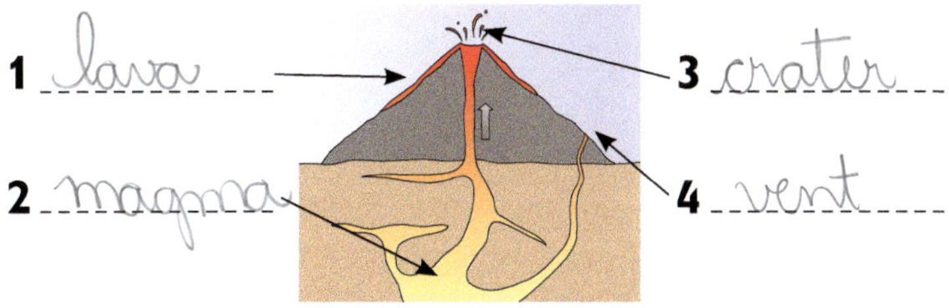

Volcanoes

A volcano is a mountain with a hole on the top. Volcanoes erupt when magma (liquid rock) from under the crust breaks through the crust. When magma reaches the earth's crust, it is called lava, but when it becomes cold, it forms rock. The bowl shape at the top of the volcano is called a crater, and the smaller holes in the side are called vents. The biggest volcano is Mauna Loa in Hawaii. It is about 10 km tall from the ocean floor to its top.

5 24 CD2 Listen. What is Mount Saint Helens? a volcano in the USA

6 25 CD2 Listen again and choose the answer.

1 Where is Mount Saint Helens?
U.S.A. / Indonesia / Australia

2 It was the worst eruption in **the world. / the U.S.A. / Indonesia.**

3 What was the date?
May 18, 1980 / March 18, 1980 / May 8, 1980

4 When did the volcano erupt?
7:30 / 8:00 / 8:30

5 How far into the sky did the cloud go?
9 km / 19 km / 90 km

Project Make a volcano.

You need:

- A water bottle
- Tape
- Cardboard (60 x 60 cm)
- Newspaper
- Flour
- A bowl
- Paint
- Scissors

How to make the volcano:

1 Cut the top of the water bottle off. Tape the bottle to the center of the cardboard.

2 Make newspaper rolls and balls to stick around the bottle.

3 Mix water and flour in the bowl to make glue. Tear the newspaper and put it into the glue.

4 Put the newspaper over the rolls to make the shape of the volcano. Don't cover the top of the bottle.

5 Wait for the paper and glue to dry completely. In the next class, paint your volcano.

Review Units 3 and 4

1 Read the letter and write the missing words.

Dear Aunt Petra,
I'm writing to tell you about the great time we had last weekend. I think Mom told you we were going to Manchester on Saturday. Well, we went to the stadium to see a soccer game, because Manchester United were playing against Liverpool. I really enjoyed it but Liverpool didn't (1) __________. They (2) __________ 1–0. On Sunday we spent the day exploring the city. We got lost because we didn't have a (3) __________. No problem! We asked a police officer for (4) __________ and he showed us where to go. We visited the Lowry Museum, which had some interesting paintings by a famous (5) __________ from Manchester, L.S. Lowry. There is a picture of one of his paintings with the letter. Hope you like it.
Yours,
Jamie

2 Listen and check (✓) the box.

26 CD2

1 Where did Paul go yesterday?

2 What did they do first?

3 What did they do in the park?

4 What did they have for lunch?

5 What was the movie about?

6 How did Paul get to the airport?

OBJECTIVES: By the end of the lesson, students will have reviewed language from Units 3 and 4 and listened to a story.

• TARGET LANGUAGE

Key language: vocabulary and language from Units 3 and 4
Additional language: *Manchester, Manchester United, Liverpool, Lowry Museum, L.S. Lowry*

• MATERIALS REQUIRED

Key vocabulary from Units 3 and 4, each word written on a small piece of paper, enough for each student in the class
Extra activity 1: The project from the previous lesson to finish, paint, paintbrushes

Warmer

- Make groups of six. Hand out a word from Unit 3 or 4 to each student. They keep their word secret. They take turns providing a definition of their word for the other students to guess. If time, regroup students and repeat.

SB44. ACTIVITY 1. *Read the letter and write the missing words.* F toward

- Tell students to open their Student's Books to page 44. Elicit that this is a letter. Ask students who wrote it (Jamie) and who he wrote it to (Aunt Petra). Tell students to read the letter quickly to find out which soccer teams were playing, which team won, and the name of the museum. Students check in pairs. Check with the class (Manchester United and Liverpool, Manchester United won, Lowry Museum). Tell students that L.S. Lowry is an artist and ask them to point to his painting on the page.
- Focus students on the activity instruction and check understanding. They silently re-read the letter and fill in the missing words. Remind them to look at the words before and after the blanks to help them. They check in pairs. Check with the class, reading the whole letter aloud. Check general comprehension of the text.

Key: 1 win, 2 lost, 3 map, 4 directions, 5 artist

SB44. ACTIVITY 2. *Listen and check (✓) the box.* F toward

- Focus students on the activity instruction and check understanding. Give students time to look through the pictures before they listen. Play the CD. Students listen and check. They check in pairs. Play the CD again. Check with the class.

Key: 2c, 3c, 4a, 5b, 6b

CD 2, 26

1. What did Paul go yesterday?

GIRL: Hi, Paul. How are you?
PAUL: Fine, thanks.
GIRL: Where were you yesterday? I didn't see you.
PAUL: No, I was in London visiting my grandpa.
GIRL: Wow!

2. What did they do first?

GIRL: What places did you visit?
PAUL: Well, the first place we went to was the Natural History Museum.
GIRL: Really?
PAUL: Yeah. It's great. It has things from all over the world.

3. What did they do at the park?

GIRL: Then where did you go?
PAUL: Well, after the Natural History Museum, we went to a park. Hyde Park.
GIRL: What did you do there?
PAUL: I flew my kite because it was really windy.

4. What did they have for lunch?

GIRL: Did you go to a restaurant for lunch?
PAUL: No. We had a picnic in the park. My grandpa makes nice sandwiches.

5. What was the movie about?

GIRL: Did you stay in the park all afternoon?
PAUL: No. It started to rain so we went to Grandpa's to watch a movie.
GIRL: Oh! What was it about?
PAUL: It was about the Titanic disaster, when a big boat hit an iceberg. It was very sad.

6. How did Paul get to the airport?

GIRL: Did you get a cab to the airport?
PAUL: No. I went to the bus station with Grandpa and we caught the bus.

WB44. ACTIVITY 1. *Read the story. Choose words from the box to complete the sentences.* F toward

Note: There are five extra words in the box.

Key: 2 restaurant, 3 quarter, 4 left, 5 wasn't, 6 walking

WB44. ACTIVITY 2. *Choose a title for this episode of* Friendly. F toward

Key: c) The best day

WB44. ACTIVITY 3. *Find the one that doesn't belong.*

Key (possible answers): 2 Cab because it's a vehicle / it isn't a place or building. 3 Stadium because it's a place or building / it isn't a direction. 4 Tsunami because it's a disaster / it isn't weather. 5 Help because it's in the present / it isn't in the past. 6 Thursday because it's a day / it isn't a month.

Extra activities: see page T103 (if time)

Ending the lesson

- Play a spelling bee. Write the months of the year on 12 pieces of thin cardboard and stick them face down on the board. Write numbers at random on the back. Make two teams. Teams take turns choosing a number. Read out the month on the thin cardboard. The team have ten seconds to spell it aloud (without looking in their books).

OBJECTIVES: By the end of the lesson, students will have reviewed language from Units 3 and 4 and played a board game.

• TARGET LANGUAGE

Key language: vocabulary and language from Units 3 and 4
Additional language: *Find your way home*
Review: language for playing games

• MATERIALS REQUIRED

Board game: Dice, colored counters
Optional: *Kid's Box AE Interactive DVD 5: The classroom* Quiz 2, *Kid's Box AE Teacher's Resource Book 5* Test Units 3–4 (pages 91–105), *Kid's Box AE Workbook 5 Language Portfolio* page 92

Warmer

- Review directions with the class. Draw a simple map on the board. Ask students to come up one by one and follow your directions with their finger on the map.

SB45. ACTIVITY 3. *Play the game.*

- Tell students to open their Student's Books to page 45. Elicit that this is a board game. Check comprehension of *Find your way home*. Focus them on the instructions and check understanding. Review game language with the class, e.g., *Move 2 squares, Go back*. Students play in groups of three. They take turns rolling the dice and moving around the board. The other students decide if the student has spelled the word correctly or not. They can help each other with interpreting the instructions.
- Monitor students as they are playing the game. The first player in each group to reach Home is the winner.

WB45. ACTIVITY 4. *Complete the sentences. Count and write the letters.*

Key: 2 hit 3, 3 outside 7, 4 October 7, 5 fire 4, 6 airport 7, 7 fog 3, 8 August 6, 9 storm 5, 10 museum 6, 11 map 3, 12 corner 6, 13 bridge 6, 14 January 7

WB45. ACTIVITY 5. *Now complete the crossword puzzle. Write the message.*

Key:

Message: streets ahead!

WB45. ACTIVITY 6. *Quiz time!*

Key: 1 The busiest airport is Heathrow. 2 It was built more than 4,000 years ago. 3 He was listening to music on the radio. 4 The Hindenburg caught fire. 5 The Richter Scale measures the size of an earthquake.

WB45. ACTIVITY 7. *Write questions for your quiz in your notebook.*

Key: Students' own answers

Extra activities: see page T103 (if time)

Optional evaluations

- Quiz 2 from *Kid's Box AE Interactive DVD 5* (*The classroom* section). This quiz can be done as a whole-class activity or as a team competition. See pages 36 and 37 of the Teacher's Booklet for the Interactive DVD.
- The test for Units 3–4 from *Kid's Box AE Teacher's Resource Book 5* (see pages 91–105) F toward

Language Portfolio

- Students complete page 92 of *Kid's Box AE Workbook 5 Language Portfolio* (I can ... Units 3 and 4).

Ending the lesson

- Students work in groups of three. They find the *Can do* Workbook sections (on pages 33 and 41) for Units 3 and 4 and write the six statements on a large piece of paper. They discuss and give examples for each *Can do* statement, checking back in the Student's Book, the Workbook or their notebooks if necessary. Elicit some examples from volunteer students in the class for each one.
- Ask students which lessons, topics and/or activities were their favorites.

3 Play the game.

Find your way home

Instructions

- Go around the board following the instructions. When you stop on a picture, spell the word. If it's right, roll again. If it's wrong, stop.

* Values - page 83 Test 3-4

5 Material things

Show what you know! What materials can you remember?

Listening **1** 27 CD2 Listen and check (✓) the materials you hear.

2 28 CD2 Listen again. Say "yes" or "no."

1 The children go to a pet store. No.
2 The mice are made of milk.
3 The teeth are made of sugar.
4 The snakes are made of paper.
5 The spiders are made of chocolate.
6 Dan's afraid of spiders.

3 Read and choose the right words.

1 The shopping mall is made **on** / **of** brick.
2 The mice **is** / **are** made of white chocolate.
3 The teeth **is** / **are** made of sugar.
4 The snake is made of **rubber** / **bone**.
5 The small black spiders are **made** / **make** of fur.
6 The spider on Dan's shoulder **is** / **isn't** real

LOOK

The mice **are made of** chocolate.
The spider **isn't made of** fur.
What **are** they **made of**?

OBJECTIVES: By the end of the lesson, students will be able to talk about objects and what materials they are made of.

● TARGET LANGUAGE

Key language: materials: *brick, white chocolate, sugar, rubber, fur, paper, bone, wood, stone, grass, leather, leaves; made of*
Review: food, animals, adjectives

● MATERIALS REQUIRED

Warmer: Classroom objects and clothes made of different materials
Extra activity 1: The CD script from Student's Book Activity 1 written on a large sheet of paper

Warmer

- Put several classroom objects on the desk and say, e.g., *This ruler's plastic.* Students correct you. (It's wood.) Do the same with other objects and clothes. Tell students the theme of Unit 5 is *Material* and write it in the center of the board.

SB46. Show what you know! *What materials can you remember?*

- Draw a circle around *Materials* on the board and write one or two of the words students said in the warmer to start the word map. Say *Show what you know … about materials.* Brainstorm materials and create a mind map on the board. Supply words in English. Students copy the mind map into their notebooks.

SB46. activity 1. *Listen and check (✓) the materials you hear.*

- Tell students to open their Student's Books to page 46 and look at the Activity 1 pictures. Elicit the names of the characters and where they are. Remind students they do the same as for the Show what you know in the previous units (check off the words they hear in the Materials mind map in their notebooks).
- Play the CD. Students listen and check. They check in pairs. Use the mind map on the board to check with the class.

CD 2, 27

Maria: This is a great new shopping mall. It's all made of brick. Look at this candy store!
Dan: Wow! Look at those mice! They're made of white chocolate.
Alex: Let's go and buy some candy.
Dan: Ahah! Do you like my new teeth?
Maria: Ugh. They're horrible. What are they made of?
Alex: Ha ha! They're made of sugar. They're great. Nice one, Dan!
Dan: Hee hee hee.
Maria: Ooh, look! These snakes are made of rubber. They're fantastic!
Alex: Yeah! Ooh, I'm going to buy one of these spiders. They're made of fur.
Dan: Really? I don't think anybody's going to be afraid of those.
Maria: Ah! Look out, Dan! There's a big black spider on your shoulder!
Dan: No, there isn't.
Alex: Oh, yes, there is. That spider isn't made of fur, Dan. It's real!
Dan: Aagghhh!
Alex and Maria: Ha ha ha!
Alex: It's OK. We were only joking!
Dan: Hmph. Well, let's go and find out what things are made of for our next ezine.
Alex: OK.
Maria: Oh, yeah.

SB46. activity 2. *Listen again. Say "yes" or "no."*

- Focus students on the Activity 2 instructions and on the sentences. Give students reading time before they listen. Play the CD. Students whisper the answer to their friend the first time they listen. Play the CD again and check, eliciting full-sentence answers from the class for the "no" responses. Check understanding of key vocabulary and add new words to the mind map.

Key: 2 no, 3 yes, 4 no, 5 no, 6 yes

CD 2, 28

Presentation

- Elicit sentence 3 again from Student's Book Activity 2 and write it on the board. Underline *made of* in the sentence. Elicit what this tells us. Say the sentence for students to repeat. Elicit from the class if *of* is stressed or unstressed (unstressed). Make sure they say it like this: /əv/. Show some of the objects from the warmer again. Introduce the question *What's it made of? / What are they made of?* to elicit responses from students using *made of.* Continue the activity in open pairs.
- Play the CD from Activity 1 again. When students hear sentences with *made of,* they raise their hands. Stop the CD and elicit what was said. At the end, elicit a story summary.

SB46. activity 3. *Read and choose the right words.*

- Focus students on the Look box.
- Focus students on the Activity 3 instruction. Remind students to read the complete sentence before they choose the correct word. Students do the activity in pairs. Pairs check with other pairs. Check with the class.

Key: 1 of, 2 are, 3 are, 4 rubber, 5 made, 6 isn't

WB46. activity 1. *Match the words with the pictures.*

Key: 2 grass, 3 stone, 4 paper, 5 brick, 6 leaves

WB46. activity 2. *Read and order the words.*

Key: 2 That skirt isn't made of chocolate. 3 What's your sweater made of? 4 Is your T-shirt made of fur? 5 Are their shoes made of wood? 6 His clothes are made of paper.

WB46. activity 3. *Answer the questions. What are they made of?*

Key: 2 They're made of wood. 3 It's made of stone. 4 It's made of fur. 5 It's made of paper. 6 It's made of grass.

WB46. activity 4. *Correct the sentences.*

Key: 2 ~~has~~ is, 3 ~~isn't~~ aren't / ~~cupcakes~~ cupcake, 4 ~~off~~ of, 5 ~~mades~~ made, 6 ~~are~~ is / ~~candy~~ candies

Extra activities: see page T104 (if time)

Ending the lesson

- Say, e.g., *Name something that's made of wood.* A student answers, e.g., *The door's made of wood.* Continue with other materials.

OBJECTIVES: By the end of the lesson, students will have had further practice using *made of* for different objects and materials.

• TARGET LANGUAGE

Key language: materials: *gold, rock, metal, plastic; cover* (v), *special, bounce, inside out, protect, drop, tire*

Review: materials

• MATERIALS REQUIRED

Photocopiable 5 (see page T94), one copy for each student

Optional: *Kid's Box AE Teacher's Resource Book 5* Unit 5 Reinforcement worksheets 1 and 2 (pages 44 and 45)

Warmer

- Give students one minute, with books closed, to write a list on a piece of paper of all the materials they remember from the previous lesson. Students swap pieces of paper with their partner. Students check their partner's work, using the mind maps in their notebooks. They award one point for materials correctly spelled. Elicit how many points each student has.

SB47. ACTIVITY 4. *Ask and answer.*

- Tell students to open their Student's Books to page 47. Focus them on the speech bubbles for Activity 4 and on the pictures. Draw students' attention to the use of *I think* and elicit that it shows the person is not sure. Point out that the bike is made of metal, but the seat is plastic or leather and the tires are rubber. Write *tire* on the board and ask a student to spell it aloud. Students work in pairs, taking turns asking and answering about the pictures. Check using open pairs. Write any new materials on the board.

SB47. ACTIVITY 5. *Listen and check.*

- Focus students on the Activity 5 instruction. Play the CD. They listen and check. They check in pairs. Play the CD again. Check with the class.

Key: 2 Snow. That's "f." 3 Bricks. That's "g." 4 Fur. That's "h." 5 Rubber. That's "e." 6 Stone. That's "a." 7 Metal. That's "b." 8 Wood. That's "d."

CD 2, 29

1.

GIRL: Is your new schoolbag made of leather?

BOY: Yes, it is.

2.

BOY: When did you make the snowman in this picture?

GIRL: We made it the last time it snowed a lot. You can only build snowmen in very cold winters because they're made of snow!

3.

GIRL: What is this wall made of?

MAN: It's made of bricks. I always use bricks when I build walls.

4.

WOMAN 1: I love your hat. Is it new? It looks very warm.

WOMAN 2: Thank you. It *is* new and it *is* very warm because it's made of fur!

5.

GIRL: What's this? Is it made of plastic?

WOMAN: No, it's called an eraser and it's made of rubber. Look! It feels soft and you can use it if you make a mistake when you write with a pencil.

GIRL: I know that!

6.

GIRL: What's your school like?

BOY: It's nice! It's very big and it has old, stone walls.

7.

GIRL: Where's your old, metal bike? You usually ride it to school.

BOY: My brother is using it today.

8.

BOY: Can I buy a pencil made of glass?

WOMAN: No! Our pencils are made of wood, like this one.

SB47. ACTIVITY 6. *Read and match.*

- Focus students on the Activity 6 pictures and elicit what they can see (hats, scarf, and shoes). Ask a student to read the first part of the text aloud. Elicit which picture it matches with (c). Continue in this way, but students silently write the match in their notebooks. Students then check in pairs. Elicit answers and the words in the text that helped them complete the match.

Key: 1c, 2d, 3f, 4e, 5b, 6a

SB47. ACTIVITY 7. *Read again and correct the sentences.*

- Focus students on the Activity 7 instruction and check understanding. Students do the task individually and then check in pairs. Check with the class.

Key: 1 The hat changes with the weather. 2 When it's raining, it has two pieces of plastic to cover his ears. 3 The sunglasses are made of special plastic. 4 The shoes can help her jump. 5 If you drop the shoes, they bounce. 6 The shoes are made of rubber.

Photocopiable 5 (see pages T89 and T94)

WB47. ACTIVITY 5. *Write the correct sentences.*

Key: 1 Our house is made of stone. 2 The boat is made of wood. 3 My book's made of paper. 4 Their tires are made of rubber.

WB47. ACTIVITY 6. *Read, look, and label the picture.*

Key: 2 windows made of water bottles, 3 roof made of grass, 4 leaves over balcony, 6 door made of wood

WB47. ACTIVITY 7. *Read and complete the text.*

F toward

Key: 2 gold, 3 bottles, 4 stone, 5 bridges, 6 thousand

Extra activity: see page T104 (if time)

Optional activity

- Unit 5 Reinforcement worksheets 1 and 2 from *Kid's Box AE Teacher's Resource Book 5* (see pages 43–45).

Ending the lesson

- Write some of the materials from this and the previous lesson in scrambled letter order for students to unscramble. Check by asking students to name something that's made of this material, e.g., *My bike tires are made of rubber.*

4 Ask and answer.

What's the school made of?

I think it's made of stone.

a 
b 
c 
d 
e 
f 
g 
h 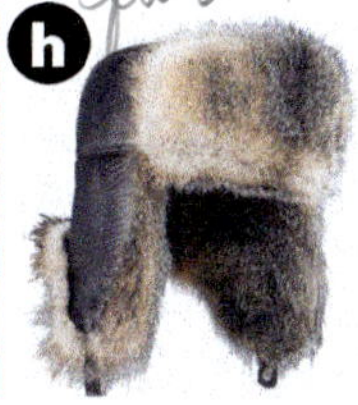

5 Listen and check.

29 CD2

Is your new school bag made of leather?

Yes, it is.

That's "c."

6 Read and match.

1 This is my favorite hat. I can wear it every day because it changes with the weather. When it's raining, it has two pieces of plastic to cover my ears.

2 When it's cold, a special scarf that is made of fur comes out to cover my neck.

3 When it's sunny, I turn it inside out, and I have a sun hat that protects me from the sun. It has some sunglasses made of special plastic to protect my eyes.

a 
b 
c 

4 These are my favorite shoes. I wear them on weekends. They are a lot of different colors.

5 When I touch one of the colors, the shoes change to that color. Look!

6 If I jump or drop the shoes on the floor, they bounce. The shoes can help me jump very high – up to two meters! This is because they are made of a special rubber called "bounce-a-lot." I'm going to bounce to the park. Goodbye.

d 
e 
f 

7 Read again and correct the sentences.

1 The hat changes every day.
2 When it's raining, it has two pieces of plastic to cover his eyes.
3 The sunglasses are made of special rocks.
4 The shoes can help her swim.
5 If you drop the shoes, they dance.
6 The shoes are made of wood.

Reading 8 Read and think. What's the most important material? Why?

http://www.cambridge.org/elt/kidsbox/ezine

Kid's Box Ezine!

home | reports | games | world | email

Kid's Box reports Materials

Materials can be man-made or natural. We make man-made materials in factories. We get natural materials from rocks in the ground, animals, and plants. Here are some interesting things made of different materials.

a

Most houses are made of bricks, stone, or wood, but Edouard Arsenault used 12,000 glass bottles to build this amazing house.

c

d

Cardboard and paper come from trees. Cardboard is stronger than paper. This tower is made of thin cardboard, and the bridge is made of paper.

Gold and silver are precious metals. This car is made of 80 kilograms of gold and 15 kilograms of silver. You have to drive it very carefully!

b

e

Most animals have fur, but sheep have wool. We use wool to make clothes. This dress is made of wool. It has animal teeth and bones on it to make it beautiful.

A lot of things are made of plastic. Today we use plastic more than any other material in the world. We must recycle plastic. "Recycle" means use it again in a different form. This chair is made of recycled plastic.

f

wood | gold | glass | cardboard | paper | wool | metal | silver | plastic

9 (CD2 30) Listen. Repeat the word and say what's made of it.

1 Glass.

Glass. That's the house.

10 Read again and answer.

1 Where do we make man-made materials?
2 How much gold is in the car?
3 How many glass bottles did Arsenault use to build his house?
4 Where does paper come from?
5 What does the dress have on it?
6 What does "recycle" mean?

OBJECTIVES: By the end of the lesson, students will have read about different man-made and natural materials from around the world.

• TARGET LANGUAGE

Key language: materials, *man-made, factory, natural, wool, recycle, precious metal, cardboard/card, bracelet*

Review: comparative adjectives, simple present

• MATERIALS REQUIRED

Warmer: A leather, plastic, and wooden bracelet and/or some metal/silver bracelets

Extra activity 2: Paper

Optional: *Kid's Box AE Teacher's Resource Book 5* Unit 5 Extension worksheet 1 (page 46)

Warmer

- Write *Materials* on the board. Hold up two objects, one made of a natural material, e.g., a wooden ruler, and another made of a man-made material, e.g., a plastic bag. Elicit from students what the two objects are made of, and ask them if they can think how the two materials are different. Show the bracelets you have brought in. Say *bracelet*, write the word on the board, and ask a student to spell it. Use the bracelets to provide other examples of man-made and natural materials to help them. When they guess (in L1), provide the words *man-made* and *natural* and write them on the board.

SB48. ACTIVITY 8. *Read and think. What's the most important material? Why?*

- Tell students to open their Student's Books to page 48. Focus them on Activity 8 and on the activity instructions. Ask a student to read them aloud. Check understanding.
- Focus students on the text and elicit that it's a webpage for *Kid's Box* ezine and that it's about materials. Students read the introduction aloud around the class.
- Focus students on the different materials at the bottom of the webpage, read them through with the class and elicit which are man-made and which are natural. Students read the texts silently and think about their answers to the question at the top. Focus on each text one at a time and discuss why each material is important. Discuss their ideas and opinions as a class. After discussing each text, elicit from the class what they think the most important material is and why. Finally, give students further reading time, check general comprehension and answer any questions they have.

SB48. ACTIVITY 9. *Listen. Repeat the word and say what's made of it.*

- Focus students on the Activity 9 instructions and on the example. Elicit the objects mentioned in the text, e.g., *house* and what it's made of (glass). Play the CD. Pause after each one for students to find the information in the text. They point to the object the first time. Play the CD again. Elicit a choral response each time.

Key: 2 Cardboard. That's the tower. 3 Paper. That's the bridge. 4 Wool. That's the dress. 5 Plastic. That's the chair. 6 Gold and silver. That's the car.

CD 2, 30

1 glass, 2 cardboard, 3 paper, 4 wool, 5 plastic, 6 gold and silver

SB48. ACTIVITY 10. *Read again and answer.*

- Focus students on the Activity 10 questions. Students work in groups of three and find the answers to / discuss the questions. Elicit answers from the class and provide any new vocabulary on the board. Discuss with students what things they recycle and where they recycle them (recycling bins at school / in the supermarket, separating their garbage at home, etc.).

Key: 1 In factories. 2 80 kilograms. 3 He used 12,000 glass bottles. 4 Paper comes from trees. 5 Animal teeth and bones. 6 "Recycle" means use it again in a different form.

WB48. ACTIVITY 8. *Choose words from the box to label the pictures.*

Note: There are two extra words in the box.

Key: 2 wool, 3 card, 4 gold and silver, 5 paper, 6 plastic

WB48. ACTIVITY 9. *Find and write eight materials.*

Key: 2 silver, 3 plastic, 4 wood, 5 cardboard, 6 paper, 7 metal, 8 wool

WB48. ACTIVITY 10. *Write the words.*

Key: 2 silver, 3 fur, 4 glass, 5 wool

WB48. ACTIVITY 11. *Look at the letters on the clock and write the words.*

Key: 2 wood, 3 coat, 4 metal, 5 silver, 6 card

Extra activities: see page T104 (if time)

Optional activity

- Unit 5 Extension worksheet 1 from *Kid's Box AE Teacher's Resource Book 5* (see pages 43 and 46).

Ending the lesson

- Play a game similar to the one in the Student's Book. Say a material, e.g., *gold*. Students give the name of something that's made of gold, e.g., *a ring*. Repeat for other materials. Students take turns calling out materials, too.

OBJECTIVES: By the end of the lesson, students will have had further practice using *made of* and *come from* and will have sung a song.

• TARGET LANGUAGE

Key language: materials, *made from / made of, come from, the ground, sand, bear, bracelet*
Additional language: *jewelry*
Review: adjectives, clothes, everyday objects

• MATERIALS REQUIRED

Extra activity 1: Encyclopedia for each group of four / the Internet for researching how many different things can be made from different materials, a large sheet of paper for each group of four
Extra activity 2: A large sheet of paper for each group of three
Optional: *Kid's Box AE Teacher's Resource Book 5* Unit 5 Song worksheet (page 48)

Warmer

- Pre-teach *jewelry*. Explain through example by showing your watch or a ring, etc., and ask students to give you further examples, eliciting bracelet, earring, etc. Write *jewelry* on the board and ask a student to spell it.
- Draw a triangle on the board and write each of these words at one of the points: *jewelry, gold, the ground.* Elicit the connection between the three, providing *come from* if necessary. Write the sentences under the triangle: *The jewelry's made of gold. Gold comes from the ground.* Check students understand the concept of *come from*. Write one or two other groups of three words. Students provide the sentences for, e.g., *ruler, wood, trees; sweater, wool, sheep.* Elicit students' own ideas.

SB49. ACTIVITY **11.** *Read and choose the right words.*

- Tell students to open their Student's Books to page 49. Focus them on the Activity 11 instruction and tell them to think again about the sentences in the warmer. Students work individually to try to complete the sentences. They check in pairs. Check with the class, discussing the processes for certain materials if students don't know where they come from. For sentences 1 and 5, elicit where these materials come from. For the other sentences, elicit everyday things that are made of these materials.

Key: 1 wood, 2 the ground, 3 trees, 4 animals, 5 sand, 6 sheep

SB49. ACTIVITY **12.** *Listen and order. Check and sing.*

- Focus students on Activity 12 and on the verses of the song. Give them reading time. Check students have read and understood the activity instructions before they listen. Play the CD. Students listen and order. They check in pairs. Play the CD again. Check with the class.
- Play the CD again for students to repeat section by section. When they are confident in their singing, sing the song right through with the class. Divide the class into eight groups. Give each group a pair of lines to sing. Repeat two or three more times, with different groups singing different lines. Play the first version on the CD and then the karaoke version.

Key: 2b, 3d, 4a, 5f, 6c, 7h, 8e

CD 2, 31

As in Student's Book and key

CD 2, 32

Now sing the song again. (Karaoke version)

SB49. ACTIVITY **13.** *Close your book. What can you remember from the song?*

- This is a memory game. Focus students on the Activity 13 instructions and on the speech bubbles. Check students know how to ask the question. They close their books and take turns asking and answering questions about the objects in the song. Tell them that there are eight objects mentioned. When one student makes a mistake, students exchange roles.

SB49. ACTIVITY **14.** *Play the game in pairs.*

- This is a guessing game. Ask students to copy the chart into their notebooks. They secretly think of five things made of each material and write them in their chart.
- Use *wood* as an example of the game. Tell students that you have written four more things on your list that are made of wood. Ask students to guess the things made of wood: *table, bookcase, boat,* and *baseball bat.* Give them a minute to do this. The class gets a point for each word.
- Students take turns playing the game in pairs. Extend the game by choosing other materials from the song.

WB49. ACTIVITY **12.** *Read. Change one letter to write a new word.*

Key: rice, nice, nine, mine, line, like, live, love, move, more, wore, work, word, wood, wool

WB49. ACTIVITY **13.** *Now write the clues for this puzzle.*

Key: Students' own answers

WB49. ACTIVITY **14.** *Find 8 mistakes in the text.*

Key: See Activity 15 key

WB49. ACTIVITY **15.** *Now write the text correctly.*

Key: Bottles are made of glass or plastic. Tables and chairs can be made of wood, plastic, or metal. People on Earth like reading books, comic books, and magazines/newspapers. These are made of cardboard and paper. Earth people get wool from sheep. I'm going to visit Earth next November. I want to get a nice big bracelet made of gold/silver/wood/plastic/metal. I can wear it when I go to parties.

Extra activities: see page T104 (if time)

Optional activity

- Unit 5 Song worksheet from *Kid's Box AE Teacher's Resource Book 5* (see pages 43 and 48).

Ending the lesson

- Sing the song from the beginning of the lesson again with students.

11 Read and choose the right words.

1 Paper and cardboard are made from **wood** / **wool** / **metal**.
2 Gold comes from **animals** / **the ground** / **trees**.
3 Wood comes from **ground** / **trees** / **flowers**.
4 Fur comes from **trees** / **sand** / **animals**.
5 Glass is made from **leaves** / **sand** / **wood**.
6 Wool comes from a **sheep** / **cow** / **bear**.

12 Listen and order. Check and sing.

31 CD2

a This table's made of wood,
And that skirt's made of grass. 4

b **From rocks, plants, or animals,**
Or from a factory. 2

c This scarf is made of wool,
And I wear it when it's cold. 6

d This chair is made of metal,
That bowl is made of glass. 3

e Some things are made of plastic
That can be strong and hard. 8

f This box is made of silver,
That watch is made of gold. 5

g **Everything's material,**
Everything we see. 1

h Books are made of paper,
Their covers are made of cardboard. 7

13 Close your book. What can you remember from the song?

14 Play the game in pairs.

wood	metal	glass	plastic	paper
pencil				

15 Focus on phonics (33 CD2)

Clare: It's time to take a break.
Dean: Let's sit on the chairs and eat our pears.
Clare: Great! But wait! Look behind that gate ...
Dean: Run, Clare! Those bears want our pears!

Speaking 16 Play the game. Choose words to make six sentences.

meet	~~knows~~	right	would	some	red	ate
sun	write	wood	read	sum	wait	sea
hour	bored	meat	pair	where	pear	hear
son	board	for	see	there	here	weight
their	four	nose	eight	our	wear	

My mom knows I like chocolate.

Knows. That's K-N-O-W-S.

Writing 17 Work with your friend. How many sentences can you write?

1. I like writing on the board.
2. Where are you going this weekend?

Joke Corner (34 CD2)

What did the snowman say to the other snowman?

"I can smell carrots!"

OBJECTIVES: By the end of the lesson, students will have practiced identifying the phonemes /eɪ/ and /eər/ and recognising alternative spellings for these sounds. They will also have completed a writing activity.

● TARGET LANGUAGE

Key language: the phonemes /eɪ/ and /eər/, describing objects
Review: house and household objects, numbers, adjectives, rhyming words

● MATERIALS REQUIRED

Extra activity 1: Eight squares of thin cardboard for each pair of students
Optional: *Kid's Box AE Interactive DVD 5: The school hall* "Junk music" episode

Warmer

- Write the following words on the board in a random order: *chair, wear, take, there, gate, bear, pear, care, break, where.* Ask students to put them into two different groups, according to their sounds. Students work in pairs, saying the words aloud to help them. Monitor and give support as necessary. Elicit the two groups (*chair, wear, there, bear, pear, care, where; take, gate, break*). Tell students that they will be practising the vowel sounds /eər/ and /eɪ/ in today's lesson. Say the sounds for students to repeat. Draw attention to the variety of spellings for the two sounds.

SB50. ACTIVITY **15.** *Focus on phonics*

- Tell students to open their Student's Books to page 50. Ask them to look at Activity 15. Play the CD. Students repeat after each line and then repeat after the whole rhyme. Repeat once more, making sure students pronounce the vowel sounds correctly. In pairs, students practice the rhyme.

CD 2, 33

As in Student's Book

SB50. ACTIVITY **16.** *Play the game. Choose words to make six sentences.*

- Focus students on the Activity 16 instructions and check understanding. Demonstrate the game in open pairs, with one or two more examples. Point out that there are two words with different spellings each time, e.g., *knows, nose.* When they hear a word, they must spell it correctly, as in the example. Students then play the game in pairs. Give them time to think of sentences before the game starts. Monitor and help where necessary.

SB50. ACTIVITY **17.** *Work with your friend. How many sentences can you write?*

- Make sure students know what to do for Activity 17. They use the words from Activity 16 to make sentences. Tell them to make interesting sentences. They can make the sentences into a story if they wish. Students work together and write the sentences in their notebooks.

SB50. JOKE CORNER

- Focus students on the Joke Corner and review the meaning of *joke*. Play the CD as students read the joke in their books. Play the joke a second time and explain if necessary.

CD 2, 34

As in Student's Book

WB50. ACTIVITY **16.** *Match the rhyming words.*

- Tell students to open their Workbook to page 50. Check they know the meaning of all the words. Go through the example and make sure students know that they have to match numbers 1 to 5 with letters a to e and 6 to 10 with f to j. Students complete the activity in pencil. Tell them to say the words aloud again to help and not to focus on the spelling.

WB50. ACTIVITY **17.** *Listen, check, and say.*

- Play the CD for students to listen and check. They compare answers in pairs. Check with the class. Play the CD again for students to listen and repeat.

Key: a4, b5, c1, d2, e3, f7, g9, h6, i10, j8

CD 2, 35

1 wool-pull, 2 year-here 3 stone-bone, 4 pear-where,
5 could-wood, 6 box-socks, 7 six-bricks, 8 wear-hair,
9 nose-goes, 10 great-ate

WB50. ACTIVITY **18.** *Read and match.*

- Before students do the activity, focus them on the Write it right box and check they understand the different points relating to describing objects.

Key: 3, 4, 1, 6, 2, 5

WB50. ACTIVITY **19.** *Write about your dream house.*

- After completing the writing activity, students draw their house on a separate piece of paper. Pin the pictures up around the room. Students then read their descriptions to the class, who listens and guesses which pictures match the descriptions.

Key: Students' own answers

Extra activities: see page T104 (if time)

Optional activity

- The "Junk music" episode from *Kid's Box AE Interactive DVD 5* (*The school hall* section). See pages 16-19 of the Teacher's Booklet for the Interactive DVD.

Ending the lesson

- Do the rhyme from the beginning of the lesson again.

OBJECTIVES: By the end of the lesson, students will have read a story, reviewed language from the unit, and completed a self-evaluation.

• TARGET LANGUAGE

Key language: language in the story, *palace*, *watchdog*
Additional language: *Cleopatra*
Review: language from the unit

• MATERIALS REQUIRED

Extra activity 2: Six strips of paper for each pair of students
Optional activity: *Kid's Box AE Workbook 5 Language Portfolio* page 99

Warmer

- Review the story so far with students. Elicit if they remember what *Sirius* is and what the date was in the last episode. Ask students what time of day it was, where the heroes were at the end of the story, and what Diggory shouted to Emily and why. Elicit their answers. (A star that showed the start of the Egyptian New Year. July 21. Night. In the secret cave. "Run to the Light." They were waiting close to a volcano.)

SB51. STORY. *Diggory Bones.*

- Tell students to open their Student's Books to page 51 and look at the first two pictures. Elicit what happened to Diggory, Emily and Brutus. Set the questions: *What does Brutus find? What is Brutus carrying? What's the inside of Brutus's bag made of? Why is this important? What happened to Cleopatra's palace? What's in the palace? What does Brutus push?* Play the CD with books closed. Students listen to find the answers. They check in pairs with books open. Check with the class. (A secret message. The Baloney Stone. Plastic. Because the Baloney Stone on Diggory's computer didn't get wet. Water covered it. Her treasures. A sleeping snake – to open the secret door.) Play the CD again. Students listen and read. Stop after each frame for students to repeat. At the end, check general comprehension by asking, e.g., *What does the writing on the wall tell them? How do they know that? How do you open the secret door? Who watches over the door? What's behind the door? Why does Diggory tell Brutus not to touch the treasure do you think?* Ask *What can you see in the treasure (in the last picture)?* to elicit *bowl, cups, bracelet, jewelry.*

CD 2, 36

As in Student's Book

WB51. ACTIVITY **20.** *Read and answer.*

Key: 2 It's made of plastic. 3 The sleeping snake. 4 Because he's an excellent watchdog. 5 They're made of glass. 6 He wants gold.

WB51. ACTIVITY **21.** *Read and order the text.*

Key: From left to right: 2, 3, 1, 5, 8, 6, 7, 4

WB51. DO YOU REMEMBER?

- Students try to do the activity first without looking back through the unit. Once they have tried to complete all the sentences, they can look back through the unit to find the answers.

Key: 2 wool, 3 metals, 4 of, 5 and 6 Students' own answers

WB51. CAN DO

- Focus students on the *Can do* section of the page. Ask a student to read the first sentence. Elicit what this means with examples and elicit/remind them of the activities they did in this unit when they talked about materials. Review what the three faces mean (not very well / OK / very well). Remind students they circle the one they think is true for them. Repeat for the second sentence, eliciting/reminding them of the activities when they talked and found out about what things were made of. Students circle the appropriate face. Repeat for the third sentence, eliciting the dream houses they wrote descriptions of.
- Say *Now show and tell your friends.* Students work in groups of three and take turns showing their work for / talking about each one.

Extra activities: see page T104 (if time)

Language Portfolio

- Students complete page 99 of *Kid's Box AE Workbook 5 Language Portfolio* (How ... is/are made).

Ending the lesson

- Ask students which rhyme/song they'd like to do again from the unit. Do it together to end the lesson.

DIGGORY BONES

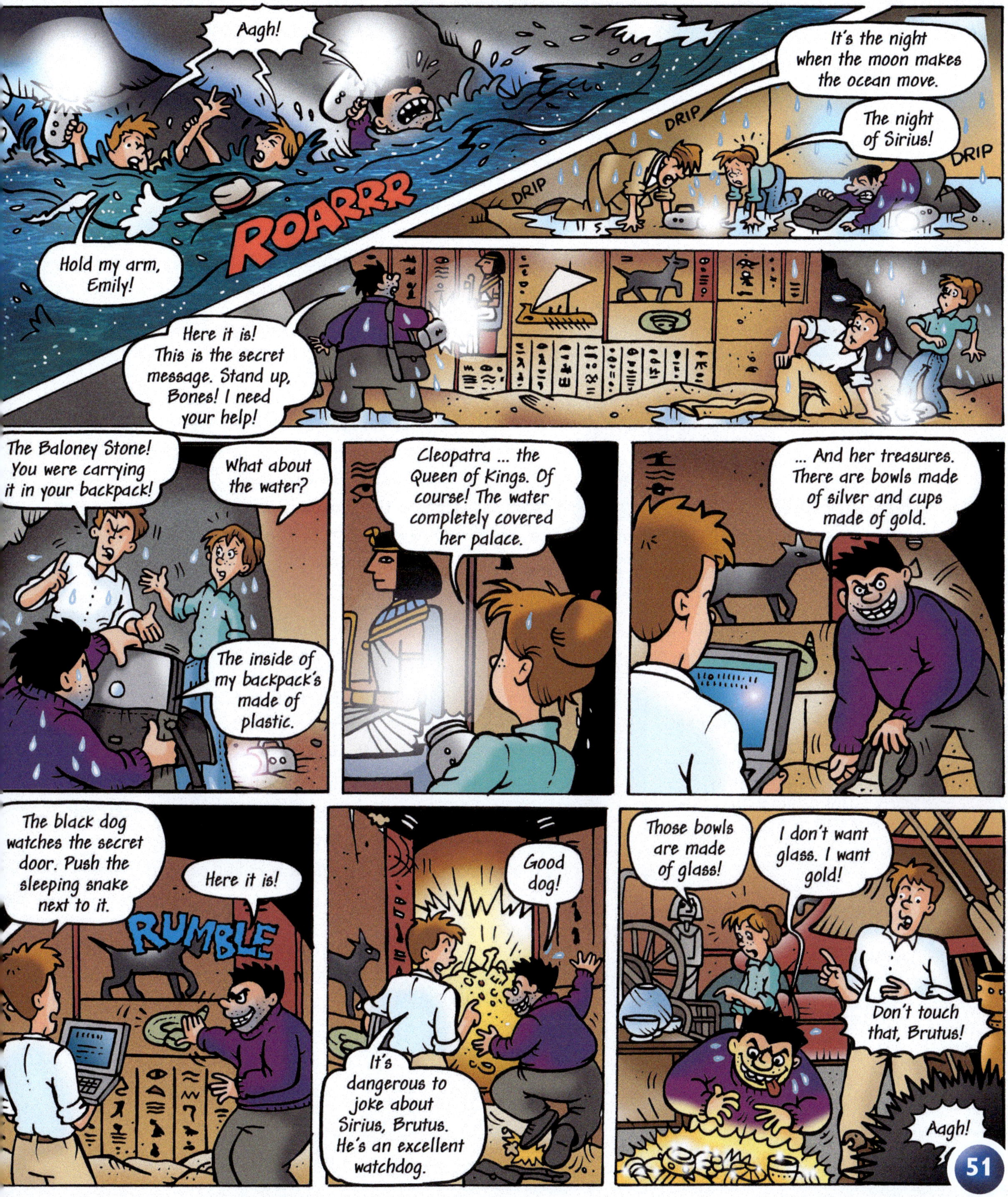

Science Recycling plastic

FACT: It takes 450 years for plastic bottles to decompose if they are put under the ground.

1 Read and do.

a) Choose a heading for each paragraph.

- What do we use plastic for?
- Why do we need oil?
- What are some of the different plastics?
- What happens to plastic when we throw it away?

b) Now answer the questions.

2 Read again and choose a title.

a) Different plastics

b) Recycling plastic

c) About plastic

3 37 CD2 Listen and label the diagram.

building	bottles and boxes	
farming	house	electronics
transportation	other	

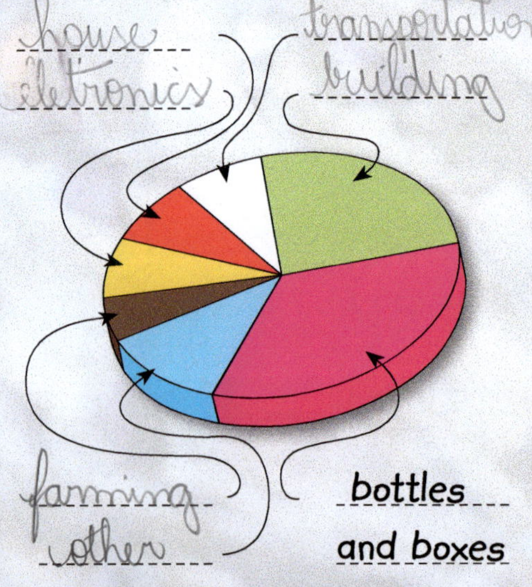

1 ______________________

Every day we throw a lot of plastic into our garbage cans. This is a problem because plastic does not change. This means that it uses a lot of space if we don't reuse it or recycle it. Did you know that half of the garbage on our beaches is made of plastic?

2 ______________________

Making plastic also uses a lot of oil. We need to use oil for two things. First, we use it as the basic material for plastic, and second, we use oil for energy to make the plastic. Because of this it is important to try to recycle different plastics. What do you recycle?

3 ______________________

Celluloid was one of the first plastics. It is made from cotton (the material that jeans are made of) and two other materials. People use celluloid to make film for movies.

Another important plastic is nylon that people use in a lot of different kinds of clothes. The word *nylon* comes from the names of two cities, New York and London.

Today the plastic that we use most is called polyethylene. We use it for bottles and boxes.

4 ______________________

We use plastic for almost everything. Think about what is around you and what you use every day. How many plastic things can you think of?

OBJECTIVES: By the end of the lesson, students will have read about different kinds of plastics, how they are made, and why they are recycled.

• TARGET LANGUAGE

Key language: *plastic, decompose, recycle, throw away, reuse, basic material, celluloid, nylon, polyethylene, diagram*

Review: materials, simple present

• MATERIALS REQUIRED

Extra activity 1: Dictionaries

Optional: *Kid's Box AE Teacher's Resource Book 5* Unit 5 Topic worksheet (page 49)

Warmer

- Write *Plastic* on the board and brainstorm with students as many things that are made of plastic as they can think of in one minute. Ask them if they think all plastic is the same (give examples from the board, e.g., *plastic bag, chair*). Ask students if they remember what plastic is made from.

SB52. FACT

- Tell students to open their Student's Books to page 52. Ask a student to read the fact. Elicit/Check understanding of *decompose*. Tell students that there are types of plastic that decompose more quickly. Ask for examples (biodegradable shopping bags). Elicit why it might be a problem if plastic takes so long to decompose.

SB52. ACTIVITY **1.** *Read and do.*

- Focus students on the Activity 1 instructions and on the pictures. Ask different students to read the headings in a) aloud. Tell them b) refers to the questions in the text. Students read the text quickly (and silently) to match. They re-read the text to answer the questions for b). They check in pairs. Check with the class.
- Read the first section through with the class, with students taking turns reading. Elicit what they think the heading is. Discuss the information, check key vocabulary, and check their opinions about the heading again. Tell them if they are correct or not. Discuss the question at the end of the section.
- Repeat the procedure for the other sections.

Key: 1 What happens to plastic when we throw it away? 2 Why do we need oil? 3 What are some of the different plastics? 4 What do we use plastic for?

SB52. ACTIVITY **2.** *Read again and choose a title.*

- Focus students on the Activity 2 instruction and on the three titles. They reread the text silently and then in pairs choose the best title. Discuss choices and reasons with the class.

Key: c) About plastic

SB52. ACTIVITY **3.** *Listen and label the diagram.*

- Focus students on the diagram. Elicit that it shows the amounts of plastic that are used for different things. Check they understand the concept of the pie chart before they do the listening.

Key: green: building, white: transportation, red: house, yellow: electrics, brown: farming, blue: other

CD 2, 37

WOMAN: Today we have with us Dr. Simon Carter who is going to talk to us about how we use plastic.

DR. CARTER: Hi. That's right. Today we use plastic for almost everything. I'm going to tell you what we use it for, and how much we use.

WOMAN: OK. Well, I see you have a diagram here to help us understand the numbers.

DR. CARTER: Yes. Now, can you see this circle has different parts? Look at the biggest part that is pink. That's a third of all the plastic we use. This part is for packaging. Packaging means all the bottles and boxes we get when we buy things from the stores and supermarkets.

WOMAN: Wow! That's a lot.

DR. CARTER: Yes, it is. Now look at the second biggest part.

WOMAN: Is that the green one?

DR. CARTER: Yes. That is for all the plastic we use in building. In our houses, plastics are very important in windows, doors and the water system.

WOMAN: I see. What are the three that are the same size?

DR. CARTER: The white one is for use in transportation. You know – cars, planes, and motorcycles. The red one is for things around the house and furniture, and the yellow one is for electronics.

WOMAN: OK. What about the last two?

DR. CARTER: The brown part is for farming, and the blue one next to it is for a lot of other different things. These include toys, shoes, mechanics, and hospitals.

WOMAN: Well, Dr. Carter, we really do use plastics for almost everything, don't we?

DR. CARTER: Yes, we do.

WB52. ACTIVITY **1.** *Look at the recycling facts. Read and write "true" or "false."*

Note: 17,500,000 = 17.5 million; 17,500,000,000 = 17.5 billion.

Key: 2 true, 3 false, 4 false, 5 true, 6 false

WB52. ACTIVITY **2.** *What should we do? Put the information in the chart.*

Key:

Things we should do	Things we shouldn't do
Give toys to friends or playgroups	Throw plastic toys away
Use plastic containers and bags again	Throw plastic containers away
Make containers into something else	Use a bag if you don't need one
Look for products made from recycled plastic	Use a lot of plastic

WB52. ACTIVITY **3.** *Write about what plastic things you use in your school and the changes you are going to make.*

Key: Students' own answers

Extra activities: see page T104/T105 (if time)

Optional activity

- Unit 5 Topic worksheet from *Kid's Box AE Teacher's Resource Book 5* (see pages 43 and 49).

Ending the lesson

- Review with students what they have done and what they have learned about in today's lesson.

OBJECTIVES: By the end of the lesson, students will have read more about recycling of plastics and completed a project.

• TARGET LANGUAGE

Key language: *piece, sort* (v), *squash, melt, should, shouldn't*
Additional language: *tip, frame, base*
Review: materials, sequencing

• MATERIALS REQUIRED

For each student, an empty CD box, scissors, glue or tape, material for decoration. Students bring in a photograph that they would like to frame or can choose a picture they like from a magazine.
Extra activity 1: Paper, stapler, colored pencils
Optional: *Kid's Box AE Teacher's Resource Book 5* Unit 5 Extension worksheet 2 (page 47)

Warmer

- With books closed, review with students what they learned about in the previous lesson. Review some of the key vocabulary.

SB53. ACTIVITY **4.** *Read and match.*

- Tell students to open their Student's Books to page 53. Focus them on Activity 4. Invite three students to read aloud one sentence each in the introductory paragraph. Check students have read the activity instruction and know what to do. They read the text quickly and silently and match the steps with the pictures. They check in pairs. Check with the class. Then check understanding of new vocabulary, e.g., *sorts, squashes.*

Key: 1a, 2d, 3c, 4e, 5b, 6f

SB53. ACTIVITY **5.** *Talk in pairs. Tell the class.*

- Focus students on the Activity 5 instructions and explanation. Elicit some ideas for how plastic items can be reused (rather than recycled). Students work in pairs. They think of all the plastic items they regularly use at home and at school and how they have reused them. Elicit ideas from students for a class discussion. If appropriate, produce a class poster with their suggestions.

Note: Remind students that it is not a good idea to reuse drink or water bottles for drinks.

SB53. PROJECT. *Make a photo frame.*

- Tell students that they are going to reuse a common plastic object. Hold up the CD case to show them. Show and name the other materials you have brought for the project. Read the project information with the class before handing anything to the students, showing the materials as they are mentioned. Hand out the materials. Students follow the instructions to make their frame. Monitor and help.

WB53. ACTIVITY **4.** FLYERS **Listening, Part 3.** *Whose things are these? Listen and look. There is one example.*
F toward

Key: Robert A, Emma F, Richard B, Katy D, Michael C

CD 2, 38

TEACHER: Hello everyone. Sarah has some things to show us today. Tell us what you have, Sarah.

SARAH: Well, I asked my family to give me some things. All the things are made of different materials. The first thing I have here today is a purse. This is mine. It's different from other purses because it's made of paper. I made it from some old comic books and put plastic on the outside.

Can you see the letter E? Now you listen and write a letter in each box.

TEACHER: That's very interesting. What else do you have?

SARAH: I asked my grandma for her gold watch, but she said it was very expensive. So I have Katy's watch. Katy is my sister. She's only four years old, so it isn't real, it's a toy. It's made of plastic. It isn't expensive, but she really likes it.

TEACHER: Yes, take care of it! Did your grandmother give you anything?

SARAH: Yes, of course she did! She gave me her comb. It's very old and really beautiful. It's made of wood and the inside of shells. She got it for her eighteenth birthday, when she was much younger. It had her name on it. It said, "Emma," – that's my grandmother's name – but we can't read it now.

TEACHER: No, but you're right. It is really beautiful. Now, who gave you that money?

SARAH: The money! It isn't real because it isn't made of metal. It's chocolate money! My younger brother Robert gave it to me. He's ten. My brother loves chocolate. He said he wants it back. He's going to eat it during the break with his friends.

TEACHER: Now what about that ball? It isn't made of rubber or plastic, is it?

SARAH: No, it isn't. It's made of glass. That's my dad's, his name's Michael. My mother gave it to him as a present. It's very heavy. He puts it on the papers on his desk.

TEACHER: I see. ... What about the hat? Is that your father's too?

SARAH: No! My dad hates that hat! It's my older brother Richard's. It's made of wool and it has a lot of colors. He wears it all the time in the winter, even with his school uniform! He's sixteen and he wants to play the guitar in a pop group. He sometimes wears really strange clothes.

Extra activities: see page T105 (if time)

Optional activity

- Unit 5 Extension worksheet 2 from *Kid's Box AE Teacher's Resource Book 5* (see pages 43 and 47).

Ending the lesson

- Review with students what they talked and read about in today's lesson and which activities they liked best from this and the previous lesson.

4 Read and match.

a

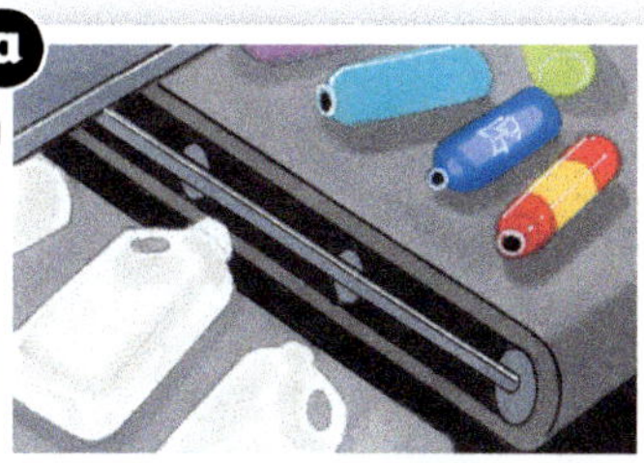

b

c

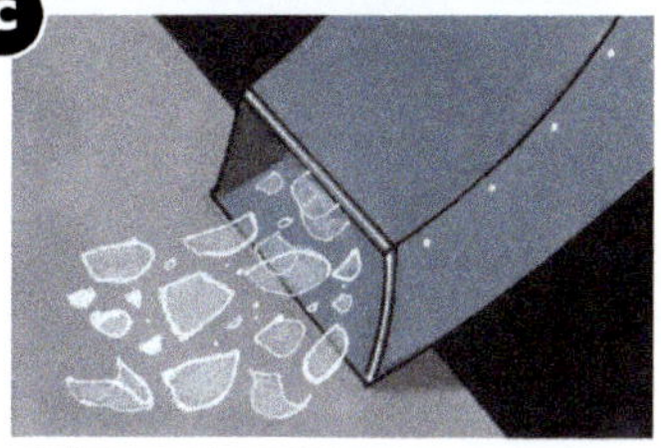

Recycling plastic

It's not easy to recycle plastic because there are hundreds of different types. How often do you drink from plastic bottles? Here are some of the things people do to recycle them.

1 First, a special machine sorts the bottles so that all of the bottles made from the same materials are together.
2 Then another machine squashes the bottles.
3 Next, another machine cuts the bottles into very small pieces.
4 Then they wash the pieces.
5 Next, they put the plastic into bags, ready for recycling.
6 Finally, they melt the plastic and use it to make a lot of new things. Sometimes they use it to make new plastic bottles!

d

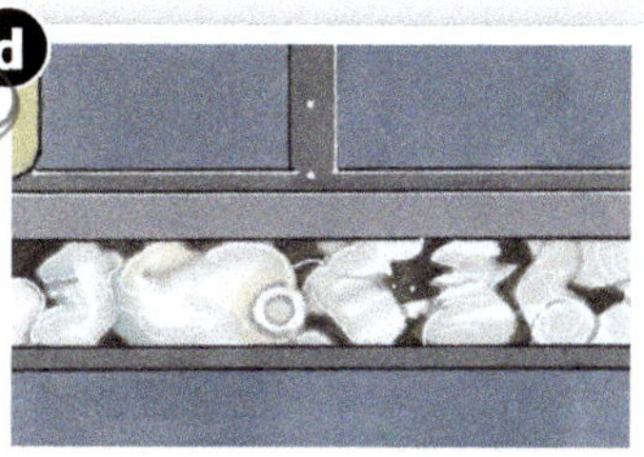

e

f

5 Talk in pairs. Tell the class.

Another thing we can do is reuse our plastic. How can you reuse some of your plastic things?

Project Make a photo frame.

You need:

- An empty CD box you can reuse
- A picture
- Scissors and glue or tape
- Things to decorate the frame

How to make the photo frame:

1 Open your CD box and take out the paper and the plastic piece where the CD goes.
TIP: Take the cover off the CD box and turn the base on its end. Then put the cover on the back of the base. The box will now stand up on its own.
2 Cut the picture to the right size.
3 Decorate the front of your frame by gluing different objects onto it. You can use stamps, old toys, flowers, or anything you want.
4 Put your picture inside the frame.

6 Senses

Show what you know! What sense words can you remember?

Listening **1** 02 CD3 Listen and check (✓) the sense words you hear.

2 03 CD3 Listen again. Who said it?

1 What does it feel like? (Maria.)
2 It feels like fur. Dan
3 It sounds like somebody falling downstairs. Alex
4 What does this smell like, Maria? Teacher
5 It smells like Alex's socks. Maria
6 What does this taste like, Alex? Teacher

3 Read and order the words.

1 a / truck. / sounds / My / car / like
My car sounds like a truck
2 feels / like / His / jacket / fur.
His jacket feels like fur
3 does / taste / What / like? / that / soup
What does that soup taste like?
4 your / mother / look / Who / like? / does
Who does your mother look like?
5 bananas. / cake / That / smells / like
That cake smells like bananas
6 does / your / What / scarf / feel / like?

LOOK

What does it **look/feel/taste/smell/sound** like?
It **looks/feels/tastes/smells/sounds** like coffee.

*Photocopiable - page T-95

OBJECTIVES: By the end of the lesson, students will be able to name and talk about the five senses.

• TARGET LANGUAGE

Key language: senses: *touch, taste, smell, sight, hearing; What does it feel/taste/smell/look/sound like? It feels/tastes/smells/looks/ sounds like …*
Review: adjectives, materials, *science club*

• MATERIALS REQUIRED

Extra activity: A black canvas or cotton bag, some objects for students to feel that they won't immediately guess, (e.g., an orange, a furry spider, a sock, a nut, a grape, a leaf, a wig)
Photocopiable 6 (see page T95), one copy for each student

Warmer

- Elicit from students the different ways we can experience the world around us. Provide one example, e.g., *We can see it.* Students give you the other senses. Provide the words in English. Tell students the theme of Unit 6 is *Senses* and write it on the board. Ask students which for them is the most important sense.

SB54. SHOW WHAT YOU KNOW! *What sense words can you remember?*

- Draw a circle around *Senses* on the board. Draw five lines from this, each ending in a circle. In these circles, write each of the five senses (touch, taste, smell, sight, hearing). Elicit something nice for one sense and write this next to the appropriate sense to start a mind map. Say *Show what you know … about senses.* Brainstorm with the class the things they experience through the different senses and create a mind map on the board. Students copy the mind map into their notebooks, including only the things they think are nice.

SB54. ACTIVITY 1. *Listen and check (✓) the sense words you hear.*

- Tell students to open their Student's Books to page 54 and look at the Activity 1 pictures. Elicit the names of the characters and where they are. Remind students they do the same as for the Show what you know in the previous units (check off the words they hear in the Senses mind map in their notebooks).
- Play the CD. Students listen and check. They check in pairs. Use the mind map on the board to check with the class.

CD 3, 02

TEACHER: In this week's science club we're going to look at the five senses. First we're going to look at the sense of touch.
MARIA: Put your hand into this box, Dan. What does it feel like?
DAN: It's very soft. It feels like fur. Is it an animal?
ALEX: No, Dan. It's my toy spider.
DAN: Not again!
ALEX AND MARIA: Ha, ha, ha!
MARIA: I didn't know we had to do the sense of hearing too.
ALEX: That's horrible! It sounds like somebody falling downstairs.
TEACHER: That's my new CD.
DAN: That's cool!
ALEX AND MARIA: Dan!
TEACHER: Now we're exploring the sense of smell. What does this smell like, Maria?
MARIA: Phoargh! That smells terrible! It smells like Alex's socks.
ALEX: Well, it's strong blue cheese, Maria.
TEACHER: And now the sense of taste. What does this taste like, Alex?
ALEX: Mmm. It … it tastes like pizza. It's great! I didn't think I liked pizza.
DAN: You do now!
ALEX: Let's find out how to make the perfect pizza for our next ezine.
MARIA AND DAN: Yes!

SB54. ACTIVITY 2. *Listen again. Who said it?*

- Read the sentences through with the class. Play the CD. Students write the names in their notebooks. They check in pairs.

Key: 2 Dan, 3 Alex, 4 Teacher, 5 Maria, 6 Teacher

CD 3, 03

Presentation

- Write sentences 1, 2, 4 and 5 from Student's Book Activity 2 on the board. Ask what they are talking about in question 1 (a toy spider). Elicit the response and if it is really an animal (no). Elicit why Dan thinks it's an animal (it feels like fur). Check the concept of *feels like*. Repeat for 4 and 5. Ask students if it is really Alex's socks (no). Ask them what it is (cheese).
- Play the CD from Activity 1 again. When students hear *feels/tastes/smells/sounds like*, they raise their hands. Stop the CD and elicit what was said (question and/or answer). At the end, elicit the story in summary from students.
- Focus students on the Look box.

Photocopiable 6 (see pages T89 and T95)

SB54. ACTIVITY 3. *Read and order the words.*

- Students complete the activity in pairs. Pairs check with pairs. Check with the class. For the questions, elicit possible answers.

Key: 1 My car sounds like a truck. 2 His jacket feels like fur. 3 What does that soup taste like? 4 Who does your mother look like? 5 That cake smells like bananas. 6 What does your scarf feel like?

WB54. ACTIVITY 1. *Read and order the words.*

Key: 2 It looks like it's going to rain. 3 That sounds like your cell phone. 4 What does this toy mouse feel like? 5 Her cake tastes like coffee. 6 What does my picture look like?

WB54. ACTIVITY 2. *Correct the sentences.*

Key: 2 ~~feels~~ feel, 3 ~~look likes~~ looks like, 4 ~~don't~~ doesn't, 5 ~~smells~~ smell, 6 ~~doesn't~~ don't

WB54. ACTIVITY 3. *Read and complete the email.* **F** toward

Key: 2 exciting, 3 shouting, 4 feel, 5 hear, 6 quickly, 7 felt

Extra activity: see page T105 (if time)

Ending the lesson

- Tell students to put their heads down on their desks and close their eyes. Make some different sounds, e.g., scrunch up some paper or write on the board. Then ask students what they all sounded like.

OBJECTIVES: By the end of the lesson, students will have had more practice talking about the five senses and what things feel, look, taste, sound, and smell like.

• TARGET LANGUAGE

Key language: senses, *What does he/she feel/look like? He/she feels/looks* + adjective, *tongue, furry*
Review: food and drink, the body, adjectives

• MATERIALS REQUIRED

Five small pieces of paper for each student, envelopes
Five objects in numbered plastic bags, one that feels soft, one hard, one light, one heavy, etc. (for Activity 7)
Optional: *Kid's Box AE Teacher's Resource Book 5* Unit 6 Reinforcement worksheet 1 (page 51) and/or Extension worksheet 1 (page 53)

Warmer

- Elicit some of the nice things students wrote for their mind maps in the previous lesson. Cover all five senses.

SB55. ACTIVITY 4. *Listen. What does it sound like?*

- Tell students to open their Student's Books to page 55. Focus them on the Activity 4 picture and elicit some of the things they can see. Ask a student to read the activity instructions aloud. Play the first one as an example and ask another student to read the speech bubble response. Check students understand what to do. Play the CD. Students say the response quietly to each other (in pairs). Play the CD again. Check with the class. Make sure they respond with the complete sentence, e.g., *It sounds like rain / someone's playing tennis.*

Key: It sounds like ... 1 a car, 2 a cat, 3 a train, 4 a lion, 5 someone's playing tennis, 6 a door, 7 someone's playing basketball, 8 rain

CD 3, 04

Sounds: 1 a car, 2 a cat, 3 a train, 4 a lion, 5 playing tennis, 6 a door, 7 playing basketball, 8 rain

SB55. ACTIVITY 5. *Play the game. What does it sound like?*

- Focus students on Activity 5 and ask a student to read the activity instructions aloud. Focus on each step of the activity and check they know what to do. Brainstorm ideas with the class for the first bullet point and help with the English words if necessary. Students secretly write their ideas and give you the pieces of paper. Put all of the small pieces of paper into a large envelope. Make two teams. A student from one team comes to the front of the class, takes a piece of paper from the envelope, looks at the word on it, and makes a sound to describe it. The other team listens and guesses what the sound comes from. Only one team member answers. Repeat for the other team. Continue, giving teams alternate turns. Award one point for a correct guess and one for the correct sound.
- Put the class into an equal number of smaller teams and divide up the words into an envelope for each team. Teams play each other.

SB55. ACTIVITY 6. *Ask and answer. What does it look like?*

- Focus students on the Activity 6 pictures. Use the question and answer prompts to talk more about the first picture. Elicit other ideas. Students play the game in pairs, taking turns asking and answering questions about the pictures (they don't have to discuss them in order). Check with the class, using open pairs. Encourage them to give a variety of answers for each one, not just guess one thing.

Key: 1 cat's nose, 2 flower, 3 hairbrush, 4 computer keyboard, 5 umbrella, 6 telescope, 7 watch/clock, 8 cell phone

SB55. ACTIVITY 7. *Ask and answer. What does it feel like?*

- Focus students on the Activity 7 instruction and remind them of the Feelie bag game if you did it in the previous lesson. Teach/Elicit *It feels (soft/hairy/furry/cold).* Say *hair-hairy, fur-furry.* Continue with *cloud, rain, fog, wind, water, dirt,* etc. Practice the new structure with students, using objects in the room (bag, desk, hair, shoes, window, etc.) before students do the activity, using the bags you have brought, as a class or in groups.

WB55. ACTIVITY 4. *How do they look? Write the answers.*

Key: 2 They look cold. 3 He looks sick. 4 She looks hot. 5 He looks frightened. 6 She looks thirsty.

WB55. ACTIVITY 5. *Read. What are they?*

Key: 2 a pea, 3 a lemon, 4 tea, 5 sausages, 6 a tiger

WB55. ACTIVITY 6. *Senses quiz. Read and answer.*

Key: 2 our nose, 3 our eyes, 4 our ears, 5 our hands/fingers, 6, 7, and 8 Students' own answers

Extra activities: see page T105 (if time)

Optional activity

- Unit 6 Reinforcement worksheet 1 and/or Extension worksheet 1 from *Kid's Box AE Teacher's Resource Book 5* (see pages 50, 51, and 53).

Ending the lesson

- Students stand up. Say the different senses quickly one after another, repeating some and saying each one more than once. When students hear the sense, e.g., *touch,* they point to or wiggle their fingertips, and so on.

4 Listen. What does it sound like?

It sounds like a car.

5 Play the game. What does it sound like?

- Think of five things that make different sounds.
- Write the words on five small pieces of paper.
- Give your pieces of paper to your teacher.
- Play the game with the class. Make the sounds and guess.
- Now play the game in groups.

6 Ask and answer. What does it look like?

What do you think number one looks like?

I think it looks like a cat's nose.

So do I.

1

2

3
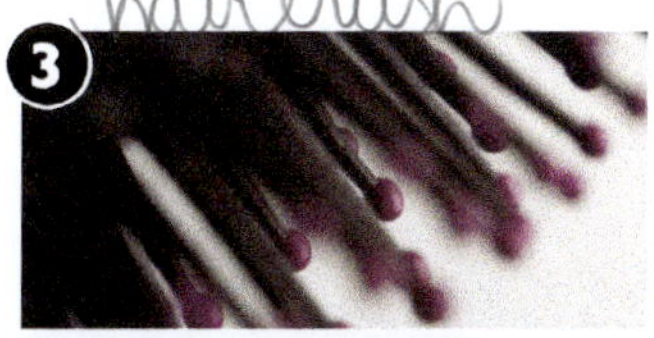

4

5

6

7
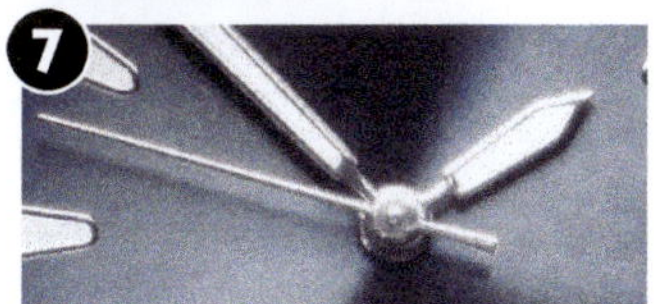

8

7 Ask and answer. What does it feel like?

Reading 8 Read and think. What would you put on your pizza?

http://www.cambridge.org/elt/kidsbox/ezine

Kid's Box Ezine! home | reports | games | world | email

We wanted to learn how to make pizza, so we went to Luigi's Italian restaurant and spoke to Mario, the cook. Before we started, we washed our hands.

Kid's Box reports Pizza

a

First we made the base. The base is made of dough. We put flour, yeast, salt, and water into a bowl, and mixed them well. Then we left the dough for an hour so it could grow.

b

Then we put tomato, cheese, salami sausage, olives, and onion on top of the base. Then we added some black pepper and cooked it in the oven for 15 minutes.

c

When it was ready, we put the pizza onto a plate. Mario uses special plates in the restaurant. They're very big, and they're made of wood.

d

You can eat pizza with your hands, but you need to cut it with a knife first. This one is round, but pizzas can also be square.

e

We had the pizza with salad. We used a big spoon and fork to mix it. Here's a picture of our delicious meal. It looks good, but it tasted even better!

flour | pizza | salt | pepper | knife | fork | spoon | plate

9 Listen. Repeat the word and find it in the text. (05 CD3) 1 Salt. — Salt.

10 Read and correct the sentences.

1 Before they started, they washed their feet.
2 They put flour, yeast, salt, and milk into a bowl.
3 They put some black chocolate on top of the pizza.
4 The plates are very big, and they're made of glass.
5 Mario used a spoon to cut the pizza.
6 They mixed the salad with a knife and fork.

OBJECTIVES: By the end of the lesson, students will have read about how to make pizza and followed a recipe.

● TARGET LANGUAGE

Key language: *recipe, flour, salt, pepper, knife, fork, spoon, plate, salami, sausage, onion, looks good, delicious, yeast, mix, dough, base, topping, olives, oven*
Review: food

● MATERIALS REQUIRED

Optional: *Kid's Box AE Teacher's Resource Book 5* Unit 6 Reinforcement worksheet 2 (page 52) and/or Extension worksheet 2 (page 54)

Warmer

- Describe a pizza for students to guess, e.g., *I'm thinking of some food. It smells yummy when it's cooking. You usually eat it with your fingers. It looks like a flat plate or a circle.* Ask if they like pizza and if any of them have made pizza at home. Tell them they're going to learn how to do it. Pre-teach *recipe*.

SB56. ACTIVITY 8. *Read and think. What would you put on your pizza?*

- Tell students to open their Student's Books to page 56. Focus them on Activity 8 and on the activity instructions. Ask a student to read them aloud. Check understanding and supply the words *topping, olives, oven,* and *delicious*..
- Focus students on the text and elicit that it's a webpage for *Kid's Box* ezine. Make sure they notice the words at the bottom of the webpage. Read the introduction first with the class. Then students read the texts silently and think about their answers to the question. Elicit the toppings mentioned in the text and discuss what students' favorite ones would be. Supply other food words if necessary. Check comprehension of the key vocabulary by referring students back to the texts. Focus on each stage of the recipe/ instructions one at a time, giving students reading time and then checking general comprehension by discussing what ingredients are used and what is happening at that stage.

SB56. ACTIVITY 9. *Listen. Repeat the word and find it in the text.*

- Focus students on the Activity 9 instructions and on the example. Check they know what to do. Play the CD. Pause after each one for students to find the word in the text. Play the CD again. Elicit a choral response each time.

Key: 2 pizza, 3 fork, 4 pepper, 5 plate, 6 flour, 7 knife, 8 spoon

CD 3, 05

1 salt, 2 pizza, 3 fork, 4 pepper, 5 plate, 6 flour, 7 knife, 8 spoon

SB56. ACTIVITY 10. *Read and correct the sentences.*

- Focus students on the Activity 10 instruction and on the sentences. Check they know what to do. They cover the text first with paper and try to correct the sentences without looking at the text. They check in pairs. Then they look at the text and check their ideas. Check with the class.

Key: 1 Before they started, they washed their hands. 2 They put some flour, yeast, salt, and water into a bowl. 3 They put some black pepper on top of the pizza. 4 The plates are very big and they're made of wood. 5 Mario used a knife to cut the pizza. 6 They mixed the salad with a spoon and fork.

WB56. ACTIVITY 7. *Choose words from the box to label the pictures.*

Note: There are two extra words in the box.

Key: 2 salt, 3 knife, 4 fork, 5 spoon, 6 plate

WB56. ACTIVITY 8. *Look and find the words.*

Key: Food words: salt, tomato, egg, pepper, rice, yoghurt, flour, lemons
Verbs: taste, eat, get up, enjoy, take off, tell, smell
Things we eat with: fork, knife
Preposition: off
Somewhere we go to eat: restaurant

WB56. ACTIVITY 9. *Read and write the answers in the puzzle.*

Key: 2 fork, 3 salt, 4 pizza, 5 plate, 6 flour, 7 knife, 8 spoon

Mystery vegetable: potatoes

Extra activities: see page T105 (if time)

Optional activity

- Unit 6 Reinforcement worksheet 2 and/or Extension worksheet 2 from *Kid's Box AE Teacher's Resource Book 5* (see pages 50, 52 and 54).

Ending the lesson

- With books closed, elicit the ingredients Mario used to make his pizza at the beginning of the lesson.
- For Extra activity 1 in the following lesson: Tell students to bring their favorite recipe (in L1) to the next lesson.

OBJECTIVES: By the end of the lesson, students will have had more practice following a recipe and will have sung a song.

• TARGET LANGUAGE

Key language: *topping, ingredients, pasta, hole, mix,* imperatives

Review: food, comparatives, language from previous lesson

• MATERIALS REQUIRED

Extra activity 1: Recipes (in L1) students have brought in

Optional: *Kid's Box AE Teacher's Resource Book 5* Unit 6 Song worksheet (page 55)

Warmer

- Write a lot of different ingredients on the board (the ones for pizza and others, too, for example, *milk, eggs, chocolate, potatoes*). Elicit from students which ones Mario used for his pizza recipe.

SB57. ACTIVITY 11. *Listen and match. Check and sing.*

- Tell students to open their Student's Books to page 57. Focus them on the pictures, rather than on the lyrics of the song. Elicit that this is Mario who they read about in the previous lesson. Focus students on the activity instructions and check understanding. Play the CD. They match the pictures with the text. They check in pairs. Check with the class. Elicit what Mario looks like and what he is doing in each picture. Play the CD again, line by line and verse by verse, for students to repeat. When students are confident with the song, they add mimes to the verse according to the pictures. Make five groups. Groups take turns singing verses and miming. Students swap groups and repeat. Play the first version on the CD and then the karaoke version.

Key: e, a, b, d, c

CD 3, 06

As in Student's Book

CD 3, 07

Now sing the song again. (Karaoke version)

SB57. ACTIVITY 12. *Listen and write the words.*

- Focus students on the Activity 12 instruction and check they realize this is a dictation. They get ready with notebooks and pencils. Play the CD. They write the words. They check in pairs. Play the CD again. Check with the class by eliciting the word and then the spelling.

Key: 2 fork, 3 flour, 4 pizza, 5 salt, 6 pepper, 7 knife, 8 spoon, 9 olives, 10 oven

CD 3, 08

1 p-l-a-t-e, 2 f-o-r-k, 3 f-l-o-u-r, 4 p-i-z-z-a, 5 s-a-l-t, 6 p-e-p-p-e-r, 7 k-n-i-f-e, 8 s-p-o-o-n, 9 o-l-i-v-e-s, 10 o-v-e-n

SB57. ACTIVITY 13. *Read and complete. Write the recipe in your notebook.*

- Focus students on Activity 13 and elicit that this is a recipe for making pasta. Tell them it's not pasta from a package, but pasta "from scratch"! Elicit what the pictured ingredients are (flour, eggs, salt, oil, olives, cheese, black pepper). Elicit what *to serve* means. Give them a hint about completing the recipe: *You need more words than the ingredients at the top.* Students work individually. They read the steps of the recipe and write the words in pencil. Remind them to look before and after the word to help them with their predictions. They check/discuss their answers in pairs. Check with the class, discussing each step one at a time to make sure they understand the process.

Key: flour, flour, eggs, eggs, fork, flour, eggs, knife, salt, plate, oil, olives, cheese, spoon, pepper

WB57. ACTIVITY 10. *Read and complete the text.*

Key: 2 Italy, 3 pizzas, 4 made, 5 cheese, 6 meal, 7 taste, 8 top, 9 cook, 10 largest, 11 meters, 12 flour, 13 900

WB57. ACTIVITY 11. *Read and order the text.*

Key: 8, 2, 1, 5, 6, 4, 7, 9, 10, 3

Extra activities: see page T105 (if time)

Optional activity

- Unit 6 Song worksheet from *Kid's Box AE Teacher's Resource Book 5* (see pages 50 and 55).

Ending the lesson

- Sing the song from the beginning of the lesson with the class again. This time, everyone mimes as groups take turns singing their verse.

11 Listen and match. Check and sing.

My name's Mario,
I'm an Italian cook.
If you want to make a pizza,
Then listen to me and look. [e]

Take salt, yeast, flour, and water,
Put them in a bowl.
Mix them all together,
And wait for it to grow. [a]

When the base is bigger,
Throw it in the air.
Use your hands to turn it,
Don't get it in your hair. [b]

Now you choose your topping,
Tomato, pepper, and cheese.
You can choose anything,
Sausage, onion, and meat. [d]

Cook for 15 minutes,
Then put it on a plate.
Cut it with a knife and fork,
Mmm. Now that tastes great! [c]

12 Listen and write the words.

2- fork | 3- flour | 4- pizza | 5- salt | 6- pepper | 7- Knife | 8- spoon | 9- olives | 10- oven

1. plate

13 Read and complete. Write the recipe in your notebook.

HW

Ingredients

For the pasta: 

To serve: 

- Put the flour onto the table.
- Make a hole in the center of the flour. Break the eggs into the hole.
- Mix the eggs with a fork. Slowly mix the flour with the eggs.
- When you have a ball of dough, mix it with your hands.
- Roll the ball of dough to make it thin. Cut it into long thin pieces with a knife.
- Put some salt in hot water and cook the pasta for about ten minutes.
- Take the pasta out of the water and put it onto a big plate.
- Add some oil, some olives, and cheese. Mix it with a spoon.
- Put some black pepper on top.
- What does it taste like?

14 (09 CD3) Focus on phonics

Daisy loves limes, lemons, and plums.
She enjoys music and playing the drums.

Lucy likes rice, salad, and sports.
She also likes science and riding her horse.

Speaking 15 Plan a party. Ask and answer.

You and your friends are going to have a party.
Talk about it. Use these words to ask questions.

Where?	What time / finish?
When?	What / eat?
How many people?	What / drink?
What time / start?	What / need?

Where are we going to have the party?

We can have it at the playground.

Or we can have it in my backyard.

OK.

Writing 16 Write about your plans for the party.

Plan for party
- backyard
- Saturday
- 20

We're going to have the party in my backyard ...

(10 CD3) Joke Corner

Why do fish live in salt water?

Because they don't like pepper.

OBJECTIVES: By the end of the lesson, students will have practiced the phonemes /z/ and /s/, planned a party and completed a writing activity.

• TARGET LANGUAGE

Key language: the phonemes /z/ and /s/, *going to*, *wh-* questions, *poem*, *diamante*, parts of speech
Review: food, clothes, adjectives, *party*, *need*, *start*, *finish*

• MATERIALS REQUIRED

Paper for each student

Warmer

- Ask students to give you some food and eating words. Write them randomly on the board. If they give you words in the singular form, change to the plural (*plates*, *forks*, etc.). Ask students to read the words on the board aloud. Put the words into two columns, one for the words containing /s/ and one for the words containing /z/. For example:
  /s/ *rice, salt, spoon, forks, plates;*
  /z/ *olives, limes, lemons, cheese, eggs, knives*. Ask students why they think the words are in two separate columns. Prompt to elicit the difference between the two sounds. Write the phonemes at the top of the relevant columns.

SB58. ACTIVITY **14.** *Focus on phonics*

- Tell students to open their Student's Books to page 58. Focus them on Activity 14. Play the CD. Students repeat after each line and then after the whole rhyme. Repeat once more, making sure students say the /z/ and /s/ sounds correctly. In pairs, students practice the rhyme.

CD 3, 09

As in Student's Book

SB58. ACTIVITY **15.** *Plan a party. Ask and answer.*

F toward

- Focus students on the Activity 15 instructions. Ask them if they like parties and when they last went to a party. Ask a student to read the prompts for the activity aloud and check students realize they will use *going to* because they are talking about plans. Read through the prompt words with the class and elicit some examples for each to give them ideas for their discussions. Make pairs. Students first decide the reason for the party (birthday, end of the week, exam results, etc.). Then they take turns asking and answering / discussing the questions and making plans. They write notes in their notebooks as they decide. At this stage, they don't need to write full sentences – only notes. Go around the class as they are working and find out about their ideas. Provide any useful vocabulary to pairs at this stage.

SB58. ACTIVITY **16.** *Write about your plans for the party.*

- Focus students on the Activity 16 instruction and on the examples and check they know what to do. Students work individually to write their plans. They swap their first draft with their partner. They check through each other's work and make suggestions for improvement/corrections. They can also remind each other what they decided about the party. Students write a final draft of their own text in their notebooks.

SB58. JOKE CORNER

- Focus students on the Joke Corner and review the meaning of *joke*. Play the CD as students read the joke in their books. Play the joke a second time and explain if necessary.

CD 3, 10

As in Student's Book

WB58. ACTIVITY **12.** *Write the words in the columns.*

- Tell students to open their Workbook to page 58. Check they know the meaning of all the words in the box. Point out the example answers and make sure students concentrate on the sounds of the underlined letters. Students complete the activity in pencil. Tell them to say the words aloud again to help.

WB58. ACTIVITY **13.** *Listen, check, and say.*

- Play the CD for students to listen and check. They compare answers in pairs. Check with the class. Play the CD again for students to listen and repeat.

Key: See audioscript below

CD 3, 11

"s" sound: Lucy, scarf, caps, dangerous, center, smell
"z" sound: Daisy, amazing, words, animals, cheese, potatoes

WB58. ACTIVITY **14.** *Read this diamante poem and answer the questions.*

- Before students do the activity, focus them on the Write it right box and check they understand what *poems* are and, in particular, what *diamante poems* look like.

Key: 1 winter, 2 Students' own answers

WB58. ACTIVITY **15.** *Look at the poem again and complete the chart.*

Key: 2 words: adjectives; 3 words; 4 words: nouns; 3 words: action verbs; 2 words: adjectives; 1 word: noun

WB58. ACTIVITY **16.** *Write your diamante poem.*

Key: Students' own answers

Extra activities: see page T105/T106 (if time)

Ending the lesson

- Do the Phoneme rhyme from the beginning of the lesson again.

OBJECTIVES: By the end of the lesson, students will have read a story, reviewed language from the unit, and completed a self-evaluation.

• TARGET LANGUAGE

Key language: language in the story, *a trap*
Review: language from the unit, imperatives

• MATERIALS REQUIRED

Extra activity 2: A black canvas or cotton bag, some objects for students to feel (different from the ones you used at the beginning of the unit) that they won't immediately guess, e.g., a wooden hinged snake, a belt, a doll's shoe
Optional: *Kid's Box AE Teacher's Resource Book 5* Unit 6 Topic worksheet (page 56)

Warmer

- Make groups of four. With books closed, students recap the story so far. Elicit a sentence from each group of four in chronological order. If they give too little information at any time, say, e.g., *But what happened before that? How did they/he get there?*

SB59. STORY. *Diggory Bones.*

- Tell students to open their Student's Books to page 59. Focus them on the story. Tell them to look quickly to find the animals in the story and the sounds they are making (spiders – tickle, snake – hiss). Set the questions: *Look at the first picture. Does Brutus feel pleased?* (No, he doesn't.) *How does Brutus feel?* (frightened/scared/afraid) *Why does Brutus feel frightened? What wants to eat the spiders? What does Diggory use his belt for? What's the dog? At the end, who falls into the snake bowl first? How do you think Emily felt?* (afraid/ scared/angry) *How do you think Diggory felt?* (angry/worried) *How do you think Brutus felt?* (pleased/ happy). Play the CD with books closed. Students listen to find the answers. They check in pairs with books open. Check with the class (He hates spiders. The snake. To get Brutus out of the snake bowl. It's the door. Emily). Play the CD again. Students listen and read. Stop after each frame for students to repeat. At the end, check general comprehension by asking, e.g., *What do you think a trap is? What woke the snake up? Why did Brutus want to get out of the snake bowl? Why did they fall into the snake bowl at the end of the episode?*

CD 3, 12

As in Student's Book

WB59. ACTIVITY **17.** *Read and answer.*

Key: 2 There are spiders and a snake inside the snake bowl. 3 Diggory uses his belt to get Brutus out of the snake bowl. 4 Diggory has The Baloney Stone now. 5 The dog is the door. 6 Brutus pushes Emily into the snake bowl.

WB59. ACTIVITY **18.** *Correct the sentences.*

Key: 2 The dangerous ancient trap is called a snake bowl. 3 Brutus hates spiders. 4 The snake woke up. 5 Diggory used his belt to help Brutus out of the snake bowl. 6 Brutus thought the dog was the door.

WB59. DO YOU REMEMBER?

- Students try to do the activity first without looking back through the unit. Once they have tried to complete all the sentences, they can look back through the unit to find the answers.

Key: 2 like, 3 fork, 4 oven, 5 Students' own answers, 6 seven

WB59. CAN DO

- Focus students on the *Can do* section of the page. Ask a student to read the first sentence. Elicit what this means, with examples, and elicit/remind them of the activities they did in this unit when they talked about the five senses. Review what the three faces mean (not very well / OK / very well). Remind students they circle the one they think is true for them. Repeat for the second sentence, eliciting/ reminding them of the activities when they talked about planning a party. Students circle the appropriate face. Repeat for the third sentence, eliciting what they remember about the diamante poem structure and the poems they wrote.
- Say *Now show and tell your friends.* Students work in groups of three and take turns showing their work for / talking about each one.

Extra activities: see page T106 (if time)

Optional activity

- Unit 6 Topic worksheet from *Kid's Box AE Teacher's Resource Book 5* (see pages 50 and 56).

Ending the lesson

- Ask students which rhyme/song they'd like to do again from the unit. Do it together to end the lesson.

DIGGORY BONES

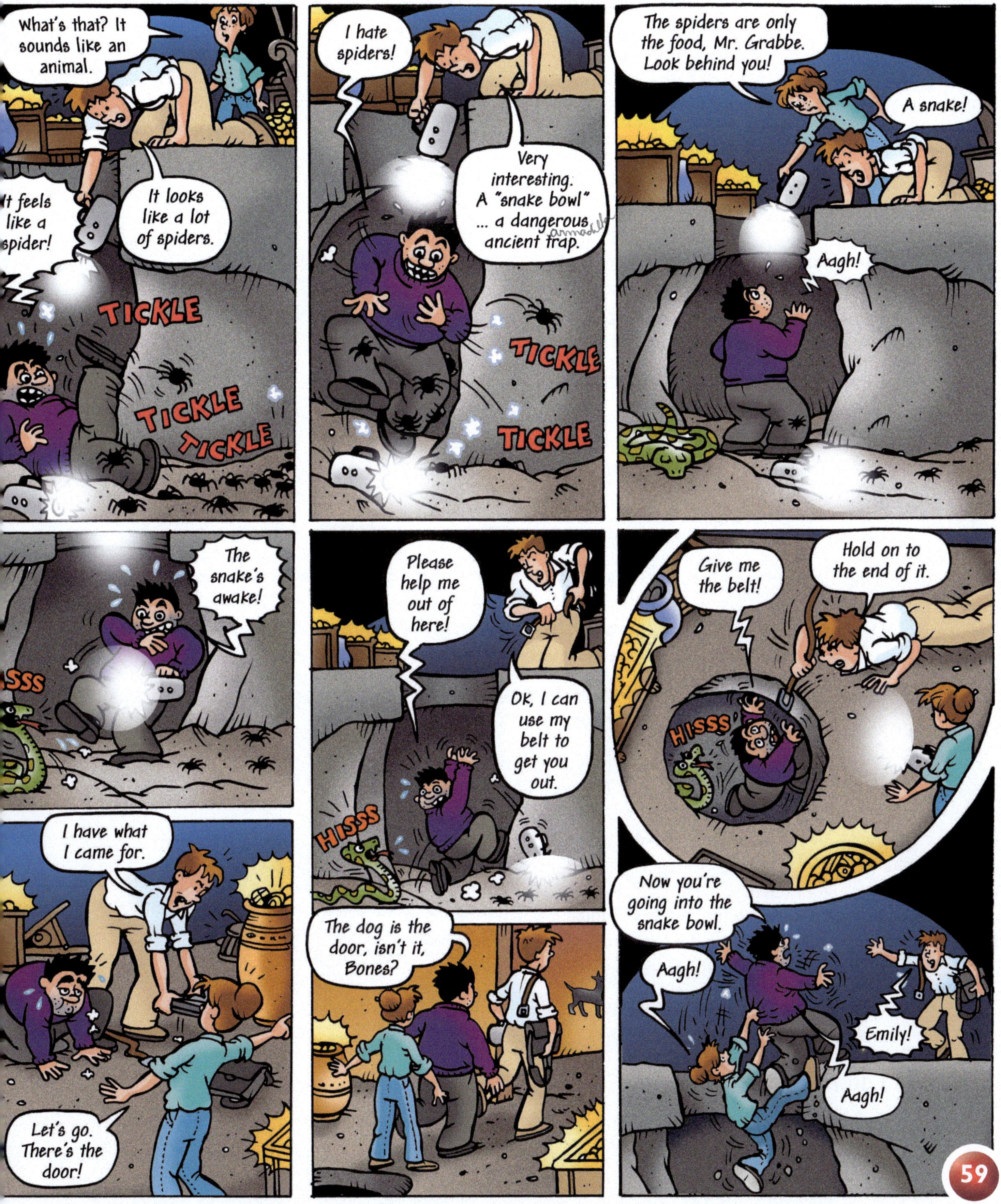

Art Optical illusions

FACT: Our eyes and brain can't always understand everything. How many legs does this elephant have?

1 Look and read. Answer the questions.

When we look at something, light travels from the object to our eye. The eye sends messages to the brain, and the brain tries to understand the message. Because the brain can't understand everything, it tries to make things simpler or easier for us to understand. Some artists play games with this and create amazing paintings and pictures that use "optical illusions." An optical illusion makes us believe we see one thing when really we see something else. It's a great surprise!

Look at these paintings. Which one do you prefer?

Donald Rust painted this picture. It is called *Bison*. Bison are big animals, similar to cows. We can see there are some bison in a field, but when we study the picture more carefully we can find some more.

How many bison are there? Where are they?

This painting is by Salvador Dali and is called *Mae West*. At first sight it looks like a woman's face, but if we look more closely, her face looks like a room with a red wall and a floor that is made of wood. Her hair looks like curtains.

What do her eyes, nose, and mouth look like?

The painting on the right is called *The Human Condition*. It was painted by Rene Magritte. Look at it very carefully.

What can you see?

When we look at it the first time, we think we are looking out of a window, but when we look at it more carefully we can see that there is a painting in front of the window.

What can you see in the painting?

2 Read again and choose a title.

a) Face painting **b)** Understanding pictures **c)** Looking out the window

OBJECTIVES: By the end of the lesson, students will have read about optical illusions and suggested a title for the text.

• TARGET LANGUAGE

Key language: *brain, optical illusion, study / look more closely/ carefully, curtains, surprise, amazing*

Additional language: *Human Condition, bison, Salvador Dali, Rene Magritte, Mae West*

Review: senses

• MATERIALS REQUIRED

Warmer: A picture in a book by an artist students might know

Rulers to check some of the optical illusions

Extra activity 1: One or two works by Escher, ideally *Relativity* and *Reptiles*, in reference books, on posters or projected onto the wall of the classroom

Extra activity 2: A long strip of paper, glue and scissors for each student. A ready-made Mobius strip: take a strip of paper, give it a half-twist, and join the ends together with glue to form a loop.

Warmer

- Show students the picture you brought with you. Elicit what it is (a picture/painting) and ask them if they know the name of the artist. Elicit other artists that they know or have heard of and ask them why they like their pictures (or maybe don't like them).

SB60. FACT

- Tell students to open their Student's Books to page 60. Focus them on the top of the page and say *Did you know … ?* Ask a student to read the fact to the class. Students look at the picture and tell you the answer. Give them time to look more closely so that they find the illusion. Tell them this is called an *optical illusion.* Elicit if they have seen other ones, e.g., on the back of cereal boxes or in magazines.

SB60. ACTIVITY **1.** *Look and read. Answer the questions.*

- Focus students on the Activity 1 instructions and on the pictures around the text. Give them time to look at the pictures to see if they can see the optical illusions in them. Discuss ideas with the class before they read.
- Focus students on the questions in bold throughout the text. Read each section with the class, stopping to discuss the question each time and to check understanding of key vocabulary. Students do not need to understand all the words in the text.

Key: Students' own answers

SB60. ACTIVITY **2.** *Read again and choose a title.* F toward

- Focus students on the Activity 2 instruction and on the three titles. They reread the text silently and then, in pairs, choose the best title. They find evidence in the text to support their choice. Discuss choices and reasons with the class.

Key: b) Understanding pictures

WB60. ACTIVITY **1.** *Read the text. What does it say? Write it correctly.*

Key: Can you understand what this sentence says? The letters are mixed so when you look at it, it is difficult to understand. Because your brain is very smart, it can read it.

WB60. ACTIVITY **2.** *Look at the pictures. What can you see?*

Key: 1 Yes, 2 a You, Me; b LIFT, 3 d, 4 They are both the same length. 5 a lion, 6 a mouse

WB60. ACTIVITY **3.** *Make your optical illusion.*

Key: White and black. No gray. Diagonal lines.

Note: The eye/brain can't see the difference between the gray-white and gray-black lines. It makes its own line.

WB60. ACTIVITY **4.** *Write about your favorite optical illusion.*

Key: Students' own answers

Extra activities: see page T106 (if time)

Ending the lesson

- Review with students what they have done and what they learned about in today's lesson.

OBJECTIVES: By the end of the lesson, students will have read more about optical illusions and completed a project.

• TARGET LANGUAGE

Key language: *optical illusions*, *show* (n.), *modern art*
Review: senses, colors

• MATERIALS REQUIRED

For each student, a pen, glue, white cardboard, scissors, string, colored pencils, compass (to draw a circle)
Extra activity 1: Paper for each student

Warmer

- Review with students what they learned about in the previous lesson and which optical illusion they thought was the smartest and why.

SB61. ACTIVITY 3. *What can you see? Talk in pairs.*

- Tell students to open their Student's Books to page 61. Focus them on the Activity 3 instructions and check they know what to do. Students work in pairs, discussing the questions for the pictures as they read. Give students time to think about / do each of the tasks.
- Focus on the texts, questions, and pictures one by one with the class. Elicit their answers to the questions and what they can see in the pictures. Some students might need help seeing the optical illusions, especially b). Encourage students to show each other. Check understanding of key words with students as they read.

Key: Students' own answers

SB61. PROJECT. *Make an optical illusion.*

- Focus students on the project and on the title and confirm that they are going to make their own optical illusions. Read the project information through with the class, showing the materials they need as they are mentioned. Check understanding of the procedure. Hand out the materials. Students work individually to make the optical illusion. Monitor and help where necessary and remind students that they can ask their friends if they are stuck. Draw a simple mouse and some cheese on the board if this helps them.
- Students show each other the optical illusions they have made and talk about what happens to the mouse and the cheese.

WB61. ACTIVITY 5. FLYERS Reading and Writing, Part 5 *Look at the picture and read the story. Write some words to complete the sentences about the story. You can use 1, 2, 3, or 4 words.* (F) toward

- Tell students to open their Workbook to page 61. Direct them to the activity instructions and check understanding. Elicit what students can see in the picture. Elicit/Pre-teach *show* and *modern art*. Go through the example. Students work in pairs. They read the story and write 1 to 4 words in each space. Monitor and help as necessary. They compare their answers in pairs. Check with the class.

Key: 1 a brother, 2 went to an, 3 people, 4 looked, 5 painting

Extra activities: see page T106 (if time)

Ending the lesson

- Review with students what they talked and read about in today's lesson and which activities they liked best from this and the previous lesson.

3 What can you see? Talk in pairs.

a) Julian Beaver drew this picture. He's sitting next to it. How did he draw it? What can you see?

b) Can you see an old woman or a young woman?

c) Say the color of these words quickly. Do you have any problems? Why?

red blue yellow purple green
yellow blue green red blue
purple green red yellow red
blue purple green red blue
yellow red blue purple red
green yellow purple blue

d) Look at this. What can you see? Are the lines straight?

e) Which two animals can you see? Which way are they looking?

Project Make an optical illusion.

You need:

- A pen
- Glue
- White cardboard
- Scissors
- String
- Colored pencils
- A compass

How to make the optical illusion:

1 Draw two circles on the cardboard.

2 Cut the circles out. On one circle, draw and color a piece of cheese. On the other, draw a mouse. Color them in.

3 Glue the circles together. Make one small hole at the top and one at the bottom.

4 Put some string through each hole and make circles with it.

5 Spin the disc quickly and watch the mouse and the cheese. They're in the same place.

Review Units 5 and 6

1 Read the text. Choose the right words and write them on the lines.

Kid's Blog

Hi everyone,

Here are a few lines to tell you about (1) our __________ soccer team. We're (2) __________ the Springfield Flyers. We (3) __________ indoor soccer on weekends, and we play against other teams from towns close to ours. There (4) __________ seven of us on the team. We always change players (5) __________ only five can play at a time.

(6) __________ week we played against the team from Fairview. They played really (7) __________, and they won 4–1. We (8) __________ the first goal, but then they scored the next four. We're going to win our next game though.

That's all for now,
Robert

1	our	we	us	5	but	because	so
2	called	calling	call	6	Next	Every	Last
3	plays	playing	play	7	well	good	beautiful
4	is	am	are	8	marked	scored	do

2 13 CD3 Listen and check (✓) the box.

1 When's David's birthday?

a 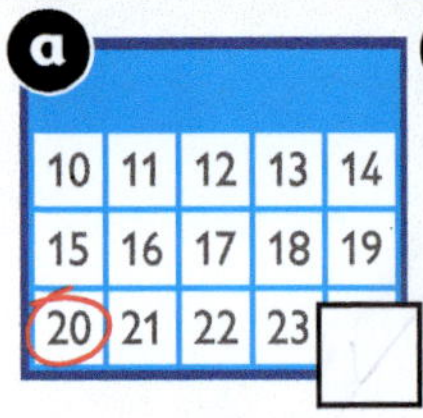

b 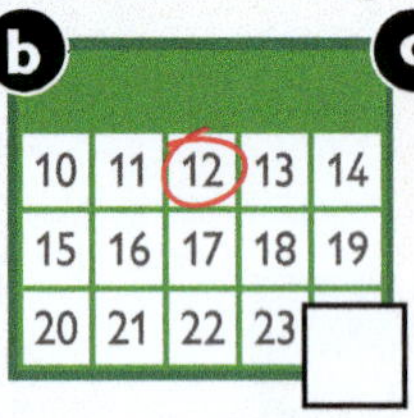

c 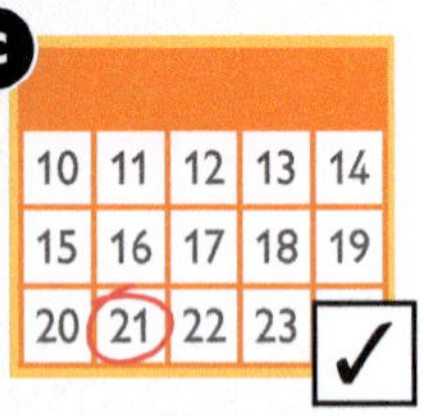

2 What's he going to do on Saturday?

a 

b 

c 

3 What time's the party?

a 

b 

c 

4 Where are they going to go?

a 

b 

c 

5 What was his favorite present last year?

a 

b 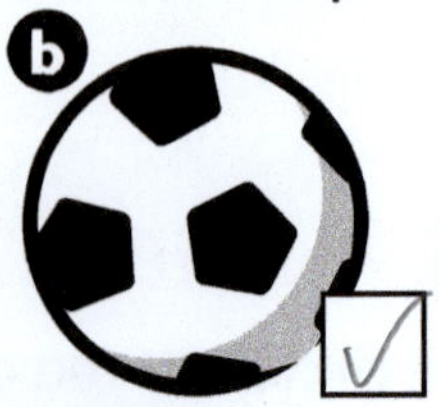

c 

6 What would he like to get this year?

a 

b 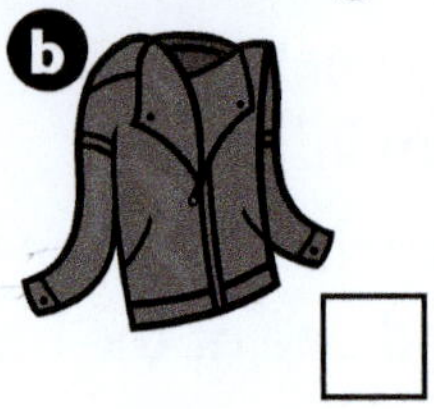

c 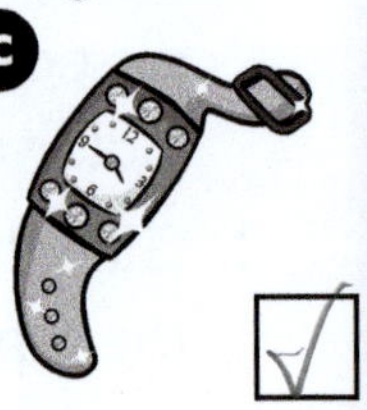

OBJECTIVES: By the end of the lesson, students will have reviewed language from Units 5 and 6 and done a listening activity.

● TARGET LANGUAGE

Key language: vocabulary and language from Units 5 and 6, *blog*

Review: sport, past tenses, *going to*

● MATERIALS REQUIRED

Key vocabulary from Units 5 and 6, each word written on a small piece of paper, enough for each student in the class

Extra activity 1: A sheet of cardboard marked out into 8 squares for each pair of students

Warmer

- Make groups of six. Hand out a word to each student. They keep their word secret. They take turns providing a definition of their word for the other students in their group to guess. If time, regroup students and repeat.

SB62. ACTIVITY 1. *Read the text. Choose the right words and write them on the lines.* F toward

- Tell students to open their Student's Books to page 62. Focus them on the text and elicit that it's an internet page and that it's a *blog*. Teach/Check understanding of *blog*. Ask students if any of them have written blogs on the Internet. Focus students on the picture and tell them this is the topic of the blog. Check students have read the activity instructions and know what to do. They read the text individually and choose which word is best for each blank. Remind them to read the words around the blanks and to look at the pronouns, nouns, and words like *Last week* before trying to choose the words.
- Students check their work in pairs / small groups. Check with the class by getting different students to read the text aloud sentence by sentence. Where several students chose incorrect answers, elicit why the word they chose doesn't work in the blank. Focus students on collocations, e.g., *score a goal*.

Key: 2 called, 3 play, 4 are, 5 because, 6 Last, 7 well, 8 scored

SB62. ACTIVITY 2. *Listen and check (✓) the box.* F toward

- Focus students on the Activity 2 instruction. Give them time to study the pictures before they listen. Play the CD and do the example first with the class. Play the rest of the CD in one go. Students listen and check. They check in pairs. Play the CD again. Check with the class.

Key: 2a, 3c, 4b, 5b, 6c

CD 3, 13

1. When's David's birthday?

MISS LAKE: Good morning, David.

DAVID: Good morning, Miss Lake. Did you know it's my birthday tomorrow?

MISS LAKE: Really? What's the date then?

DAVID: It's January 21.

2. What's he going to do on Saturday?

DAVID: I'm not going to have a party tomorrow, though.

MISS LAKE: Why not?

DAVID: Because we have school tomorrow. But I am going to have a party on Saturday. All my friends are coming.

3. What time's the party?

MISS LAKE: That's good. What time's your party going to start?

DAVID: It's going to be in the afternoon, at half past three.

4. Where are they going to go?

MISS LAKE: Are you going to have the party in your house?

DAVID: No, we're not. Not this year.

MISS LAKE: What are you going to do?

DAVID: We're going to the movies. We're going to see *Shep 5*.

5. What was his favorite present last year?

MISS LAKE: And do you think you're going to get a lot of presents?

DAVID: I don't know. I did last year.

MISS LAKE: Which was your favorite?

DAVID: It was this soccer. Do you like it?

MISS LAKE: Yes. It's nice!

6. What would he like to get this year?

MISS LAKE: And what would you most like to get this year?

DAVID: I'd love a gold watch.

MISS LAKE: A gold watch?

DAVID: OK … a silver one!

WB62. ACTIVITY 1. *Read the story. Choose words from the box to complete the sentences.* F toward

Note: There are five extra words in the box.

Key: 2 like, 3 made, 4 plastic, 5 felt, 6 pizza

WB62. ACTIVITY 2. *Choose a title for this episode of* Friendly. F toward

Key: b) A sweet dress

WB62. ACTIVITY 3. *Find the one that doesn't belong.*

Key (possible answers): 2 Wool because it isn't food. 3 Eyes because they aren't a verb/sense. 4 Bracelet because you don't eat with it. 5 Stone because it doesn't come from an animal. 6 Glass because it doesn't come from trees.

Extra activities: see page T106 (if time)

Ending the lesson

- Play a game of *Time bingo*. Draw 12 clocks on the board, each showing a different time. Write a number under each clock. Students draw a 2 x 2 bingo square in their notebooks and write a number in each square corresponding to four of the clocks. Call out the times quickly at random. Students cross out numbers that correspond to the clocks. The first student to cross out all four shouts *Bingo!* Elicit the times from the student before declaring him/her the winner.

OBJECTIVES: By the end of the lesson, students will have reviewed language from Units 5 and 6 and played a game.

• TARGET LANGUAGE

Key language: vocabulary and language from Units 5 and 6
Review: language for playing games

• MATERIALS REQUIRED

Board game: Dice, colored counters
Ending the lesson: Large sheet of paper for each group of three
Optional: *Kid's Box AE Interactive DVD 5: The classroom* Quiz 3, *Kid's Box AE Teacher's Resource Book 5* Test Units 5–6 (pages 106–120), *Kid's Box AE Workbook 5 Language Portfolio* page 93

Warmer

- Write *Materials* on the board and brainstorm all the materials students can remember, with books closed, in two minutes. It is not necessary to write the words on the board.

SB63. ACTIVITY 3. *Play the game.*

- Tell students to open their Student's Books to page 63. Elicit that this is a board game. Focus them on the instructions and check understanding. Elicit what the seven materials are (metal, paper, wood, flour, glass, wool, plastic) and get them to make a list in their notebooks. Students play in groups of four. They take turns throwing the dice and moving around the board, saying what the item is and what it is made of. The other students decide if the student has done this correctly or not. They can help each other with interpreting the instructions. If they are right, they have another turn, crossing off the materials on their list. If they make a mistake, they stop. If they stop on something made of a material they have, they miss a turn. The winner is the first person to get seven things made of different materials.
- Monitor students as they are playing the game.

Note: It is acceptable for students to describe *flour* as a material here.

WB63. ACTIVITY 4. *Complete the sentences. Count and write the letters.*

Key: 2 taste 5, 3 knife 5, 4 Wool 4, 5 weak 4, 6 like 4, 7 ears 4, 8 spoon 5, 9 Silver 6, 10 plastic 7, 11 Wood 4, 12 made 4, 13 thirsty 7, 14 plate 5

WB63. ACTIVITY 5. *Now complete the crossword puzzle. Write the message.*

Key:

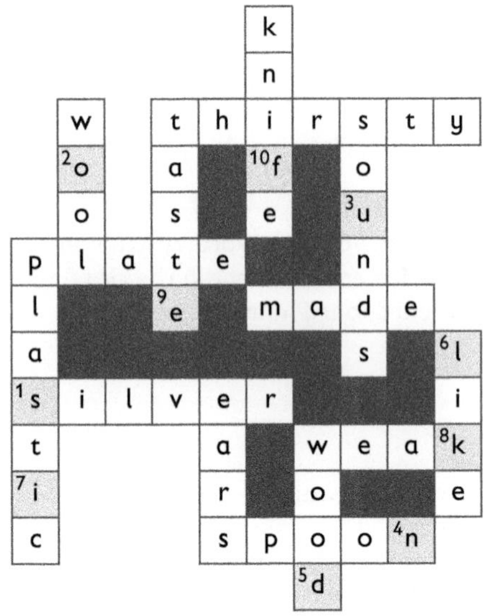

Message: sounds like fun!

WB63. ACTIVITY 6. *Quiz time!*

Key: 2 It's made of glass bottles. 3 It's used to make movies. 4 Strong blue cheese smells like Alex's socks. 5 It makes pizzas. 6 It looks like a woman's face and a room.

WB63. ACTIVITY 7. *Write questions for your quiz in your notebook.*

Key: Students' own answers

Extra activities: see page T106 (if time)

Optional evaluations

- Quiz 3 from *Kid's Box AE Interactive DVD 5* (*The classroom* section). This quiz can be done as a whole-class activity or as a team competition. See pages 36 and 37 of the Teacher's Booklet for the Interactive DVD.
- The test for Units 5–6 from *Kid's Box AE Teacher's Resource Book 5* (see pages 106–120) F toward

Language Portfolio

- Students complete page 93 of *Kid's Box AE Workbook 5 Language Portfolio* (I can ... Units 5 and 6).

Ending the lesson

- Students work in groups of three. They find the *Can do* Workbook sections for Units 5 and 6 (pages 51 and 59) and write the six statements on a large sheet of paper. They discuss and give examples for each *Can do* statement, checking back in the Student's Book, the Workbook, or their notebooks if necessary. Elicit some examples from volunteer students in the class for each one.
- Ask students which lessons, topics and/or activities were their favorites.

3 Play the game.

Collect the materials

Instructions

- The winner is the first person to get seven things made of different materials.
- Roll the die and move your counter. Say what you can see and what it's made of. If you're right, take another turn. If you're wrong, stop.
- If you stop on something made of a material that you have, miss a turn.

7 Natural world

Show what you know! What nature words can you remember?

Listening **1** 14 CD3 Listen and check (✓) the nature words you hear.

2 15 CD3 Listen again. Say "yes" or "no."

1 They have five days to write their ezine project. (No.)
2 Dan thinks they should put some sunblock on.
3 A man's taking glass bottles and plastic bags out of the lake.
4 He has to do this every day.
5 People should put their garbage in the garbage cans.
6 The kids shouldn't tell their friends about the problem.

LOOK

People **should take** their garbage with them.

They **shouldn't leave** it on the grass.

What **should** we **do** about this?

3 Read and match.

1 It's very hot
2 When the sun is strong
3 We shouldn't leave
4 We should always
5 We shouldn't throw our
6 What should we

a do to help?
b our garbage on the grass.
c garbage into lakes or rivers.
d clean up after a picnic in the country.
e so we should put our hats on.
f we should use sunblock.

OBJECTIVES: By the end of the lesson, students will be able to talk about the natural world and give advice using *should* and *shouldn't.*

• TARGET LANGUAGE

Key language: advice: *should/shouldn't*; *natural world, nature, garbage, path*
Review: materials, country, clothes, weather, *sunblock, lake, have to,* suggestions: *Let's*

• MATERIALS REQUIRED

Extra activity 1: The CD script from Student's Book Activity 1 written on a large sheet of paper
Optional: *Kid's Box AE Teacher's Resource Book 5* Unit 7 Reinforcement worksheet 1 (page 58)

Warmer

- Introduce the topic of the natural world by eliciting from students what kinds of things they can see in the country. Tell students the theme of Unit 7 is the *Natural world* (nature) and write it in the center of the board.

SB64. SHOW WHAT YOU KNOW! *What nature words can you remember?*

- Draw a circle around *Natural world* on the board and write one or two of the words students said in the warmer to start a mind map. Say *Show what you know … about the natural world.* Brainstorm nature words and create a mind map on the board. Supply words in English where necessary. Students copy the mind map into their notebooks.

SB64. ACTIVITY 1. *Listen and check (✓) the nature words you hear.*

- Tell students to open their Student's Books to page 64 and look at the Activity 1 pictures. Elicit the names of the characters and where they are.
- Play the CD. Students listen and check. They check in pairs. Use the mind map on the board to check with the class.

CD 3, 14

Dan: This is great! A day in the country!
Alex: Yeah, but we only have two more days to write our next ezine project and we don't have a topic. What should we write about?
Maria: I don't know, but it's very hot, so we should put our hats on.
Dan: Phew! You're right. The sun is strong. I think we should put some sun cream on, too. Here you go.
Maria: Thanks, Dan. Do you want some, Alex?
Alex: Uh. Eh? Look! What's that man doing? Let's go and see.
Alex: Excuse me. Can you tell me what you're doing?
Man: Sure. I'm taking the glass bottles and plastic bags out of the lake because they're dangerous for wild birds. I have to do this every week.
Dan: That's terrible! People should put their garbage in the cans. They shouldn't leave it on the grass or throw it in the lake.
Maria: What should we do about this? Can we do anything to help?
Man: Well, most people don't know that this is a big problem for birds and other animals, so you should tell your friends and family about it.
Alex: Yeah. We should write about it in the ezine.
Dan: Come on! We have a job to do.

SB64. ACTIVITY 2. *Listen again. Say "yes" or "no."*

- Focus students on the Activity 2 instructions and on the sentences. Give students reading time before they listen. Check students understand the key vocabulary in the sentences. Play the CD. Students whisper the answer to their friend the first time they listen. Play the CD again and check, eliciting full-sentence correct answers from the class for the "no" responses. Elicit from students any new words to add to the mind map.

Key: 2 Yes. 3 Yes. 4 No. (He has to do this every week.) 5 Yes. 6 No. (They should tell their friends about the problem.)

CD 3, 15

Presentation

- Elicit sentences 5 and 6 (the uncorrected versions) from Activity 2 and write them on the board. Underline *should/shouldn't* in each sentence.
  Elicit what this tells us. Say the sentences for students to repeat. Elicit other things we should or shouldn't do in the country.
- Play the CD from Activity 1 again. When students hear sentences with *should/shouldn't,* they raise their hands. Stop the CD and elicit what was said. Elicit the question *What should we do?* and write it on the board. Elicit a story summary.
- Focus students on the Look box.

SB64. ACTIVITY 3. *Read and match.*

- Focus students on the Activity 3 instruction. Students do the activity in pairs. Check and replay the CD if necessary.

Key: 1e, 2f, 3b, 4d, 5c, 6a

WB64. ACTIVITY 1. *Read and match.*

Key: 3, 5, 1, 6, 4, 2

WB64. ACTIVITY 2. *Think and write "should" or "shouldn't."*

Key: 2 shouldn't, 3 should, 4 should, 5 shouldn't, 6 should

WB64. ACTIVITY 3. *Correct the sentences.*

Key: 2 ~~to~~, We should walk on the paths. 3 ~~should~~ shouldn't, We shouldn't drop our garbage. 4 ~~always should~~ should always, We should always use garbage cans. 5 ~~of~~, We shouldn't play with animals in fields. 6 ~~We's~~ We, We shouldn't drink water from rivers.

Extra activities: see page T106 (if time)

Optional activity

- Unit 7 Reinforcement worksheet 1 from *Kid's Box AE Teacher's Resource Book 5* (see pages 57 and 58).

Ending the lesson

- Ask students *What should you do at the end of the lesson?* Students respond with sentences, using *should* and *shouldn't.*

OBJECTIVES: By the end of the lesson, students will have had more practice giving advice and sung a song.

• TARGET LANGUAGE

Key language: advice: *should/shouldn't*; question form: *Should … ?*; things/animals in the natural world: *bear, cow, tree, field; problem*

Additional language: *(is) after me*

Review: action verbs, adverbs

• MATERIALS REQUIRED

One piece of A4 card for each group of four

Extra activity 2: One piece of paper for each student

Optional: *Kid's Box AE Teacher's Resource Book 5* Unit 7 Song worksheet (page 62)

Warmer

- Elicit the title of the unit (Natural world) and elicit some of the things you should and shouldn't do to protect the environment. (Remind students of the impersonal use of *you*.) Write two of the examples they give on the board: one positive and one negative. Focus students on the verb following *should/shouldn't* and elicit what kind of word it is (infinitive without *to*).

SB65. ACTIVITY 4. *Listen and complete. Check and sing.*

- Tell students to open their Student's Books to page 65. Focus them on the song and the words in the box. Elicit that these are all infinitives without *to* that students use to complete the song. Give students time to read through the song silently and to try to predict some of the words before playing the CD. Play the CD. The first time they listen, students don't write anything. They listen, look, and think. They then discuss the song in pairs and add any words they can remember. Play the CD again for students to complete the song. They check again in pairs. Play the CD, stopping after each verse to check the verbs and understanding of key vocabulary. Play the CD a fourth time, line by line and then verse by verse, for students to repeat. Make two groups: one that asks the questions and one that answers. They sing the song in role. Play the first version of the song on the CD and then the karaoke version. Repeat, with groups changing roles.

Key: put, clean, stop, climb, go, walk, run, jump

CD 3, 16

As in Student's Book and key

CD 3, 17

Now sing the song again. (Karaoke version)

SB65. ACTIVITY 5. *Look and choose the right answer.*

- Focus students on Activity 5 and on the instruction. Check they know what to do. In pairs, they look at each picture and choose the correct answer. (The aim of the questions is to trigger discussion. The right answer isn't always clear.) Pairs check with pairs. Check with the class. If students have different ideas, elicit their reasons. Elicit another sentence of advice (positive or negative) for each picture from students.

Key (possible answers): 1a, 2b, 3a, 4a, 5b, 6a

SB65. ACTIVITY 6. *Play the "should" game.*

- Tell students they are going to play a game. Focus them on the Activity 6 instruction and on the speech bubbles. Elicit other situations/prompts where someone responds with advice, e.g., *I'm hungry/thirsty/tired. We're having a picnic in the country. / I have a toothache / a headache. English is difficult. I don't understand this word. / The sun's very strong. / It's my mom's birthday tomorrow.* Make groups of four. Hand each group a piece of thin cardboard. They cut it into eight pieces and write a different prompt on each. Encourage them to include their own ideas.
- Groups take turns reading prompt cards aloud for other groups to respond. Give points for a) grammatically correct responses and b) appropriate ones.

WB65. ACTIVITY 4. *Match the problems with the correct advice.*

Key: 2b, 3a, 4e, 5c, 6d

WB65. ACTIVITY 5. *Think and write advice.*

Key: Students' own answers

WB65. ACTIVITY 6. *Answer the questions.*

Key: Students' own answers

Extra activities: see page T106 (if time)

Optional activity

- Unit 7 Song worksheet from *Kid's Box AE Teacher's Resource Book 5* (see pages 57 and 62).

Ending the lesson

- Sing the song from the beginning of the lesson again.

4 Listen and complete. Check and sing. (16 CD3)

Dictation

go	stop	~~drop~~	jump	climb	run	clean	walk	put

You shouldn't drop your garbage,
You should put it in a garbage can.
You shouldn't leave it on the ground,
You should clean up everything.
Here comes the bear, here comes the bear!
It's coming for your lunch!

Should I move or should I stop **?**
Should I climb **that tree?**
I should do something now.
That bear / cow is after me.

You shouldn't go across the field,
You should walk around.
You shouldn't go too close to that cow,
It can push you to the ground.
You should run …
You should jump quickly!

5 Look and choose the right answer. (Possible answers)

1

a) They shouldn't play close to a busy road.
b) They should play carefully.

2

a) He should brush his teeth.
b) He should go to the dentist.

3

a) They should go home.
b) They should wait under a tree.

4

a) They should put their garbage in the garbage can.
b) They shouldn't eat sandwiches outdoors.

5

a) They should walk quietly through the field.
b) They shouldn't go into the field.

6

a) She should wash her hands before she eats.
b) She should wash her hands after she eats.

6 Play the "should" game.

I have an exam tomorrow.

You should go to bed early.

You should study.

You should eat a healthy breakfast.

Reading 7 Read and think. What should you do to help?

http://www.cambridge.org/elt/kidsbox/ezine

Kid's Box Ezine!

home | reports | games | world | email

There are about 1,000 endangered species of animals and birds, and even more species of insects in danger, like butterflies. We should protect them so that they do not become extinct.

Kid's Box reports
Nature Watch

a

b

Two of the world's most famous endangered animals are also famous for their stripes. They are mountain zebras and Siberian tigers. They need big forests to live in, but these forests are smaller nowadays because people cut trees down for wood.

To help protect the tigers in Russia, they made two National Parks. These also protect them from people who want to catch them for their beautiful striped fur.

c

This is the nine-spotted ladybug beetle. It has four black spots on each wing and one in the middle of its body. It lives in North America, and it is an endangered species.

The Lost Ladybug Project asks people to take photos of this beetle if they see it.

d

Frogs are in danger all over the world. The frog in the picture is Lehmann's poison frog. It is found in Colombia. It has red, orange, or yellow stripes.

People named 2008 the "Year of the Frog."

e

Butterflies are beautiful flying insects. This butterfly is the purple spotted butterfly. It has white spots on its purple wings. Every year millions of butterflies fly to a different place. Some die when cars hit them.

In 2007, the Taiwanese government closed a busy highway to protect the purple spotted butterfly!

extinct | wings | spots | spotted | stripes | striped | butterfly | insect | beetle

8 18 CD3 Listen. Repeat the word and find it in the text. 1 Wings. Wings.

9 Read again and answer.

1 How many endangered species are there?
2 Which animal has red, orange, or yellow stripes?
3 Which animal has a spotted body and wings?
4 Where does the Lehmann's poison frog live?
5 Which animal has white spots on its wings?
6 What did they do to protect butterflies in Taiwan?

OBJECTIVES: By the end of the lesson, students will have read and talked about endangered species.

• TARGET LANGUAGE

Key language: *endangered species, extinct, insect, protect, striped, stripes, spots, spotted, zebra, forest, beetle, wing, butterfly, national park, poison, in danger*

Additional language: *Siberia, Russia, North America, Colombia, Taiwan, extinction, highway*

Review: *should*, animals, adjectives, parts of speech

• MATERIALS REQUIRED

Extra activity 1: A large world map, an A4 photocopy of a map of the world for each student, small pieces of paper

Extra activity 2: Paper for each pair of students

Optional: *Kid's Box AE Teacher's Resource Book 5* Unit 7 Reinforcement worksheet 2 (page 59), *Kid's Box AE Workbook 5 Language Portfolio* page 100

Warmer

- Pre-teach *spotted* and *striped*, using students' clothes or other objects in the room. Then ask students to think of any animals they know that are spotted or striped. Ask different students to write the words on the board and to spell them out.

SB66. ACTIVITY 7. *Read and think. What should you do to help?*

- Tell students to open their Student's Books to page 66. Focus them on Activity 7. Tell them to skim the text quickly to find any spotted or striped animals they mentioned in the warmer. Elicit from the class.
- Focus students on the activity instructions. Ask a student to read them aloud. Check understanding. Focus students on the text and elicit that it's the webpage for *Kid's Box* ezine and that it's about animals and nature. Read the introduction aloud to students and use the context to elicit what they think *endangered species* means. Teach the meaning of this phrase. Pre-teach *highway*. Say *It's a big road where cars can drive fast.*
- Focus students on the words at the bottom of the webpage, read them through with the class and elicit/check understanding. Students read the texts silently and think about their answers to the question for each situation. They briefly compare their ideas in pairs. Focus on each text one at a time. Discuss what the problem is, what has happened, and what advice they would give. Discuss their opinions as a class. Finally, give students further reading time, check general comprehension, and answer any questions they have.

SB66. ACTIVITY 8. *Listen. Repeat the word and find it in the text.*

- Focus students on the Activity 8 instructions and on the example. Play the CD. Pause after each word to give students time to find the word in the text. They point to the word in the text. Play the CD again. Elicit a choral response each time.

Key: 2 extinct, 3 spotted, 4 insect, 5 striped, 6 spots, 7 stripes, 8 butterfly, 9 beetle

CD 3, 18

1 wings, 2 extinct, 3 spotted, 4 insect, 5 striped, 6 spots, 7 stripes, 8 butterfly, 9 beetle

SB66. ACTIVITY 9. *Read again and answer.*

- Focus students on the Activity 9 questions. Students work in groups of three and find the answers to / discuss the questions. Elicit answers from the class and provide any new vocabulary on the board. Discuss with students other endangered animals that they know of, what they look like, and what, if any, steps are being taken to protect them. Focus on local species if possible.

Key: 1 about 1,000, 2 Lehmann's poison frog, 3 the nine-spotted ladybug beetle, 4 in Colombia, 5 the purple spotted butterfly, 6 They closed a busy highway.

WB66. ACTIVITY 7. *Choose words from the box to label the pictures.*

Key: 2 Siberian tiger, 3 nine-spotted ladybug beetle, 4 Lehmann's poison frog, 5 purple spotted butterfly

WB66. ACTIVITY 8. *Unscramble and write the words.*

Key: 2 butterfly, 3 insect, 4 spot, 5 stripe, 6 fur, 7 tail, 8 body, 9 beetle

WB66. ACTIVITY 9. *Now match the words with the definitions.* F toward

Key: 2 fur, 3 wings, 4 tail, 5 body, 6 butterfly, 7 insect, 8 spot, 9 stripe

WB66. ACTIVITY 10. *Write the words in the chart.*

Key:

adjectives	verbs	prepositions	nouns
extinct	recycle	into	extinction
spotted	appear	over	wing
warm	explore	across	stripe

- Students can write more words for each group in their notebooks.

Extra activities: see page T107 (if time)

Optional activity

- Unit 7 Reinforcement worksheet 2 from *Kid's Box AE Teacher's Resource Book 5* (see pages 57 and 59).

Language Portfolio

- Students complete page 100 of *Kid's Box AE Workbook 5 Language Portfolio* (An endangered animal).

Ending the lesson

- Brainstorm with students a mind map on the board of all the new words they learned about animals today.

OBJECTIVES: By the end of the lesson, students will have described pictures of animals and further practiced giving advice, using *should* and *shouldn't*.

• TARGET LANGUAGE

Key language: measurements, descriptions, numbers, *female, male, bat, riverbank, habitat, ocean, pond, stream, disappear, You can … , I think we should/shouldn't … , I agree, I don't agree.*

Additional language: *endangered animals*

Review: animals, comparative adjectives, colors

• MATERIALS REQUIRED

Extra activity 1: A large sheet of paper for each group of four, colored markers

Extra activity 2: Word processors for groups to write their texts and reference materials / the Internet

Optional: *Kid's Box AE Teacher's Resource Book 5* Unit 7 Extension worksheet 1 (page 60)

Warmer

- Describe one of the animals from the previous lesson for students to guess with books closed. Students can then take turns describing an animal, in particular what it looks like, e.g., *spotted/striped*, for the class to guess.
- Write on the board: *ocean, lake, stream, river.* Ask *Which do you think is bigger, a pond or a lake? A stream or a river?* Explain that ponds and streams are smaller than lakes and rivers. Ask students to make sentences with *bigger* and *smaller*, using the words on the board.

SB67. ACTIVITY 10. *Look at the pictures. Describe them to your friend.*

- Tell students to open their Student's Books to page 67. Focus them on the Activity 10 instructions, pictures, and speech bubbles. Check understanding of *male* and *female*. Check students know what to do. They take turns saying sentences describing the pictures. Monitor and prompt where necessary. Elicit descriptions from the class.

SB67. ACTIVITY 11. *Listen. Write words or numbers.*

- Focus students on the information for Activity 11. Check they realize it's about the same butterfly as in Activity 10. Give students reading time and check understanding of key vocabulary, e.g., *measure*. Play the CD. Students complete. They check in pairs. Play the CD again. Check with the class.

Key: 1 birdwing butterfly, 2 20, 3 30, 4 brown with white spots on its wings, 5 brown with blue stripes on its wings

CD 3, 19

MARY: Oh, hello, Mr. Burke. Can I ask you some questions? Is that OK?

MR. BURKE: Hello, Mary. Yes, of course. What about?

MARY: Well, it's about a butterfly I want to do my project on. I have some information, but I want to find out some more.

MR. BURKE: OK. Which butterfly is it?

MARY: It's called the Queen Alexandra's birdwing butterfly.

MR. BURKE: Oh, yes. I know the one. It's an endangered species from Papua New Guinea, isn't it?

MARY: That's right. Its habitat is getting smaller and smaller every year. Can you tell me about it, please?

MR. BURKE: OK. What do you want to know?

MARY: Well, I read in a book that it's the biggest butterfly in the world. Is that right?

MR. BURKE: Yes, it is. But the male is smaller than the female. From one edge of the male's wing to the other it can measure 20 centimeters.

MARY: 20 centimeters. But the female's bigger?

MR. BURKE: Yes, it is. Its wings can measure 30 centimeters.

MARY: Wow! That's a big butterfly! What about their colors?

MR. BURKE: Well, both butterflies are brown. The female has some small, white spots on its wings.

MARY: And the male?

MR. BURKE: It's brown, too, but it has blue stripes on its wings.

MARY: That's really interesting. Thanks very much, Mr. Burke.

SB67. ACTIVITY 12. *Read and complete.*

- Focus students on Activity 12. Ask them to look at the text quickly and to tell you what it's about (advice on what to do to make the world a better, cleaner place). Check understanding of the words in the box. Students do the task individually and then check in pairs. Check with the class. Check general comprehension of the text as well as of individual words, e.g., *riverbank*.

Key: 2 extinct, 3 should, 4 yard, 5 trees, 6 butterflies

SB67. ACTIVITY 13. *Look at the pictures. Talk about what you should do.*

- Focus students on the Activity 13 pictures. Ask two students to read the speech bubbles. Elicit other ideas for one or two of the other pictures. Elicit/Provide a response for disagreement and write it on the board, e.g., *I don't agree with you.* Students work in groups of three. They take turns making suggestions for each picture and responding, either agreeing or disagreeing.

Key: Students' own answers

WB67. ACTIVITY 11. *Match the pictures of endangered animals with the words.*

Key: 2c, 3e, 4g, 5d, 6b, 7f, 8h

WB67. ACTIVITY 12. *Now find out one fact about each of the endangered animals in Activity 11.*

Key: Students' own answers

WB67. ACTIVITY 13. *Now make a quiz for your friends.*

Key: Students' own answers

WB67. ACTIVITY 14. *Read and order the story.*

Key: 4, 8, 1, 3, 6, 5, 2, 7

Extra activities: see page T107 (if time)

Optional activity

- Unit 7 Extension worksheet 1 from *Kid's Box AE Teacher's Resource Book 5* (see pages 57 and 60).

Ending the lesson

- Write key words from the unit so far in scrambled form on the board. Students work individually with books closed to write each word correctly. They check in pairs before you check with the class. Check the meanings of the words.

10 Look at the pictures. Describe them to your friend.

The female is brown.

The male is more beautiful than the female.

Queen Alexandra's birdwing butterfly

Male

Female

11 19 CD3 Listen. Write words or numbers.

Mary's project

Name of butterfly	1 Queen Alexandra's birdwing butterfly
Wings measure (Male)	2 20 cm
Wings measure (Female)	3 30 cm
Description (Female)	4 brown white white spots on its wings
Description (Male)	5 brown white blue stripes on its wings

12 Read and complete.

~~thousands~~ should yard butterflies trees extinct

There are (1) thousands of endangered species in the world. *Endangered* means there is time to help them before they disappear. They are not (2) extinct. So what should we do? We (3) should take care of our world and ask everybody to help make it a cleaner place for animals and insects to live in. We should make oceans, ponds, streams, and the air much cleaner than they are now … and you can help, too! (Teacher correct with ss)

You can:

- help clean and protect the habitat in your (4) yard, close to your house, or on your school ground.
- build homes for animals in (5) trees.
- plant trees and flowers where insects like (6) butterflies can live.
- help projects to plant riverbanks with plants that make the ground stronger and give animals a habitat.

13 Look at the pictures. Talk about what you should do. Ss' own answers.

I think we should recycle all bottles.

Yes, I agree.

14 Focus on phonics

Spots and **stripes** – **cats** and **dogs**,
Black and **white** – **fish** and **frogs**.
Pink and **green** – **dogs** and **cats**,
Legs and **wings** – **birds** and **bats**!

Speaking 15 Ask and answer.

What should you do?

1 You see someone throwing paper onto the floor. What should you do?
a) Tell them they dropped it. **b)** Do nothing. **c)** Pick it up and recycle it.

2 You see a man making a fire in a field.
a) Do nothing. **b)** Call the fire department. **c)** Tell an adult.

3 You're going to go shopping at the supermarket.
a) Take some old plastic bags. **b)** Buy a lot of candy.
c) Use a lot of plastic bags from the supermarket.

4 You find some money in the street.
a) Put it in your bag. **b)** Take it to the police station. **c)** Do nothing.

5 You see a strange bag on a bus.
a) Tell the bus driver. **b)** Do nothing. **c)** Pick it up.

6 You see a man climbing through the window of the house next door.
a) Do nothing. **b)** Call the police. **c)** Stop and talk to him.

Writing 16 Write your questionnaire.

- Work in pairs and write another questionnaire.
- Think of six problems.
- Think of three possible solutions to each problem.
- Write them out like the ones above.
- Now you can ask your friends the questions.

Joke Corner

Why did the man throw the butter out of the window?

To see the butterfly.

OBJECTIVES: By the end of the lesson, students will have practiced saying and identifying weak forms of *and* and completed a writing activity.

• TARGET LANGUAGE

Key language: weak form of *and*, advice: *should, shouldn't;* collocations with *and*

Review: natural world, materials, clothes, school

• MATERIALS REQUIRED

Extra activity 1: Write the following words, each on a piece of paper: *cats, dogs, spots, stripes, fish, frogs, bats, birds, black, white, sharks, whales, burger, fries, gold, silver, salt, pepper, knife, fork, shoes, socks.* You will need one word for each student. If you have more than 22 students, add one or more pairs of words. If you have fewer, take away pairs of words.

Warmer

- Write these words on one side of the board: *black, socks, burger,* and these on the other: *fries, shoes, white.* Ask students to match them for you and elicit, e.g., *black and white.* Repeat for students, making the *and* very weak. Repeat for the other two pairs. Ask students what happens to the *and* between the words (it almost disappears) / has the vowel sound /ə/.

SB68. ACTIVITY **14.** *Focus on phonics.*

- Tell students to open their Student's Books to page 68. Ask them to look at Activity 14. Play the CD. Students repeat after each line and then after the whole rhyme. Repeat once more, making sure students say the pairs of words and pronounce the weak form of *and* correctly. In pairs, students practice the rhyme.

CD 3, 20

As in Student's Book

SB68. ACTIVITY **15.** *Ask and answer.*

- Focus students on the questionnaire in Activity 15. Do the first question with the class as an example. Make sure students realize there is no one correct answer, so they need to think about which they would do and why. Students work in pairs. They take turns reading out the questions and then saying which answers they prefer. Monitor and prompt the discussions by asking, e.g., *Why?* Go through the questionnaire as a class, having students raise their hands to see how many students have chosen the different answers and asking different students to give reasons for their choices.

Key: Students' own answers

SB68. ACTIVITY **16.** *Write your questionnaire.*

- Focus students on Activity 16. Read the activity instructions through with the class and check they understand what to do. Brainstorm some other problems to get them started. Monitor and help students prepare their questionnaires in pairs. Make groups of six for students to ask and answer with their friends.

SB68. JOKE CORNER

- Focus students on the Joke Corner and review the meaning of *joke.* Play the CD as students read the joke in their books. Play the joke a second time and explain if necessary.

CD 3, 21

As in Student's Book

WB68. ACTIVITY **15.** *Write the opposites.*

- Tell students to open their Workbooks to page 68. Make sure they know the meaning of all the words in the box. They work in pairs and write their answers in pencil. Do not confirm answers at this stage.

WB68. ACTIVITY **16.** *Listen, check, and say.*

- Play the CD for students to listen and check. Check with the class. Play the CD again for students to listen and repeat. Make sure they are using the weak form of *and.*

Key: See audioscript below

CD 3, 22

1 young and old
2 hot and cold
3 black and white
4 day and night
5 short and long
6 weak and strong
7 present and past
8 first and last

WB68. ACTIVITY **17.** *Read and number the parts of the letter.*

- Before students do the activity, focus them on the Write it right box and check they understand what the six points mean with reference to polite letters.

Key:

2. March 15, 2015
3. Mrs. Smith
4. I'm writing to ask you for information about recycling bins at our school.
5. Regards
6. Emily Wood

WB68. ACTIVITY **18.** *Now write a letter to Mrs. Green about recycling. Ask her for information about the recycling bins.*

Key: Students' own answers

Extra activities: see page T107 (if time)

Ending the lesson

- Do the Pairs rhyme from the beginning of the lesson again.

OBJECTIVES: By the end of the lesson, students will have read a story, reviewed language from the unit, and completed a self-evaluation.

• TARGET LANGUAGE

Key language: language in the story, *parents*

Additional language: *Queen Hetepheres*

Review: language from the unit, adjectives, colors

• MATERIALS REQUIRED

Photocopiable 7 (see page T96) copied onto thin cardboard, one copy for each pair of students, scissors, envelopes

Optional: *Kid's Box AE Teacher's Resource Book 5* Unit 7 Topic worksheet (page 63)

Warmer

- Elicit from students what they remember about the snake bowl from the last episode of the story: what was living there, what the animals looked like, and who went down into the snake bowl at the end of the episode.

SB69. STORY. *Diggory Bones.*

- Tell students to open their books to page 69. Focus them on the story and check who is in the snake bowl in the first frame. Set the questions: *How many snakes does Diggory say are in the snake pit? How does he describe them? Why does Brutus want to turn on the computer? What is at the bottom of the ladder?* Play the CD with books closed. Students listen to find the answers. They check in pairs with books open. Check with the class. (Two. One has spots and stripes but the other doesn't, i.e. Brutus. To find instructions to get out of the snake bowl. The butterfly room of Queen Hetepheres / thousands of butterflies.)
- Play the CD again. Students listen and read. Stop after each frame for students to repeat. At the end, check general comprehension by asking, e.g., *What advice does Brutus give Diggory about his daughter? Who is the weak, ugly snake with no spots and stripes? Why doesn't Diggory need instructions to get out of the snake bowl? Why should Emily be careful on the ladder? What's in the room? What color are the spots on the butterflies' wings? What do the butterflies want to protect?*

CD 3, 23

As in Student's Book

Photocopiable 7 (see pages T89 and T96)

WB69. ACTIVITY **19.** *Read and answer.*

Key: 2 Because it's old and not very strong. 3 It takes them to the famous butterfly room of Queen Hetepheres. 4 They're orange and black striped with white spots on their wings. 5 He shouldn't touch anything. 6 young butterflies/insects

WB69. ACTIVITY **20.** *Read and order the text.*

Key: From left to right: 5, 1, 9, 8, 4, 3, 2, 7, 6

WB69. DO YOU REMEMBER?

- Students try to do the activity first without looking back through the unit. Once they have tried to complete all the sentences, they can look back through the unit to find the answers.

Key: 2 shouldn't, 3 photographs, 4 stripes, 5 cold, 6 address

WB69. CAN DO

- Focus students on the *Can do* section of the page. Ask a student to read the first sentence. Elicit what this means with examples and elicit/remind them of the activities they did in this unit when they described insects and animals. Review what the three faces mean (not very well / OK / very well). Remind students they circle the one they think is true for them. Repeat for the second sentence, eliciting/reminding them of the activities when they talked about things they should and shouldn't do. Students circle the appropriate face. Repeat for the third sentence, eliciting information about the letters they wrote.
- Say *Now show and tell your friends.* Students work in groups of three and take turns showing their work for / talking about each one.

Extra activity: see page T107 (if time)

Optional activity

- Unit 7 Topic worksheet from *Kid's Box AE Teacher's Resource Book 5* (see pages 57 and 63).

Ending the lesson

- Ask students which rhyme/song they'd like to do again from the unit. Do it together to end the lesson.

DIGGORY BONES

23 CD3

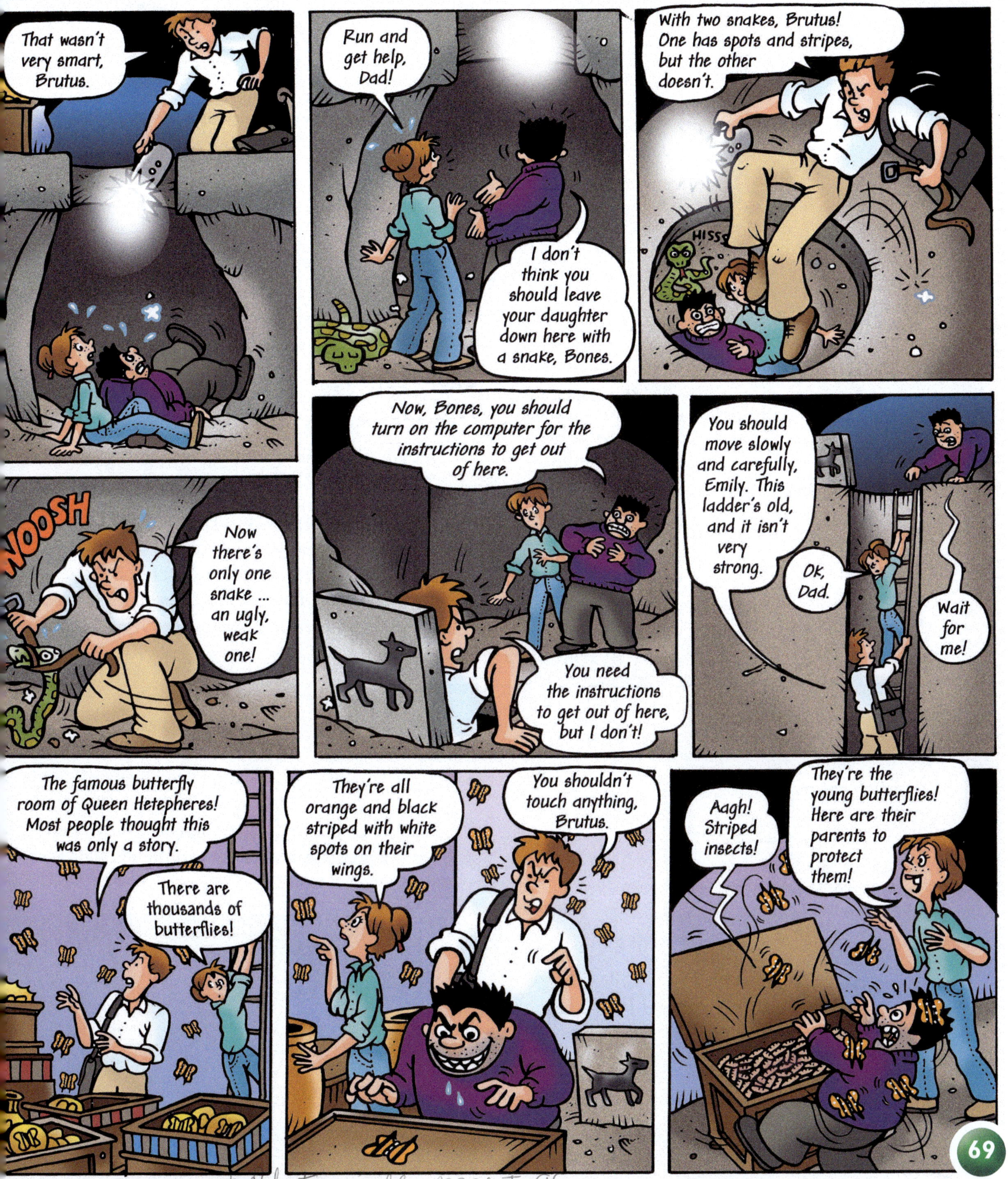

*Photocopiable - page T-96

Science Extinction

FACT: **Some scientists think that in the last 600 years more than 44,000 different insects have become extinct.**

1 Read and answer.

1. Give three reasons animals become extinct.
2. When did the last dinosaurs die?
3. Why did big animals disappear?
4. What did the asteroid do?
5. What happened to the weather?

2 Read again and find words that mean:

1. a family of animals
2. when an animal family dies
3. a big rock from space
4. when the earth moves
5. the opposite of "die"

3 Make a mind map.

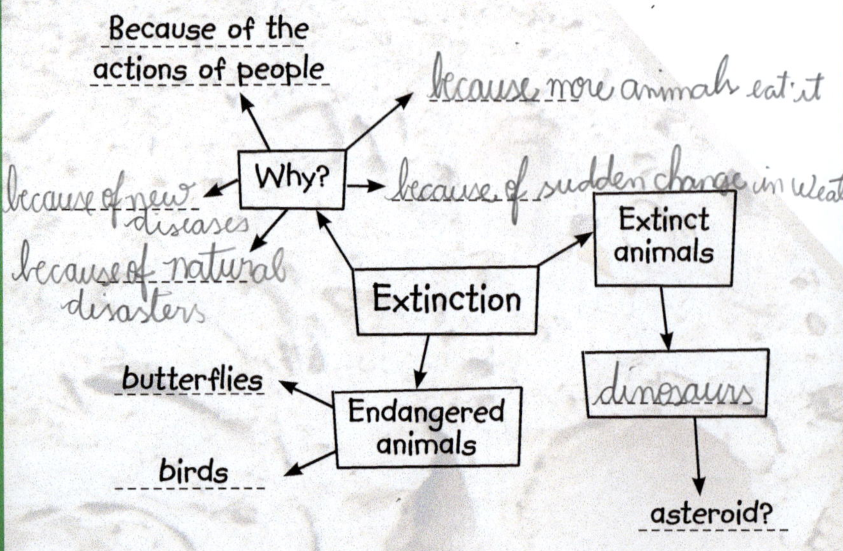

Extinction

Animals can become extinct when all of their species or family die. When an animal family is in danger of extinction, we call it an endangered species.

A species can become extinct because of many different things:

- more animals eat it
- sudden changes in the weather
- natural disasters
- new diseases
- the actions of people

The most famous extinct animals are the dinosaurs, which died out more than 65 million years ago. People have different ideas about why the dinosaurs became extinct.

Before they disappeared, there was a lot of plate movement. This means that there were volcanic eruptions, earthquakes, tsunamis, and changes in the ocean level. The earth also got colder. These things killed a lot of dinosaurs, but something else happened that killed all animals over 25 kg and a lot of smaller plants and animals.

The most popular idea is that an asteroid, an enormous rock from space, hit the earth and made a big hole. It also started a lot of fires, earthquakes, tsunamis, and storms. The weather became colder, so a lot of plants died. Bigger animals didn't have anything to eat, so they couldn't live.

OBJECTIVES: By the end of the lesson, students will have read about reasons for animal extinctions and about the extinction of the dinosaurs.

• TARGET LANGUAGE

Key language: *dinosaur, asteroid, disease, die out, disappear*
Additional language: *space, Diplodocus, Archaeopteryx*
Review: natural disasters, adjectives, animals

• MATERIALS REQUIRED

Extra activity 1: Reference books on the extinction of the dinosaurs / relevant internet sites, a large sheet of paper for each group
Extra activity 2: Reference books on extinct animals
Optional: *Kid's Box AE Teacher's Resource Book 5* Unit 7 Extension worksheet 2 (page 61)

Warmer

- Write *Extinct animals* on the board and brainstorm with students some of the extinct animals that they know. For each animal, ask students if they know when it became extinct and why. Accept general figures for when. Ask students if they think animals are becoming extinct now.

SB70. FACT

- Tell students to open their Student's Books to page 70. Focus them on the top of the page. Ask a student to read the fact to the class. Elicit their responses to the fact, in particular the number of insects that have become extinct.

SB70. ACTIVITY **1.** *Read and answer.*

- Focus students on the Activity 1 instruction and on the pictures.
- Ask different students to read the questions aloud. Don't explain words in the text at this stage. Students read the text quickly (and silently) to find answers to the five questions. They check and discuss their answers in pairs. Check with the class.
- Read the first paragraph through with the class, with students taking turns reading. Discuss the information in the paragraph and check understanding of key vocabulary. Elicit any other information about anything mentioned in the paragraph. Repeat the procedure for the other paragraphs.

Key: 1 Three of the following reasons: more animals eat them, sudden changes in the weather, natural disasters, new diseases, the actions of people, 2 more than 65 million years ago, 3 The most popular idea is that an asteroid hit the earth. 4 It made a big hole and started a lot of fires, earthquakes, tsunamis, and storms. 5 It became colder.

SB70. ACTIVITY **2.** *Read again and find words that mean:*

- Focus students on the Activity 2 instructions and check they understand what to do. Do the first one as an example with the class. Students re-read the text silently to find the words. Then they check in pairs. Check with the class.

Key: 1 species, 2 extinction, 3 asteroid, 4 earthquake, 5 live

SB70. ACTIVITY **3.** *Make a mind map.*

- Focus students on Activity 3 and elicit what this is (a mind map). Elicit other ideas for each section, reminding students to look back at the text to find the information they need. Students copy the mind map into their notebooks and develop the other sections. Go around the class and make suggestions as to what students can include where necessary.

Key:

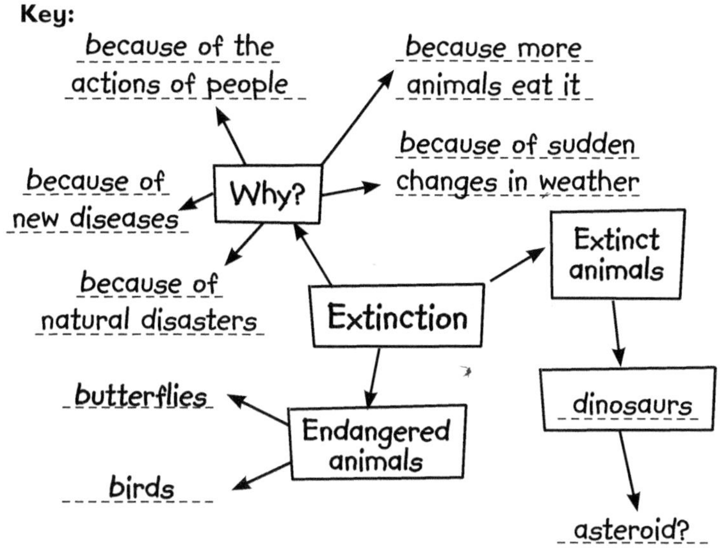

WB70. ACTIVITY **1.** *Read the fact sheet and complete the text.*

Key: 2 fifty, 3 Germany, 4 30, 5 wings, 6 three, 7 hundred, 8 animal, 9 meat

WB70. ACTIVITY **2.** *Now read and write about the Diplodocus.*

Key: Students' own answers

Extra activities: see page T107 (if time)

Optional activity

- Unit 7 Extension worksheet 2 from *Kid's Box AE Teacher's Resource Book 5* (see pages 57 and 61).

Ending the lesson

- Review with students what they have done and what they have learned about in today's lesson.

OBJECTIVES: By the end of the lesson, students will have read about fossils and completed a project.

• TARGET LANGUAGE

Key language: *fossils, fossilized, footprint, go hard, knead*
Review: animals, body parts

• MATERIALS REQUIRED

Reference books on local fossil findings, local museum information sheets, the Internet, etc. If possible, invite a local archeologist to the class.
For each student, flour, salt, water, a bowl; for the class, things to make fossil prints out of, e.g., leaves, shells, cooked and washed bones
Optional: *Kid's Box AE Interactive DVD 5: The school hall* "Fossil hunt" episode

Warmer

- With books closed, review with students what they learned about in the previous lesson. Review key vocabulary. Ask students how we know so much about dinosaurs today. Elicit/Pre-teach *fossil*. Ask students if they have seen any fossils and, if so, what they were of. Check students understand how fossils are made.

SB71. ACTIVITY **4.** *Read and match.*

- Tell students to open their Student's Books to page 71. Focus them on the Activity 4 pictures and elicit what they are (fossils). Check students know what to do. They read the text quickly and silently to match the pictures with the five words in bold in the text. They check in pairs. Check with the class.
- Read the text through with the class, with students taking turns reading. Discuss the information and check understanding. Elicit more information about dinosaur (or other) fossils.

Key: a footprints, b eggs, c teeth, d skin, e bones

SB71. ACTIVITY **5.** *Find out more.*

- Focus students on the Activity 5 instructions and tell them they are going to find out more about dinosaur fossil finds in their country. Students work in groups, using the reference books and/or museum information sheets and/or internet sites to find out the necessary information. If you can, invite a local archeologist to come and give a talk to the class. This can be done in L1 and then students can select relevant information to write / talk about in English.

SB71. PROJECT. *Make a fossil print.*

- Tell students that they are going to make a fossil print for their project today. Show and name the materials you have brought for the project. Read the project information before handing anything to the students, showing the materials as they are mentioned. Hand out the materials to individual students. They follow the instructions to make their fossils and then place them in a cool, dry place. Remind students to write their initials on their fossils when they are still soft. Monitor and help where necessary.

WB71. ACTIVITY **3.** FLYERS **Listening, Part 1.** *Listen and look. There is one example.* F

- Tell students to open their Workbook to page 71. Elicit what they can see. Point out the example. Play the CD. Students check in pairs. Play the CD again. Check with the class. Elicit the name they didn't use (Sarah).

Key: George – next to Harry, Betty – girl eating an apple, Katy – girl drinking orange juice, Holly – next to kangaroos, spotted dress, Richard – in shorts, subject of photograph

CD 3, 24

HARRY: Hi, Mom. Come and look at this!
MOM: What is it, Harry?
HARRY: It's a picture from our field trip. We went to the zoo.
MOM: Oh, yes. That's you – in front of the elephants. You are wearing your gray jacket.

Can you see the line? This is an example. Now you listen and draw lines.

1.
MOM: Who is standing next to you?
HARRY: With the jeans and the striped T-shirt?
MOM: Yes, who's that?
HARRY: That's my friend, George.
MOM: He likes the elephants, too!

2.
MOM: Tell me who else is in the picture.
HARRY: Well, can you see the girl who's eating an apple?
MOM: Yes, she has a T-shirt with a butterfly on it.
HARRY: That's right. She's Betty.
MOM: Oh, OK. I like her T-shirt.

3.
MOM: Who's the girl with brown hair?
HARRY: The girl who's eating an apple?
MOM: No, not her. She's drinking some orange juice.
HARRY: That's Katy. She's new, but she's very friendly.

4.
MOM: Who are these children next to the kangaroos?
HARRY: You know the girl in the polka-dotted dress!
MOM: Really?
HARRY: That's Holly. She came to my party last year.
MOM: You're right. I remember now.

5.
MOM: That boy looks happy.
HARRY: Who? The one who's wearing shorts?
MOM: Yes.
HARRY: That's Richard. The teacher is taking a picture of him.

Extra activities: see page T107 (if time)

Optional activity

- The "Fossil hunt" episode from *Kid's Box AE Interactive DVD 5* (*The school hall* section). See pages 20–23 of the Teacher's Booklet for the Interactive DVD.

Ending the lesson

- Review with students what they talked and read about in today's lesson and which activities they liked best from this and the previous lesson.

4 Read and match.

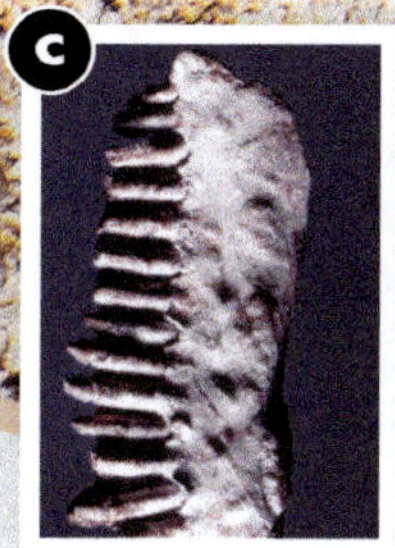

We know about dinosaurs because of fossils. Fossils are made from old bones or parts of animals or plants that change into rocks over a very long time. The most important fossils are from parts of the body or from footprints.

Fossils include:

1 Bones: These fossils are the most important when we want to learn about dinosaurs. Archeologists found the first dinosaur bone in 1818 and they find more and more every day.

2 Teeth: These tell us about what different dinosaurs ate.

3 Eggs: Archeologists found the first fossilized dinosaur eggs in France in 1869.

4 Skin: Some dinosaurs had hard thick skin, like crocodiles.

5 Footprints: Dinosaur footprints were normally made in sand. They are important because they tell us about different things, including:

- how big and how fast a dinosaur was
- if the dinosaur walked on two or four legs
- the bones in the dinosaur's foot

5 Find out more.

Are there any dinosaur fossils in your country? See what you can find out.

Project Make a fossil print.

You need:

- 2 cups of flour
- ½ cup of salt
- ¾ cup of water
- A bowl
- Things to make fossils of (leaves, shells, rocks, cooked and washed chicken leg bones)

How to make your fossil print:

1 Measure and mix together the flour, salt, and water to make a salt dough.

2 Knead the dough for five minutes and make it into balls with your hands.

3 Press your objects into the balls of dough. Make one print in each ball.

4 Put your fossils in a place where they can dry and go hard.

8 World of sports

Show what you know! What sports can you remember?

Listening 1 25 CD3 Listen and check (✓) the sports words you hear.

2 26 CD3 Listen again. Complete the sentences.

1 Today's the school prize day.
2 Good luck in the race, Alex .
3 He's jumped over the sand.
4 He hasn't climbed over the wall .
5 He's lost the race .
6 He's stopped to help a friend .

3 Read and choose the right words.

1 **We're** / **We've** going to give the prize to the winners of the ezine competition.
2 I've **ever** / **never** won any prizes!
3 **You've** / **You haven't** almost finished!
4 He's **cross** / **crossed** the water.
5 He **haven't** / **hasn't** lost.
6 We've **doing** / **done** it!

LOOK

We**'ve done** it.
He **hasn't lost**.
Have you ever **won** a prize?

OBJECTIVES: By the end of the lesson, students will have reviewed sports vocabulary and will be able to talk about their experience of playing sports.

• TARGET LANGUAGE

Key language: present perfect to express: experience with *ever, never* / present relevance, following *It's the first time …* ; *celebrate, obstacle race*, regular and irregular verbs

Review: sports and sports competitions, school, *should*

• MATERIALS REQUIRED

Extra activity 1: The CD script from Student's Book Activity 1 photocopied for every student in the class, the CD script written on a large sheet of paper for display

Warmer

- Mime one or two sports that students know. When they guess, write the sport, e.g., *tennis*, on the board. When there are three or four sports on the board, elicit the headword, *Sports*, and write it in the center of the board.

SB72. SHOW WHAT YOU KNOW! *What sports can you remember?*

- Draw a circle around *Sports* on the board and write the sports from the warmer to start a mind map. Say *Show what you know … about sports*. Brainstorm with the class in two minutes the sports words they can remember and create a mind map on the board. Supply words in English where necessary. Students copy the mind map into their notebooks.

SB72. ACTIVITY 1. *Listen and check (✓) the sports words you hear.*

- Tell students to open their Student's Books to page 72 and look at the Activity 1 pictures. Elicit the names of the characters, where they are, and what they're doing (listening to the principal, who is speaking from a platform outside their school). Remind students they do the same as for the Show what you know in the previous units (check off the words they hear in the Sports mind map in their notebooks).
- Play the CD. Students listen and check. They check in pairs. Use the mind map on the board to check with the class. Elicit why the friends are so excited (they won the ezine competition).

CD 3, 25

TEACHER: Today's the school prize day. First we're going to have our yearly obstacle race. Then we're going to give the prize to the winners of the ezine competition. Runners should go to the starting line.

MARIA: Good luck in the race, Alex.

DAN: Have you ever won a sports prize?

ALEX: I've never won any prizes!

MARIA: He's doing really well.

DAN: Yeah. He's jumped over the sand and he's crossed the water, but he hasn't climbed over the wall. Come on, Alex! You've almost finished!

DAN: What's he doing? He's stopping. I can't believe it. He's lost the race.

MARIA: He hasn't lost, Dan. He's stopped to help a friend.

PRINCIPAL: Good job, Sarah. You've won this year's race. Now, I have the names of the winners of the ezine competition here. They are Maria, Dan, and Alex for the *Kid's Box* ezine.

DAN: We've done it! We've done it!

ALEX: It's the first time I've won a prize!

MARIA: Well, I think we should celebrate. Let's write one more project for the ezine. Let's do it on sports.

DAN AND ALEX: OK.

SB72. ACTIVITY 2. *Listen again. Complete the sentences.*

- Focus students on Activity 2. In pairs, they try to predict what the missing words are. Play the CD again. Students listen for the missing words. They check in pairs.

Key: 1 school, 2 Alex, 3 jumped, 4 wall, 5 race, 6 friend

CD 3, 26

Presentation

- Write sentences 3–6 from Student's Book Activity 2 on the board. Focus students on the new structure (present perfect) in each sentence and underline it. Focus on the form and how the tense is made (auxiliary *have* + past participle). Use concept questions to check students understand the meaning of each sentence. Show students that, e.g., *He's* in sentence 3 is a contraction of *He has*. Make sure students notice that the time, i.e. *when*, is not stated in any of the sentences and that these are things that have only just happened.
- Play the CD from Activity 1 again. When students hear the present perfect, they raise their hands. Stop the CD and elicit what was said (question and/or answer). Elicit a story summary.
- Focus students on the Look box.

SB72. ACTIVITY 3. *Read and choose the right words.*

- Focus students on the first sentence of Activity 3. Tell them to choose the right words: *We're* or *We've*. Elicit the answer as a full sentence. Elicit what the full form of each one is (*We are / We have*). Students complete the activity in pairs, checking with other pairs if necessary. Check with the class by eliciting the full sentence.

Key: 1 We're, 2 never, 3 You've, 4 crossed, 5 hasn't, 6 done

WB72. ACTIVITY 1. *Are these verbs regular or irregular? Write "R" or "I".*

Key: R: believe, stop, play, jump, finish, wash
I: make, meet, catch, win

WB72. ACTIVITY 2. *Make negative sentences.*

Key: 2 She hasn't won a prize. 3 They haven't played basketball. 4 He hasn't climbed the highest mountain. 5 You haven't won the game. 6 We haven't made a kite.

WB72. ACTIVITY 3. *Match the pictures with the text.*

Key: From left to right: 5, 2, 1, 4, 3, 6

Extra activities: see page T108 (if time)

Ending the lesson

- Elicit from students things in their lives they haven't done, but that they would like to. Start with an example, e.g., *I've never visited London, but I'd like to go and see Buckingham Palace.*

OBJECTIVES: By the end of the lesson, students will have had more practice with the present perfect.

● TARGET LANGUAGE

Key language: present perfect for recently completed actions and question forms, contrasting uses of *going to* future, present continuous and present perfect

Review: sports, ordinal numbers, action verbs

● MATERIALS REQUIRED

Optional: *Kid's Box AE Teacher's Resource Book 5* Unit 8 Reinforcement worksheet 1 (page 65)

Warmer

- Ask students *What have you done today?* to review present perfect. Provide some examples to help them if necessary. Write some of their responses on the board.

SB73. ACTIVITY 4. *Choose words to talk about the pictures.*

F toward

- Tell students to open their Student's Books to page 73. Focus them on the first set of pictures in Activity 4 and on the speech bubbles. Ask three students to read them. Check students realize they relate to each picture and that the pictures are in a sequence. Students work in pairs and make sentences about the other pictures using the words in the box. Check sentences, writing the examples on the board for students to copy:

***Going* to future**		**Present continuous**		**Present perfect**
They're going to wash the car.	→	*They're washing the car.*	→	*They've washed the car.*

- Remind students of the meaning of the present perfect: something has just happened (and we can see that it has just happened).

Key: 2 a They're going to wash the car. b They're washing the car. c They've washed the car. 3 a He's going to jump over the bar. b He's jumping over the bar. c He's jumped over the bar. 4 a She's going to cook pasta. b She's cooking pasta. c She's cooked pasta. 5 a She's going to paint the wall. b She's painting the wall. c She's painted the wall. 6 a They're going to walk up the mountain. b They're walking up the mountain. c They've walked up the mountain.

SB73. ACTIVITY 5. *Listen and answer the questions.*

- Focus students on the Activity 5 instruction and on the questions. Give students time to read the questions. Play the CD. Students listen and write their answers. They check in pairs. Play the CD for them to check. Play the CD, stopping after each section to elicit the sentence.

Key: 1 She's opened the box. 2 They've closed their suitcase. 3 He's skipped for 32 hours, 23 minutes and 5 seconds / set a new world record. 4 He's answered the question correctly. 5 They've finished their exam. 6 He's climbed to the top of the climbing wall.

CD 3, 27

1.

GIRL: Look at that box. It's old and made of wood. It looks really interesting. Should we open it?

BOY: I don't think we should.

GIRL: Well, I'm going to open it.
Ooh … It's very difficult.
It's open! Wow! Look what's inside!

2.

WOMAN: Can you help me, please? I can't close this suitcase.

BOY: Oof! It's very full.

WOMAN: I know. Can you sit on it, please?
Great! That's it. We've done it. Now we can go.

3.

MAN 1: He's done it. That's a new world record. He's skipped for 32 hours, 23 minutes and 5 seconds. Congratulations! How do you feel?

MAN 2: I feel great.

4.

TEACHER: Who was the first man to walk on the Moon? Michael?

MICHAEL: Uh, was it Neil Armstrong?

TEACHER: That's right, Michael. Good work!

5.

TEACHER: Put your pencils down, please. You've finished your exam.

BOY AND GIRL: Yay!

6.

INSTRUCTOR: OK, Robert, put your right hand up above your head. Put your left foot on the green rock. You're nearly at the top of the climbing wall. Now, put your left hand up to the top. That's it. Good work!

ROBERT: I've done it! I've climbed to the top!

SB73. ACTIVITY 6. *Read and order the words.*

- Focus students on the Activity 6 instruction. Students write the sentences and then check in pairs. Check with the class.

Key: 1 He's visited his grandmother this afternoon. 2 Have you ever played basketball? 3 She's never been ice skating before. 4 He hasn't done his homework. 5 We've won first prize! 6 Have they entered the competition?

WB73. ACTIVITY 4. *Answer the questions.*

Key: 2l, 3p, 4h, 5a, 6b, 7e, 8t
What's the word?: alphabet

WB73. ACTIVITY 5. *Now make your word puzzle.*

Key: Students' own answers

WB73. ACTIVITY 6. *Write the correct form of the verbs in the email.*

Key: 2 talked, 3 studied, 4 finished, 5 happened, 6 decided, 7 stopped, 8 started, 9 raced, 10 won

WB73. ACTIVITY 7. *Look at the pictures. Write the questions.*

Key: 2 What has he done? 3 What has he done? 4 What has she done? 5 What have they done? 6 What has she done?

WB73. ACTIVITY 8. *Now answer the questions.*

Key: 2 He's won a cup. 3 He's dropped some eggs. 4 She's brushed her hair. 5 They've visited the Tower of London. 6 She's cleaned the floor.

Extra activities: see page T108 (if time)

Optional activity

- Unit 8 Reinforcement worksheet 1 from *Kid's Box AE Teacher's Resource Book 5* (see pages 64 and 65).

Ending the lesson

- Mime a sequence of actions, along the lines of Student's Book Activity 4. Students give the sentences as you mime. Students take turns doing similar mimes for the class.

4 Choose words to talk about the pictures.

wash jump paint cook walk ~~start~~

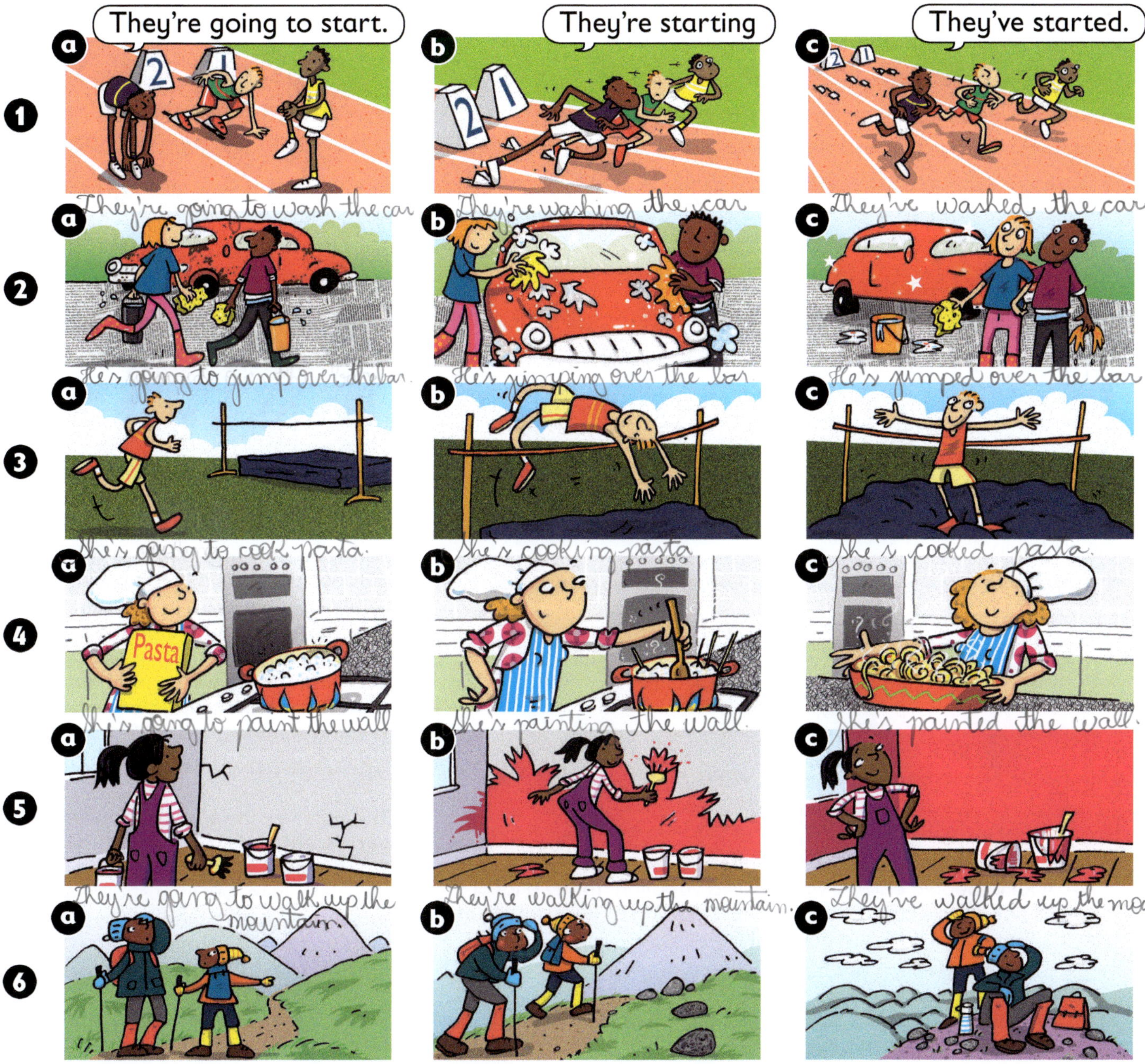

5 Listen and answer the questions.

27 CD3

1 What has she done?
2 What have they done?
3 What has he done?
4 What has Michael done?
5 What have they done?
6 What has Robert done?

6 Read and order the words.

1 this / afternoon. / visited / He's / his / grandmother
2 you / Have / ever / basketball? / played
3 never / ice skating / before. / been / She's
4 He / his / hasn't / done / homework.
5 won / first / We've / prize!
6 entered / the / Have / they / competition?

Reading **7** Read and think. What time of year do people play your favorite sport?

http://www.cambridge.org/elt/kidsbox/ezine

Kid's Box Ezine!

home | reports | games | world | email

When we play some sports, we need the right weather.

Kid's Box reports

Sports for all seasons

a

b

Track and field is a sport that we usually do outside. It's difficult to do in the cold and rain so, in school, we do track and field in the summer. A lot of adults play golf in the summer, but they can play it in the winter, too!

c

d

e

Some sports are only winter sports because we need snow and ice. A lot of people enjoy a winter skiing vacation. Today a lot of young people like snowboarding, too. Sledding is also a lot of fun in the winter. You can sled down a hill.

f

There are other sports that you can play in any season. In England and most of Europe, cycling is a very popular sport. A lot of people cycle in the spring, fall, and winter, not only in the summer. Some people have racing bikes and enter competitions. The most famous bicycle race is the Tour de France, which is in the summer.

The dates for the seasons are different in different parts of the world. In Europe, North America, and Asia, spring is from March to June, but in Australia, Africa, India, and South America, it is from about September to December.

golf | track and field | snowboarding | skiing | sledding | hill | cycling | spring | summer | fall | winter

8 28 CD3 Listen. Repeat the word and say the letter.

1 Skiing.

Skiing. That's "c."

9 Read and correct the sentences.

1 In school they do track and field in the fall.
2 Adults always play golf in the winter.
3 For winter sports we need fog and rain.
4 People go sledding in the summer.
5 The Tour de France is usually in the fall.
6 Spring comes between fall and winter.

OBJECTIVES: By the end of the lesson, students will have read about sports that people do in different seasons.

● TARGET LANGUAGE

Key language: sports: *golf, track and field, snowboarding, skiing, sledding, cycling, racing; hill, season, spring, summer, fall, winter, tournament, adult*

Review: weather, months

● MATERIALS REQUIRED

Extra activity 2: Reference books / the Internet, a large sheet of paper for each pair of students, colored markers

Optional: *Kid's Box AE Teacher's Resource Book 5* Unit 8 Reinforcement worksheet 2 (page 66)

Warmer

- Elicit some sports onto the board. Ask students what time of year they play these sports. Review/Introduce the seasons. Ask students if the seasons happen at the same time of year all over the world. Review what they know about seasons in the across from hemisphere to their own.

SB74. ACTIVITY 7. *Read and think. What time of year do people play your favorite sport?*

- Tell students to open their Student's Books to page 74. Focus them on Activity 7. Tell them to skim the text quickly to find the months for spring in the countries that are mentioned in the text. Elicit from the class. Focus students on the activity instruction and on the question. Ask a student to read them aloud. Check understanding. Focus students on the text and elicit that it's the webpage for *Kid's Box* ezine and that it's about sports for all seasons.
- Focus students on the words at the bottom of the webpage, read them through with the class and check understanding. Students read the texts silently and think about their answer to the question. They briefly compare their ideas in pairs. Focus on each text one at a time. Discuss what the sports are and what time of year people usually do them. Elicit if any of these sports are any student's favorite. Finally, give students further reading time, check general comprehension, and answer any questions they have. Ask students when professional soccer players play soccer. Ask students to give another word for *soccer* to elicit *football*. Explain that this is the word used outside the USA for soccer. Ask a student to write it on the board and another to spell it aloud. Ask students to give another word for *ride a bike* to elicit *cycle*. Ask a student to write it on the board and another to spell it aloud. Say *Put your hand up if you like cycling. Put your hand up if you cycle to school.*

SB74. ACTIVITY 8. *Listen. Repeat the word and say the letter.*

- Focus students on the Activity 8 instructions and on the example. Play the CD. Pause after each one to give students time to find the picture. They point to the picture in the text the first time. Play the CD again. Elicit a choral response each time.

Key: 2 Racing bikes / Cycling. That's "f." 3 Snowboarding. That's "d." 4 Golf. That's "b." 5 Track and field. That's "a." 6 Sledding. That's "e."

CD 3, 28

1 skiing, 2 cycling, 3 snowboarding, 4 golf, 5 track and field, 6 sledding

SB74. ACTIVITY 9. *Read and correct the sentences.*

- Focus students on the Activity 9 instruction and on the sentences. Check they know what to do. Students work individually and correct each sentence. They write the correct version in their notebooks. They check in pairs. Elicit corrections from the class and provide any new vocabulary on the board.

Key: 1 In school they do track and field in the summer. 2 Adults usually play golf in the summer. 3 To do winter sports we need snow and ice. 4 People go sledding in the winter. 5 The Tour de France is always in the summer. 6 Spring comes between winter and summer.

WB74. ACTIVITY 9. *Choose words from the box to label the pictures.*

Note: There are two extra words in the box.

Key: 2 snowboarding, 3 sledding, 4 cycling, 5 track and field, 6 golf

WB74. ACTIVITY 10. *Write the seasons.*

Key: 2 spring, 3 fall, 4 winter (Note: This does not apply to the tropics.)

WB74. ACTIVITY 11. *Write the sports words in the chart.*

Key:

winter sports	ball sports	other sports
ice-skating	soccer	sailing
sledding	Ping-Pong	cycling
skiing	basketball	horseback riding
ice hockey	tennis	track and field

WB74. ACTIVITY 12. *What are the sports? Write the words in the puzzle.*

Key: 2 soccer, 3 cycling, 4 sledding, 5 horseback riding, 6 skiing

Mystery sport: tennis

Extra activities: see page T108 (if time)

Optional activity

- Unit 8 Reinforcement worksheet 2 from *Kid's Box AE Teacher's Resource Book 5* (see pages 64 and 66).

Ending the lesson

- Call out the seasons one by one (but not in order). Students say what sports they like doing in each season.

OBJECTIVES: By the end of the lesson, students will have had further practice reading and writing about sports and sung a song.

• TARGET LANGUAGE

Key language: *snowboard*, present perfect (experience), simple past, sports and sports equipment, definitions, *race against the clock*

Review: colors, adjectives, clothes

• MATERIALS REQUIRED

Extra activity 1: Small pictures from vacation brochures to enable students to make up stories – you will need about five pictures for each group of four

Optional: *Kid's Box AE Teacher's Resource Book 5* Unit 8 Song worksheet (page 69)

Warmer

- Give students two minutes to think of as many sports as they can that begin with different letters of the alphabet. Elicit from the class.

SB75. ACTIVITY 10. *Listen and write the words.*

- Tell students to open their Student's Books to page 75. Focus them on the Activity 10 instruction and check they know what to do (write the words as they hear them spelled). Focus them on the example and tell them what the word group is going to be: sports and seasons. Students close their books. Play the CD. Students listen and write in their notebooks. They check in pairs. Play the CD again. Students open their books. Check with the class.

Key: 2 skiing, 3 fall, 4 sledding, 5 track and field, 6 spring, 7 cycling, 8 racing

CD 3, 29

1 g-o-l-f, 2 s-k-i-i-n-g, 3 f-a-l-l, 4 s-l-e-d-d-i-n-g,
5 t-r-a-c-k-a-n-d-f-i-e-l-d, 6 s-p-r-i-n-g, 7 c-y-c-l-i-n-g,
8 r-a-c-i-n-g

SB75. ACTIVITY 11. *Listen and order. Check and sing.*

- Focus students on the first part of the Activity 11 instructions. Give them time to read the lines from the song before they listen. Play the CD. Students listen for the order. They check in pairs. Play the CD again. Check with the class. Check general understanding and key vocabulary, e.g., *race against the clock*, before students start to sing the song. Play the CD a third time, for students to repeat in pairs of lines, and then as a whole. Divide the class into seven groups. Each group sings a pair of lines. Play the first version on the CD and then the karaoke version. Groups change roles and repeat.

Key: 2d, 3c, 4g, 5b, 6a, 7f

CD 3, 30

As in Student's Book and key

CD 3, 31

Now sing the song again. (Karaoke version)

SB75. ACTIVITY 12. *Read and complete. Answer the questions.*

- Focus students on the pictures for Activity 12. Tell the class these are pictures from Jane's vacation. Elicit where she was and what she did (using the pictures only). Focus students on the words in the box and on the text. They read the text silently and put the correct words in the blanks, using the pictures to help them. They check in pairs. Check with the class before they move on to the questions. They write the answers to the questions in their notebooks.

Key: 2 skiing, 3 sledding, 4 snowball, 5 snowboarding, 6 hill, 7 snowboard

Key: 1 She went to the mountains. 2 She went with her family. 3 They went skiing every morning. 4 Her older brother Frank went sledding with her. 5 They tried to play volleyball with a snowball. 6 They all went snowboarding together.

WB75. ACTIVITY 13. *Write the sports.*

Key: 2 basketball, 3 snowboarding, 4 sailing, 5 waterskiing, 6 golf

WB75. ACTIVITY 14. *Now write definitions for six more sports.*

Key: Students' own answers

WB75. ACTIVITY 15. *Read and complete the chart.*

Key:

Name	Richard	Sally	Robert
House number	1	2	3
Thing for the snowman	carrot	scarf	hat

WB75. ACTIVITY 16. *Choose the story. Then draw your snowman in your notebook.*

Key: Students' own answers

Extra activities: see page T108 (if time)

Optional activity

- Unit 8 Song worksheet from *Kid's Box AE Teacher's Resource Book 5* (see pages 64 and 69).

Ending the lesson

- Sing the song from the beginning of the lesson again with the students.

10 Listen and write the words. (29 CD3)

1. golf / 2. skiing / 3. fall / 4. sledding / 5. track and field / 6. spring / 7. cycling / 8. racing

11 Listen and order. Check and sing. (30 CD3)

a Some like playing soccer,
Some like watching it. [6]

b We've skated in the park,
We've made a ball to throw. [5]

c We've played golf with Grandma,
We've raced against the clock. [3]

d We've skied down a mountain,
We've climbed up a rock, [2]

e **We love sports, swimming, sailing, running!**
We love sports,
We love to do it all. [1]

f It's good to move your body,
DON'T JUST SIT! [7]

g We've played badminton and tennis,
We've gone sledding in the snow, [4]

12 Read and complete. Answer the questions.

Dictation

sledding	skiing	~~mountains~~	hill	snowboarding	snowboard	snowball

This morning Jane is coming home from her vacation in the (1) mountains with her family. She's had a great time. During the week her mother and father went (2) skiing every morning, but Jane and her older brother Frank went (3) sledding. After lunch Jane and her brothers played in the snow. They tried to play volleyball with a big (4) snowball, but it was very difficult because the snow was too soft. On the last day they all went (5) snowboarding together. Jane's parents and brothers kept falling and rolling down the (6) hill, but Jane was pretty good at it. She wants to buy a (7) snowboard and go to the mountains again next year.

1 Where did Jane go on vacation? She went to the mountains.
2 Who did she go with? She went with her family.
3 What did her parents do every morning? They went skiing every morning.
4 Which of Jane's brothers went sledding with her? Her older brother Frank went sledding with her.
5 What did they try to play volleyball with? They tried to play volleyball with a snowball.
6 What did they all do on the last day of their vacation? They all went snowboarding together.

13 Focus on phonics

Where have they played?
They've played in the sea.
What have they made?
A cup for tea!

What have they bought?
They've bought a dish.
What have they caught?
They've caught a fish!

Speaking 14 Find someone who …

Have you ever been skiing? — No, I haven't.

Have you ever played golf? — Yes, I have.

Questionnaire

Find someone who …	Names	
has been skiing.		
has played golf.	Peter	Sally
has won a prize.		
has climbed a mountain.		
has entered a competition.		
has played volleyball.		

Writing 15 Write a report about your class.

I spoke to ten people in my class about things they have done.
Three of them have been skiing …

Joke Corner

What do you call a snowball in the summer?

No ball!

OBJECTIVES: By the end of the lesson, students will have practiced rhyming words and past tense forms (regular and irregular). They will also have completed a writing activity.

● TARGET LANGUAGE

Key language: rhyming words, past participles, present perfect (experience) + short answers, simple past, *find someone who ... , enter a competition*

Review: sports, activities, action verbs

● MATERIALS REQUIRED

Optional: *Kid's Box AE Teacher's Resource Book 5* Unit 8 Extension worksheet 1 (page 67)

Warmer

- Elicit from students some of the things they have done in their lives / today. Write the sentences on the board, putting irregular verbs on one side and -*ed* past endings on another. Elicit that some of the verbs are irregular, some regular. Focus them on the sounds of the verb endings in the -*ed* columns (/t/, /d/, /ɪd/).

SB76. ACTIVITY 13. *Focus on phonics*

- Tell students to open their Student's Books to page 76. Focus them on Activity 13. Play the CD. Students repeat after each line and then after the whole rhyme. Repeat once more, making sure students say the past forms correctly. In pairs, students practice the rhyme.

CD 3, 32

As in Student's Book

SB76. ACTIVITY 14. *Find someone who ...*

- Focus students on the Activity 14 questionnaire and on the speech bubbles. Ask a student to read the first prompt aloud (*Find someone who has been skiing*) and another to read the question in the speech bubble (*Have you ever been skiing?*). Check students' understanding that they have to make and ask a question like this each time. Elicit what the other questions are. Check that they understand *enter a competition*. Teach short answers: *Yes, I have. / No, I haven't.* Students copy the questionnaire into their notebooks. They walk around the classroom, asking the questions. Instead of *Peter* and *Sally*, they write the names of classmates who have done the activities. Monitor to check students are asking full questions.

SB76. ACTIVITY 15. *Write a report about your class.*

- Focus students on Activity 15 and on the sample report. Elicit some of the information students found out, using the formula in the report, e.g., *I spoke to ... people in my class about things they have done. ... of them have ... , ... of them ...*
- Students work individually and write their reports in their notebooks.

SB76. JOKE CORNER

- Focus students on the Joke Corner and review the meaning of *joke*. Play the CD as students read the joke in their books. Play the joke a second time and explain if necessary.

CD 3, 33

As in Student's Book

WB76. ACTIVITY 17. *Match the rhyming words.*

- Tell students to open their Workbook to page 76. Check they know the meaning of all the words and elicit the infinitives of the irregular verbs (1 wear, 2 say, 4 fly, 6 catch, 8 hear, 9 win, 10 feel, 11 stand, b buy, c make, l do). Go through the example and make sure students know that they have to match numbers 1 to 6 with a to f and 7 to 12 with g to l. Students complete the activity in pencil. Tell them to say the words aloud to help and not to focus on the spelling.

WB76. ACTIVITY 18. *Listen, check, and say.*

- Play the CD for students to listen and check. They compare answers in pairs. Check with the class. Play the CD again for students to listen and repeat.

Key: 1d, 2e, 3f, 4a, 5c, 6b, 7j, 8k, 9l, 10i, 11g, 12h

CD 3, 34

1 wore – four, 2 said – head, 3 skated – waited, 4 flew – through, 5 played – made, 6 caught – bought, 7 laughed – craft, 8 heard – word, 9 won – done, 10 felt – belt, 11 stood – should, 12 smiled – child

WB76. ACTIVITY 19. *Find and circle information about what, when, where, and why. Make four circles in total.*

- Before students do the activity, focus them on the Write it right box and check they understand how to write emails and how they are different in layout and tone from letters.

Key:
When: on the weekend
Where: in Springfield
Why: They love soccer.

WB76. ACTIVITY 20. *Now write your email about something that happened on the weekend.*

Key: Students' own answers

Extra activities: see page T108 (if time)

Optional activity

- Unit 8 Extension worksheet 1 from *Kid's Box AE Teacher's Resource Book 5* (see pages 64 and 67).

Ending the lesson

- Do the rhyme from the beginning of the lesson again.

OBJECTIVES: By the end of the lesson, students will have read a story, reviewed language from the unit, and completed a self-evaluation.

• TARGET LANGUAGE

Key language: language in the story, *invent, handball*

Review: language from the unit

• MATERIALS REQUIRED

Optional: *Kid's Box AE Teacher's Resource Book 5* Unit 8 Extension worksheet 2 (page 68)

Warmer

- Review the whole Diggory Bones story so far with the class. Give them clues about each episode, e.g., *Where was Diggory in the first episode? Do you remember what the bones were?* If students can't remember, let them open their Student's Books to look. Tell them this is the last episode. Elicit their ideas for how the story is going to end.

SB77. STORY. *Diggory Bones.*

- Tell students to open their Student's Books to page 77. Focus them on the story. Tell them to look quickly to see if their predicted endings of the story are in fact what happens. Set the questions: *How do they get out of the butterfly room? Why did the Ancient Egyptians paint sports on the walls? Does Brutus get the treasure?* Play the CD with books closed. Students listen to find the answers. They check in pairs with books open. Check with the class. (They go through a door. They loved sports. / They're trying to tell people something. No, he loses it all.) Check understanding of *invent* and *handball*. Play the CD again. Students listen and read. Stop after each frame for students to repeat. At the end, check comprehension by asking: *Why does Diggory tell Brutus to close his mouth? What sports did the Ancient Egyptians invent? How does Sir Doug know how to find Diggory and Emily? Why did Brutus lose the treasure?*

CD 3, 35

As in Student's Book

WB77. ACTIVITY 21. *Read and answer.*

Key: 2 No, he hasn't. 3 hockey and handball, 4 from the snake bowl, 5 It says that you can't take the treasure and live.

WB77. ACTIVITY 22. *Who said it? Read and match.*

Key: b3, c4, d1, e1, f2

WB77. DO YOU REMEMBER?

- Students try to do the activity first without looking back through the unit. Once they have tried to complete all the sentences, they can look back through the unit to find the answers.

Key: 2 won, 3 played, 4 Summer, 5 Students' own answers, 6 Bye

WB77. CAN DO

- Focus students on the *Can do* section of the page. Ask a student to read the first sentence. Elicit what this means with examples and elicit/remind them of the activities they did in this unit when they talked about things they've done. Review what the three faces mean (not very well / OK / very well). Remind students they circle the one they think is true for them. Repeat for the second sentence, eliciting/ reminding them of the activities when they talked about different sports. Students circle the appropriate face. Repeat for the third sentence, eliciting what they remember about writing an email.
- Say *Now show and tell your friends.* Students work in groups of three and take turns showing their work for / talking about each one.

Extra activities: see page T108 (if time)

Optional activity

- Unit 8 Extension worksheet 2 from *Kid's Box AE Teacher's Resource Book 5* (see pages 64 and 68).

Ending the lesson

- Ask students which rhyme/song they'd like to do again from the unit. Do it together to end the lesson.

DIGGORY BONES

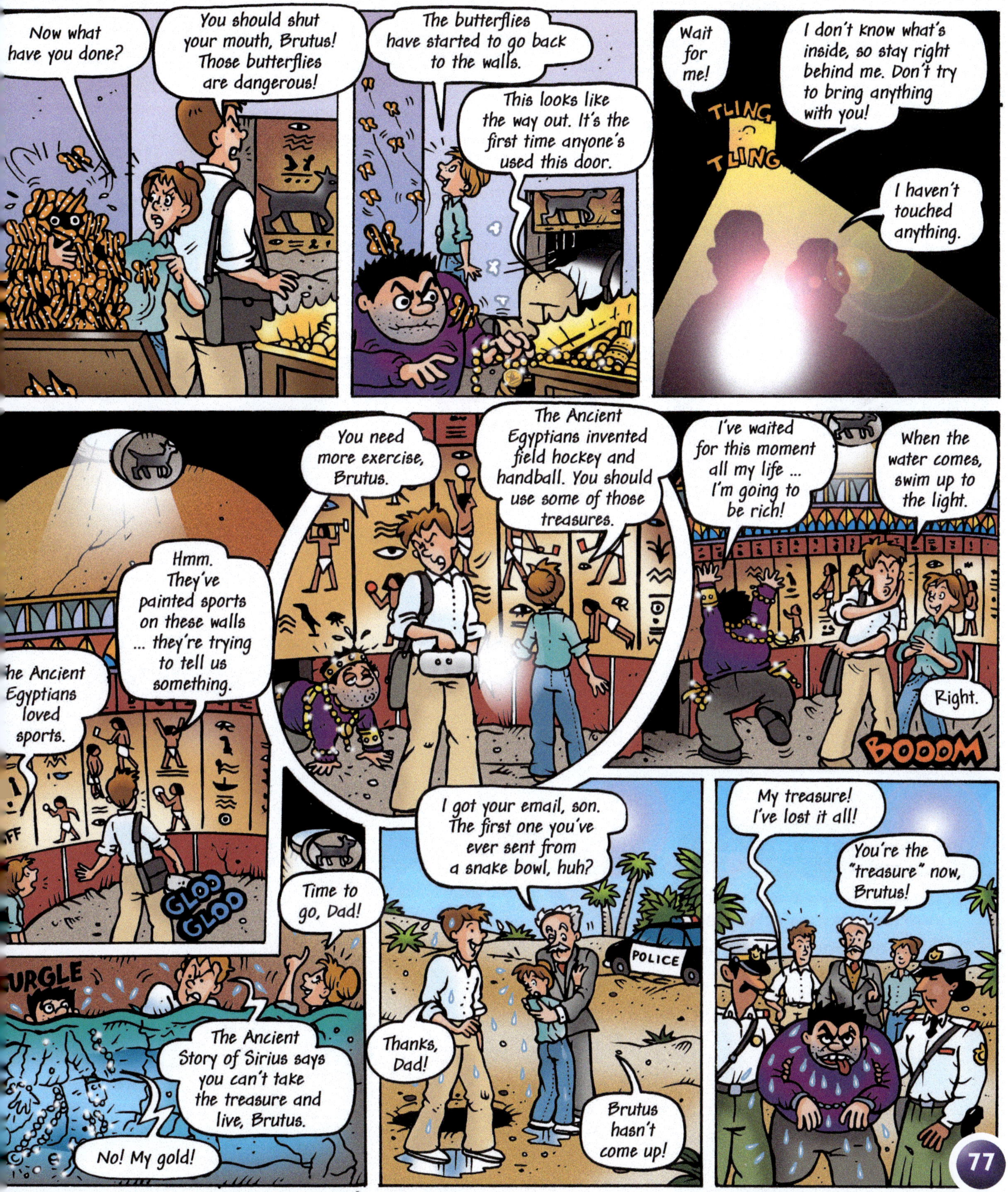

Art Olympic design

FACT: **The Olympic Games happen every four years. 204 different countries competed in the 2012 Olympics in 26 different sports.**

1 Read and match.

1 Can you see the picture with five different colored circles? This is called a logo. It is for the Olympic Games. The circles represent five different continents of the world. ( )

a london

2 Each country also has another logo for its games. The Beijing 2008 logo shows a person dancing. This was the old logo for the city, but it also represents all the different sports at the Olympics. ( )

3 The picture for London plays with the numbers 2012. It is a modern picture, because people wanted young people to watch the games and play more sports. ( )

b Beijing 2008

4 The logo for Rio 2016 shows three people and uses the three colors of Brazil's flag. The shape the people are making looks like Sugarloaf Mountain in Rio. Do you like it? ( )

c Rio2016

d

2 Ask and answer.

1 What's a logo?

2 How many circles are there in the Olympic logo? Why?

3 What's the person doing in the Beijing logo?

4 Which city uses numbers in its logo?

5 What colors are used in the Rio logo for 2016? Why?

6 Which is your favorite logo? Why?

Project 1 Design your Olympic logo.

Work in groups. Imagine the next Olympic Games are going to be in your city.

1 Think of a design for a logo.

2 Make a poster to show your design.

3 Show the class and decide on the best logo.

OBJECTIVES: By the end of the lesson, students will have read about the Olympic Games and completed a project.

• TARGET LANGUAGE

Key language: *Olympic Games, Paralympics, disability, logo, design*, numbers, definitions
Additional language: *Beijing, London, Rio, Brazil*
Review: sports

• MATERIALS REQUIRED

A large sheet of paper for each pair of students, colored markers
Optional: *Kid's Box AE Teacher's Resource Book 5* Unit 8 Topic worksheet (page 70)

Warmer

- Draw the Olympic logo (five circles) on the board and elicit if students know what it stands for. If not, tell them it's the logo of the Olympic Games. Teach *logo*. Briefly elicit what they know about the Olympic Games, e.g., the most recent games, winter and summer games, some of the sports.

SB78. FACT

- Tell students to open their Student's Books to page 78. Ask a student to read the Fact to the class. Elicit their responses to the facts, in particular the number of sports events in the games.

SB78. ACTIVITY 1. *Read and match.* F toward

- Focus students on the Activity 1 instruction and on the pictures.
- Don't explain words at this stage. Students read the text quickly (and silently) to match the pictures with the paragraphs. They check and discuss their answers in pairs. Check with the class.
- Read the first paragraph through with the class, with students taking turns reading parts aloud. Discuss the information in the paragraph and check understanding of key vocabulary. Elicit any other information they know about anything mentioned in the paragraph. Repeat the procedure for the other three paragraphs.

Key: 1d, 2b, 3a, 4c

SB78. ACTIVITY 2. *Ask and answer.*

- Focus students on the Activity 2 instruction and on the questions. Students cover the text with a piece of paper. They take turns asking and answering the questions. When they have finished all the questions, they take away the paper and look at the text again to check their answers. Check briefly with the class.

Key: 1 a picture, 2 five, because they represent the five continents, 3 The person's dancing. 4 London, 5 green, yellow, and blue, They are the colors of the Brazilian flag. 6 Students' own answers

SB78. PROJECT 1. *Design your Olympic logo.*

- Focus students on the project and confirm that they are going to design an Olympic logo for their closest big city. Brainstorm what is important and/or special about their city and its history to help them with planning their designs. Read the project information through with the class and check understanding of the procedure. Students work in pairs to design their logos. Monitor and help where necessary. Hand out the large sheets of paper only when students have produced a design. Pairs present and display their logos, giving reasons for the elements in the design. The class votes for the best logo.

WB78. ACTIVITY 1. *Choose words from the box to complete the text.* F toward

Note: There are two extra words in the box.

Key: 2 always, 3 athletes, 4 well, 5 started, 6 countries

WB78. ACTIVITY 2. *Invent a sport for the next Olympics.*

Key: Students' own answers

WB78. ACTIVITY 3. *Now use the information in your mind map to write a letter to the Olympic Committee telling them about your sport.*

- Students can also draw their Olympic sport if time.

Key: Students' own answers

Extra activities: see page T108 (if time)

Optional activity

- Unit 8 Topic worksheet from *Kid's Box AE Teacher's Resource Book 5* (see pages 64 and 70).

Ending the lesson

- Review with students what they talked and read about in today's lesson and which activities they liked best.

OBJECTIVES: By the end of the lesson, students will have read more about the Olympic Games and completed a project.

• TARGET LANGUAGE

Key language: *medal, silver, gold, bronze, front, back, 24-carat gold, % (per cent), dragon, must*

Additional language: *Nike, stadium, jade, precious stone, compass*

• MATERIALS REQUIRED

For each student, a piece of thin cardboard, a compass, a ruler, a pencil and pens, glue, scissors, string or ribbon, reference materials, the Internet

Extra activity 1: Paper for each student, colored pencils

Warmer

- Review with students what they learned about in the previous lesson and what they remember about the different logos.

SB79. ACTIVITY 3. *Read and answer.*

- Tell students to open their Student's Books to page 79. Focus them on the text. Ask a student to read the title aloud and check understanding. Elicit what the students can see in the pictures. Pre-teach *gold, silver, bronze, medals*, and *front* and *back*. Focus on the Activity 3 instruction and on the questions. Students work in pairs. They read the questions and then read the text silently. They try to answer the questions together. Tell them not to worry if they can't answer them all. Check with the class. Ask students to take turns reading each paragraph of the text aloud and then focusing on the questions for that paragraph, checking key vocabulary and pronunciation as you do so.

Key: 1 They must be at least 68 mm across and 3 mm thick. 2 There is at least 92.5% silver. 3 Nike, the Greek goddess of winning, 4 the city where the games are that year, 5 a circle of jade, 6 green

SB79. PROJECT 2. *Design an Olympic medal.*

- Focus students on the project and confirm that they are going to design an Olympic medal to go with the logo they designed for their city in the previous lesson. Remind them that the medal and the logo shouldn't be the same, but that they should reflect similar ideas about the city and its history. Read the project information through with the class and check understanding of the procedure. Hand out the project materials. Students work individually. First they draw the front of their medals. Then they produce a design for the back of the medals, using reference materials / the Internet. Monitor and help where necessary. Students make their medals and display them in front of their logos from the previous lesson. If time, individuals present their medals to the class and the class decides on the best medal for each logo.

WB79. ACTIVITY 4. FLYERS Reading and Writing, Part 4 *Read the text. Choose the right words and write them on the lines.* F toward

- Tell students to open their Workbook to page 79. Focus them on the activity instructions and the example. They complete the text by choosing from the words at the bottom of the page. They check in pairs. Elicit answers. Ask students to explain their choices.

Key: 1 These, 2 the, 3 are, 4 skiing, 5 people, 6 race, 7 third, 8 exciting, 9 of, 10 more

Extra activities: see page T108 (if time)

Ending the lesson

- Review with students what they talked and read about in today's lesson and which activities they liked best from this and the previous lesson.

3 Read and answer.

1 How big must the Olympic medals be?
2 How much silver is there in the gold and silver medals?
3 Who is on the front of the Olympic medals?
4 Who decides what goes on the back of the medals?
5 What was on the back of the medals for the Beijing games in 2008?
6 What color is jade?

How are the Olympic medals made?

Each Olympic medal must be at least 68 mm across and 3 mm thick. The gold and silver medals must be at least 92.5% silver. There are six grams of 24-carat gold covering each gold medal. The bronze medals contain a mixture of different metals, including silver.

The front of the medal

Since 1928, there has been a picture of Nike, the Greek goddess of winning, on the front of every medal.

For the 2004 games in Athens, a new front was designed. It had a new picture of Nike flying into the Greek stadium to give the winners their prizes.

The back of the medal

The back of every medal is different for each Olympic Games and is designed by the city where the games are. The medal for the Beijing 2008 Olympic Games had a circle of a green precious stone called jade. Jade is important in China because it means something is beautiful and excellent. The top of the medal looks like a dragon, which shows somebody is strong.

Project 2 Design an Olympic medal.

You need:

- A piece of thin cardboard
- A compass
- A ruler
- A pencil and pens
- Glue
- Scissors
- String or ribbon

How to make your medal:

1 Draw two circles on a piece of thin cardboard. Use a compass to make them exactly 68 mm.
2 Cut out the circles.
3 Draw the goddess Nike on one circle. This is the front of the medal. Then draw your own design for the back of the medal on the other circle.
4 Glue the circles together and use the compass to make a hole at the top.
5 Put string or ribbon through the hole to finish your medal and show it to the class.

Review Units 7 and 8

1 Look at the picture. Talk about it in pairs.

It's a sunny day.

They're outside a restaurant.

Daisy

Sally

Vicky

Fred

John

Paul

Jack

2 36 CD3 Listen and draw lines. There is one example.

3 Read the story. Choose a word from the box. Write the correct word next to numbers 1–5. There is one example.

~~kicked~~	sandwiches
water	quiet
have	shouldn't
are	can clothes
sand	dangerous

I went to the beach with Sam and his dad last weekend. We took a picnic and a ball. We were playing soccer on the beach when I _kicked_ the ball into the ocean! It was soon far out in the (1) _water_ !

"Can you swim?" Sam asked.

"No, I've never learned to swim!" I answered. "Can you swim?"

"Yes," said Sam, and he started swimming.

The waves were huge.

Sam's dad started shouting at him, "(2) _Have_ you seen the flag? You shouldn't swim when there is a red flag!"

Sam's dad swam toward him and pulled him back to the beach.

"Sorry, Dad," Sam said. "The ocean was (3) _dangerous_ !"

"Um. Should we have our picnic, now?" I said.

We went to get our picnic, but it wasn't there.

"You (4) _shouldn't_ leave food on the beach!" Sam's dad said. "The birds always eat it. Look!"

It was true. We saw a lot of big white birds eating our (5) _sandwiches_ .

Now choose the best name for the story.

Check (✓) one box.

- A day at the beach ☑
- The dangerous birds ☐
- A nice swim ☐

* Photocopiable – page T-97

OBJECTIVES: By the end of the lesson, students will have reviewed language from Units 7 and 8 and done speaking, reading, and listening activities.

• TARGET LANGUAGE

Key language: vocabulary and language from Units 7 and 8, describing pictures: *in the foreground, in the background, in the center, on the left, on the right, on the left of, on the right of*

Review: descriptions, people, clothes, activities, food, directions

• MATERIALS REQUIRED

Warmer: Key vocabulary from Units 7 and 8, each word written on a small piece of paper, enough for each student in the class

Photocopiable 8 (see page T97), one photocopy for each pair, cut into two parts

Warmer

- Make groups of six. Hand out a word on to each student. They take turns providing definitions of their words for the other students in their group to guess. Regroup students and repeat.

SB80. ACTIVITY 1. *Look at the picture. Talk about it in pairs.* F toward

- Tell students to open their Student's Books to page 80. Focus them on the picture. Tell them to ignore the people's names around the picture for now. Use this to pre-teach/review language for picture description, e.g., *I can see … in the foreground, in the background, in the center, on the left (of), on the right (of).* Write the key language on the board. Elicit some sentences from different students to demonstrate the activity. Students work in pairs and talk about the picture. Monitor and give ideas where necessary. Elicit the description of the picture from the whole class.

SB80. ACTIVITY 2. *Listen and draw lines. There is one example.* F toward

- Focus students on the Activity 2 instructions and on the names. Play the CD and do the example with the class. Play the rest of the CD in one go. Students listen and draw lines. They check in pairs. Play the CD again. Check with the class.

CD 3, 36

BOY: What are you looking at, Uncle Paul?
MAN: It's a photograph of me when I was younger.
BOY: Who are you?
MAN: I'm the little boy, playing with the plastic car.
BOY: Is that Aunt Daisy riding the bike?
MAN: That's right. Daisy loved her bike.
BOY: Who are the people sitting at the table next to you?
MAN: Well, the man who's eating the piece of bread is your grandfather, Jack, when he was younger. He's wearing a yellow T-shirt.
BOY: Is the woman who's drinking water my grandmother?
MAN: No, that's your grandfather's sister, Sally.
BOY: Who's the other man? The one who's putting butter on his bread?
MAN: He was a friend of Sally's, but I can't remember his name.
BOY: Is my mom in the photograph?
MAN: No, she wasn't born when this photograph was taken.
BOY: Do you know the names of the other people, Uncle Paul?
MAN: Well, yes, I do, or at least three of them. Can you see the man in the uniform?
BOY: The police officer standing on the corner?
MAN: Yes. His name's Fred. He was one of your grandad's school friends.
BOY: Oh! Really?
MAN: Yes. And the waiter with the striped T-shirt is John. He lived in the house next to us.
BOY: And who is the third person you know?
MAN: Well, John, the waiter, is talking to a woman with long hair. She's named Vicky. She's a teacher. She taught math to me and your mom and your Aunt Daisy.
BOY: Wow! You know them all.

SB80. ACTIVITY 3. *Read the story. Choose a word from the box. Write the correct word next to numbers 1–5. There is one example.* F toward

- Ask a student to read the instructions aloud. Do the example with the class by asking another student to read the first three lines of the story aloud. Briefly review how students know this word is correct (verb following *I*). Remind students to think carefully about which words to use by looking at the words around each blank. Give a time limit for students to complete the activity individually. Students check in pairs. Check with the class.

Key: 1 water, 2 Have, 3 dangerous, 4 shouldn't, 5 sandwiches

SB80. *Now choose the best name for the story. Check (✓) one box.*

- Focus students on the second part of the activity. Give them thinking time before they check one of the boxes. Check opinions around the class, eliciting reasons for their answers.

Key: A day at the beach

Photocopiable 8 (see pages T89 and T97)

WB80. ACTIVITY 1. *Read the story. Choose a word from the box. Write the correct word next to numbers 1–6.* F toward

Note: There are five extra words in the box.

Key: 2 ride, 3 were, 4 skis, 5 sled, 6 snowman

WB80. ACTIVITY 2. *Choose a title for this episode of* Friendly. F toward

Key: b) Snowy disaster!

WB80. ACTIVITY 3. *Match the questions with the answers.*

Key: 5, 6, 2, 1, 3, 4

Extra activity: see page T109 (if time)

Ending the lesson

- Describe someone in the class for the other students to guess, e.g., *This student has dark hair and is wearing …* Students can then take turns giving descriptions for the class to guess.

OBJECTIVES: By the end of the lesson, students will have reviewed language from Units 7 and 8 and played a game.

• TARGET LANGUAGE

Key language: vocabulary and language from *Kid's Box AE 5*
Review: language for playing games

• MATERIALS REQUIRED

Warmer: The following questions on a large sheet of paper, each one in scrambled order:

1 *What do they look like?*
2 *When did you go snowboarding?*
3 *What does it feel like?*
4 *What do they sound like?*
5 *What should we do with them?*
6 *What would you like?*
7 *How many times a week do you go to school?*
8 *What's the name of the fifth month?*

Board game: Dice, red and blue counters

Warmer

- Display a large sheet of paper with scrambled questions. Students work in pairs to unscramble them and write them in their notebooks. Elicit the questions from students and write them on the board. Elicit one or more possible answers.

SB81. ACTIVITY 4. *Play the game.*

- Tell students to open their Student's Books to page 81 and erase the board. Elicit that this is a board game. Focus students on the instructions and check understanding. If they land on a circle that is their color, they ask a related question. Their partner decides if the question is correct or not. If it is correct, the questioner receives 3 points. If not, he/she loses a point. Students play in pairs. They take turns throwing the dice and moving around the board, asking the questions. Be ready to give your verdict in any disputes. Encourage students to be inventive with their questions – there are many different possibilities.
- Monitor students as they are playing the game. At the end of the game, the player with the most points in each pair is the winner.
- Fast finishers can play again, changing color.

Key (possible questions): 1 What time / When do you go to bed? 2 What does a lime look like? 3 What should we do with plastic, glass bottles, etc? 4 What did you have for breakfast? 5 What does it feel like? 6 What's (the name of) the eighth month? 7 How old is he? 8 How many books are there in your bag / on the table, etc.? 9 How often / many times a day do you brush your teeth? 10 Where did you go yesterday? 11 What does it taste like? 12 What color are the socks? 13 How do you go to school? 14 Why did you phone me / leave me a message? 15 What does it sound like? 16 Can I help you? / Which book would you like? 17 Who's that / this? / your favorite teacher? 18 Who did you have lunch with yesterday? 19 How many days are there in a year? 20 How many medals have you won?

WB81. ACTIVITY 4. *Complete the sentences. Count and write the letters.*

Key: 2 ever 4, 3 extinct 7, 4 done 4, 5 spotted 7, 6 have 4, 7 should 6, 8 dinosaur 8, 9 wings 5, 10 jumped 6, 11 Games 5, 12 stripes 7, 13 fur 3, 14 golf 4

WB81. ACTIVITY 5. *Now complete the crossword puzzle. Write the message.*

Key:

					f						e	
		s	[1]h	o	u	l	d		h		[5]v	
		p			r			[3]g	a	m	e	s
	g	o	l	f					v		r	
		t				d	o	n	e			w
		t				i				j		[2]i
		[6]e	x	t	i	n	c	t		u		n
		d				o				m		g
						s	t	r	i	p	e	s
						a				e		
d	i	[4]f	f	i	c	u	l	t		d		
						r						

Message: high five

WB81. ACTIVITY 6. *Quiz time!*

Key: 1 They should recycle it. 2 a beetle, 3 because an asteroid hit the earth, 4 He hasn't won any races. 5 in the winter, 6 in London, in England

WB81. ACTIVITY 7. *Write questions for your quiz in your notebook.*

Key: Students' own questions and answers

Extra activities: see page T109 (if time)

Optional evaluations

- Quiz 4 from *Interactive DVD 5* (*The classroom section*). This quiz can be done as a whole-class activity or as a team competition. See pages 36 ans 37 of the Teacher's Booklet for the Interactive DVD.
- The test for Units 7–8 from *Kid's Box AE Teacher's Resource Book 5* (see pages 121–135) F toward

Ending the lesson

- Students work in groups of three. They find the *Can do* Workbook sections for Units 7 and 8 and write the six statements on a large piece of paper. They discuss and give examples for each *Can do* statement, checking back in the Student's Book, the Workbook or their notebooks if necessary. Elicit some examples from volunteer students in the class for each one.
- Ask students which lessons, topics and/or activities were their favorites.

4 Play the game.

What's the question?

Instructions

- Play in pairs. One player is red, and the other is blue. In turns, go around the board. Read the answer and ask the question. If your question is right, score three points. If it's wrong, lose one point. Make a note of the points in your notebook.

Respect in the classroom

1 Look at the picture. What's wrong? Talk to your friends.

Look at "a." What do you think is wrong?

She doesn't have her book for the class.

2 37 CD3 Listen and check. Say the letter.

He's worried because he's late.

That's "d."

1.d / 2.a / 3.j / 4.b / 5.h / 6.i / 7.f / 8.g / 9.e / 10.c

3 Ask and answer.

Ss' own answers

1 What should the children do to start their class on time?
2 Which of the things in the picture do you never do?
3 Which of the things in the picture do you sometimes do?
4 What should you do to be a better student?

OBJECTIVES: By the end of the lesson, students will have read and talked about appropriate behavior in the classroom.

• TARGET LANGUAGE

Key language: *values, respect, classroom, What do you think is wrong?*

Review: classroom objects, simple past, adjectives: *worried, late, hungry, angry, tired, happy, unhappy; should/shouldn't, never, sometimes, always, because, better, before, during, after, contract, must / must not, correctly*

• MATERIALS REQUIRED

Extra activity 2: The following sentence halves written on separate pieces of paper (one set of 14 pieces of paper for each pair of students): *I should arrive / on time. / I shouldn't forget / the things I need for class. / I should eat / a good breakfast. / I should listen / to the teacher. / I shouldn't / talk to my friends. / I should go to bed / early on school nights. / I shouldn't eat / in class.*

Warmer

- Stand at the front and yawn as if you are very tired. Look around for the things you need (bags, book, board pen), saying *Where's my pen? Did I forget my books today?* etc. as if you are not ready for class. Try to make this seem serious. Stop and ask students in L1 what they think about your behaviour. Elicit that it isn't the right way for the teacher to start the class. Say *There are things a teacher should do before class and in the class. And there are things students should do, too.* Tell students they are going to talk about these things in today's lesson.

SB82. ACTIVITY 1. *Look at the picture. What's wrong? Talk to your friends.*

- Tell students to open their Student's Books to page 82. Focus on the heading *Values* and elicit the meaning. Read the lesson title and check that students understand *respect*. Elicit things students can see in the picture, e.g., *pencil case, bag, ruler* and what the pictures in the thought bubbles show, e.g., an angry face, someone texting in bed late at night.
- Ask volunteers to read the speech bubbles. Ask how the girl who's forgotten her book feels (unhappy). Students work in pairs or small groups to talk about the rest of the children marked by letters. Do not confirm answers.

SB82. ACTIVITY 2. *Listen and check. Say the letter.*

- Play the CD. Students listen and check their answers to Activity 1. Play the CD again, pausing after each sentence for students to say the letter (as in the model speech bubble). Play the CD again and check comprehension. Ask, e.g., *How does girl "a" feel? (unhappy) Why? (because she forgot her book).*

Key: 1d, 2a, 3j, 4b, 5h, 6i, 7f, 8g, 9e, 10c

CD 3, 37

1. He's worried because he's late.
2. She's unhappy because she forgot to bring her book.
3. He's hungry because he didn't have breakfast.
4. He's angry because they're playing with his pencil case.
5. He's angry because his friend's eating in class.
6. He's tired because he went to bed late.
7. She's happy because she's talking to her friend.
8. They're unhappy because the girls are talking.
9. She's unhappy because her school bag's messy.
10. They have his pencil case and they think it's funny.

SB82. ACTIVITY 3. *Ask and answer.*

- Read the activity instruction and the questions. Students work in pairs. They take turns answering each question. Elicit ideas and have a brief class discussion. Elicit/Explain that even if each person only does one wrong thing, put together this makes it difficult for everyone to learn. Behaving well in class is about respect for the teacher and for the other students.

WB82. ACTIVITY 1. *Read and choose the answer.*

- Tell students to open their Workbook to page 82. Focus on Activity 1. Point out that this is a quiz. Go through the questions and options, reviewing the meaning of *never, sometimes, always, before,* and *after.* Students choose their answer individually by circling a, b or c. They compare answers in pairs. Elicit recommended answers without judging or being too authoritarian and have a brief class discussion.

Key: Students' own answers

WB82. ACTIVITY 2. *Write a class contract.*

- Focus students on Activity 2. Read the activity instruction and check comprehension of *contract.* Ask a student to read the example sentence. Elicit/Explain why we use *must* or *must not* in a contract (these are rules, not advice). Work together with the class to agree on and elicit rules 2 to 5, e.g., *We must speak English, … listen to the teacher, … come to class with the right things.* Point out that for sentence 6 you need to agree on the rewards students will get if they keep to the contract. Discuss these, agree and write them on the board, e.g., *We can play a game. We can sing the song again.* Students copy the sentences for the contract into their Workbooks.

Key: Students' own answers

Extra activities: see page T109 (if time)

Ending the lesson

- Books closed. Write the title *Respect in the classroom* in the center of the board. Elicit the things students should/shouldn't do to show respect in class and make a mind map.

OBJECTIVES: By the end of the lesson, students will have read and talked about the role of the emergency services.

• TARGET LANGUAGE

Key language: *break (her) leg, hit (her) head, fall off (my bike), hero(es)*

Additional language: *emergency services, cycle, dark, lights, clearly, hill, suddenly, thanks to them, X-ray, operate, ambulance, accident, save (someone's) life, team, on fire, catch thieves, robbery*

Review: simple past and past progressive, *help, hospital, helmet, driver, doctor, nurse*

• MATERIALS REQUIRED

Extra activity 1: Five pieces of paper (A5 size) for each student

Warmer

- Write *emergency services* and *911* on the board. Elicit/Explain what emergency services are (police, fire, ambulance) and that 911 is the emergency phone number in the U.S. Ask students if there is a similar system in their country / what number they should call in an emergency. Ask who helps us in an emergency. Elicit *police / police officers, firefighters, doctors, nurses, ambulance drivers.*

SB83. ACTIVITY **1.** *Read and answer the questions.*

- Tell students to open their Student's Books to page 83. Direct them to the article and the photograph. Elicit that the girl is being interviewed. Choose students to read the title and the introduction. Check comprehension of *heroes*. Read through the questions and make sure students understand *break her leg* and *hit her head*. Tell them not to worry about new vocabulary, but to focus on answering the questions. Students read the text, then talk about the questions in pairs. Check with the class and explain any new words.

Key: 1 She fell off her bike. 2 because she wasn't wearing a helmet, 3 a car driver, ambulance drivers, doctors and nurses

SB83. ACTIVITY **2.** *Listen and say "firefighter," "doctor," "police officer," or "ambulance driver."*

- Choose a student to read the activity instruction. Check comprehension of the four jobs and practice pronunciation. Talk briefly in English about where each person works and the things they do. Tell students that there may be more than one answer for each sentence. Play the CD. Students whisper the answer(s) to a partner. Play the CD again, pausing to elicit ideas.
- If time, organize a discussion in small groups. Write some of the following questions on the board: *When did you last see a doctor? What do police officers do? Would you like to be a firefighter? Why? / Why not? Do you know anyone who has had an accident? What happened?*

Key: (possible answers): 1 doctor, 2 firefighter, 3 police officer, 4 doctor/nurse, 5 ambulance driver, 6 police officer, 7 police officer, 8 doctor

CD 3, 38

1. She works with a team of nurses.
2. She carries people out of buildings on fire.
3. He looks for and catches thieves.
4. When she works at night, she has to sleep at the hospital.
5. He has to drive people to the hospital quickly and safely.
6. He goes to schools to teach young people to use the Internet safely.
7. When there is a robbery at a bank, he arrives quickly.
8. She has to operate to save people's lives.

WB83. ACTIVITY **1.** *Read and order the text.*

- Tell students to open their Workbook to page 83. Focus on Activity 1. Students work in pairs to put the lines in order. Check with the class. Ask, e.g., *Who is Harry? What happened to him? What did the firefighters have to do? What did the police officers do? How long did he stay in the hospital?*

Key: 4, 8, 14, 2, 11, 6, 13, 3, 7, 10, 9, 12, 1, 15, 5

Completed **text:** Last week William's dad, Harry, / had a bad car accident. His car hit a / truck and he couldn't get out of / his car. Firefighters had to cut the car door / and pull Harry out. Police / officers called the hospital and / told the nurses about Harry and his / accident. The police officers drove Harry / to the hospital with the ambulance / to help stop the traffic. At / the hospital a team of doctors and / nurses worked together to save / Harry's life. Now, two weeks later, Harry is / much better. He's going to leave / hospital and go home to his family.

WB83. ACTIVITY **2.** *Write a letter to thank the firefighters.*

- Focus on Activity 2. Check comprehension of the instructions and the words in the box. Students write a first draft of their letter in their notebooks. Monitor and help as necessary. Students compare letters. When you have checked their drafts, students copy them into their Workbooks.

Key: Students' own answers

Extra activities: see page T109 (if time)

Ending the lesson

- Review what students have learned in the lesson. Ask if there are any other people/professions they think are heroes and why.

People who help us

1 Read and answer the questions.

1 How did Holly break her leg? 2 Why did she hit her head? 3 Who helped her?

Holly's heroes

It's a rainy day, and there are gray clouds in the sky. Holly's walking to school. She has a history exam. A lot of young people might feel unhappy or worried, but not Holly. Holly's just happy she can walk to school.

Last year Holly was in the hospital for four weeks, and she had to learn to walk again. We ask Holly about her heroes.

So, Holly, can you tell us what happened to you last year?

I was cycling home from my friend's house after school. It was dark, and I didn't have any lights, so I couldn't see clearly. I was going very quickly down a hill when suddenly a cat ran across the road in front of me. I tried not to hit it, but I fell off my bike.

How terrible! Then what happened?

Well, I can't remember. I hit my head because I wasn't wearing a helmet. People told me what happened. I fell badly and broke my leg in two places.

How did you get to the hospital?

A driver saw me on the ground and stopped his car. He called for an ambulance, and they took me to the closest hospital. I arrived in less than ten minutes.

Wow! That was fast.

Yes. Thanks to them, the doctors and nurses could work quickly. I had an X-ray, and then they had to operate for four hours, but they saved my leg. Then I had to learn to walk again.

So you have a lot of heroes: the ambulance drivers and the team of doctors and nurses.

Yes, but also the driver who stopped to call the ambulance. I want to say thank you to everyone who helped me. When I grow up, I want to be a doctor or nurse because I'd like to help other people, too.

2 38 CD3 Listen and say "firefighter," "doctor," "police officer," or "ambulance driver."

Tell the truth but don't hurt

1 Read and choose answers. Ss' own answers

1 **Your friend has a new haircut, and you think it looks awful. When he asks you what you think, you say:**

a) "It looks terrible. I don't like it."
b) "It's OK, but I prefer the old haircut."
c) "It looks amazing! It's perfect for you."

2 **Your mom spent all afternoon making a special dinner, but you don't like it. What do you do?**

a) You eat it and ask for more.
b) You make a horrible face and say you don't want to eat it.
c) You tell her that it's nice, but it's not your favorite meal. Suggest a meal that she can make more quickly and easily.

3 **You're shopping with a friend who wants to buy a new dress. She tries on a dress that looks awful on her. She asks you what you think. What do you do?**

a) You say the dress doesn't look very nice, and you find a different dress for her to try.
b) You say that the dress looks nice and tell her to buy it.
c) You tell her the dress looks horrible and you're bored with shopping.

4 **A new boy in your class invites you to play tennis on Saturday afternoon. You'd like to go to the movies with some friends. What do you do?**

a) You say, "Sorry, I can't. I want to go to the movies with my friends."
b) You make a horrible face and say, "I hate tennis!"
c) You smile and say, "Thanks very much, but I want to go to the movies with some friends on Saturday. Would you like to come with us?"

5 **You have a friend who sometimes smells bad after his tennis lesson. What's the best way to help him?**

a) Make a horrible face and say, "You smell bad. Take a shower!"
b) Give him a box of shower gel and deodorant for his birthday.
c) Talk about him with the other students and laugh.

6 **Your dad doesn't have a job. He lost it last year, and your parents are worried about money. It's your birthday soon, and you want a big party, but your parents say that you can't have one this year. What do you do?**

a) You tell your parents that you understand and it isn't important.
b) You get angry and stay in your room all day.
c) You tell your parents that you understand. You ask your friends to bring some lemonade and chips to the park so you can have a small party.

2 Talk about your answers with your friend. Are they the same or different?

3 Discuss these questions. Ss' own answers

1 Is it important to always tell the truth?
2 Are there some situations where it's OK not to tell the truth?
3 How can we say things to help our friends and not hurt their feelings?

OBJECTIVES: By the end of the lesson, students will have read and talked about telling the truth / telling white lies.

• TARGET LANGUAGE

Key language: *tell the truth / tell a lie, hurt someone's feelings*
Additional language: *haircut, make a face, shower gel, deodorant, tell a little white lie, kind, unkind*
Review: *look (great/horrible), smell (bad)*

• MATERIALS REQUIRED

Extra activity 1: Paper for each pair of students
Extra activity 2: White chalk or white tape (for making a line on the floor)

Warmer

- Say *Listen and do "thumbs up" for true and "thumbs down" for false.* Tell students some things about yourself, some true, some false, e.g., *I went on vacation to London last year. I'm really good at playing volleyball. I have five children.* Make sure the false things are not too obvious. Students respond to each sentence with "thumbs up" or "thumbs down." See if they all agree / if they can tell when you are lying. Reveal which sentences were false.

SB84. ACTIVITY 1. *Read and choose answers.*

- Tell students to open their Student's Books to page 84. Focus on the lesson title and check comprehension. Explain that they are going to take a quiz about telling the truth. Pre-teach new vocabulary from the quiz questions and options, e.g., *haircut, make a face, shower gel.* Ask the students to read and answer the questions on their own by writing a letter for each question in their notebooks.
- Monitor as students read, and help as necessary but do not go through the answers at this stage.

SB84. ACTIVITY 2. *Talk about your answers with your friend. Are they the same or different?*

- Students reread the quiz in pairs and compare their answers for each question. Encourage them to give reasons for their choices.

SB84. ACTIVITY 3. *Discuss these questions.*

- Focus on Activity 3. Choose three students to read the questions. Check comprehension of *situation* and *hurt someone's feelings*. Students discuss the questions in small groups, then have a class discussion. Ask students which words/actions are *kind* and *unkind* and remind them to think about other people's feelings. Teach the expression *(tell a) little white lie.*

WB84. ACTIVITY 1. *Read and answer the questions.*

- Tell students to open their Workbook to page 84. Focus on Activity 1. Read the activity instruction and the questions. Students answer individually then compare answers in pairs. Check with the class.

Key: 1 It can make them feel bad or unhappy. 2 because we don't want to hurt someone, 3 and 4 Students' own answers

WB84. ACTIVITY 2. *Imagine a situation and write about telling a little white lie.*

- Focus students on Activity 2 and on the activity instruction. Remind students of the situations in the quiz in the Student's Book and the language used to describe them. Point out that they need to imagine a situation in the past when someone told a little white lie. Brainstorm other possible situations when it would be better to tell a white lie than tell the truth. Write notes on the board if necessary. Students write about their chosen situation in their notebook. Monitor and help with new vocabulary. They copy their ideas into the Workbook individually, then compare in pairs or small groups.

Key: Students' own answers

Extra activities: see page T109 (if time)

Ending the lesson

- Write the following phrases from the lesson on the board, split into two halves and mixed up, as shown:

1 tell the	*a) face*
2 tell a	*b) truth*
3 tell a little	*c) feelings*
4 hurt someone's	*d) lie*
5 make a	*e) white lie*

Students copy and match the phrases in pairs. Check with the class. Elicit an example sentence for each phrase.

Key: 1 tell the truth, 2 tell a lie, 3 tell a little white lie, 4 hurt someone's feelings, 5 make a face

OBJECTIVES: By the end of the lesson, students will have read problem letters and advice. They will have discussed moral dilemmas and given advice with *should/ shouldn't*.

• TARGET LANGUAGE

Key language: *value (v), friendship, marks, cheat (v)*
Additional language: *fail/pass (an exam), out of ten, make a mistake, steal, shopping mall*
Review: *the best, should/shouldn't, You (don't) have to … , It's better to … , It's a good idea to … , going to,* imperatives, simple past, present perfect, adjectives

• MATERIALS REQUIRED

Warmer: Example of a "problem page" from a magazine or newspaper (in English or L1)
Extra activity 2: Large pieces of paper, colored markers

Warmer

- Show the class an example of a "problem page" from a magazine or newspaper. Ask students if they ever read these pages and point out that they are usually made up of letters and replies. Explain/Remind students that in English the experts who answer such letters are often called Agony Aunts (or Uncles). Tell students they are going to read some letters from a problem page in today's lesson.

SB85. ACTIVITY 1. *Read the letters and answer the questions.*

- Tell students to open their Student's Books to page 85. Focus on the lesson title and elicit a translation of *Value your friendships*. Point to the picture of Betty and Robert and explain that they are an agony aunt and agony uncle. Read the activity instruction and questions 1 to 3 aloud. Check comprehension of *marks* and *cheat*. Pre-teach *fail (an exam)* and *out of ten*. Students read the problem letter and answer the three questions in pairs. Check with the class. Repeat the process with questions 4 and 5.

Key: 1 Yes, he does. 2 No, he doesn't. 3 She takes pictures of the book on her cell phone. 4 If you cheat, you learn very little. 5 No, they don't.

SB85. ACTIVITY 2. *Discuss these questions.*

- Focus students on Activity 2. Choose two students to read the paragraphs of the letter aloud. Check comprehension of new vocabulary (*make a mistake, popular, unkind*). Read through the questions with the whole class and make sure they know that they need to give their own opinions. They discuss in pairs or small groups. Monitor and encourage students to speak in English. Elicit ideas from pairs/groups and have a class discussion about loyalty, friendship, and forgiveness. Students can write Betty and Robert's answer to Katy for homework.

WB85. ACTIVITY 1. *Write the sentences and questions.*

- Tell students to open their Workbook to page 85. Read the activity instruction and go through the example. Students work in pairs to reorder the rest of the sentences and questions. Check with the class.

Key: 2 I didn't tell the truth. 3 Who should he speak to? 4 My best friend cheats in exams. 5 I've made a really big mistake. 6 What should I do?

WB85. ACTIVITY 2. *Read the letter and answer the questions.*

- Focus on Activity 2. Read the activity instruction. Pre-teach *shopping mall*. Check comprehension of *steal*. Students read the letter individually and answer the questions. They compare answers in pairs. Elicit ideas and have a class discussion, if time.

Key: Student's own answers

- Ask the following questions: *Is there a difference between stealing big and little things? Why shouldn't we steal? Are cameras the only reason for not stealing, or should the "camera" be inside us?*

WB85. ACTIVITY 3. *Write a reply to Daisy.*

- Focus on Activity 3. Read the activity instruction. Remind students of the reply letter from Betty and Robert to Richard in the Student's Book. Give them time to re-read this letter and write useful phrases on the board (e.g., *You (don't) have to … , It's better to … , I'm sorry that … , It's (not) a good idea to … , You should/shouldn't … , Don't worry about … , This situation is difficult.*). Students write a reply in their notebooks first. They compare with a partner. When you have checked their work, they copy their reply into the Workbook.

Key: Students' own answers

Extra activities: see page T109 (if time)

Ending the lesson

- Ask students if they would ever write a letter to a problem page. Elicit reasons for their answer. Ask who they talk to if they have problems like the ones they have read about in the lesson.

Value your friendships

1 Read the letters and answer the questions.

Dear Betty and Robert,

I work really hard at school and I always study a lot for my exams, but I don't get good marks. I don't fail, but I get 5, 6, or sometimes 7 out of 10.

My best friend, Emma, gets the best marks in the school, but she cheats. She takes pictures of the book on her cell phone and uses them in the exams. I'm really unhappy about this.

Should I do the same as my friend and get better marks or should I tell the teacher that she cheats in exams? Please help me decide.

Yours,

Richard

Dear Richard,

When you work hard at school and study for your exams, you are learning things. I'm sorry that you don't get the good marks that you want. It's better to work hard and learn things than cheat and learn very little. It's not a good idea for you to do the same as Emma. You should feel good because you're passing your exams. Do your best and don't worry about other people's marks.

This situation is difficult. You don't have to tell the teacher that your friend is cheating. Emma can't always cheat – one day someone is going to catch her.

Yours,

Betty and Robert

1 Does Richard work hard at school?
2 Does he get good marks?
3 How does Emma cheat in the exams?
4 What do Betty and Robert think about cheating?
5 Do they think that Richard should get the same marks as other students?

2 Discuss these questions.

1 Is Sarah right to be unhappy? Why?
2 What do you think Katy should do?
3 What do you think Sarah should do?

Dear Betty and Robert,

I'm really unhappy because I've made a huge mistake with my best friend, Sarah. There's a group of very popular girls in my class. They're cool and funny, and everyone wants to be friends with them. They asked me to go out with them last Saturday. I was really excited, but it was Sarah's birthday.

I didn't go to Sarah's party, and now she's unhappy with me. Now she doesn't want to be my friend. I've started to see that the popular girls are boring and unkind, and I don't like going out with them. I want to be Sarah's best friend again. What should I do?

Yours,

Katy

Grammar reference

Student's Book

1

What time is it?
It's 6 o'clock.

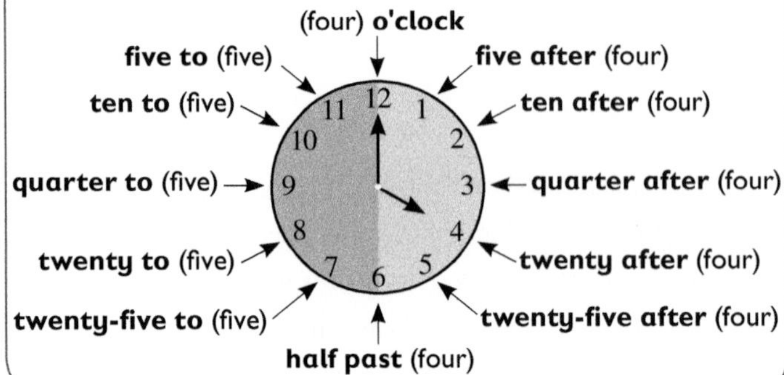

2

We use *going to* to talk and write about the future.

Affirmative	Negative (n't = not)	Question
I**'m going to work** hard.	I**'m not going to work** hard.	**Am** I **going to work** hard?
She**'s going to work** hard.	She **isn't going to work** hard.	**Is** she **going to work** hard?
They**'re going to work** hard.	They **aren't going to work** hard.	**Are** they **going to work** hard?

3

right	She turned **right**.
left	They took the second street on the **left**.
across	They looked and listened carefully before they walked **across** the street.
along	We walked **along** the street.
straight ahead	He didn't turn. He drove **straight ahead** to the end of the road.
corner	I turned at the **corner**.
past	You have to walk **past** the park.

4

We use the past progressive to describe what was happening in the past.

Affirmative	Negative (n't = not)	Question
I **was reading** a book.	I **wasn't reading** a book.	**Was** I **reading** a book?
We **were reading** a book.	We **weren't reading** a book.	**Were** we **reading** a book?

5

We use *made of* to describe materials.

Affirmative	Negative (n't = not)	Question
It**'s made of** metal.	It **isn't made of** metal.	**Is** it **made of** metal?
They**'re made of** metal.	They **aren't made of** metal.	**Are** they **made of** metal?

6

We use verb + *like* to describe things.

Affirmative	Negative (n't = not)	Question
It **sounds like** a train.	It **doesn't sound like** a train.	**Does** it **sound like** a train?
They **sound like** cats.	They **don't sound like** cats.	**Do** they **sound like** cats?

7

We use *should* to give and ask for help or advice.

Affirmative	Negative (n't = not)	Question
I **should tell** my teacher.	I **shouldn't tell** my teacher.	**Should** I **tell** my teacher?
He **should tell** his teacher.	He **shouldn't tell** his teacher.	**Should** he **tell** his teacher?

8

We use the present perfect to talk and write about things we did any time up to now.

Affirmative	Negative (n't = not)	Question
They**'ve visited** London.	They **haven't visited** London.	**Have** they **visited** London?
She**'s visited** London.	She **hasn't visited** London.	**Has** she **visited** London?

Grammar reference

Workbook

ANSWER KEY

WB86. ACTIVITY 1. *Write the times.*

Key: 2 quarter to eight, 3 five to eight, 4 five after eight, 5 twenty-five after eight, 6 ten to nine

WB86. ACTIVITY 2. *Read and write.*

Key: 2 No, she isn't. She's going to eat some meat. 3 No he isn't. He's going to have lunch at home. 4 No we aren't. We're going to get up late. 5 No, I'm not. I'm going to buy a new comic book. 6 No, it isn't. It's going to snow.

WB86. ACTIVITY 3. *Read and choose the right words.*

Key: 2 past, 3 right, 4 across, 5 left, 6 corner

WB86. ACTIVITY 4. *Read and order the words.*

Key: 2 Was Sarah skiing in the mountains? 3 I wasn't taking a bath. 4 David was sailing to an island. 5 Emma and Harry were running through the park. 6 Were you waiting at the bus stop?

WB87. ACTIVITY 5. *Answer the questions.*

Key: 2 It's made of paper. 3 They're made of leather. 4 It's made of wool. 5 They're made of glass. 6 It's made of gold.

WB87. ACTIVITY 6. *Complete the sentences.*

Key: 2 like, 3 cheese, 4 feel, 5 It

WB87. ACTIVITY 7. *Read and write "Yes, you should." or "No, you shouldn't."*

Key: 2 No, you shouldn't. 3 Yes, you should. 4 No, you shouldn't. 5 Yes, you should. 6 No, you shouldn't.

WB87. ACTIVITY 8. *Write questions and answers.*

Key: 2 Have they ever entered a competition? No they haven't. 3 Has he ever played Ping-Pong? No, he hasn't. 4 Have they ever made a snowman? Yes, they have. 5 Have you ever seen the Olympics? No, I haven't.

Teaching notes for Photocopiables

Unit 1 page 11

- Hand out a copy of Photocopiable 1 (see page T90) to each student. Students complete the schedule information in the top section of the photocopy as they wish.
- Make pairs. Students don't look at each other's papers. They take turns asking and answering questions about Peter and Sally and complete the schedule at the bottom of the photocopy with their partner's information. Remind them to use the prompts in the speech bubbles. When they have finished, students look at each other's work to check.

Unit 2 page 22 (see also page T22, Student's Book Activity 17 and 18)

- Copy Photocopiable 2 (see page T91) twice, onto thin cardboard. Cut out the cards before the lesson. (If you have a class of, e.g., 26, you will only need to use 13 of the cards from Photocopiable 2 – two copies of each).
- Hand out one card to each student. On the board write in example speech bubbles *What are you going to do on … ?* and *I'm going to …* . Tell students they need to find the person who has the same plans as they have on their card. The students mingle and ask and answer questions to find out who their partner is. Monitor and make sure they are speaking English and not simply comparing cards. When students have found their partner, they check with you, and then sit down. They will work together on Student's Book Activity 18.

Unit 3, page 30

- Hand out a copy of Photocopiable 3 (see page T92) to each pair, part A to StudentA, part B to StudentB. StudentA starts reading until he/she comes to a blank, and then StudentB takes over. They continue like this until the end of the text. The first time, they don't try to write anything, but just read and listen to get the general sense of the text. The second time, they complete their text, writing in the words their partner says. At the end, they compare texts to check. See below for completed text.

Unit 4, page 39

- Hand out Photocopiable 4 (see page T93), one copy cut in half for each pair. Demonstrate the activity on the board. Students work individually, keeping their work secret. They check one thing each child in the chart was doing when an earthquake struck (including themselves in the "me" row).
- Students work in pairs. They take turns exchanging information about Harry, Katy, William, Betty, and themselves, by asking and answering questions like the examples at the top of their chart. They put an "x" in the appropriate box for their partner's answers. Monitor and check that they are not looking at each other's papers. When they have asked about all the children, they compare charts, to check.

Text for Photocopiable 3

London Bridge

The Romans made the first bridge in London over the River Thames. It was the only bridge over the Thames until 1750. London Bridge was also important because it had houses and stores on it. There were about 400 stores on the old bridge.

In the 1820s, a new London Bridge was built over the Thames. They tore down the old bridge. In 1968 another London Bridge was opened. An American bought the old bridge and took it to Lake Havasu in Arizona, U.S.A. Today a lot of people visit the London Bridge in Arizona.

Unit 5, page 47

- Hand out a copy of Photocopiable 5 (see page T94) to each student. Check students remember the clothing words. Individually, each student completes the chart at the top of the page with materials that the different children's clothes are made of.
- Make new pairs. Students don't look at their partner's chart. They take turns asking and answering questions and to complete the chart at the bottom of the page. Each time they have the same information as their partner, they call out *Snap!* Students compare their charts at the end.

Unit 6, page 54

- Hand out a copy of Photocopiable 6 (see page T95) to each student. They study the pictures individually and think about their responses to the questions. After about three minutes, put students into groups of four for a discussion. Remind them of the structure to use, e.g., *I think it looks like a face.* Encourage students to discuss the drawings in detail, e.g., *These look like eyes and this looks like a nose.* Monitor groups as they are working. Students write their friends' ideas on the lines.
- After the groupwork, go through the worksheet with the class, discussing each picture.

Unit 7, page 69

- Hand out a copy of Photocopiable 7 (see page T96) to each pair of students. Check all the words and discuss together the connections between the words in columns 1 and 2, e.g., *hair – fur, spots – stripes, birds – bats*, etc. and columns 3 and 4. Students then cut out the word cards and place them face down on their desks. They take turns turning over two cards at a time. The student who turns over the cards says the two words aloud. If they are a pair, he/she keeps them. If not, he/she turns them face down again and the other student has a turn. At the end, the student in each pair with the most pairs of cards is the winner.
- Students put their cards in envelopes at the end of the game. Collect the envelopes so the students can play again in another lesson.

Unit 8, page 80

- Hand out a copy of Photocopiable 8 (see page T97) to each pair of students (one part to each student). Remind them how to do the crossword puzzle: they have to provide the definition for their partner and ask their partner for definitions to complete all the clues. Remind students not to look at each other's crossword puzzles. Monitor and help where necessary. Students compare completed crossword puzzles at the end.

Key: Across: 2 park, 7 spotted, 8 plant, 11 butterfly, 13 insect, 14 ground, 16 striped, 18 sea, 19 frog, 20 lake;
Down: 1 trees, 3 field, 4 dinosaur, 5 countryside, 6 forest, 9 leaf, 10 river, 12 extinct, 14 grass, 15 wing, 17 duck

Photocopiable 1

Name: ____________________

1 Peter and Sally are in different classes at the Park Road School. Complete their schedules for Monday. Use these words.

English	math	science	geography
history	computer studies	art	music

	Peter	Sally
8:15		
9:10		
10:30		
11:25		
1:30		
2:25		
3:20		
4:15		

2 Ask and answer. Complete.

What does Peter have at quarter after eight?

He has music.

	Peter	Sally
8:15		
9:10		
10:30		
11:25		
1:30		
2:25		
3:20		
4:15		

Photocopiable 2

Name: ____________________

I'm going to play volleyball on Wednesday afternoon. I'm going to do my homework on Saturday morning.	I'm going to play volleyball on Wednesday afternoon. I'm going to have a party on Saturday morning.	I'm going to play volleyball on Wednesday afternoon. I'm going to go shopping on Saturday morning.
I'm going to play volleyball on Wednesday afternoon. I'm going to read a comic book on Saturday morning.	I'm going to read a comic book on Wednesday afternoon. I'm going to go shopping on Saturday morning.	I'm going to read a comic book on Wednesday afternoon. I'm going to do my homework on Saturday morning.
I'm going to read a comic book on Wednesday afternoon. I'm going to get up late on Saturday morning.	I'm going to read a comic book on Wednesday afternoon. I'm going to go shopping on Saturday morning.	I'm going to go shopping on Wednesday afternoon. I'm going to play volleyball on Saturday morning.
I'm going to go shopping on Wednesday afternoon. I'm going to get up late on Saturday morning.	I'm going to go shopping on Wednesday afternoon. I'm going to read a comic book on Saturday morning.	I'm going to go shopping on Wednesday afternoon. I'm going to watch TV on Saturday morning.
I'm going to have a party on Wednesday afternoon. I'm going to get up late on Saturday morning.	I'm going to have a party on Wednesday afternoon. I'm going to watch TV on Saturday morning.	I'm going to have a party on Wednesday afternoon. I'm going to read a comic book on Saturday morning.

Photocopiable 3

A London Bridge

The ________ made ________ ________ ________ in London over ________ ________ ________ . ________ ________ ________ ________ bridge over the Thames ________ ________ . London Bridge was ________ ________ ________ it had houses ________ ________ ________ ________ . There were about ________ ________ ________ the old bridge.
________ ________ ________ , a new London Bridge ________ ________ over the Thames. ________ ________ ________ the old bridge. ________ ________ , ________ London bridge was opened. ________ ________ ________ ________ old bridge and took ________ ________ ________ Havasu ________ Arizona, ________ . Today a lot of people ________ ________ London Bridge in ________ .

B London Bridge

________ Romans ________ the first bridge ________ ________ ________ the River Thames. It was the only ________ ________ ________ ________ until 1750. ________ ________ ________ also important because ________ ________ ________ and stores on it. ________ ________ ________ 400 stores on ________ ________ ________ .
In the 1820s, ________ ________ ________ ________ was built ________ ________ ________ . They tore down ________ ________ ________ . In 1968, another ________ ________ ________ ________ . An American bought the ________ ________ ________ ________ it to Lake ________ in ________ , U.S.A. ________ ________ ________ ________ visit the ________ ________ ________ Arizona.

Photocopiable 4

A

B: What was Harry doing when the earthquake struck?
A: He was watching TV when the earthquake struck.

	watch TV 	sing in the shower 	talk on the phone 	do homework 	read a book 	use the computer 
Harry	✓					
Katy						
William and Betty						
me						
my friend						

B

A: What was Harry doing when the earthquake struck?
B: He was talking on the phone when the earthquake struck.

	watch TV 	sing in the shower 	talk on the phone 	do homework 	read a book 	use the computer 
Harry			✓			
Katy						
William and Betty						
me						
my friend						

Photocopiable 5

Name: ____________________

1 Write the material words in the boxes.

	ring	gloves	shoes	belt	coat
Richard					
Sarah					
Katy					

2 Ask and answer and complete.

What's Richard's ring made of?

It's made of plastic.

	ring	gloves	shoes	belt	coat
Richard					
Sarah					
Katy					

Photocopiable 6

Name: ------------------------

Ask three friends. Write your friends' answers.

1 What does this look like?

2 What does this look like?

3 What does this look like?

4 What does this look like?

5 What does this look like?

6 What does this look like?

Photocopiable 7

Name: ____________________

hair	fur	cats	dogs
spots	stripes	fish	frogs
bats	birds	teeth	tails
black	white	sharks	whales
fish	chips	gold	silver
salt	pepper	knife	fork
shoes	socks	pencil	paper

Photocopiable 8

A

Down ↓

1 Very big plants. There are a lot in a forest.
15 Most birds and insects use this to fly.
17 A bird which loves water. It lives near rivers and lakes.

Across →

7 An adjective to describe an insect with spots.
8 It lives and grows, but it isn't an animal. A flower's one.
11 It can fly, but it isn't a bird. It's beautiful and it loves flowers.
13 This isn't an animal or a plant. Lizards like to eat them.
14 This is the floor when we're outside.
18 A very big area of salt water.
19 This animal can swim and jump very well. It lives near rivers and lakes.

B

Down ↓

3 There's a lot of grass here. Cows and sheep are usually in one.
4 This animal was called "The terrible lizard." It's extinct now.
5 Not in the city. We can go here for a picnic.
6 There are a lot of trees here.
9 This is green. We can see it on a plant.
10 There's water here, but it isn't the sea or a lake.
12 An adjective to describe plants or animals which don't exist any more.
14 Cows eat this.

Across →

2 In a town or a city, we can play here.
16 An adjective to describe an insect with stripes.
20 There's water here, but it isn't a river or the ocean.

Extra activities

Welcome to our ezine

Page 4

- **Extra activity 1: Making friends**

Make pairs. If possible, pair students who don't know each other very well. Elicit some questions to find out personal information, e.g., *When's your birthday? Where do you live? Do you have brothers and sisters? What's your favorite band?* Either do this orally, or write the questions on the board. Individually, students choose and write six questions to ask their partner on a piece of paper. They then take turns asking and answering the questions. They write the answers under the questions. They write their friend's name at the top of the paper, decorate it, and then display it on the board.

- **Extra activity 2: Word race**

This is an extension of Workbook page 4 Activity 1. Divide the class into groups of four. Give a large piece of paper to each group. They divide it into four. Tell students you will give them time limits to write other lists, as in Activity 1. Each time you say a category, give students two minutes to write as many words as they can think of in one part of the paper. Remind them to do it quietly so the other groups don't hear. At the end of the activity, groups swap papers with other groups. Brainstorm mind maps onto the board for each category. Students can be creative, but you must decide if their words are acceptable or not. The groups with the most words in each of the categories are the winners. Suggested categories: *things we eat, things we drink, things we carry, things we ride, things we play, things we take care of.*

Page 5

- **Extra activity 1: Profiles**

Students use the information they found out about in Student's Book Activity 6 to write a short profile of their partner. They use the texts in Student's Book Activity 4 as a model. Remind them to use the third person, e.g., *She likes riding …* . Students display their texts.

- **Extra activity 2: Mime game**

Introduce the game by miming one of the activities from the lesson, e.g., *playing the guitar.* Choose eight students to come to the front. Together they very quietly choose eight activities to mime to the class. They take turns miming the activities (they can include activities that are not from the lesson). The class watches and silently writes the activities in their notebooks. They don't speak. Students swap notebooks. The eight students redo their mimes one by one and the class says the activity. Students correct their partner's work. Repeat with another eight students and eight new activities.

Page 6

- **Extra activity 1: Ezine page**

Students work in groups of four to create their own ezine page about their school, using the texts and pictures on the Student's Book page as a model. They should include drawings and text. Display the posters around the class. Decide who wins "the prize."

- **Extra activity 2: Dictionary game**

Elicit all the school words from the lesson (including school subjects) and write them as a mind map on the board. Students copy the mind map into their notebooks. In pairs, students write each word from the mind map on a separate piece of paper. They then arrange the words in alphabetical order. Pairs check with pairs. In groups of four, students place one set of word cards down on their desks. Hand out dictionaries: one for each pair. Pairs take turns turning over words. Both pairs then race to find the word in the dictionary. The pair who finds the word first reads out the definition and "wins" the word. The game continues until all the words have been won.

Page 7

- **Extra activity 1: School song**

Students work in groups of four to write a new verse for the School song. Monitor and help the different groups. Some groups may only want to change a few words; others may feel confident enough to rewrite the verse.

Groups perform their verses, e.g., Group A sings their verse; the whole class sings a chorus; Group B sings their verse; the whole class sings a chorus, and so on around the class.

- **Extra activity 2: Word poems**

Demonstrate the activity for the class. Choose a subject and write the word vertically on the board with the first letter at the top and the last at the bottom. Elicit/Write a word or phrase for each one so the poem looks like this:

***M**ultiply*
***A**dd*
***T**hat's*
***H**andy*

Students work in groups of four to create their own poems using other subjects. Groups display their poems for the class.

Page 8

- **Extra activity 1: About our schedules**

Students work in groups of four. They put their schedules on their desks and look for similarities and differences. They all stick their schedules on a large sheet of paper and write sentences underneath about what they found, e.g., *We all have two math lessons a day. No one has science on Monday. Only (name) has tennis on his/her schedules.* Groups take turns coming to the front, holding up their poster, and reading out their sentences to the class. Display the posters on the wall.

- **Extra activity 2: Writing together**

Put students into pairs or groups of four. They read through the texts each of them wrote for Workbook Activity 19 and try to correct any mistakes. Remind them to use pencil and not pen on each other's work. Tell students that this is a cooperative activity, not a competitive one: they are trying to help each other. Students then rewrite their own texts on a piece of paper.

Page 9

- **Extra activity 1: Role play**

Make groups of three. Students read through the Student's Book story in their groups. They take turns being the three different characters. More confident students can role play the story for the whole class.

- **Extra activity 2: Fill in the words**

Students close their Student's Books. Display a large sheet of paper with the blanked out text (see page T9) on the board. Students work in pairs to complete the text with the key words. Give them a time limit. They write the missing words in a list in their notebooks. Students swap notebooks with other pairs for correcting. Check with the class.

Key: 1 writing, 2 understand/read, 3 Rosetta, 4 languages, 5 languages, 6 understand/read, 7 Rosetta, 8 understand/read, 9 hieroglyphics

Unit 1

Page 10

• Extra activity 1: Matching game

Dictate the following times to students: *2:15, 10:30, 4:10, 5:40, 6:45, 12:30, 11:25, 7:55*. Hand out two sheets of colored paper / thin cardboard one white, one blue, to each pair. They divide and then cut each one into eight squares. On the white paper / cardboard they write each time in words, e.g., *quarter after two*; on the blue one they draw clocks to show the different times.

Make groups of four. Students put their cards face down on the table and mix them around. They take turns turning over one white and one blue card. The student says the time on each one aloud. If they match and the student has said them correctly, he/she keeps the pair. If they are not a match or if the student has made a mistake, then he/she turns the cards face down again. Game continues until all the cards have been matched.

• Extra activity 2: My day

Students work individually and write a sequence similar to Workbook Activity 3 for their day in their notebooks. They write the sentences on different lines. At the end of each sentence, they draw a clock showing the time. They swap their notebooks with a partner and check each other's work.

Page 11

• Extra activity: Talking about yesterday

Write *Today* in a box on the board with the following verbs underneath: *have, start, catch, finish, get dressed, go, begin, come, wake up, get up, eat, drink, put, take*. Write *Yesterday* in a box on the board and elicit one example from the list, e.g., *have–had*, and write *had* in the box. Students work in pairs to write the other words in the past. Elicit from pairs and complete the box on the board.

In their pairs, students write four sentences on strips of paper about the time they do/did things in the day: two in the present and two in the past. Collect the strips of paper. Make four teams. They line up, with the student at the front facing the board. Erase the board and write only *Yesterday* on one side and *Today* on the other. Read out a sentence at random. According to whether the sentence is in the present or the past, the students at the front of each team run and touch the correct word on the board. The first to do so wins a point for their team. The runners go to the back of the line. Continue with the other sentences until everyone has had at least one turn.

Page 12

• Extra activity 1: TV show survey

Elicit the question for finding out favorite shows from students (*What's your favorite TV show?*). Elicit possible responses, e.g., the name of the show or *I don't have one*.

Students prepare a five-column by seven-row survey chart. They write *Question* at the top of column 1, and *Name* at the top of the other four columns. Down the left-hand side they write six questions to ask their friends. Make sure they notice that we say *What's your favorite TV sports/cartoon/news/quiz show?* But we say *What's your favorite TV series/documentary?* (without using *show*).

Students move around the class, asking the six questions of four friends. They note their answers. Discuss with the class which their favorite shows are.

• Extra activity 2: Making a TV show

Students work in groups of four. They choose a TV show they know well, e.g., a series, a quiz, a comedy or a news show. They write a short script, to include all four students in the group. They rehearse their scripts. Monitor and help groups at this stage, providing input on language and content. When all the groups are ready, they perform their show extracts for the class. Photograph or film their efforts.

Page 13

• Extra activity 1: Reading race

Make groups of four. Give each group their questions (see page T13) and give them reading time. Put copies of a newspaper TV schedule on the wall where groups cannot read them from their desks. Tell the class the rules and demonstrate the race with an example question.

Rules: The groups read the first question, then one student from each group goes to the TV schedule to find an answer. They have to remember the answer, come back to their group, tell them, and they record it on their paper. Only one student can be away from the group at any one time. Students take turns as the "runner" and the "writer." Start the race. Note the time that each group finishes (let them all finish). Groups swap papers. Correct as a class for groups to score each other's answers. The group with the most correct answers (including spelling) is the winner.

• Extra activity 2: Presentations

Students use the information from Workbook Activity 14 to prepare and give short oral presentations to the class (one to two minutes). They should make notes before their presentation and can use these when they are speaking, but they shouldn't write the complete text to read aloud. You can spread the presentations over several days or students can present in small groups.

Page 14

• Extra activity 1: Comparing information

Make new groups of four that do not contain any of the pairs from Student's Book Activity 17. Students use their notes about their friend to report to the group. They take turns reporting one piece of information, e.g., *Luca watches TV seven times a week*. If another student has found out the same information about their friend, they can add it, e.g., *Oh, Gemma watches TV seven times a week, too*. After they have all orally reported about their friends, tell groups to put away their notebooks. Hand out large sheets of paper to each group. They prepare group posters about their friends' TV habits, using the information from Activity 17. They can organize/present the posters in whatever way they like, apart from writing texts (that they are going to do for Activity 18). Students display their posters on the wall.

• Extra activity 2: Writing together

Put students into pairs or groups of four. They read through the texts each of them wrote for Workbook page 14 Activity 19 and try to correct any mistakes. Remind them to use pencil and not pen on each other's work. Tell students that this is a cooperative activity, not a competitive one: they are trying to help each other. Students then rewrite their own texts on a piece of paper.

Page 15

• Extra activity 1: Role play

Make groups of five. Students decide on their roles and then read through the Diggory Bones story in their groups. They extend parts of the story as they wish, e.g., the interview with Diggory. They prepare and practice their role plays as a group and perform their stories for the whole class.

- **Extra activity 2: The news**

Students work in pairs. They use the information from the previous episode, this episode, and their imagination to extend the news item about the professor and the Baloney Stone, so that it lasts about one minute. Set up a news desk at the front of the class for the pairs to read their news items. Vote as a class for the best, funniest, most imaginative news item.

Page 16

- **Extra activity 1: Our cartoon**

Students work in pairs or groups of four. Organize the groups so that there is a balance of different creativity, artistic ability, writing ability, etc. in each one. They discuss their ideas for a cartoon and then transfer their ideas to paper for presentation/display. Provide prompts on the board, e.g.

Name:
Themes:
Characters:
Technique: (cell animation, models, hand-drawn)
Example of storyline:
Example drawings of some of the characters:

Students present their ideas to the class. Vote for the best cartoon idea.

- **Extra activity 2: Class survey**

Students use the questionnaire from Workbook Activity 1 as the basis of a class survey. Students work in pairs and ask each other the questions. They record the information. Make new groups of six. Students report the information they found out from their partner to the group. The group collates the information onto a grid. Collate the class survey onto the board.

Page 17

- **Extra activity 1: My personal timeline**

Students work individually to make a timeline about their own lives. Brainstorm with the class some key points in students' lives, e.g., *starting school, moving to a new place, learning to walk, learning to swim, starting English*. Students draw their own timeline on a large piece of paper with the heading *My personal timeline*, divide it into years and then write the information above or below the relevant sections. They illustrate the information. Students compare timelines.

- **Extra activity 2: CLIL vocabulary**

Elicit the new words and phrases from the two lessons on cartoons onto the board. Check students understand them and know how to say them. In their vocabulary books, students write the heading *Cartoons*. They write the new words, phrases, and expressions from the lessons, either as a mind map, or as a list. At the bottom of the page, they write some of the things they did in the lessons, e.g., *I learned about how cartoons are made. I made my own flipbook*. If time, students can illustrate the page.

Unit 2

Page 18

- **Extra activity 1: Sentence parts**

Students work in pairs. They write at least six sentences using *going to*, including questions, negatives, and affirmatives. They write each one on a strip of paper and cut it up, as in Student's Book Activity 3. They swap their sentences with another pair, who try to sequence them correctly.

- **Extra activity 2: Number code**

Show students how to create their own number code for the letters of the alphabet. They write the letters A to Z in a row and numbers above each letter in any order they want, e.g., just even numbers (A = 2, B = 4, C = 6, etc.), or starting at 26 (A = 26, B = 25, etc.). Students work in pairs. They make up their code and then each write a message in the code (by writing the numbers that represent the letters). Then they swap messages and decode them.

Page 19

- **Extra activity 1: Song time**

Brainstorm ideas for other verses for the song, e.g., *going to work all night, and do it right / teach them sums, and make it fun.* Students work in threes. They rewrite a verse and illustrate it with an amusing picture. Groups sing their verses and display their work.

- **Extra activity 2: My Calendar**

Students write their own imaginary calendars (using Sam's in Workbook Activity 7 as a model) for the next weekend. They include times and also add their own ideas. Students work in pairs. Students take turns asking and answering questions about each other's calendars and write a note in their calendar about what their friend is doing when.

Page 20

- **Extra activity 1: Disappearing text**

This activity uses one of the texts from Student's Book Activity 8. Either write one of the shorter texts or part of one of the longer texts on the board in the lesson, or reveal the text you wrote on the board beforehand. Ask students to take turns reading it aloud (books closed). Erase the jobs from the text. Ask students to read it aloud again, filling in the words that have been erased. Continue, erasing a different class of words each time until there are only a few words left, e.g., proper nouns.

- **Extra activity 2: Famous people's lives**

Elicit names of famous people from the students' home country, e.g., cooks, actors, writers, sportspeople. Choose one of the people you are familiar with and elicit what students know about his/her life. Write notes about the person's life on the board. Students use the notes to write a short biography of the person in their notebooks, similar to the ones on Student's Book page 20.

Page 21

- **Extra activity 1: Predictions**

Students work in groups of six. They draw a chart like the one in Student's Book Activity 14, putting their name at the top of the list and then their friends' names down the side. They have an extra column on the right (for the jobs). Brainstorm ideas and put them into a mind map about what students love doing, to give them ideas. Students write what they love doing in the column next to their own name. Elicit/Provide the questions: *What do you love doing? What are you good at?* Students take turns asking the questions of the others in their group and noting the answers in the middle column. Students use the information to complete the third column alone. Then they discuss their predictions as a group, e.g., *I think you're going to be ...* . Discuss students' predictions for each other as a class.

- **Extra activity 2: Guess the job**

Play the CD from Student's Book Activity 11 again. Students work in pairs. They write a short dialog, that gives clues about a job, but that doesn't say exactly what it is. Encourage students to be creative and funny. Pairs role play their dialogs for the class to guess the job.

Page 22

- **Extra activity: What's the job?**

Students use the texts they wrote for Workbook Activity 19 in a guessing game. They look back through their texts and cross out the actual job. Ask for six volunteers. They come to the front. The students take turns reading their texts aloud. The rest of the class listens in silence and writes down what they guess the job is. They do this for all six. At the end, check the answers with the students at the front. Repeat with six more volunteers.

Page 23

- **Extra activity 1: Role play**

Make groups of five. Students decide on their roles and then read through the story in their groups. They extend parts of the dialogue in their groups as they wish, e.g., Sir Doug can go to the library, too. They prepare and practice their role plays as a group and peform their stories for the whole class.

- **Extra activity 2: Job alphabet**

Students divide a piece of paper into 26 squares. They write a letter of the alphabet in the corner of each square. The squares should be big enough to write at least one word in. At the top of the page, they write *Jobs*. Students look back through the unit to find all the jobs they can that begin with different letters of the alphabet. They write the words in the appropriate places. Students discuss and compare.

Page 24

- **Extra activity 1: Draw and label**

Students copy the diagrams from Student's Book Activities 2 and 3 into their notebooks and label them. Underneath, they write about their own teeth, saying how many incisors, canines, premolars, and molars they actually have.

- **Extra activity 2: Other animals and their teeth**

Make groups of four. Students use reference books and/or the Internet to find out other amazing facts about animals and their teeth. Before the activity, brainstorm some animals and questions with the class to give them ideas, e.g., *Do snakes have teeth? How big was a dinosaur tooth? Do any other animals brush their teeth? Can any animals regrow their teeth? What animals have tusks?*

Students find out the information in their groups and transfer it onto a poster. They can draw pictures of the animals. Display the posters on the wall. Students walk around the room and look at all the posters. They find what they think is the most amazing fact and write it in their notebooks.

Page 25

- **Extra activity 1: Brushing my teeth**

Students write the text on brushing their teeth from Student's Book Activity 5 in the correct order in their notebooks. Once they have done this, they rehearse brushing their teeth in this way, allocating timings to the different activities.

- **Extra activity 2: CLIL vocabulary**

Elicit the new words and phrases from the two lessons on teeth onto the board. Check students understand them and know how to say them. In their vocabulary books, students write the heading *Teeth*. They write the new words, phrases, and expressions from the lessons, either as a mind map, or as a list. At the bottom of the page, they write some of the things they did in the lessons, e.g., *I did an experiment. I learned about the different teeth people have. I know how to brush my teeth correctly.*

Review Units 1 and 2

Page 26

- **Extra activity 1: Songs and chants**

Sing one of the songs or do one of the chants from Units 1 and 2.

- **Extra activity 2: Phoning Peter**

Tell students they are going to write the telephone conversation between Sarah and Peter (see Student's Book Activity 1). Give them time to re-read the conversation in the Student's Book first and elicit the things that Sarah needs to ask Peter. Write the beginning of the phone call on the board:

Peter: Hello?
Sarah: Hi, Peter. It's Sarah. …

Students work in pairs to continue the conversation. Tell them to use their imagination. (Will Peter say "yes" or "no"? Does he have a different suggestion about where to go?) Monitor and help with language. Students practice their phone call. Ask volunteer pairs to perform their call for the class.

Page 27

- **Extra activity 1: Vocabulary review**

Students look back through Units 1 and 2, checking they have noted all the key vocabulary in their vocabulary books. They write example sentences for any words they find difficult to remember. Finally, they create mind maps for the unit themes: *TV shows* and *Jobs*.

- **Extra activity 2: Games and activities**

Students choose one of the games or activities from Units 1 and 2 to do again.

Unit 3

Page 28

- **Extra activity 1: Following directions**

Organize the tables in the classroom so that there are "roads" for students to walk along and corners and turnings. Place labels on some of the tables, e.g., *museum, station, supermarket*.

Demonstrate the activity by giving simple directions for a student to follow. In pairs, students write a short set of directions for another student to follow around the class. All students start with *You are outside/at the (place)* and they have to take the person to a certain place in the "city" (classroom). They can choose where to start. Write prompts on the board, e.g., *Take the …, Turn …* . Pairs take turns giving directions to another student.

- **Extra activity 2: Now draw the map**

Students work in pairs and draw and label a map of the part of the city as described in Workbook Activity 1. They can add to the map, but all the features mentioned in the text must be there and correct. Students swap maps. Read the text aloud to the class. They follow on the friend's map, as if they are the bus driver, to check.

Page 29

- **Extra activity 1: Correct the mistakes**

Focus students on the map in Student's Book Activity 4. Tell them you are going to give them some directions to follow. Display the large sheet of paper (see page T29). Students read and follow the directions to find the mistakes. They check in pairs. Check with the class.

- **Extra activity 2: How to get there**

Tell students that a friend is going to visit their house or school and needs directions from, e.g., the train station, or the bus stop. Provide a simple email format on the board for them to complete:

Hi (name)
It's great that you are coming to visit. Here are the directions so you can find my house/school easily.
You start at … (lines for directions)
Here's my cell phone number in case you get lost.
Good luck and see you soon
(Name)

Page 30

- **Extra activity: London posters**

Review what students thought were the most exciting things about London from the warmer and from the reading. Tell students they are going to make a poster, in groups of four. The poster is to promote London and to make people of their age want to go there, so it has to be exciting, colorful, and interesting. Students can use reference books and the Internet to find information. They can print pictures off the Internet, but they have to write their own text. Give them planning and research time and then time to prepare their posters. Display the posters around the classroom or the school.

Page 31

- **Extra activity 1: Drawing a map**

Students draw a map to illustrate their directions from Student's Book Activity 14. They then write the directions underneath it.

- **Extra activity 2: Ten questions**

In pairs, students make a quick mind map of all the jobs they can remember, then secretly choose one of them. Pairs take turns coming to the front. The rest of the class can ask ten *yes/no* questions to guess their job. If the class does not guess in ten, the pair of students scores 1 point. If the class do guess, the pair who guesses correctly wins 1 point.

Page 32

- **Extra activity 1: Spelling**

Students work in pairs. StudentA closes his/her book. StudentB says a word from Workbook Activity 18. StudentA says the word and tells StudentB if it has the sound /s/, /ʃ/, or /ʧ/. StudentA then writes the word in his/her notebook, thinking carefully about the spelling. StudentB checks StudentA's spelling. Then they swap roles. Repeat two or three times.

- **Extra activity 2: Pelmanism**

Students close their books. Hand out a photocopy of the 12 words in Workbook Activity 18 to pairs of students. They cut them into 12 cards. They put the cards face down on the desk. Students take turns turning over two cards and saying the words. If the words have the same sound (the ones that are underlined), he/she keeps the pair. If not, he/she turns them face down again. When most or all of the cards are paired up, students check with another pair.

Page 33

- **Extra activity 1: Role play**

Make groups of four. Students decide on their roles and then read through the story in their groups. They extend parts of the dialog in their groups as they wish, e.g., Sir Doug can go to Egypt, too / Brutus is doing a different job. They prepare and practice their role plays as a group and perform their stories for the whole class.

- **Extra activity 2: Following directions**

Organize the tables in the classroom so that there are "roads" for students to walk along and corners and turnings (similar to Extra activity 1 for page 28). Students make labels for places in the city and place them on some of the charts, e.g., *museum, station, supermarket*. Demonstrate the activity by giving simple directions for a student to follow. In pairs, students write a set of directions for another student to follow around the class. Students can start the directions wherever they like, e.g., *You are outside the museum / at the school*, and they have to take their partner to a certain place in the "city" (classroom). Write prompts on the board, e.g., *Take the …* , *Turn …* . Pairs take turns giving directions to another student.

Page 34

- **Extra activity 1: Cavemen**

Brainstorm with the class what they know about cavemen: what they wore, where they lived, what they ate, how they hunted, what they looked like, etc. Students use the information to write a short text in their notebooks about cavemen. They can personalize, e.g., imagine they are a caveman for a day.

- **Extra activity 2: The Industrial Revolution**

Use pictures to brainstorm key aspects of the Industrial Revolution with the class (trains, factories, mechanization, cities, speed, and ease of travel). Students work in groups of four. They choose one aspect of the Industrial Revolution, e.g., the railways / the first steam train, and find out about it, using reference books / the Internet. They present their information on a poster with pictures and a short text and groups take turns talking to the class about what they learned.

Page 35

- **Extra activity 1: What we did for the project**

Students reflect on and then write about what they did for the project: what they talked about, how they decided what to include and why, the process of drawing the city plan (was it difficult?), the name they chose and why.

- **Extra activity 2: CLIL vocabulary**

Elicit the new words and phrases from the two lessons on cities onto the board. Check students understand them and know how to say them. In their vocabulary books, students write the heading *Cities*. They write the new words, phrases, and expressions from the lessons, either as a mind map, or as a list. At the bottom of the page, they write some of the things they did in the lessons, e.g., *I learned about the history of cities. I learned about the Industrial Revolution. I created a plan for a new city in my group.*

Unit 4

Page 36

- **Extra activity 1: Role play**

Display the CD script from Student's Book Activity 1 on the board. Make groups of four. Students take turns being the different characters and role play the story.

- **Extra activity 2: Timeline**

Students put the sentences from Workbook Activity 3 on timelines, using the same colors as before.

Page 37

- **Extra activity 1: Palms up or down?**

Students work individually and write sentences about things they were doing / that happened to them during the previous week. Some must be true; others can be false. They write six sentences in all. Supply some examples, e.g., *I was shopping with my mom when I saw a tiger in a tree*. Make groups of four. Students take turns reading their sentences to the group. The students guess true or false, but they don't say it. They put one hand down on the table, palm up for true, palm down for false. Correct guesses win a point. Elicit the strangest true sentences from students at the end.

- **Extra activity 2: Survey**

Students prepare a five-column x seven-row survey chart in their notebooks. Students write six questions in the left-hand column, beginning *What were you doing at … ?* and adding times. They interview four people, write their names at the top, and then write their answers in the relevant column using the past progressive.

Page 38

- **Extra activity 1: Important dates in my life**

Draw a life timeline on the board for an imaginary student(Sylvia). Mark six dates along the timeline, e.g., *Born on June 27, 1995, Baby brother born in 1998, Started school in September 2000, Learned to swim in February 2001, Moved to a different house on October 31, 2003, Got my pet dog Frankie on December 25, 2005.*

Elicit sentences from the class about Sylvia's life. Check they say the days correctly (use of *in*, *on*, pronunciation of months, ordinals, years, etc.). Students work individually. They draw a timeline for themselves in their notebooks and mark six points along it. Make groups of four. Students take turns telling each other about the events in their lives. They find out if they have any dates or events in common. Students write sentences about the six events in their lives under the timeline.

- **Extra activity 2: Date bingo**

Write 16 complete dates on the board, e.g., *October 15, 2003.* Students draw a 2 x 2 bingo grid in their notebooks and choose four dates. They write one in each square in their notebooks. Call out the dates at random. Students cross out ones that they hear. The first student to cross out all four is the winner, if they can then say all four dates correctly.

Page 39

- **Extra activity: The other hemisphere**

Display a world map or show students a globe. Teach *the northern hemisphere* and *the southern hemisphere*. Ask students if they have ever visited friends or relations in the other hemisphere. If they have, ask them what the weather was like in the month they visited. Write the months of the year horizontally on the board. Above the months (for the northern hemisphere), mark in the seasons. Below the months (for the southern hemisphere), mark in the seasons. Ask students, e.g., *When it's summer for us, what season is it in the southern/northern hemisphere?* (winter). *What do you think people do then?* Repeat for another season. Students copy the chart into their notebooks. In pairs, they discuss what people do in the different months in the other hemisphere. Check students are using the simple present. Elicit their ideas.

Page 40

- **Extra activity 1: Recording survey information**

Students write sentences about their three friends in their notebooks using the information they gathered in the survey in Student's Book Activity 15, e.g., *At 8:45 yesterday morning, Joanna was walking to school with her brother.*

- **Extra activity 2: Writing together**

Put students into pairs or groups of four. They read through the texts each of them wrote for Workbook Activity 18 and try to correct any mistakes. Remind them to use pencil and not pen on each other's work. Tell students that this is a cooperative activity, not a competitive one: they are trying to help each other. Students then rewrite their own texts on a piece of paper.

Page 41

- **Extra activity 1: Role play**

Make groups of three. Students decide on their roles. Play the CD of the Diggory Bones story. Students repeat in role. They read through the story in their groups. They repeat twice more, changing roles each time.

- **Extra activity 2: Birthday chart**

Display the birthday chart (see page T41). Tell students when your birthday is, write the date and your name on a piece of paper, and stick it in the appropriate segment of the birthday chart. Students work in pairs. They ask their friend when their birthday is and write their name and the date on a small piece of paper. Students then stick the paper in the correct part of the birthday chart. Discuss with the class, e.g., *Look. There are no birthdays in February. How many of you have birthdays in April?*

Page 42

- **Extra activity 1: Catch me if you can**

Students work in pairs. StudentA closes his/her book. StudentB starts reading one of the texts from the Student's Book page. He/She makes a deliberate mistake, e.g., *The plates under the earth are always moving quickly.* When StudentA correctly spots the mistake, he/she gains a point. StudentB continues until the end of the text. Then students swap roles.

- **Extra activity 2: My own wordsearch puzzle**

Students look back through Unit 4 to find ten words connected with disasters. They make a wordsearch puzzle including the ten words and write the words underneath (scrambling the letters). Students swap wordsearch puzzles with their partner and find the ten words. Pairs then review the words from both wordsearch puzzles together.

Page 43

- **Extra activity 1: Write about your volcano**

Students write a personal report on how they made the volcano in the lesson, including what was easy and what was difficult. They use the connectors *First, then, next, lastly.* Students write the first draft and then swap with a partner for correction. Students then write a revised draft.

- **Extra activity 2: CLIL vocabulary**

Elicit the new words and phrases from the two lessons on the Earth's surface onto the board. Check students understand them and know how to say them. In their vocabulary books, students write the heading *The Earth's surface.* They write the new words, phrases, and expressions, either as a mind map, or as a list. At the bottom of the page, they write some of the things they did in the lessons, e.g., *I learned how volcanoes got their name. I know what the Richter Scale measures. I made a volcano.*

Review Units 3 and 4

Page 44

- **Extra activity 1: Project Part 2**

Complete the project on volcanoes with the class.

- **Extra activity 2: Songs and chants**

Sing one of the songs or do one of the chants or rhymes from Units 3 and 4.

Page 45

- **Extra activity 1: Vocabulary review**

Students look back through Units 3 and 4, checking they have noted all the key vocabulary in their vocabulary books. Students can check and compare. They write an example sentence for any words they find difficult to remember. Finally, they create mind maps for the unit themes: *City life* and *Disasters.*

- **Extra activity 2: Games**

Students choose one of the games from Units 3 and 4 to play.

Unit 5

Page 46

- **Extra activity 1: Role play**

Display the CD script from Student's Book Activity 1 on the board. Make sure all the students can see it. Make groups of three. They take turns role playing the story, using mime, e.g., for the spider.

- **Extra activity 2: What's it made of?**

Students work in groups of four. They each select six things (from their bags, their clothes, etc.) to ask questions about using *made of*. If they are not sure what the object is made of or how to say it in English, they can check with you / their dictionaries. Students take turns asking their friends in their groups about the objects they have chosen, e.g., *What's my watch made of?* At the end of the activity, elicit what was the most common material in their group.

Page 47

- **Extra activity: My imaginary house**

Brainstorm ideas with students as to what houses are made of. Explore many different possibilities from around the world with the class. Individually, students draw a picture of an imaginary house or one from somewhere in the world and write a text about it, using the text from Workbook Activity 6 as a model. Students swap texts and read about their partner's house.

Page 48

- **Extra activity 1: Natural or man-made**

Students each make a list of the clothes and objects that they are wearing, e.g., *watch*, *jewelry*, *glasses*. Next to the object, they write what it's made of. Then they categorize the information into two columns: *man-made* and *natural*, and see which they have more of. Students compare with their friends.

- **Extra activity 2: Find the one that doesn't belong**

Demonstrate the activity for students. Write on the board: *car, jewelry, ruler, shoes*. Elicit which one doesn't belong: there may be more than one answer, e.g., shoes can't be made of metal, but the others can; cars can't be made of wood, but the others can. Students work in pairs. They write a list on paper of six groups of four words, each with one item that doesn't belong. In their notebooks, they write their answer for each one. They swap papers with another pair and take turns saying which thing they think doesn't belong for each group. Encourage students to be inventive. Monitor and help.

Page 49

- **Extra activity 1: Finding out**

Write a source material on the board, e.g., *wool*. Ask the class how many things they can think of that are made of wool, or have wool as part of their content. Elicit their ideas, e.g., *clothes, mattresses, blankets*. Make groups of four. Each group needs an encyclopedia and/or access to the Internet or school library. Give each group a source material to research: they have to find as many things as they can that are made of / contain that material. Suggested source materials: metal, trees, wool, animals (but not their fur/hair), plants or parts of plants (not trees). Students have about ten minutes to do their research. They collate their information onto a poster and present their findings to the class.

- **Extra activity 2: Material chains**

Students work in groups of three to make material chains. They work on one piece of paper. They start with a material, e.g., wood, and draw an oval around it like a link in a chain in the center of the paper.

Students take turns making other links, either to the left or to the right, with something that's made of/from the material, e.g., paper, or that the object comes from. For example, the link from paper could be plants (leaves – papyrus) as paper can be made from that, too. Give students thinking time as they play the game. It will encourage them to think laterally. Provide suggestions.

Page 50

- **Extra activity 1: Picture a sound**

Elicit words from the lesson with the phonemes /eɪ/ and /eə/. Write them on the board, including *take, break, great, wait, gate, ate, chair, pear, Clare, bear, wear* and *where*. Students work in pairs. Hand out eight pieces of thin cardboard to each pair. They choose four of the words on the board. For each of the four words, one student writes the word on a piece of cardboard and the other student draws a picture representing the word (e.g., StudentA writes *bear* on a card, StudentB draws a bear on a different card). Make sure students swap so that they each do two drawings and write two words.

Make groups of four. Students put their cards together so they have 16 cards. They mix them up, turn them face down and play a game of matching pairs: students take turns turning over two cards at a time. If they get a matching word and picture they say the word and take the two cards at a time. If the cards don't match, they turn them over and it is the next student's turn.

- **Extra activity 2: Writing together**

Put students into pairs or groups of four. They read through the texts each of them wrote for Workbook Activity 19 and try to correct any mistakes. Remind them to use pencil and not pen on each other's work. Tell students that this is a cooperative activity, not a competitive one: they are trying to help each other. Students then rewrite their own texts on a piece of paper.

Page 51

- **Extra activity 1: A different ending**

Make groups of three. Play the CD of the Diggory Bones story. Students repeat in role. Students then work together to rewrite the final two frames. They write the new story in their notebooks. They then practice the role play. Groups perform their role plays for the whole class.

- **Extra activity 2: Who said it?**

Students look back through the episodes of the Diggory Bones story. In pairs, they find six short phrases that people said. They write the phrases on six strips of paper. Collect the strips from students. Make four teams. Teams allocate numbers to their team members, starting from *1*. If the smallest team has, e.g., six members, and the others have seven, then the larger teams will number *1–6* and then start at *1* again. Select a strip and call a number at random, e.g., *Four*. A team member with that number has to answer. Read out the quotation from the story. The first to answer correctly with the name of the speaker wins a point for their team. Repeat, calling a different number and reading a new quotation each time. If there are two number 1s in a team, only one can answer at any one time.

Page 52

- **Extra activity 1: Alternatives to plastic**

Refocus students on the question at the end of the text in the Student's Book (How many plastic things can you think of?). Put students into groups of four. Tell them to think about the time between when they got up this morning and now and to list all the plastic things they have used during that time. Provide dictionaries if they need them to check vocabulary. Students draw a line vertically down a sheet of paper. They head one side *Plastics* and list the plastic objects there. They head the other side *Alternatives*. They try to think of an alternative material or object for each plastic one. For example, in the *Plastics* column they have written *cup*. In the *Alternatives* column they could write *glass*. At the end of the activity, elicit how many plastic objects they couldn't find alternatives for. Ask other groups for their ideas.

- **Extra activity 2: The most useful plastics**

If students did Extra activity 1, they work in the same groups of four. They look at the list of plastic items they wrote and rank them in order of how useful they are (1 is the most useful; 5 is the least useful). They should come to a group decision. If they didn't do Extra activity 1, students work in groups of four. They brainstorm all the plastic things they have used that day and then allocate them to the number scale 1–5.

Elicit ideas from groups and compare their rankings.

Page 53

- **Extra activity 1: Our ideas for reusing plastic**

Students write a personal report on the making of the picture frame. They can use the instructions to provide them with a framework.

On a piece of paper, students write up at least one more idea for reusing a plastic item. They write it as a set of instructions with simple pictures. Make a class book of ideas. Display the book and encourage students to try out their friends' ideas.

- **Extra activity 2: CLIL vocabulary**

Elicit the new words and phrases from the two lessons on plastics onto the board. Check students understand them and know how to say them. In their vocabulary books, students write the heading *Plastics*. They write the new words, phrases, and expressions from the lessons, either as a mind map or as a list. At the bottom of the page, they write some of the things they did in the lessons, e.g., *I learned the names for different plastics. I know how plastic is recycled. I made a picture frame from recycled plastic.*

Unit 6

Page 54

- **Extra activity: Feelie bag**

Put objects in a feelie bag before the lesson so students don't see them. Invite students to the front one by one. They put their hand in the feelie bag (without looking) and feel for one object. They describe it using the key language, e.g., *It feels like an animal.*

Page 55

- **Extra activity 1: What things looked like**

Students review what they and the class said for Student's Book Activity 6. In their notebooks, they write sentences for each picture in the activity, e.g., *I think picture 6 looks like (a door handle).*

- **Extra activity 2: Riddles**

Write the prompts for a riddle on the board like this:

I look/sound/taste/feel like ______________.
I am ________________.
I come in ________________ (colors).
You can ________________.
I always/sometimes/never ________________.
What am I?

Students work in pairs. They write a riddle on a piece of paper. Pairs put their riddles on the walls as you number them. Students go around the classroom, reading the riddles, and writing the number of the riddle and their guess of the answer in their notebooks. At the end of the activity, the pair who wrote each riddle gives the correct answer so the class can check.

Page 56

- **Extra activity 1: My favorite pizza**

Students use the model in the reading text in Student's Book Activity 8 sections a, b, and c to write an account of how to make their favorite pizza. They can illustrate their writing with a picture of their pizza.

- **Extra activity 2: Pizza role play**

The students are going to order their favorite pizza over the phone. Elicit a sample conversation onto the board for students to use, e.g.

Hello. Ace Pizzas here.
Hi. I'd like to order a pizza, please.
Fine. Go ahead.
Well, I'd like (mushrooms, green pepper) and a lot of (cheese) but no (onions). I don't like (onions).
Right. That's (repeats order but with a mistake).
No, I'd like (repeats again).
Got it. (repeats correctly)
Do you want anything to drink?
Yes, please. (An orange juice.)
And what's the address for delivery?
(gives address)
Fine. It'll be about a quarter of an hour.

Students prepare and then do their role plays in pairs. They can swap roles if time. More confident students can role play their conversations for the class.

Page 57

- **Extra activity 1: My favorite recipe**

Elicit and write up the key words from the recipe, e.g., *mix, put, roll, take, add, cut*. Add other words students might need, e.g., *weigh*. Ask students to get out the recipes they brought with them. Go around the room, looking at the different recipes. Choose the least complex ones. Students work in groups of four. They work together to write one or two of the recipes from their group in English. Help the groups with key words and simplify recipes if necessary. Groups swap their recipes with other groups and read the different recipes.

- **Extra activity 2: Recipe word maps**

Write *Ingredients* on one side of the board and *Processes* on the other. Draw a circle around each one. Elicit one or two ingredients from this and the previous lesson e.g., *flour, eggs*, and start a mind map for *Ingredients*. Do the same for *Processes*, eliciting, e.g., *mix, cut*. In pairs, students make mind maps of all the ingredients and processes from this and previous lessons in their notebooks.

Page 58

- **Extra activity 1: /z/ and /s/ words**

After Workbook Activity 13, students copy the /z/ and /s/ columns from the board into their notebooks. They make pairs. One student(A) closes their book. StudentB says a word from one of the lists, for their partner to say either *Daisy* or *Lucy*. StudentB says six more words. Then they swap roles.

- **Extra activity 2: Writing together**

Put students into pairs or groups of four. They read through the poems each of them wrote for Workbook Activity 16 and try to correct any mistakes. Remind them to use pencil and not pen on each other's work. Tell students that this is a cooperative activity, not a competitive one: they are trying to help each other. Students then rewrite their own poems on a piece of paper for display.

Page 59

- **Extra activity 1: Role play**

Make groups of three. Students decide on their roles. Play the CD of the Diggory Bones story. Students repeat in role. They then read through the story in their groups. They repeat twice more, changing roles each time. Students decide on final roles and practice their role plays as a group and/or perform their role plays for the whole class.

- **Extra activity 2: Feelie bag**

Play the Feelie bag game again with students. See Extra activity for page 54.

Page 60

- **Extra activity 1: Tricks of the eye**

Make pairs. Introduce the artist Escher and show students his pictures one at a time. First of all, show them a picture for only a short time. Ask them what they can see. Elicit descriptions from students. Then show them the picture for a longer time so that they can study the optical illusion. Discuss what the illusion is in the picture and how what they see is actually impossible.

- **Extra activity 2: Mobius strip**

Show students the Mobius strip you made (see below) and how it only has one side and one edge. Draw a line along the middle of one side and show students where the line ends up. Tell students you are going to cut the strip along the middle. Ask them what they think will happen to it, e.g., will it fall apart / make two strips? Cut the strip in half along the line and show them how it becomes one loop with two half-twists in it.

Hand out a strip and some glue to each student. They take the strip of paper and join the ends to make a loop, after giving one end a half-twist so it joins up with the other one upside down. Students can then see how their strip only has one edge/side. If they want, they can also cut it along the middle to make one loop with two twists.

Students write in their notebooks about how they made the Mobius strip and what its properties are.

Page 61

- **Extra activity 1: Write about your optical illusion**

Students write a personal report on how they made their optical illusion and what the trick was at the end. If they understand how it worked, they can write about this too in their report. They structure their report using the connectors *first, then, next, lastly*. Students write the first draft of their texts on paper and then swap with a partner. They correct and give suggestions to each other. Students then write a revised draft in their notebooks.

- **Extra activity 2: CLIL vocabulary**

Elicit the new words and phrases from the two lessons on optical illusions onto the board. In their vocabulary books, students write the heading *Optical illusions*. They write the new words, phrases, and expressions from the lessons, either as a mind map or as a list. At the bottom of the page, they write some of the things they did in the lessons, e.g., *I looked at pictures by different artists and saw optical illusions in their pictures. I made my own optical illusion.*

Review Units 5 and 6

Page 62

- **Extra activity 1: Picture a sound**

Students play the Picture a sound game again. See Extra activity 1 for page 50.

- **Extra activity 2: Songs and chants**

Sing one of the songs or do one of the chants from Units 5 and 6.

Page 63

- **Extra activity 1: Vocabulary review**

Students look back through Units 5 and 6, checking they have noted all the key vocabulary in their vocabulary books. Students can check and compare. They write an example sentence for any words they find difficult to remember. Finally they create mind maps for the unit themes: *Material things* and *Senses*.

- **Extra activity 2: Games**

Students choose one of the games from Units 5 and 6 to play.

Unit 7

Page 64

- **Extra activity 1: Role play**

Display the CD script from Student's Book Activity 1 on the board. Make sure all the students can see it. Make groups of four. Play the CD again as they read silently. Students take turns role playing the story in their groups. More confident groups can perform their role plays for the class.

- **Extra activity 2: More sentence halves**

In pairs, students use the sentence stems from Student's Book Activity 3 and complete them with their own ideas. For sentence 1, they need to add *so* to the stem so it reads: *It's very hot, so …* . Make groups of four (two pairs). Students take turns reading their *should/shouldn't* sentences to the other pair and check they make sense and are grammatically correct.

Page 65

- **Extra activity 1: Written advice**

Elicit and write eight situations/prompts you used for Student's Book Activity 6 on the board. Students copy the prompts into their notebooks. For each prompt, they write one piece of advice with *should* and one with *shouldn't*. Encourage them to think of new ideas (not just to use the advice from the game).

- **Extra activity 2: Helping each other**

Elicit some other problems, using the ideas in Workbook Activity 4 as examples. The problems can be real or funny. Using the texts from Workbook Activity 4 as a model, students individually write a *Dear Pamela* letter on a piece of paper, leaving room for the answer at the bottom. Students fold their letters in half and swap letters with another student in the class. They write answers to each other's letters at the bottoms of the papers, using *should* or *shouldn't*. Students swap letters again and read the answers.

Page 66

- **Extra activity 1: Where do they live?**

Display a map of the world and elicit the names of the countries students read about in Student's Book Activity 7. Write them on the board. Ask students to come and show you where the countries are on the map. Hand out A4 world maps to students so they can find the countries on their maps. Students work individually. They write simple facts about each endangered animal from Student's Book Activity 7 on small pieces of paper. Provide a model for students on the board, e.g.

Animal: Siberian tiger *Habitat: forests in Russia*
Description: striped fur *Status: endangered*

Students do the same for each animal that's mentioned in the text. They stick the paper on the edge of the map and draw a line from the paper to the country on the map.

- **Extra activity 2: Guessing game**

Provide a definition of an animal for students to guess, e.g., *I'm thinking about a small animal. It's not an insect. It has eight legs. It lives in houses and outside. Sometimes these animals are very hairy.* (spider). Students then work in pairs to write a definition on paper of another animal. They write the animal in brackets. Collect the pieces of paper for a team game. Make three teams. Students number the people in their team, starting at *1*. Choose a definition and call out a number at random. The students with that number on the teams can answer. The others have to stay quiet. Read the definition and give the three students ten seconds to answer. Award one point for the first team member to answer correctly. Repeat with other definitions.

Page 67

- **Extra activity 1: The school environment**

Focus students on the *You can ...* section of Student's Book Activity 12. Tell them to imagine they have to make suggestions about the school. Elicit some ideas for protecting habitat, recycling, etc. Students work in groups of four. They produce a poster for display in the school about ways of taking care of the natural world in the school and protecting the environment. They present their ideas as in the model, i.e. *You can ...* . Groups present their posters to the class before they are displayed.

- **Extra activity 2: Endangered animals**

Divide the class into eight. Give each group one of the endangered animals from Workbook Activity 11. They use reference books / the Internet to find out as much as they can about it. They co-write a short text on the computer about the animal (description, habitat, why it's endangered, etc.) and insert a picture. Print out all the texts to make a class booklet.

Page 68

- **Extra activity 1: Find your partner**

Hand out the pieces of paper (see page T68) to the students. Tell them not to shout out their word to the class or show their word to anyone. Clap your hands. Students walk around the room, whispering their word to students as they pass them. When they find their partner, they stand together at the side of the room. When everyone has found their partner, go quickly around the room asking students to say their word pairs. Tell them they must say the weak form of *and* and put the words in the right order, e.g., *a burger and fries,* not *fries and a burger.*

- **Extra activity 2: Writing together**

Put students into pairs or groups of four. They read through the letter each of them wrote for Workbook Activity 18 and try to correct any mistakes. Remind them to use pencil and not pen on each other's work. Tell students that this is a cooperative activity, not a competitive one: they are trying to help each other. Students then rewrite their own letters on a piece of paper.

Page 69

- **Extra activity: Role play**

Make groups of three. Students decide on their roles. Play the CD of the Diggory Bones story. Students repeat in role. They read through the story in their groups twice more, changing roles each time. Students decide on final roles and practice their role plays as a group and/or perform their role plays for the whole class.

Page 70

- **Extra activity 1: The extinction of the dinosaurs**

Elicit from students what the text in the Student's Book tells us about the extinction of the dinosaurs. Remind students that this is "the most popular idea" or theory, but that there are others, too. Tell them they are going to find out about some of the other ideas or theories. Make groups of four and give each group a reference book / list of relevant internet sites and a large sheet of paper. Give groups a fixed time to do their research. They make notes on what they find out. Groups then prepare another mind map, but this time with *Extinction of the dinosaurs* at its center. They present the information they found out on their mind maps and display them around the class. Give groups time to read other groups' information and then discuss the main findings as a class.

- **Extra activity 2: Find out and write about an extinct animal**

Elicit any extinct animals that students know. If they say *dinosaurs*, elicit different types and some information about them, e.g., what they looked like, what they ate. Find out if students know the names of any animals that have become extinct more recently, e.g., the dodo. Elicit and then write points on the board to help students with their research: *animal's name, type of animal, where it lived, what it looked like, what it ate, why it became extinct.* Hand out reference books. Students can work individually or in pairs. They write notes for each point about an extinct animal. Then they use their notes to write a text about the animal in their notebooks.

Page 71

- **Extra activity 1: Write about your fossil prints**

Students write a personal report on how they made their fossil prints, what they used to make them, what was easy, and what was more difficult. They use the connectors *first, then, next, lastly*. Students write the first draft and then swap with a partner for correction. Students then write a revised draft.

- **Extra activity 2: CLIL vocabulary**

Elicit the new words and phrases from the two lessons on extinct animals onto the board. Check students understand them and know how to say them. In their vocabulary books, students write the heading *Extinct animals*. They write the new words, phrases, and expressions from the lessons, either as a mind map, or as a list. At the bottom of the page, they write some of the things they did in the lessons, e.g., *I learned some of the reasons for animal extinctions. I read about fossils. I made some of my own fossil prints.*

Unit 8

Page 72

- **Extra activity 1: Find the present perfect**

Hand out photocopies of the CD script (see page T72) from Student's Book Activity 1. Tell students to underline all the uses of the present perfect in the text. They work in pairs. Display a large sheet of paper with the CD script on it and go through the answers carefully with the class, underlining the examples on the paper.

- **Extra activity 2: In my life**

Brainstorm with students some of the more unusual things they have done in their lives, e.g., won a swimming prize, climbed a mountain, been snowboarding. Students head the page in their notebooks *In my life* and then write at least six things they've done in their lives. Students then make groups of three and take turns telling their friends things they've done. Discuss as a class by asking one student in a group to tell you some of the things the other students in their group have done, using *He/She has …*

Page 73

- **Extra activity 1: Talking about actions**

Refer back to Student's Book page 73 Activty 4 and say that you're going to play a game. Demonstrate, e.g., pick up a board pen to elicit *You're going to write on the board.* Write on the board to elicit *You're writing on the board.* Move away from the board to elicit *You've written on the board.* In groups of three, students think of at least two mimes they can do to practice this sequence of structures. They work quietly so the other groups don't hear. Groups take turns miming one of their sequences. Then elicit sentences from the rest of the class for each stage of the action.

- **Extra activity 2: What we've done in the lesson**

Students work in pairs and write at least six sentences about what they have done in the lesson. Tell them to start at least one sentence with *I*, one with the name of one friend, one with the name of two or more friends, and another with *We*. All the sentences should be in the present perfect. Put two pairs together so they can compare sentences.

Page 74

- **Extra activity 1: When people do sports**

Students transfer the information in Activity 7 into a chart in their notebooks, showing when people do different sports.

- **Extra activity 2: Unusual sports**

Find out if students know about any unusual sports from their region or other parts of the world. Make a list together, adding your suggestions. Tell them they are going to research an unusual sport. Students work in pairs. Students use reference books / the Internet to find out information about their sport, e.g., which countries/seasons it's played in, how many people play it, where it's played, e.g., on a court, if it's a team sport, if it's played with rackets and/or balls, how it's scored. They write the name of the sport at the top of a poster and find a picture of the sport to put in the center. Then they write the information they found out around the picture. Students display their posters.

Page 75

- **Extra activity 1: Vacation stories**

Tell students you have some pictures for them about vacations and that they have to make up a story using the pictures. They can add scenes in between the pictures if they like (they don't need to draw them). Put students into fours and hand out a set of pictures to each group. They invent a story around the pictures, adding characters and names. They practice telling the story using the past. Go around the class and listen to the groups' stories.

- **Extra activity 2: Mind maps**

Students extend the sports mind maps they started at the beginning of the unit to include all the sports words they learned in the subsequent lessons.

Page 76

- **Extra activity 1: Writing together**

Put students into pairs or groups of four. They read through the reports each of them wrote for Student's Book Activity 15 and try to correct any mistakes. Remind them to use pencil and not pen on each other's work. Tell students that this is a cooperative activity, not a competitive one: they are trying to help each other. Students then rewrite their own reports in their notebooks.

- **Extra activity 2: *-ed* endings**

Students work in pairs. They look back through the lesson and find all the verbs in the Student's Book and in the Workbook that have *-ed* at the end of the simple past or past participle. For each verb, they work out whether the letters are pronounced /t/, /d/, or /ɪd/. They check their lists in pairs and then as a class.

Page 77

- **Extra activity 1: Diggory's email**

Brainstorm ideas with the class about Diggory's email, e.g., it told Sir Doug what was happening, where they were, about Brutus, to come quickly, to bring the police. Remind students about "Write it right: Emails" from the previous lesson. Students work in pairs to write the email from Diggory.

- **Extra activity 2: Role play**

Divide the class into nine groups. Each group takes one of the episodes of the Diggory Bones story from the Student's Book to review and to role play. If possible, let each group come up to the CD player one at a time and listen to their episode again at low volume. Students practice and prepare their performance. Groups perform their role plays in sequence for the rest of the class.

Page 78

- **Extra activity 1: Write about your logo**

Students write a personal report on how they decided on the design for their logo, e.g., what aspects of the city and its history influenced them in the design and what the different elements of their design represent. They include the actual design in their report and refer to various sections of it. Students write the first draft and then write a revised draft in their notebooks.

- **Extra activity 2: Paralympic sports**

Students find out and write about two Paralympic sports.

Page 79

- **Extra activity 1: My medal**

Students use the reading text from the Student's Book as a model and write about the front and the back of their medals, describing what is on each side and why. They draw a picture of the designs for the front and back of their medal under the text.

- **Extra activity 2: CLIL vocabulary**

Elicit the new words and phrases from the two lessons on Olympic Games onto the board. In their vocabulary books, students write the heading *Olympic Games*. They write the new words, phrases, and expressions from the lessons, either as a mind map, or as a list. They write some of the things they did in the lessons, e.g., *I read about the Olympic Games in different countries. I designed an Olympic logo with my friends. I learned about the Paralympic Games. I designed a medal to match my logo.*

Review Units 7 and 8

Page 80

- **Extra activity: Songs and chants**

Sing one of the songs or do one of the chants from Units 7 and 8.

Page 81

- **Extra activity 1: Vocabulary review**

Students look back through Units 7 and 8, checking they have noted all the key vocabulary in their vocabulary books. Students can check and compare. They write an example sentence for any words they find difficult to remember. Finally, they create mind maps for the unit themes: *Natural world* and *World of sports*.

- **Extra activity 2: Games**

Students choose one of the games from Units 7 and 8 to play.

Values

Page 82

- **Extra activity 1: Contract for the teacher**

Students work in pairs. They write a contract for the teacher, based on the one they wrote for Workbook Activity 2. Monitor and help with new vocabulary. Choose your favorite sentences from the contracts and invite students to share them with the class.

- **Extra activity 2: Make rules**

Give out sentence halves (see page T82) to each pair of students (one set of 14 pieces of paper per pair). The students put the sentences together. Early finishers can write the completed sentences in their notebooks. Check with the class.

Page 83

- **Extra activity 1: Which job?**

Give five pieces of paper to each student. Tell them to write a different job from the lesson on each piece of paper as follows: *doctor, nurse, ambulance driver, police officer, firefighter.* Say a sentence about one or more of the jobs. Students hold up one or more of their pieces of paper to match the sentence. Example sentences (answers in brackets): e.g., *They work in a hospital. (nurse, doctor); They sometimes work at night. (all the jobs); They rescue people from traffic accidents. (ambulance driver, firefighter, police officer); They have to drive quickly for work. (ambulance driver, firefighter, police officer); They operate on people. (doctor); They aren't afraid of heights. (firefighter); They run after thieves. (police officers); They interview people. (police officers)*

- **Extra activity 2: Role play emergency call**

Write the first line of an emergency phone call on the board, as follows:

Hello. Which service do you need – police, fires, or ambulance?

Students work in pairs to write the rest of the conversation. Tell them that the operator (the first person to talk) needs to find out what happened and where the person lives. Write some useful phrases for the operator on the board, e.g., *Don't worry. Please calm down. It's going to be OK.* Monitor and help with the writing. When you have checked their work, students role play their conversation in the same pairs. Ask volunteers to perform their role play for the class.

Page 84

- **Extra activity 1: Quiz question**

Students work in pairs. They write a question about a moral dilemma, with three options (a, b, c), similar to the ones in the quiz in Student's Book Activity 1. Monitor and help with language. Pairs swap their questions with another pair, who decide which option they would choose. They exchange ideas.

- **Extra activity 2: Truth or white lie?**

You will need a large space such as a gymnasium for this activity. Draw a long white line or use white tape to separate the space into two halves. The students all stand on the line. Point to one side of the line and say *This side is for telling the truth.* Point to the other side and say *This side is for telling a little white lie.* Remind students what *white lie* means.

Describe a situation, similar to the ones in the Student's Book quiz Activity 1, e.g., *Your grandmother gives you a hat she made for your birthday. You don't like it.* The students have to decide if they would tell the truth or tell a white lie in that situation, and jump to the appropriate side of the line. See how many students end up on each side of the line and ask individuals to explain their choice. Repeat with different situations.

Page 85

- **Extra activity 1: Ask Betty and Robert**

Students do a role play in groups of three. One student plays the role of an interviewer on a TV show. The other two students are Betty and Robert (the agony aunt and uncle from the Student's Book). Give students time to prepare for the role play – the "interviewer" thinks of questions to ask Betty and Robert (about their lives, their work, the advice they give). Betty and Robert invent a personal life. Are they husband and wife, brother and sister, or do they just work together? What did they study? Do they always agree on advice? Monitor and help with the planning stage. Students then act out the interview in their groups.

- **Extra activity 2: Posters**

Remind students of the subject of Richard's problem letter in the Students' Book (cheating). Students work in groups of three or four. Give each group a large piece of paper. Ask them to design a poster with the title *Don't cheat.* They draw a picture to illustrate a situation where someone is cheating (at school, in a game, or a sport). They write a caption in English, e.g., *It's better to work hard.* Display the finished posters in the classroom.

Extra project ideas

Unit 1 Making models

You will need:
Colored modeling clay for students to make their own *Wallace and Gromit*-type characters, a digital camera, a printer, large sheets of paper.

For this project, students work in pairs or small groups to make a group of model characters out of modeling clay. They make the characters, and produce a brief description of each character and possible ideas for stories.

Tell students what the focus of the project is (making models). If you have time to make a model of your own before the lesson, show it to them. Write the steps of the project on the board for students to copy into their notebooks:

Step 1: Make pairs / small groups.
Step 2: Decide which characters you are going to make. You can invent them or use characters you've seen on TV.
Step 3: Brainstorm the characteristics of each character and typical storylines before you decide what the characters will look like. Make notes of your ideas.
Step 4: Divide up the characters into the number of people in your group. Ask your teacher for the clay. Each person makes at least one model. Make name labels for your characters. Put each character on an empty table one at a time and photograph it from different angles, using the digital camera. Print out some images for the poster.
Step 5: Each person writes a character sketch of their character on paper. Swap texts in your group and check for content and grammar.
Step 6: As a group, write a typical storyline for your, group of characters. Write/Stick final versions of the texts and photographs on large sheets of paper. Put the models on a table or a desk against the wall with the name labels and display the posters behind them.
Step 7: Present your models and your ideas to the class.

Remind students that the characters need to be quite small so they don't take too long to make. Monitor and guide students as they are working, making sure they all keep on task, don't take too long on any one step, and don't try to be too ambitious. Help students with their drafts. Provide models for texts on the board or on paper, as appropriate. Encourage students to swap their work for peer correction at Step 5.

Each group should have time to make their presentation to the rest of the class. Leave the posters and models on display in the classroom. If possible, display them around the school for other students, teachers, and parents to see.

Unit 2 Find out what's good for your teeth

You will need:
Reference books, the Internet, large sheets of paper, glue, colored pencils and markers, paints, scissors, dictionaries.

For this project, students work in pairs or small groups to research food that is good for their teeth / less good for their teeth. They produce a poster that they display as they make their class presentation. Posters should be a mix of pictures and text (their own, not copied from the Internet / reference books).

Tell students what the focus of the project is (food that is good for their teeth and food that is less good for their teeth). Write the steps of the project on the board for students to copy into their notebooks:

Step 1: Make pairs / small groups.
Step 2: Plan your project as a group. Think about what you want to find out and how you want to display the information.
Step 3: Research different foods and dental health using the Internet and reference books. Make notes about what you find out.
Step 4: Divide up the information into the number of people in your group. Each person finds pictures to illustrate their information. Plan the poster.
Step 5: Each person writes a draft of their text on paper. Swap texts in your group and check for content and grammar.
Step 6: Write final versions of the texts on paper. Stick the pictures and texts on the poster.
Step 7: Present your poster to the class.

Monitor and guide students as they are working, making sure they all keep on task, don't take too long on any one step and don't try to be too ambitious. Help students with their drafts. Provide models for texts on the board or on paper, as appropriate. Encourage students to swap their work for peer correction at Step 5.

Each group should have time to make their presentation to the rest of the class. Leave the posters on display in the classroom. If possible, display them around the school for other students, teachers, and parents to see.

Unit 3 City research project

You will need:
Reference books, the Internet, paper, stapler, glue, colored pencils and markers, scissors, dictionaries.

For this project, students work in pairs or small groups to research another famous city in the world and its history. They produce a booklet that they display as they make their class presentation. Booklets should be a mix of pictures and text (their own, not copied from the Internet / reference books).

Tell students what the focus of the project is (a famous capital city and its history). If you have time to make a booklet of your own before the lesson, show it to them. Write the steps of the project on the board for students to copy into their notebooks. Brainstorm capital cities if appropriate.

Step 1: Make pairs / small groups.
Step 2: Decide which capital city to research.
Step 3: Research the city using the Internet and reference books. Make notes about what you find out. Don't forget to find out about its past as well as its present.
Step 4: Plan the booklet (how many pages, order of information, cover, etc.). Divide up the information into the number of people in your group. Each person finds pictures to illustrate their information.
Step 5: Each person writes a draft of their text on paper. Swap texts in your group and check for content and grammar.
Step 6: Write final versions of the texts. Arrange and make the booklet.
Step 7: Present your booklet to the class.

Monitor and guide students as they are working, making sure they all keep on task, don't take too long on any one step, and don't try to be too ambitious. Give them ideas for how to sequence the information in their booklets and for the covers. Help students with their drafts. Provide models for texts on the board or on paper, as appropriate. Encourage students to swap their work for peer correction at Step 5.

Each group should have time to present their information and booklet to the rest of the class. Leave the booklets on display in the classroom. If possible, display them around the school for other students, teachers, and parents to see.

Unit 4 A local disaster

You will need:
Reference books, the Internet, large sheets of paper, glue, colored pencils and markers, scissors, dictionaries.

Note: This may be a topic that needs to be treated with sensitivity.

For this project, students work in pairs or small groups to research a disaster that has affected their country or region in the last 100 years. They produce a poster that they display as they make their class presentation. Posters should be a mix of pictures and text (their own, not copied from the Internet / reference books).

Tell students what the focus of the project is (a disaster that has affected their country or region in the last 100 years). If you have time to make a poster of your own before the lesson, show it to them. Write the steps of the project on the board for students to copy into their notebooks. Provide information on disasters in the region for the class at the beginning of the lesson for them to choose and research. If groups particularly want to research a disaster that happened in another part of the world, they can do that.

Step 1: Make small groups.
Step 2: Decide which disaster to research.
Step 3: Research the disaster using the Internet and reference books. Make notes about what you find out, including facts and figures.
Step 4: Divide up the information into the number of people in your group. Each person finds pictures to illustrate their information. Plan the poster.
Step 5: Each person writes a draft of their text on paper. Swap texts in your group and check for content and grammar.
Step 6: Write final versions of the texts on paper. Stick the pictures and texts on the poster.
Step 7: Present your poster to the class.

Monitor and guide students as they are working, making sure they all keep on task, don't take too long on any one step, and don't try to be too ambitious. Help students with their drafts. Provide models for texts on the board or on paper, as appropriate. Encourage students to swap their work for peer correction at Step 5.

Each group should have time to make their presentation to the rest of the class. Leave the posters on display in the classroom. If possible, display them around the school for other students, teachers, and parents to see.

Unit 5 Recycling bins

You will need:
Cardboard boxes, strong glue, paints, colored pencils and markers.

For this project, students work in pairs or small groups to produce a recycling bin for their school. They produce a bin that they display as they make their class presentation. The bins will then be placed around the school for actual use.

Tell students what the focus of the project is (making recycling bins for the school). If you have time to make a bin of your own before the lesson, show it to them. Write the steps of the project on the board for students to copy into their notebooks. You will need to check that there is a local company (private or public) that will come and take the recycled material away.

Step 1: Make pairs / small groups.
Step 2: Decide what your recycling bin is for and what it is going to look like.
Step 3: Decide where your bin is going to be placed in the school and check with the teachers/principal that this is OK.
Step 4: Divide up the tasks into the number of people in your group. It is important that each person takes part in making the bin, its lettering and logo, and its decoration. You can use pictures to decorate your bin as well. Make your bin.
Step 5: As a group, write a draft of a text about the bin and about the importance of recycling that will be displayed next to the bin. Check the text carefully for content and grammar.
Step 6: Write a final version of your text on paper.
Step 7: Present your bin to the class.
Step 8: Site your bin in the school and display the text. If possible, present your bin to the school beforehand, for example at a school assembly.

Monitor and guide students as they are working, making sure they all keep on task, don't take too long on any one step, and don't try to be too ambitious. Help students with their draft texts. Provide models for texts on the board or on paper, as appropriate.

Each group should have time to make their presentation to the rest of the class. Leave the bins on display in the classroom for a short period before they are sited around the school.

Arrange for the bins to be checked and emptied regularly.

Unit 6 Menus

You will need:
Sample menus for ideas, magazines with food pictures, cardboard, sticky plastic, glue, colored pencils and markers, scissors, dictionaries, a printer.

For this project, students work in pairs or small groups to produce a menu for a restaurant that specializes in tasty, healthy food. They produce a menu that they display as they make their class presentation. Menus should include the restaurant name, be colorful, and include prices and a range of foods and drinks.

Tell students what the focus of the project is (to produce a menu for a restaurant that specializes in tasty, healthy food). If you have time to make a menu of your own before the lesson, show it to them. Write the steps of the project on the board for students to copy into their notebooks:

Step 1: Make pairs / small groups.
Step 2: Decide what kind of healthy food you are going to offer in your restaurant. Decide on the categories on the menu, e.g., appetizers, main courses, snacks, desserts, drinks.
Step 3: Brainstorm food and drink ideas for each category. Remember the focus is health and taste. Make notes.
Step 4: Divide up the tasks into the number of people in your group. Each person finalizes the dishes/drinks in their category, including names and prices. Plan the menu and decide on the name of the restaurant and its logo.
Step 5: Each person writes a draft of the dishes/drinks in their category, including the price, on paper. Swap texts in your group and check for content and grammar and if you agree on the names and prices.
Step 6: Agree the final contents and order of the menu. Write the final version on thin cardboard and decorate the menu with pictures, etc. Turn the menu over, write the name of the restaurant, and draw the logo. Cover both sides with sticky plastic.
Step 7: Present your menu to the class. Groups take time to study each other's menus.

Monitor and guide students as they are working, making sure they all keep on task, don't take too long on any one step, and don't try to be too ambitious. Help students with their drafts and with the prices.

Each group should have time to make their presentation to the rest of the class. Leave the menus on display in the classroom. If possible, display them around the school for other students, teachers, and parents to see.

Unit 7 Animal extinctions around the world

You will need:
Reference books, a world map, the Internet, large sheets of paper, glue, colored pencils and markers, a printer, scissors, dictionaries.

For this project, students work in pairs or small groups to research animal extinctions, including highly endangered animals in different continents of the world. Each group will focus on a different part of the world. They produce a poster that they display as they make their class presentation. Posters should be a mix of pictures and text (their own, not copied from the Internet / reference books).

Tell students what the focus of the project is (animal extinctions, including highly endangered animals in different continents of the world). If you have time to make a poster of your own before the lesson, show it to them. Write the steps of the project on the board for students to copy into their notebooks:

Step 1: Make pairs / small groups.
Step 2: Decide which part of the world you are going to focus on. Your teacher will tell you what the choices are.
Step 3: Research the part of the world, using the Internet and reference books to find out about animals in the region that have recently become extinct or that are highly endangered. Make notes about what you find out. Choose one or two animals.
Step 4: Divide up the information into the number of people in your group. Each person finds out more about their animal, e.g., what it eats/ate, its habitat, why it became extinct / is endangered.
Step 5: Share ideas, find pictures, and plan the poster.
Step 6: Either alone or in groups, write a draft of the text for each animal, including what should be done to protect the animal now or to stop similar extinctions in the near future. Check the texts carefully for content and grammar.
Step 7: Write final versions of the texts on paper. Stick the pictures and texts on the poster.
Step 8: Present your poster to the class.

Monitor and guide students as they are working, making sure they all keep on task, don't take too long on any one step, and don't try to be too ambitious. Help students with their drafts. Provide models for texts on the board or on paper, as appropriate.

Each group should have time to make their presentation to the rest of the class. Leave the posters on display in the classroom. If possible, display them around the school for other students, teachers, and parents to see.

Unit 8 Olympic athletes in our country

You will need:
Reference books, the Internet, paper, stapler, glue, colored pencils and markers, scissors, dictionaries, word processor, printer.

For this project, students work as a class to find out what the medal total was for their country in the last Olympic Games (Summer, Winter, and Paralympics). Then students work in three groups (Summer, Winter, and Paralympic Games) and each student researches one medal-winning athlete. Each group produces a booklet (each studentis responsible for one page) that they display as they make their class presentation. Booklets should be a mix of pictures and students' own text.

Tell students what the focus of the project is (Olympic athletes from their country). If you have time to make a sample page of a booklet before the lesson about one local athlete, show it to them. Write the steps of the project on the board for students to copy into their notebooks:

Step 1: As a class, research what the medal total was for your country in the last Olympic Games. How many gold, silver, and bronze medals were won? How many medals were won in the last Summer, Winter, and Paralympic Games? Who won them? For what sports?
Step 2: Make three groups. Your teacher will give you your focus (Summer Games, Winter Games, Paralympic Games). Decide which medal-winning athletes you are each going to research.
Step 3: Research the person and their sport and find out as much as you can about their medal-winning performance, using the Internet and reference books. Find out where they live in your country. Make notes about what you find out and find pictures to illustrate your page of the booklet.
Step 4: Share the information with the rest of your group. Plan the booklet so that you write a page each.
Step 5: Each person writes a draft of their text on paper. Swap texts in your group and check for content and grammar.
Step 6: Write or type final versions of the texts and stick pictures on each page. Make the booklet and the cover.
Step 7: Present your booklet to the class, with each student talking about their athlete.

Monitor and guide students as they are working, making sure they all keep on task, don't take too long on any one step, and don't try to be too ambitious. Help students with their drafts. Provide models for texts on the board or on paper, as appropriate. Encourage students to swap their work for peer correction at Step 5.

Each group should have time to make their presentation to the rest of the class. Leave the booklets on display in the classroom. If possible, display them around the school for other students, teachers, and parents to see. Invite one of the athletes featured in the booklets to the school, if possible, to talk to the students.

Evaluation 1

Listening Part 5

Name: ....

Listen and color and write. There is one example.

Evaluation 2

Speaking Part 2

A

Boy's name	Jim
When / go on vacation	August
What / like best	swimming
Vacation fun / exciting	fun
What date / come home	24th

Girl's name	
When / go on vacation	
What / like best	
Vacation fun / exciting	
What date / come home	

Summer vacations

Winter vacations

B

Summer vacations

Winter vacations

Boy's name	
When / go on vacation	
What / like best	
Vacation fun / exciting	
What date / come home	

Girl's name	Susie
When / go on vacation	January
What / like best	snowboarding
Vacation fun / exciting	exciting
What date / come home	13th

Evaluation 3

Reading and Writing Part 5

Name: ....

Look at the picture and read the story. Write 1, 2, 3 or 4 words to complete the sentences about the story.

Sam and his pet mice

My name is Sarah and I have an older brother named Sam. He loves animals and he has a lot of pets. He has five mice and three rabbits. The rabbits live in the garden. They are black and their fur feels very soft. Sam keeps the mice in cages in his bedroom. His favorite mouse is gray. It's called Jerry. I like the rabbits, but I don't like the mice.

Last Saturday morning, Sam was in his bedroom playing with his mice. Suddenly, he came running downstairs into the living room. "Mom, Dad, Sarah!" he shouted. "I can't find Jerry." Dad came in from the kitchen. "Oh, no," he said. "Tell us what happened." "I played with Jerry," said Sam. "And then I put him in his cage. After a few minutes, I looked for him in his cage and he wasn't there. I think I forgot to close the door."

"I have an idea," I said. "Jerry's favorite things to eat are carrots and cheese. Let's put a carrot and some cheese in his cage. When he gets hungry, he'll go home." "That's a good idea," said Dad. Sam went into the kitchen and got some cheese and a carrot. He went to his bedroom to put them in the bowl in Jerry's cage. Then we heard a noise. It sounded like Sam was laughing. "Jerry's in his cage and his bowl is already empty. Now he's waiting for his dinner!"

Examples

Sarah has an older brother called Sam.

Jerry is Sam's favorite mouse.

Questions

1 Sam's mice live in his bedroom in ....

2 Sarah prefers ....

3 Dad was in the .... when Sam ran downstairs.

4 After Sam .... , he put him back in the cage.

5 Sam didn't remember to ....

6 Jerry loves eating ....

7 Sam said that Jerry was in the cage and there was nothing in ....

Name: ....

Read the letter and write the missing words. Write one word on each line.

Dear Aunt Mary

Example I am ___writing___ to tell you about my trip to the Olympic Games. I went with my friend's

1 family and we travelled there ________________ plane. Everything was very exciting, but I

2 liked the track and field ________________ . I am

3 sending you a photograph ________________ shows a medal ceremony. You can see that

4 our country ________________ all three medals: gold, silver and bronze. I had a fantastic time.

5 See you ________________

Paula

Thanks and Acknowledgments

The authors and publishers acknowledge the following sources of copyright material and are grateful for the permissions granted. While every effort has been made, it has not always been possible to identify the sources of all the material used, or to trace all copyright holders. If any omissions are brought to our notice, we will be happy to include the appropriate acknowledgments on reprinting.

The authors and publishers would like to thank the following for permission to reproduce photographs:

p.6(a,b,c): © Stephen Bond; p.6(d): Alamy/© Lennello Calvetti; p.6(e): Shutterstock/© Titov Dmitry; p.6(f): Alamy/© Steve Vidler; p.11: © Stephen Bond; p.12(a): Rex Features/ © Universal/Everett; p.12(b): Rex Features/© Steve Meddle; p.12(c): Alamy/© Image Source; p.12(d): Shutterstock/© Nazarino; p.12(e): Shutterstock/© Florian Ispas; p.12(f): Rex Features/© Roderick Barker-Benfield; p.12(f): Getty Images/© AFP: p.12(g): Rex Features/© Monkey Business Images; p.13(1): Rex Features/© Steve Meddle; p.13(2): Alamy/© Peter Phipp/Travelshots.com; p.13(3): Alamy/© Image Source; p.13(4): Corbis/© David Spurdens; p.16(background): Shutterstock/© Mhatzapa; p.16(T): Rex Features/© 20th Century Fox/Everett; p.16(a): Alamy/© AF Archive; p.16(b): Rex Features/© Everett Collection; p.16(c): Kobal Collection/© Universal; p.16(BL): Alamy/© Meblankress; p.16(C): Corbis/© Sergio Gaudenti/Kipa; p.16(CR): Getty Images/© Time & Life Pictures; p.16(BR): Corbis/© Louis Quail/In Pictures; p.17(TR): Topfoto; p.17(TL): Rex Features/© Everett Collection; p.17(CR): Kobal Collection/© Dreamworks LLC; p.17(B): © Stephen Bond; p.20(a): Rex Features/© Stewart Cook; p.20(b): Alamy/© CBW; p.20(c): Getty Images/ p.20(d): Rex Features/© Julian Makey; p.20(e): Alamy/ Kolvenbach; p.20(f): Shutterstock/© BrAt82; p.22: © Stephen Bond; p.24(background): Shutterstock/© Trendywest; p.24(T): © The Museum of London; p.24(TR): Shutterstock/© Vipman; p.24(a): Shutterstock/© Pressmaster; p.24(b): Alamy/© Henry E Iddon; p.24(c): Alamy/© Moodboard; p.25(TR):Alamy/© YAY Media AS; p.25: © Stephen Bond; p.30(a): Alamy/© Steve Vidler; p.30(b): Alamy/© Jack Sullivan; p.30(c): Alamy/© Bob Masters; p.30(d): Alamy/© Andrew Holt; p.30(e): Alamy/© Geoff A Howard; p.30(f): Alamy/© Anthony Kay/Loop Images; p.30(g): Shutterstock/© Justin Black; p.30(h): Shutterstock/© Kamira; p.34(background): Shutterstock/© Yunjun; p.34(a): Shutterstock/© Viacheslav Lopatin; p.34(b): Shutterstock/ © Stuart Monk; p.34(c): Alamy/© Sean Pavone; p.34(d): Shutterstock/ © Upthebanner; p.34(BR): Alamy/© UIG/DeAgnosti; p.35: © Stephen Bond; p.38(a): Corbis/© Bettmann ; p.38(b): Alamy/© GL Archive; p.38(c): Corbis/© Daniel Aguiler; p.38(d): Shutterstock/© Warren Goldswain; p.38(e): Getty Images; p.38(f): Shutterstock/© Barry Tuck; p.39: © Stephen Bond; p.42(background): Getty Images/© Digital Vision; p.42(T): Corbis/© Andrew Cowin/Travel Ink; p.43: © Stephen Bond; p.44(TR): Shutterstock/© Naipung; p.44(L): Alamy/© Howard Barlow; p.44(R): Bridgeman Art Library/© Private Collection; p.47(a): Alamy/© Anna Stowe; p.47(b): Shutterstock/© Blazej Lyjak; p.47(c): Shutterstock/© Mrsiraphol; p.47(d): Alamy/© O. Digoit; p.47(e): Alamy/© Anton Starikov; p.47(f): Shutterstock/© Smith; p.47(g): Alamy/© Mira; p.47(h): Shutterstock/© Karkas; p.48(a): Used with kind permission of Réjeanne Arsenault; p.48(b): Press Association/ © Rajanish Kakade/AP; p.48(c): Alamy/© K-Photos; p.48(d); Getty Images/© AFP; p.48(e): © Trustees of the British Museum; p.48(f): Shutterstock/© Blanscape; p.49: © Stephen Bond; p.52(background): Shutterstock/© Bogdan Ionescu; p.52(T): Shutterstock/© Pics Five; p.52(TR): Getty Images; p.52(CL): Shutterstock/© Flasioo; p.52(CR): Shutterstock/© Elnur; p.52(B): Shutterstock/© Huyangshu; p.53: © Stephen Bond; p.55(TR): © Stephen Bond; p.55(1): Shutterstock/ © Bofotolux; p.55(2,3): © Stephen Bond; p.55(4): Shutterstock/ © Yeko Photo Studio; p.55(5): Shutterstock/© Tamara Kulikova; p.55(6): Shutterstock/© Trekandshoot; p.55(7): Shutterstock/© Anteromite; p.55(8): Shutterstock/© Berislav Kovacevic; p.55(B): © Stephen Bond; p.56(ALL): © Stephen Bond; p.60(background): Superstock/© Ingram Publishing; p.60(TR): © Donald Rust; p.60(L): © Salvador Dali, Gala-Salvador Dali Foundation DACS, London 2009; p.60(BR): © National Gallery of Art, Washington DC, USA/Lauros/Giraudon/The Bridgeman Art Library, ©ADAGP, Paris and DACS, London 2009; p.61(TL): Alamy/© Justin Kase z11z;l p.61(CL): Corbis/ Swim Inc 2m, LLC: p.61(C): © DK Images; p.61(B): © Stephen Bond; p.63(wool hat): Shutterstock/ © Lucy Liu; p.63(bread): Shutterstock/© Anna Breitenberger; p.63(doll): Alamy/© D Hurst; p.63(earrings): Shutterstock/© Africa Studio; p.63(window): Shutterstock/© Pavels; p.63(airplane): Shutterstock/ © Ugorenkov Aleksandr; p.63(toy car): Alamy/© Emmanuel Lattes: p.63(door): Shutterstock/© Scorpp; p.63(belt): Shutterstock/ © SS1001; p.63(robot): Getty Images/© CSA Plastok; p.63(scarf): Shutterstock/© Adisa; p.63(knife): Shutterstock/© Tischenko Irina; p.63(notebook): Shutterstock/© Theeradech Sanin; p.63(mirror): Shutterstock/© James Steidl; p.63(cake): Shutterstock/© Noonday; p.63(bag): Shutterstock/© M Unal Ozmen; p.63(trophy): Shutterstock/ © Boris Rabtsevich; p.63(box): Shutterstock/ © RT Images; p.63(ring): Shutterstock/© Johnny Lye; p.63(bike): Shutterstock/© Horiyan; p.63(cup): Shutterstock/© Danny Smythe; p.63(eraser): Shutterstock/ © PicsFive; p.63(bin bag): Shutterstock/© Hans Slegers; p.63(bottle): Shutterstock/© Anaken 2012; p.63(jumper): Shutterstock/© Chamille White; p.63(shoes): Shutterstock/© Patricia Hofmeester; p.63(paper bag): Shutterstock/© Naypong; p.63(silver bracelet): Getty Images/ iStock/ppart; p.63(toy train): Shutterstock/© VHdtlm; p.63(chair): Shutterstock/© Photobac; p.763(truck): Alamy/© Gabe Palmer; p.63(comic): Alamy/© Boy Kyrpos; p.63(spoon): Shutterstock/© Stephen Rees; p.63(pizza): Shutterstock/© Kesu; p.63(watch): Shutterstock/ © Maraze; p.63(glass): Shutterstock/© Mariyana M; p.66(a): Shutterstock/© Eco Print; p.66(b): Shutterstock/© Andrey Khrolenok; p.66(c): Getty Images/EyeEm/Ahmed Nooh; p.66(d): Ardea/© Thomas Marent; p.66(e): Alamy/© Danita Delimont; p.67(ALL): Nature Picture Library/© Bristol City Museum; p.70(background): Shutterstock/ © Sergiy Artsaba; p.70(T): Getty Images/© Stocktrek Images; p.70(B): Corbis/© Mike Agliolo; p.71(a): Alamy/© Hoberman Collection; p.71(b): Science Photo Library/© Sinclair Stammers; p.71(c): Corbis/© Reuters; p.71(d): Getty Images/© Ken Lucas/Visuals Unlimited; p.71(e): Corbis/© Louie Psihoyos; p.71: © Stephen Bond; p.74(a): Alamy/© Janine Weidel Photo Library; p.74(b): Alamy/© INDASCO Photography; p.74(c): Getty Image/© Scott Markewitz; p.74(d): Corbis/© David Spurdons; p.74(e): Alamy/© Kuttig-People; p.74(f): Getty Images/Lonely Planet Images/Angus Oborn; p.78(background): Shutterstock/ Andrey Armyagov; p.78(TR): Rex Features/© Brice Adams/Daily Mail; p.78(a): Alamy/© One-Image Photography; p.78(b): Alamy/© Grzegory Knec; p.78(c,d): Alamy/© Concept Media; p.78: © Stephen Bond; p.79(L, R): Rex Features/© Top Photo Group; p.79(c): Alamy/© Image Broker; p.79: © Stephen Bond; p.83: Shutterstock/© Monkey Business Images.

Stephen Bond: commissioned photography

The authors and publishers are grateful to the following illustrators:

FLP; Graham Kennedy; Gywneth Williamson; Jo Taylor, c/o Sylvie Poggio; John Woodcock, c/o Thorogood kids; Lisa Smith, c/o Sylvie Poggio; Melanie Sharp, c/o Sylvie Poggio; Moreno Chiacchiera, c/o Beehive; Teresa Tibbetts, c/o Beehive; Ken Oliver, c/o Art agency; Christian Cornia, c/o Advocate Art; Alan Rowe

The publishers are grateful to the following contributors:

Lynne Rushton: Editor
Alison Prior: picture research and art direction
Wild Apple Design Ltd: page design
Blooberry: additional design
Lon Chan: cover design
John Green and Tim Woolf, TEFL Audio: audio recordings
Songs written and produced by Robert Lee, Dib Dib Dub Studios.
hyphen S.A.: publishing management, American English edition